IMAGES OF INVENTION
Essays on Irish Writing

THE IRISH LITERARY STUDIES SERIES

1 *Place, Personality & the Irish Writer*. Andrew Carpenter (editor)
2 *Yeats and Magic*. Mary Catherine Flannery
3 *A Study of the Novels of George Moore*. Richard Allen Cave
4 *J. M. Synge & the Western Mind*. Weldon Thornton
5 *Irish Poetry from Moore to Yeats*. Robert Welch
6 *Yeats, Sligo & Ireland*. A. Norman Jeffares (editor)
7 *Sean O'Casey, Centenary Essays*. David Krause & Robert G. Lowery (editors)
8 *Denis Johnston: A Retrospective*. Joseph Ronsley (editor)
9 *Literature & the Changing Ireland*. Peter Connolly (editor)
10 *James Joyce: An International Perspective*. Suheil Badi Bushrui & Bernard Benstock (editors)
11 *Synge: the Medieval & the Grotesque*. Toni O'Brien Johnson
12 *Carleton's Traits and Stories & the 19th Century Anglo-Irish Tradition*. Barbara Hayley
13 *Lady Gregory: Fifty Years After*. Ann Saddlemyer & Colin Smythe (editors)
14 *Women in Irish Legend, Life & Literature*. Edited by S. F. Gallagher (editor)
15 *'Since O'Casey' & Other Essays on Irish Drama*. Robert Hogan
16 *George Moore in Perspective*. Janet Egleson Dunleavy (editor)
17 *W. B. Yeats, Dramatist of Vision*. A. S. Knowland
18 *The Irish Writer & the City*. Maurice Harmon (editor)
19 *O'Casey the Dramatist*. Heinz Kosok
20 *The Double Perspective of Yeats's Aesthetic*. Okifumi Komesu
21 *The Pioneers of Anglo-Irish Fiction, 1800–1850*. Barry Sloan
22 *Irish Writers & Society at Large*. Masaru Sekine (editor)
23 *Irish Writers & the Theatre*. Masaru Sekine (editor)
24 *A History of Verse Translation from the Irish 1789–1897*. Robert Welch
25 *Kate O'Brien, A Literary Portrait*. Lorna Reynolds
26 *Portraying the Self, Sean O'Casey and the Art of Autobiography*. Michael Kenneally
27 *W. B. Yeats & the Tribes of Danu*. Peter Alderson Smith
28 *Theatre of Shadows: Samuel Beckett's Drama 1956–76*. Rosemary Pountney
29 *Critical Approaches to Anglo-Irish Literature*. Michael Allen & Angela Wilcox (editors)
30 *'Make Sense Who May': Essays on Samuel Beckett's Later Works*. Robin J. Davis & Lance St. J. Butler (editors)
31 *Cultural Contexts and Literary Idioms in Contemporary Irish Literature*. M. Kenneally (editor)
32 *Builders of My Soul: Greek and Roman Themes in Yeats*. Brian Arkins
33 *Perspectives of Irish Drama and Theatre*. Jacqueline Genet & Richard Allen Cave (editors)
34 *The Great Queens. Irish Goddesses from the Morrigan to Cathleen ni Houlihan*. Rosalind Clark
35 *Irish Literature and Culture*. Michael Kenneally (editor)
36 *Irish Writers and Politics*. Okifumi Komesu & Masaru Sekine (editors)
37 *Irish Writers and Religion*. Robert Welch (editor)
38 *Yeats and the Noh*. Masaru Sekine & Christopher Murray
39 *Samuel Ferguson: the Literary Achievement*. Peter Denman
40 *Reviews and Essays of Austin Clarke*. Gregory A. Schirmer (editor)
41 *The Internationalism of Irish Literature & Drama*. Joseph McMinn (editor)
42 *Ireland and France, A Bountiful Friendship: Literature, History and Ideas*. Barbara Hayley & Christopher Murray (editors)
43 *Poetry in Contemporary Irish Literature*, Michael Kenneally (editor)
44 *International Aspects of Irish Literature*, Toshi Furomoto (editor)
45 *A Small Nation's Contribution to the World*, Donald E. Morse, Csilla Bertha, Istvàn Pàllffy (eds.)
46 *Images of Invention. Essays on Irish Writing*. A. Norman Jeffares
47 *Literary Inter-Relations: Ireland, Egypt, and the Far East*. Mary Massoud (editor)
48 *The Irish Writers and their Creative Process*. Jacqueline Genet and Wynn Hellegouarc'h (editors)
49 *Rural Ireland, Real Ireland?* Jacqueline Genet (editor)

IMAGES OF INVENTION
Essays on Irish Writing

A. Norman Jeffares

Irish Literary Studies: 46

COLIN SMYTHE
Gerrards Cross, 1996

British Library Cataloguing in Publication Data

A catalogue record for this book is available from
the British Library

ISBN 0-86140 362-X

Produced in Great Britain
Printed and bound by T J Press (Padstow) Ltd. Cornwall

CONTENTS

Acknowledgements   vii

Introduction   ix

SWIFT AND THE IRELAND OF HIS DAY   1

SWIFT: THE PRACTICAL POET   19

ASPECTS OF SWIFT AS A LETTER WRITER   46

FARQUHAR'S FINAL COMEDIES   76

GOOD-NATURED GOLDSMITH   90

THE VICAR OF WAKEFIELD   106

THE WILD IRISH GIRL   115

LADY MORGAN'S O'DONNEL   123

MATURIN THE INNOVATOR   131

READING LEVER   150

YEATS AND THE WRONG LEVER   164

LEVER'S LORD KILGOBBIN   179

TORRENS: AN IRISHMAN IN SOUTH AUSTRALIA   188

BLUNT: ALMOST AN HONORARY IRISHMAN   201

GEORGE MOORE: PORTRAIT FOR RADIO   220

SOMERVILLE AND ROSS: AN INTRODUCTION   251

YEATS'S GREAT BLACK RAGGED BIRD   260

MEMORIES OF MAUD GONNE   277

THE FORTUNES OF RICHARD MAHONY:
AN ANGLO-IRISHMAN RECONSIDERED   282

JOYCE'S PRECURSORS   289

JOYCE'S 'DONE HALF BY DESIGN'   310

THE REALIST NOVEL IN IRELAND 1900-1945   314

Notes   323

Index   337

ACKNOWLEDGEMENTS

'Swift and the Ireland of His Day', *Irish University Review*, II, 2, Autumn 1972

'Farquhar's Final Comedies', Introductions to editions of *The Recruiting Officer* (1973) and *The Beaux Stratagem* (1972), Oliver & Boyd

'Goodnatured Goldsmith', *Hermathena*, CXIX, 1975

The Vicar of Wakefield, *Goldsmith the Gentle Master*, ed. Sean Lucy, Cork University Press, 1984

'Maturin the Innovator', *Huntingdon Library Quarterly, 1958*

'Reading Lever', *Charles Lever: Towards a Reassessment*, ed. Tony Bareham, Colin Smythe, 1991

'Yeats and the Wrong Lever', *Yeats, Sligo and Ireland*, Colin Smythe, 1980

'Lord Kilgobbin', *Essays and Studies,* collected by Robert Ellrod, Murray for the English Association, 1975

'Torrens: An Irishman in Australia', *Australia & Ireland: Bicentenary Essays*, ed. Colm Kiernan, Gill & Macmillan, 1986

'George Moore: Portrait for Radio', Australian Broadcasting Commission, 1987

'Somerville and Ross: An Introduction', Australian Broadcasting Commission, 1986

'Yeats's Great Black Ragged Bird', *Hermathena*, CXVIII, Winter 1979

'Memories of Maud Gonne', *Yeats Annual*, 1991

'*The Fortunes of Richard Mahoney* Reconsidered', *The Sewanee Review*, Winter 1979

'Joyce's Precursors', *James Joyce: The Artist and the Labyrinth*, ed. Augustine Martin, Ryan Publishing, 1990

'The Realist Novel in Ireland 1900-1945', *The Genius of Irish Prose*, ed. Augustine Martin, RTE and Mercier Press, 1985

INTRODUCTION

I grew up in a city of talkers and selfdramatisers. Talk was expected to be entertaining: speech cost nothing and the common stock
was rich. Vocabulary was extensive, spiced with sayings, phrases,
snatches of song or dramatic dialogue echoing from Shakespeare
down to Dion Boucicault, oaths, imprecations and prayers.
Invention was lively, Gaelic echoes irradiated Hiberno-English,
and the flat Dublin accents were not drowned in the noise of thick
modern traffic.

In the twenties there was still the sound of ironshod drays, still
the clop of hoofs, still the hoarse hooting of ships downriver and of
Guinness barges as they lowered their funnels under the city's
bridges in a cloud of steam. Cabs, outside cars, high-swung deliv-
ery vans and bicycles moved easily through streets not yet filled
with the pervasive convergence of private cars, which, even into
the thirties, could be easily parked. There were no official bus
stops, the few buses responding – somewhat at the whim of individualistic drivers – to requests to stop from passengers within or
would-be passengers without. The newsboys cried 'Harolomail';
the shawlies chanted 'Fine vi'lets, fine vi'lets, a peddy a budch the
vi'lets'.

There was also the sound of talk. There was time to chat when
friends or acquaintances happened on each other in the street. In
pubs, people talked many a novel away, many a play, many a short
story, while spoken biographies were brief and often bitchy.

Was it ever greatly different? As a child Swift heard the city's
background noises in Hoey's Court, as later he did in the Deanery,
where, as in Stella's lodgings in Ormond Quay, good conversation
flourished. Farquhar and Goldsmith experienced an oasis of quiet
within Trinity's walls, though Goldsmith ventured outside them,
playing his flute and selling his songs, and Farquhar swaggered
out to the taverns, gaining in them the reputation of a rake and
atheist. Lady Morgan held her fashionable salon in Kildare Street,
Maturin his in York Street, though Lever, when in the money,
moved out to Templeogue. Torrens exported himself to South
Australia with a capacity for oratory and argument – as well as
vision – built into him as an undergraduate in Trinity where he was
known as 'Radical Torrens'. Another Dubliner, the fictional Richard

Mahony, also an emigrant, returned briefly to Dublin, cutting his visit to three days, depressed by the stagnation and decay of the city which he now saw, after seventeen years away, through antipodean eyes. But there were seasonal visitors who enjoyed the capital, among them Somerville and Ross, and Lady Gregory (whose friend Wilfrid Scawen Blunt's acquaintance with Dublin was brief; he spent much of his time in Ireland in gaol). George Moore made his house in Ely Place a bastion from which he sallied into the city to capture some of Dublin's citizens and incarcerate them in the sharply malicious and amusing prose of *Hail and Farewell!*. Maud Gonne, entering with enthusiasm into plans to free Ireland, first stayed in a central position, taking rooms in Nassau Street where her talkative visitors included Charles Oldham and Douglas Hyde. Later she set up house in Coulson Avenue in Rathgar, and then moved back again to the city, acquiring 73 St Stephen's Green. In the twenties and thirties Yeats, too, settled in the city in a central area known for good talk from the eighteenth century on, Merrion Square.

Joyce was to create a lasting image of modern city life in his use of Dublin and its characters. Dublin shaped the childhood of Elizabeth Bowen, who wrote well of it in *Seven Winters*. Her experiences of life in Herbert Street – south Dublin – are in contrast with those told by Austin Clarke in *Twice Round the Black Church*, set in what the southern inhabitants called 'the North Side', just as life in Moore's Ely Place, south of the Liffey, differed from that of Joyce's Eccles Street, north of the river. Some of the social nuances still remain, as does the now lessening difference between Rathgar and Rathmines.

The authors I discuss here, though most of them were, in Oscar Wilde's phraseology, great talkers, took the trouble to write. They captured the flying thoughts of conversation, of wit and humour, set down political and philosophical ideas, interpreted and portrayed the lasting and the ephemeral, and wrote with the ease and elegance, the overflowing inventiveness of lively speech.

Fife Ness   A.N.J.

To Adèle and Christopher

SWIFT AND THE IRELAND OF HIS DAY

'We are come to fine things here in Dublin', wrote William Molyneux, 'and you would wonder how our city increases sensibly in fair buildings, great trade, and splendour in all things – in furniture, coaches, civility, housekeeping, etc.' He was writing in 1683 to his brother Thomas who had graduated from Trinity College, Dublin that year and gone to Leyden to increase his knowledge of medicine. William was twenty-seven and full of enthusiasm. He was promoting 'the rudiments of a society', drawing up rules for it modelled on those of the Royal Society, to which he was himself elected in 1685 – and of which his brother Thomas also became a Fellow. William and ten or twelve of his friends met regularly in Dublin to discuss 'philosophical, methodical and mathematical matters', and they formed the Dublin Philosophical Society, which first met at the lodgings of the Provost of Trinity College. One of the most active was Sir William Petty, anatomist, statistician, economist, surveyor, and inventor of a famous double-bottomed ship which was remarkably steady in high seas in its first year but sank in a storm in its second. William Molyneux, a mathematician and astronomer, was secretary, and among the members were William King, later Archbishop of Dublin, and St George Ashe, later Provost of Trinity. (Both men played not-insignificant parts in Swift's life). Other members became archbishops, bishops and professors; they were the *virtuosi* of Dublin. And for a time their society flourished; a laboratory was erected, a garden for plants established, experiments conducted and papers were read; but the period of the Society's active life was brief (no entry was recorded in its Minute Book after 1686, and two attempts to revive the Society within the next twenty years proved vain). It had flowered during the period of relative peace Ireland experienced after the Restoration. The country was beginning to recover slightly from its experience of the brutality of Cromwellian conquest and the rapaciousness of its aftermath, the Cromwellian Settlement, a confiscation and plantation of land – eleven million acres, Sir William Petty calculated, out of a total twenty million acres of Irish land had been confiscated in this attempt to colonise Ireland permanently and perpetuate Cromwell's Commonwealth.

After Cromwell's death in 1658, and once the monarchy had

been restored in 1660 by the army leaders, the Church and
Parliament of Ireland were also restored and some restitution was
made. William Molyneux had been four years old at the
Restoration. He was educated at Trinity College, Dublin during
Seele's Provostship, a period when discipline was tightened up
and the College buildings improved. He graduated in 1674 and
then read law in London, where he developed his interest in science. His friendships lay among men who sought scientific knowledge and economic improvement, and his optimistic view of
Dublin's development was coloured by what he had experienced
in London. There were signs that the *virtuosi* could develop a similar group which, even though small, would affect the life of their
country. But these hopes and ambitions suffered sadly during the
reign of James II. The *raison d'etre* of the Protestant garrison, of
which Molyneux was, in effect, a member, was undermined by a
Catholic king who had set aside the Test Act and thus was admit-
ting Catholic officers into the army. In Ireland Lord Clarendon was
recalled by James from the Lord Lieutenancy after a year because
he could not agree with the policy of Catholicising the Irish bench
and the army; this policy the Earl of Tyrconnel, the new Lord
Deputy, pushed forward. He had the army in his control, and when
James fled to France on the coming to power of William and Mary
in England and hence in Ireland, there was a curious situation in
which the King *de jure*, who had been, as Professor Curtis pointed
out:

King *de facto* in all three Kingdoms [was] appearing in arms against a king
whom the English and Scottish parliaments had made monarch *de facto*.
According to the accepted Constitutional position, however, which had
prevailed ever since Henry VIII took the title of King of Ireland, the latter
kingdom had been inseparably annexed to however was King *de facto* of
England. On this theory, which naturally was resented on the Irish side,
was based the Claim of the English Commonwealth, of Cromwell and then
of William III and the English Parliament, to rule in Ireland.[1]

Events leading up to the war of 1689-91 were disturbing. Many of
the Protestants left Ireland, fearing that Tyrconnel's measures
would lead to a repetition of the situation of 1641. The intellectuals
found pressure was sharply brought to bear on them. Tyrconnel
withdrew the governmental grant to Trinity College, having failed
to get a Catholic appointed to a lectureship; the King ordered the
college to admit a Catholic to a fellowship but was resisted. By
1689 most of the students had left the College. When the war was
finally over, the siege of Londonderry, the battle of the Boyne, the

battle of Aughrim, the siege and treaty of Limerick and the naval battle of La Hogue having been written into history, the era of the Protestant ascendancy had begun and was to last until the Act of Union of 1800.

Molyneux became M.P. for the University of Dublin in 1692 and no doubt hoped that the country could return to the conditions it had known before James had come to the throne. But the 'great trade and splendour in all things' of which he had written so enthusiastically to his brother in 1683 were no longer in existence. The parliament in which he sat was entirely Protestant, because an Act of 1691 passed by the English Parliament was extended to Ireland, and this required members of both houses to take an oath of allegiance (which in effect debarred Catholics from parliament until Catholic emancipation in 1829). From 1695 to 1727 the Irish Parliament was busy with the Penal Code, which was punitive and preventive in its disabling statutes, excluding Catholics from the army, from office and from civil employment. There was a fear of Catholicism, and of France; Jacobite feelings remained strong in Ireland, and Protestant intellectuals remembered that James had turned Trinity College into a prison for Dublin Protestants.

In all this aftermath of the war when measures were designed to preserve the Protestant Ascendancy and the connection with England, a paradox soon appeared. The garrison of Protestants was being treated as a colony. Molyneux, who had seen the wealth of England, turned a cold analytical eye on the situation. Why should the self-interest of England hinder his country's recovery and economic development? For this was what was happening – the economic situation was rapidly deteriorating. And the deterioration was caused by English restrictions on Irish trade. The 'Irish Cattle Bill' of 1666 forbade the importation of Irish cattle into England. This led to the expansion of an Irish trade with the continent, which had been encouraged by Ormonde. But the Navigation Acts of 1663 and 1670 (not the first Act of 1651) forbade direct exportation from Ireland to the colonies; and direct import from them to Ireland was forbidden in an Act of 1696. These measures made impossible the creation of a shipping fleet and excluded Ireland from trading with the rest of the Empire – except through England – for over a century. Scotland and Ireland were ruled out of an English preserve. All this was bad enough for Ireland, but in addition the English woollen merchants decided to crush the Irish woollen trade by allowing Irish manufactured woollen goods to be exported only to England, where they were liable to heavy duties, and so could not compete with the English woollen industry.

Molyneux applied his common sense to the question, and came up with the obvious answer: that the problem was one of government. He realised that England's measures were damaging Ireland's trade and industry. As these were largely in the hands of the Protestant ascendancy England was, in fact, damaging her own garrison. When he wrote *The Case of Ireland's being bound by Acts of Parliament in England, Stated (1698)* he was expressing the point of view of the colonists, who felt they were being ill-treated: they could obviously avoid the damaging effects of English selfishness if they controlled their own destinies. 'The subject therefore', wrote Molyneux, 'of our present disquisition shall be *How far the Parliament of England may think it reasonable to intermeddle with the affairs of* Ireland *and bind us up by Laws in their House.*'[2]

The situation was obscure. As always in Irish history, the past was very important, but Molyneux realised there *was* a starting point; 1167 was as clear cut for Ireland as 1066 for England. In his *Case* he dealt with three English kings, arguing that when Henry II first introduced the laws of England into Ireland, at a public assembly of the Irish in Lismore, he allowed them the freedom of Parliaments 'to be held in Ireland as they were held in England'. King John at the request and by the consent of the Irish appointed the laws of England to be of force in Ireland. He did this not as King of England but as Lord of Ireland: his English crown came by descent from his brother Richard who had no regal power in Ireland 'and what his Brother had could not descend to him'. Henry III gave Ireland a Magna Charta and in the twelfth year of his reign provided 'that all the Laws of England should be observ'd in Ireland'. He summed up this point by arguing that from these three kings onward England and Ireland have 'been both govern'd by the like forms of Government under one and the same supreme Head, the *King of England;* yet so, as both Kingdoms remain'd separate and distinct in their several Jurisdictions under that one Head, as are the Kingdoms of *England* and *Scotland* at this Day without any *Subordination* of one to the other'. He argued further that the laws of England that became established in Ireland included the great 'Law of Parliament' by which all laws received sanction, 'the Free Debates and Consent of the People, by themselves, or their chosen Representatives'. This, he thought, was the foundation of future legislation in Ireland, and was shown by Parliaments being so early convoked in Ireland.

The present situation created confusion and uncertainty. He continued:

We are supremely bound to obey the *Supream Authority* over us; and yet we are not permitted to know *Who* or *What* the same is; whether the *Parliament of England*, or *that of Ireland*, or *Both*; and in what Cases the *One*, and in what the *Other*: Which *Uncertainty is* or may be made a Pretence at any time for *Disobedience*. It is not impossible but the different Legislations we are subject to, may enact different, or contrary Sanctions: Which of these must we obey?[3]

He had earlier rejected Ireland's colonial status with decision: 'Of all the Objections raised against us, I take this to be the most extravagant.' And he went on, breathlessly almost, to enumerate some of the absurdities:

It seems not to have the least *Foundation* or *Colour* from Reason or Record: Does it not manifestly appear by the *Constitution of Ireland*, that 'tis a *compleat Kingdom* within it self? Do not the Kings of *England* bear the *Stile of Ireland* amongst the rest of their Kingdoms Is this agreeable to the Nature of a *Colony*? Do they use the Title of Kings of *Virginia, New England,* or *Mary-Land*? Was not *Ireland* given by *Henry* the Second in a Parliament at *Oxford* to his Son *John,* and made thereby an *absolute Kingdom, separate* and wholly *independent* of *England,* 'till they both came United again in time, after the Death of his brother *Richard* without Issue? Have not Multitudes of Acts of Parliament both in *England* and *Ireland* declared Ireland *a compleat Kingdom*? Is not *Ireland* stiled in them all, the *Kingdom* or *Realm* of *Ireland*? Do these *Names* agree to a *Colony*? Have we not a Parliament, and Courts of Judicature? Do these *things* agree with a *Colony*?[4]

This was a heart-felt cry in the midst of an argument generally put forward most carefully and cautiously, one which culminated in an appeal to England to realise the inconvenience to itself of assuming this power, 'asserting this the Jurisdiction' over the Kingdom of Ireland. Molyneux realized the English fears caused by conditions on the continent and by the links which existed between Ireland and France; he regarded the outcries which greeted the breaking of the Edict of Nantes as justified, but he pointed out that the breaking of Ireland's constitution was a matter of over five hundred years' standing. And he ended with a plea that Rights of Parliament should be preserved as sacred and inviolable wherever they are found.

The Case of Ireland, Stated is the case of the Anglo-Irish Protestants – for the Anglo-Irish Catholics had regarded James rather than William as their leader – poised in an awkward position between powerful Protestant England and dangerous Catholic Ireland.

They had reduced the power of the Catholics, and were in a

position of power in relation to them, as they were themselves in
the power of England. In Ireland Catholics were debarred from
Parliament by the Act of 1691, but the Protestant members of the
Irish Parliament had not protested; they remembered the Attainder
Act through which James's Irish Parliament planned a virtual *coup
d'état* of Ireland by the Catholics. William was lenient to the
Catholics; in the Treaty of Limerick civil articles allowed to
Catholics the religious and civil rights which had existed in the
time of Charles II. But the Irish Parliament refused to confirm this
part of the Treaty, and surrendered to England their right to origi-
nate money bills and did this in order to get permission to create
the penal laws. These laws forbade Catholics to practise law, to
hold offices under the Crown, to hire more than two apprentices,
to belong to the guilds, to purchase land, to hold a lease for more
than thirty-one years, to bequeath land to their eldest sons, to hold
their land for more than their lifetime if any member of their family joined the established Protestant Church of Ireland, to send
their children to a seminary in Ireland or abroad, to possess or
carry arms, to own a horse worth more than five pounds, to celebrate mass, if a priest, unless registered with the government
(which involved taking an oath which declared James II had no
right or title to the crown), to remain in Ireland, if of the higher
orders of Catholic clergy. The Catholics, the 'mere Irish' as they
were called, were regarded as hewers of wood and drawers of
water, a conquered people.

Their conquerors unfortunately did not always live among
them. In 1641 fifty-nine per cent of the land had been owned by
Catholic Irish; by 1703 they owned but fourteen per cent. The Civil
War and the Revolution had brought confiscation and plantation
on a large scale. These abstract words obscure the injustice and
inhumanity involved in these operations. Englishmen had
obtained estates and some had sold them to other English specula-
tors; they tended to live in England where they were often joined
by Anglo-Irish of longer standing. The estates were let on long
leases; the tenants often became absentees themselves, subletting
the land to other tenants, who often continued the process, and the
result was that the actual worker of the land had to pay far too
high rents. There was also a practice by which land was auctioned
to the highest bidder for short term leases. So there was no security of tenure; improvements made by the tenant led to higher rents;
and irresponsible tenants who had bid up the price of a short term
lease produced the minimum to meet their exorbitant rents. The
whole system of land tenure, as well as the landlords' policy of

extending grazing rather than maintaining tillage militated against the country's achieving any improvement. This situation could have altered for the better within Ireland even if her general economic development was certain to have been restricted by England.

The theory behind this restriction was that if Ireland were too prosperous England would suffer. Sir William Temple, in 'An Essay upon the Advancement of Trade in Ireland'[5], wrote firmly that where Irish trade interfered with English the interest of trade in England should prevail over the encouragement of Irish trade. He was worried by the effects of England's legislation against the importation of Irish cattle into England in 1666, which were perhaps unforeseen by English politicians and resulted in an increase of Irish trade with the continent. Temple cast a jaundiced eye on the Irish woollen trade; his attitude anticipated the Woollen Act of 1699 which effectively destroyed this Irish industry. England did little to compensate for this by encouraging the linen trade as had been agreed.

England's power in Ireland was maintained by the appointment of Englishmen to positions in government and church – the Duke of Ormonde was the only holder of the office of Lord Lieutenant in the first fifty years of the eighteenth century who was born in Ireland. These Englishmen tended to advance England's interest; the native Catholics were powerless to oppose them. And the Anglo-Irish, as *The Case of Ireland, Stated* demonstrates, were in a position of some complexity. They owed their loyalty to the Crown but not the Parliament of England: yet they were the descendants of Englishmen: their rights had been guaranteed by Henry II and as Englishmen they had the rights of subjects in constitutional monarchy; they were not a colony. But the real difficulty in their position was that they were not interested in the rights of the Catholic Irish. Nor indeed were they interested in the rights of the Protestant dissenters in the North, whom they realised they need not appease, because they thought these Presbyterians would be forced to support them through fear of the Catholics. This happened in 1704 when the Sacramental Test Act was added to laws against Catholics; it prevented Presbyterians taking civil and military posts but, as the Secretary of State wrote to the Earl of Nottingham, who had added the Test clause to the Popery Bill, the Dissenters made some noise when they heard the news of the Test being added, but met with 'as little encouragement, and even those gentlemen were so sensible of the great advantages occurring by the Bill for suppressing the Popish Interest, that they have almost declined any further talk about it'.[6]

Such were the results of religious and political warfare: poverty, prejudice, suspicion, self-interest, and sheer stupidity. Molyneux failed to convince the English, and the English Parliament declared his book seditious. But it provided a reasonable argument based on views that had been held since 1641. Then the Irish Parliament had declared that it was independent of the English Parliament, and indeed there was an anonymous manuscript in circulation in this period entitled *A Declaration Setting Forth How, and by What Means, the Laws and Statutes of England, from Time to Time, Came to be of Force in Ireland*[7] which asserted that the king was supreme head of the body politic in Ireland, but that the Parliament of England had no more jurisdiction in Ireland than it had in Scotland. Ireland was a free and distinct kingdom in itself.

These views lay deep in the resident Protestant Anglo-Irish sub-conscious. How deeply is revealed in Swift's attitude to Ireland once he lived in Dublin and realised just how unique Ireland's 'singular condition' was, and what de facto colonial status meant to any man of independent mind.[7] The Protestant Ascendancy, of its nature, created a particular kind of independence. The survival of the Ascendancy depended upon it having a powerful, dominating independence, for it lived in an anarchic country, despising the native Catholic Irish and disliking the Presbyterian Scots. The independent-minded Irish Protestant had several courses open to him: if he possessed land he could become a kind of Irish Squire Western on his estates, or else leave others to sublet them, while he lived in London: he could draw his money from some sinecure; or if without private means, he could be a proletarian farmer (small, poor Protestant farmers did exist!). If either ambitious or desperate he could seek employment for his talents in England; and ultimately in the late eighteenth and early nineteenth centuries he could find himself in the role of a patriotic leader.[8]

How did Swift fit into this pattern of eighteenth century life? The historian William Hartpole Lecky remarked that the curse of Swift was to have been born an Irishman and a man of genius and to have used his talents for his country's good. What was it like to have been born an Irishman and a man of genius in 1667? And how did Swift use his talents for his country's good?

Swift's life had always an element of battling against odds about it. 'But I am not content' he might have answered, many times over, if some of his successes were pointed out to him. The dice must have seemed to him to have been loaded against him from the start. As he told Pope late in life he had when young more desire to be famous than ever since. His endeavours to distinguish himself were 'only for want of a great title and fortune' that he might be used like a lord by those who had an opinion of his parts. Like so many who have seen the light of day in Ireland he was not born to be content with the second best.

There was a feeling of unfairness from the beginning. The Swift family took pride in the loyalty of Thomas Swift, the parson of Goodrich in Herefordshire, to Charles I, even if there was little comfort in the fact that he had, in Swift's words, been persecuted and plundered two hundred and fifty times by the barbarity of Cromwell's hellish crew.[9] It is not without significance that Swift, at the age of fifty-nine, took the trouble to visit his grandfather's church in England, to set up a tablet to his memory in it and to present the church with a chalice used by his grandfather. This grandfather, Thomas Swift, never recovered his living under the Commonwealth; his sons went to Ireland in 1658 just before the Restoration to try to rebuild the family fortunes. They were led by the view of other Englishmen that things were good in Ireland. Jonathan Swift's father and mother contracted in Dublin what their son later called a 'very indiscreet' marriage: the consequences of which he felt, he said, not only through the whole course of his education but during the greatest part of his life. The father died before his son was born, and before he could make a sufficient establishment for his family. The boy was taken to Whitehaven for three years by his Irish foster nurse, then, at six, he was sent to Kilkenny College, his mother having returned to her home in Leicester.

A family resentment against Puritans and Dissenters was virtually inbuilt into the young Swift, and the school to which he was sent would have inculcated strong Anglican principles into him. Kilkenny College was founded by the eighth earl of Ormonde, a member of the great family, Anglo-Irish in the best sense of the word, which kept up its interest in the school and in Trinity College, Dublin. Swift learned the classics and rhetoric there; and prayers, scriptural readings, the catechism and attendance at the Cathedral reinforced the academic teaching. Swift did not mention his schooldays much: 'I formerly used to envy my own happiness when I was a schoolboy, the delicious holidays, the Saturday afternoon, and the charming custards in a blind alley.' He said he never considered 'the confinement ten hours a day, nouns and verbs, the terror of the rod, the bloddy [sic] noses and broken shins'[10]. It was probably a boyhood of frustration, summed up in a hauntingly sad vignette: 'I remember when I was a little boy I felt a great fish at the end of my line which I drew up almost to the ground, but dropped it, and the disappointment vexeth me to this very day, and I believe it was the type of all my future disappointments.'[11]

The school's gospel of hard work was also preached at Trinity College, Dublin where Swift proceeded in 1682. Though we now know, thanks to Professor Ehrenpreis, that he did 'passably well in College but not so well as the septuagenarian Swift could have wished', Swift's comment on his own 'dullness and insufficiency' is important; for he thought that it was through the ill-treatment of his nearest relations that he was 'so discouraged, and sunk in his spirits that he neglected some parts of his academick studyes, for which he had no great relish by nature and turned himself to reading history and poetry'.[12]

Swift obviously disliked abstract philosophy and formal rhetoric, while delighting in language and literature. Apart from his annoyance at his relatives – probably occasioned by his uncle Godwin losing his money in the ironworks at Swadlingbar[13] with, no doubt, an ensuing shortage in Swift's own funds – the unsettled state of affairs in Ireland must have made academic work appear, in modern student jargon, irrelevant. Much of the syllabus must have seemed rather dreary drudgery to Swift anyway. Not only the syllogistic disputes which were part of the course but the students who pursued success in them smacked of dullness. In 1687 Swift was neglecting his work, and frequenting the town. He cut his lectures in mathematics; in 1688 he joined in starting tumults in college; he had insulted the Junior Dean, and he and another student had to beg his pardon publicly on bended knees.

This behaviour no doubt reflects the troubled state of the times, and their effect on university life. James II's interfering with the English universities' appointments and Tyrconnel's attempting to do the same in Dublin did not leave university staff and students unaffected. The annual pension paid to Trinity College had been withdrawn when James II arrived in Ireland. Fuel and food were scarce, but one meal a day being served in the College, while some of the plate was sold and the manuscripts sent to England, where many of the students and Fellows had fled by 1689, Swift and Congreve among them. Molyneux himself sailed for Chester in 1689.

There was probably more, however, to Swift's discontent as an undergraduate than any immediate lack of funds from his relatives or the disturbing situation in the country. He must have realised very clearly that there was no guarantee that either academic brilliance (which he was not demonstrating) or plodding application (which he obviously found abhorrent) would necessarily be rewarded in any spectacular way. He was, in short, all too clearly aware that he lacked money and influence. He admired distinction; his instincts were scholarly. He respected and liked men of the calibre of St George Ashe, his tutor, (despite his satirising, indeed ridiculing, in *A Tale of a Tub* and *Gulliver's Travels* the 'natural philosophy' in which Ashe was so deeply interested and which he had sought to encourage through his writings and his secretaryship of the Dublin Philosophical Society); but he had too much pride to stoop to the obvious and dull routes which might further him in finding a career. This pride underlies many of the apparent contradictions in his character. Professor Ehrenpreis cleverly instances Swift's attitude (perhaps privately jealous, perhaps contemptuous, certainly publicly indifferent) to his contemporary at college, Peter Browne, who succeeded notably in a conventional way. Swift's recipe for himself was difficult:

> Beat not the path which vulgar feet have trod
> But give the vigorous fancy room.

And so his early poetry records a young man aware of his ability, yet lacking in confidence, experiencing in poetry the same disappointment that had greeted his fishing:

> In vain, I tug and pull the oar
> And when I almost reach the shore
> Straight the Muse turns the helm, and I launch out again.

Swift's paternal and maternal grandfathers, his paternal great-grandfather, and great-great-grandfather and two uncles were clergymen. His elder cousin Thomas, whose childhood was so like Swift's (his father died when he was five, the widow was badly off; the Irish uncles brought him up in the same way as Jonathan, with what was obviously a good education at Kilkenny College and Trinity College, Dublin) was destined for the Church. Trinity College was regarded as a nursery of clergymen by Ormonde, who thought the Church of Ireland should be staffed by its graduates[14], and it did indeed absorb a large number of them. The church was thus not an unexpected or an unlikely career for Swift: there were however, it seems, more graduates produced than potential preferment warranted. And, as well as the uncertainty of success in such a sphere – many of Swift's able contemporaries and friends did not rise very far in the Church – Swift himself had a scruple of entering the Church merely for support.[15] He did not do so until he had had the offer of an administrative post in government. Pride again, and not so much a theologically sinning kind of pride as a species of self-respect. Short of money and influence, he had nonetheless to feel he was making a free choice.

Had Swift entered the Church immediately on his twenty-third birthday (or earlier, had he obtained a benefice) he might have been less aware of the second-best element in his choice. But two factors obtrude: the first, the obvious insecurity of property in Ireland and the pressures of England on Irish political life: the second, his experience of gracious living in England at Moor Park, Sir William Temple's house, and his enjoyment there of the company of Temple himself, a man of polite learning and literary genius, a diplomat and courtier, who disliked natural philosophy, who traced the events of history to the personalities of heads of states, who strove to end or prevent wars, and whose public life received its rewards and its disillusionments. (The parallels with Swift's own subsequent career and many of his ideas are obvious.)

With his social standards and his literary ambitions kindled by his first stay under Temple's roof, Swift felt the pressure of making a living the more strongly, and, once he could live 'without being driven into the church for a maintenance, he .... resolved to go to Ireland and take holy orders',[16] But he had added by this time a desire, surely, for fame in literature. Literary success would not bring him large sums of money, but it might (indirectly in its effects) bring about his being used like a lord.

Though Temple had offered Swift the post which enabled him to seek a clerical position instead, he was not given to active help as a patron. Swift had earlier decided to take orders but not, he told his uncle, till the king – to whom he had been carrying messages for Temple – gave him a prebendary. Though Temple promised the certainty of this to Swift he was slower than Swift would have wished: 'Though he promises me the certainty of it, because, I suppose, he believes I shall leave him and upon some accounts he thinks me a little necessary to him.'[17] They parted on bad terms; Swift did not, however, foresee he would have to apply to Temple – in the letter which Temple's sister marked as his 'penitential letter' – for a testimonial as to his 'good life and behaviour' in the three years previous to his application in Dublin in 1694 to be ordained. There had been a good deal of slackness in its administration but now the Irish church was tightening up. And it certainly needed to. So the behaviour and character of candidates for ordination were looked into.

Swift had seen something of the power and dignity, as well as the difficulties, of the Anglican church in England: now he was to experience its weakness in Ireland. The established Church of Ireland was in a difficult position, as he realised, remarking bitterly that his sermons 'were calculated for a church without a company or a roof'. As prebend of Kilroot, in the diocese of Down and Connor, he was in charge of the united vicarages of Kilroot and Templecorran and the rectory of Ballynure. There was a church at Templecorran, one in bad repair at Ballynure and a ruin at Kilroot, where the hundred parishioners were Scottish Presbyterians – in 1695 there was 'not one natural Irish in the parish'. The same situation applied in Templecorran, and things were little better in Ballynure. The previous incumbent was William Milne, a Scot; charged with non-residence, incompetence and incontinence, and suspended by the ecclesiastical commission of 1693, he had been deprived of the living but allowed £20 per year from the income of the prebend, which amounted to £100, no doubt to Swift's annoyance. The rectorial tithes of Kilroot were impropriate to a lay holder, the Earl of Donegal; those of Templecorran were in the possession of the See of Connor. It is uncertain whether Swift had a manse or glebe house in any of his parishes. Surrounded by Presbyterians, close only to the urban life of Belfast and the scanty civilized society it afforded, it is small wonder Swift grew weary in 'a few months' of the cold damp scenery of Belfast Lough, and returned to Moor Park in 1696, there to thwack or finish off his thwacking of the Dissenters in *A Tale of a Tub*.[18]

The contrast was indeed strong. And moreover the very ordinary observations he had made, as he pointed out in a letter to his cousin's husband, with going half a mile beyond the university, had taught him experience enough not to think of marriage 'till I settle my fortune in the world which I am sure will not be in some years'.[19] As a student, short of money, as a young graduate not unattractive to women, nor averse to flirtation, he was now back with his patron, but at the end of his second and final long period at Moor Park which lasted from 1696 to Temple's death in 1699, he failed to obtain the prebend of Canterbury the King had promised Temple he would give him.

Swift returned to Ireland as chaplain to the Earl of Berkeley. He was appointed to livings in Meath – a union of three parishes, the rectory of Agher and the vicarages of Laracor and Rathbeggan. He was made prebendary of Dunlavin in St Patrick's Cathedral. (He did not receive the rich living of Ratoath which his predecessor in Laracor refused to vacate.) The diocese of Meath was in nearly as bad a state from the Church of Ireland point of view as Down and Connor had been. A few years before, the then Bishop of Meath had reported that only forty-three of the 197 parish churches were in repair, and that only forty of his fifty-five clergy were in residence.

In the North of Ireland Swift had been surrounded by Presbyterians; now he was surrounded by Roman Catholics. There was the same story of decaying churches, lack of manses or glebes, non-residence of priests and consequent neglect of parishes, impropriations of tithes and temporalities in a bad way. Laracor seems to have brought Swift in £100 (potential) a year, reduced by a salary to his curate and a crown rent. The church at Laracor was in reasonable repair and Swift built a parsonage there. He complained to 'Varina' (in a letter designed to dissuade her from the idea of marriage, dated 4 May 1700) that 'the place of residence .... they have given me is within a mile of a town called Trim, twenty miles from hence, and there is no other way but to hire a house at Trim, or build one on the spot; the first is hardly to be done, and the second I am too poor to perform at present.' His performance of his parochial duties was incidental. He took care, however, to choose good curates; he increased the size of the glebe by at least twenty acres; and he bought for the living some impropriate tithes (of Effernock in the next parish). Agher, which probably had few or no Protestants in it, brought him in about £20 per annum and Rathbeggan, which seems to have had no Protestants at all in it, about £50 (His other income was a few pounds from his Dunlavin prebend).

Swift enjoyed one aspect of Laracor, the very human one of 'improving'. His *Journal to Stella* often records his pleasure in the place and his work 'cutting down willows, planting others, scouring my canal and every kind of thing',[20] He thought lyrically of Laracor from London:

'Oh, that we were at Laracor this fine day! the willows begin to peep and the quicks to bud. My dream's out: I was dreamed last night that I eat ripe cherries. And now they begin to catch the pikes, and will shortly the trouts (pox on these ministers), and I would fain know whether the floods were ever so high as to get over the holly bank or the river walk; if so, then all my pikes are gone; but I hope not. Why don't you ask Parvisol these things, sirrahs? And then my canal, and trouts, and whether the bottom be fine and clear?'[21]

Eel and trout fishing there appealed to him. In October 1710 he regarded Westminster as à sort of monastic life and . . . liked Laracor better'. The next month he hoped Ormonde would give him an addition to Laracor. He thinks in 1711 of making his canal

fine in the summer, 'as fine as I can. I am afraid I shall see great
neglects among my quick-sets. I hope the cherry trees on the river-
walk are fine things now'.[22] In February and March he worried
about the trees, ' . . . I would fain be at the Beginning of my
Willows growing. Percival tells me that the Quicksetts upon the
flatt in the Garden, do not grow so well as those famous ones on
the Ditch. They want digging about them; The Cherry trees by the
River side my Heart is sett upon'.[23] In June he remarked that 'riding to Laracor gives me short sighs as well as you. All the days I
have passed here have been dirt to those'. In November 1711 he
was weary of courts and wanting his journeys to Laracor. In July
1712 he asks the ladies to visit Laracor and give him an account of
the garden, river, holly and cherry trees – in August he makes the
same request – he laments his work among people in London in
September 1712, instead of being among his canal and river walk
and willows. After Swift escaped being killed in London by the
booby-trapped bandbox sent to Oxford,[24] he wished himself even
more and more among his willows. He writes in April 1712 – after
he had been awarded the Deanery of St Patrick's – that he will not
give up Laracor. It was not, one likes to think, simply because he
felt a need of the income from the living, but out of a genuine love
of what he had done with the place.

Money and fame he needed always – not so much in the vulgar
sense as in being treated like a lord by those whose appreciation
would be worth having – and now he was to move into a position
where, having acquired a living with some money, he was to experience literary and political fame in London. His position in St
Patrick's Cathedral gave him influence, and, no doubt, some experience of committee work. By 1705 he was actively engaged in a
successful campaign to elect Stearne to the Deanery. At the close of
this period of his life he was to press equally successfully against
strong opposition for Stearne's appointment to the episcopal
bench, thus himself attaining the Deanery.[25]

The story of his work in London for the Irish Church, and his
pamphleteering work for the Tory Ministry and for peace, is sufficiently well known. But once he had failed in his ambition 'to live
in England, and with a competency to support me with honour' he
returned to Dublin in 1714 to comparative quiet, hoping to keep his
'resolution of never medling with Irish Politics'. This quiet lasted
but six years, till 1720. But he *had* meddled earlier. Once he had
returned to Ireland in 1699 and established himself at Laracor he
was, almost inevitably, faced with the problem of independence.
His quest for money, for fame, for power, are all caught up in what

we admire him for most of all: his passionate, savage defence of liberty.

An independent-minded intellectual in Ireland, without money or land, was bound to realize in 1700 that the industry, trade and commerce of his country were being actively hindered in the interest of the neighbouring wealthier island. Swift followed Molyneux's example: he drew upon his arguments and welded them into his own view of the political and economic situation in which Ireland found herself in relation to England. His view was more complex than that of Molyneux: the situation itself was now more complex. To Molyneux's reasoning he added his own brand of allegory: the events which triggered off *The Story of the Injured Lady, in a Letter to her Friend, with her Answer*[26] were those leading to the Union of England and Scotland which took place on 1 May 1707.

Union with England might have satisfied Swift: it would have meant equality for a proud man who resented Ireland's colonial status, in comparison with Scotland's apparent gain. His dislike of Protestant dissent in Scotland also motivated him in his dislike for the Union as *The Story of the Injured Lady* shows. This allegory depicts Ireland as the Lady, ruined by England, the Gentleman who is casting her off and about to marry her rival, Scotland. The Lady describes her Rival as devoid of 'Virtue, Honesty, Truth or Manners' and we learn that the Gentleman's steward [Charles] was knocked on the head as the result of a dispute caused by her conduct. 'Half by Force and half by Consent' is how the Lady became the Gentleman's mistress – he has behaved like a Conqueror to her. She has replaced her old Servants with his favourites and paid the latter when they reside with him. She has accepted the Gentleman's Steward [William] to manage her estate, but the Gentleman behaves even more authoritarianly, making her tenants sell their goods across the River [the Irish Sea] in his Townmarket, paying duty on both sides. The allegory covers the economic restraints and the political problems: the latter seem to Swift just as they did to William Molyneux; 'The Gentleman pretends that whatever Orders he shall think fit to prescribe for the future in his family, he may, if he will, compel mine to observe them, without asking my Advice or hearing my Reasons'. This is a reference to England's interpretation of Poyning's Law of 1387. The Lady is loyal to the Gentleman; she is not interested in offers from others, i.e., the Pretender and France, and she just wants to be free of the persecution of the Gentleman, to manage her little fortune to her best advantage. Where Molyneux wished the remedy to come from

England, however, Swift's views rest more upon self-help. The Lady is advised to call her tenants – Parliament – together and with them to resolve to have no further dependence on the Gentleman except by the old agreement that they shall have the same Steward and that she shall regulate her household 'by such Methods as you shall both agree to'. Further, to resolve not to carry goods to his market unless she pleases, nor to be hindered in carrying them elsewhere; to insist that her servants [the landlords] live at home or forfeit their places; and to make such leases to tenants that they cannot break.

Swift's dislike of dissent had been sorely tried during his negotiations in London on behalf of the Irish Church, to obtain the remission of 'the First Fruits and Twentieth Part', a tax which the Queen had remitted for the English but not the Irish Church. He had discovered that the Whig Ministry intended to appease the Irish dissenters by repealing the Sacramental Test Act. It appeared in November 1708 as if the Irish Church was going to receive the Queen's Bounty (as the remission of the First Fruits was called) and it also appeared that the Irish Bishops were going to be asked (as a quid pro quo) to refrain from opposing the removal of the Test Act. Swift wrote *A Letter from a Member of the House of Commons of Ireland to a Member of the House of Commons in England*, which was published in January 1709. This ironic letter looks forward to Swift's later Irish pamphlets in its proposal to sacrifice Ireland's economy to England.

It was not, however, until the Whig government passed the Declaratory Act of 1720 that Swift resumed his strenuous political writing on behalf of liberty. This law defined Ireland as a depending kingdom. This in Swift's words was a Law *to bind Men without their own Consent*. He replied with *A Proposal for the Universal Use of Irish Manufacture, in Cloths and Furniture of Houses & utterly Rejecting and Renouncing Every Thing wearable that comes from England* in which he proclaimed that a traveller in Ireland would hardly think himself in a Land where *Law, Religion,* or *common Humanity is* professed. Swift began to be regarded as their defender by his parishioners, the weavers of Dublin, and as a patriot by the Irish people. There followed the *Drapier Letters*, and in them Swift reaches the same pitch of indignation as Molyneux before him:

Were not the People of *Ireland* born as *Free* as those of *England?* Is not their *Parliament* as fair a *Representative* of the *People* as that of *England?* And hath not their Privy Council as great or greater share in the Administration of Publick Affairs? Are they not Subjects of the same King? Does not the same

Sun shine on them? Have they not the same *God* for their Protector? Am I
a *Free-Man* in *England*, and do I become a *Slave* in six Hours by crossing the
Channel?[27]

The guilt for Ireland's condition of poverty was shared between
England and Ireland. Poverty and lowness of spirit in Ireland arose
from the loss of liberty occasioned by hardship.

Swift became a powerful force in Irish politics. There followed
various *Proposals* until his anger overflowed in *A Modest Proposal* of
1729, with its condemnation of landlords, the idle rich, the poor,
the dissenters, the papists, the absentees, the shopkeepers, the beg-
gars. In this Swift advocates, other expedients and advice having
failed, the fattening of children under two for food. This was his
saeva indignatio at its most devasting level. In his earlier *Letter to the
Archbishop of Dublin* the patriot found he could not reflect upon the
singular condition of the country without some emotion and without often examining those animals which came in his way 'with
two legs and human faces' and wondering whether they 'clad, and
erect, be of the same species with what I have seen very like them
in England, as to the outward Shape but differing in their notions,
natures, and intellectuals more than any two kinds of Brutes in a
forest, which any men of common prudence would immediately
discover by persuading them to define what they mean by Law,
Liberty, Property, Courage, Reason, Loyalty or Religion.[28]

Swift followed upon early North American anticolonialist writers, and upon William Molyneux the Irish patriot and even Bishop
Berkeley in *The Querist*, but he was the first writer to become more
than provincial, more than anti-colonial in his speech in favour of
liberty. 'What I did for this country' he wrote in 1734, in universal
words we could also apply to his work for subsequent readers
everywhere 'was from perfect Hatred of Tyranny and Oppression.'
And he had shown the way to later Anglo-Irishmen who moved
into more extreme concepts of nationalism: these ideas arose out of
Swift's patriotism, the patriotism he could not, in the end, resist,
and which triumphed briefly in 1782 in that all too-short flowering
of the Ascendancy, to be crushed after 1798 and the Act of Union
of 1800. The repeal of the Declaratory Act marked the best moment
of the Anglo-Irish when they might have become more than an
ascendancy, when Grattan proclaimed in the Dublin Parliament:
'Spirit of Swift! Spirit of Molyneux! Your genius has prevailed.'[29]

SWIFT: THE PRACTICAL POET

Like several of his literary countrymen Swift was a late developer.
Goldsmith and Yeats, for instance, seemed as children to be worry-
ingly slow to respond to the stimuli of adult conversation in the
one case, to the orthodox requirements of education in the other.
Not so Swift, who claimed (admittedly when he was in his forgetful seventies) that at the age of three he could read any chapter in
the Bible; it was as a poet that he was a late developer. On the evidence of the odes Swift wrote in his early twenties, largely in the
style of Cowley, Dryden was right to remark, 'Cousin Swift, you
will never be a poet'. Swift was writing these poems to advertise
his abilities to the world outside Moor Park; but those abilities did
not show to advantage in these complex and formal exercises in a
florid mode that was already going out of fashion. When he wrote
what pleased him, he was 'Cowley to myself and can read it a hundred times over.'

Swift found composition difficult, writing to his cousin Thomas
Swift in May 1692 that he seldom wrote more than two stanzas of
a Pindaric Ode in a week; he altered them a hundred times, though
he did not believe himself 'a laborious dry writer'. Writing his
'Ode to Dr William Sancroft' was proving almost impossible; he
could not finish it for his life, he wrote, he had done nine stanzas
and didn't like half of them, 'nor am I nigh finished, but there it
lies and I sometimes add to it and would wish it were done to my
desire'. He was trying to be too clever; his poetic wit was too
much, even for its creator. 'Egad', he told his cousin, 'I cannot write
anything easy to be understood though it were but in praise of an
old shoe.' He was over thirty when he first wrote poetry effectively: 'Mrs Harris's Petition' is successful because Swift had found his
own way of writing.

In this lively poem Swift shows his capacity to adopt the identity and capture the speech of others, demonstrates his ability to tell
a story in verse and shares with his readers his amusement at
Frances Harris's loss of her purse (and of the parson himself) in a
not unkindly way. He had broken away from fashionable poetic
convention and given his sense of humour its head. He had already
found his way to general satire in 'Verses Wrote in a Lady's Ivory
Table-Book' and to satiric comment upon particular individuals in

19

'The Problem' and 'The Discovery'.

'The Problem' burlesques classical deities, Jove and Cupid being involved in this account of how three ladies decide to try which of them the Earl of Romney loves (a subtitle in a transcript read 'that Sidney Earl of Romney stinks, when he is in love'). Romney, Lord Lieutenant of Ireland in 1692, was Lord Justice in 1697, and had failed to recommend Swift to the King for preferment (probably in 1699) and Swift was getting his own back. The poem is vigorous, its couplets crisp, and its imagery, linking sex with the scatological, something which Swift was to employ at intervals, is more surprising than schoolboyish, for it is forgivably witty. The ladies

> Ambitious of a regent's heart
> Spread all their charms to catch a fart!
> Watching the first unsavoury wind,
> Some ply before and some behind.
> My Lord, on fire amidst the dames
> Farts like a laurel in the flames.
> The fair approach the speaking part,
> To try the back way to his heart.
> For, as when we a gun discharge
> Although the bore be ne'er so large,
> Before the flame from muzzle burst,
> Just at the breech it flashes first:
> So from my Lord his passion broke,
> He farted first, and then he spoke.

'The Discovery' is a milder affair. In it Swift, who had gone to Ireland as chaplain to Lord Berkeley, and had briefly acted as his secretary also, was making much of a conversation between Lord Berkeley and Arthur Bushe, who was secretary to Berkeley when he was Lord Justice. Swift disliked Bushe; he thought he had been elbowed out of the position of secretary by him and that Bushe had prevented him from becoming Dean of Derry (a post for which in any case he would probably hardly have seemed qualified at the time); and so Bushe is satirised with his 'new state-airs'. He is 'His Lordship's premier minister' which leads to him being 'held as needful as his clyster'. Berkeley is 'wise', though it is suggested that bargaining over hay and oats is beneath his dignity.

Absorption into Lord Berkeley's household in Dublin Castle provided Swift with the friendly companionship and with it the to-and-fro of teasing that he always enjoyed, particularly with attractive, intelligent young women. His friendship with the Lord Justice's daughter, Lady Betty Berkeley, was to prove a lasting one.

To an incomplete poem Swift wrote in Berkeley Castle in Gloucester in the summer of 1702, 'A Ballad on the Game of Traffic' (describing Lord and Lady Berkeley and members of their household playing cards) a note in the Faulkner edition of 1735 tells us 'Lady Betty Berkeley finding this ballad in the author's room unfinished' added the final stanza:

> With these is Parson Swift,
> Not knowing how to spend his time,
> Does make a wretched shift,
> To deafen 'em with puns and rhyme.

Swift replied with 'A Ballad to the Tune of the Cutpurse', secure enough now to be able to laugh at himself for being unable to complete a poem:

> Even so Master Doctor had puzzled his brains
> In making a ballad, but was at a stand,
> He had mixed little wit with a great deal of pains;
> When he found a new help from invisible hand.

And he was able, too, to treat the young girl with raillery:

> And though some malicious spirit did do't
> You may know by the hand, it had no cloven foot.

In April 1701 Lord Berkeley was dismissed from his post as Lord Justice and returned to England. Swift accompanied him. He persuaded Hester (or Esther) Johnson, whom he called Stella, and Rebecca Dingley, who had been members of Sir William Temple's household at Moor Park, to move to Ireland, where, he pointed out, their money would go further. They arrived in Dublin in August 1701, Swift returning to the city in September. The ladies' presence there was an ample compensation for the loss of the Berkeleys' company. As the 1702 poems show, Swift had become not only rector of Laracor (near Trim in County Meath) and the associated parishes of Agher and Rathbeggan and prebend of Saint Patrick's Cathedral, Dublin, but 'Master Doctor', having received a DD from Trinity College, Dublin, in 1702. In Dublin he was able to maintain something of the companionship he had enjoyed at Moor Park, where he had known Stella since he was about twenty-one and she six. He had taught her to write and guided her reading. Now that Stella was twenty, she was 'looked upon as one of the most beautiful, graceful and agreeable young women in London, only a little too fat', her hair was 'blacker than a raven and every feature of her face in perfection'.

Swift regarded Stella's judgement highly; he appreciated her advice and he delighted in her wit. He was not, however, content to remain a country clergyman in Ireland and went to London in 1702, becoming acquainted with the Whig lords, who at the time were not in a position to aid his career, and whom he had defended in *A Discourse of the Contests and Dissentions between the Nobles and Commons in Athens and Rome, with the Consequences they had upon both these States*, of which he let it be known he was the author.

A Tale of a Tub was published anonymously in 1704 though Swift's authorship of it was also known; his reputation grew in London with the success of the Bickerstaff papers. His literary friendships there developed. By 1707 he became intimate with Addison and Steele. Congreve, his contemporary at Kilkenny and Trinity, was also a friend. The Church of Ireland entrusted him with negotiating the Remission of the First Fruits. His confidence in his own powers was being borne out by the confidence others were placing in him, and sufficiently so for him to develop his powers of abuse in verse. 'The Description of a Salamander' gives Lord Cutts a hard time of it; he is described as a snake in human form. Sir John Vanbrugh is treated with raillery in two poems, but later, though Swift categorised him as a good natured fellow, he had 'a long quarrel' with Swift about the verses on his house: 'we were very civil and cold'. Ridicule and irony did not always appeal to the recipient of them, but Swift was not affected by this: he pressed on with the mockery of Partridge the Almanac-Maker.

Swift viewed literature's traditions with a sceptical eye. In 'Apollo outwitted', a poem .to 'Ardelia' (later to become Anne, Countess of Winchelsea) Phoebus Apollo approaches the nymph, who, sceptical like her creator, can guess – and see through – his business:

> He in the old celestial cant,
> Confessed his flame, and swore by Styx,
> Whate'er she would desire, to grant;
> But wise Ardelia knew his tricks.

'Baucis and Philemon', an imitation of a story in the eighth book of Ovid's *Metamorphoses*, carries on this lighthearted adaptation of the classical inheritance but it is a poem marked by an increasing surety of technique. Swift now uses antitheses and balance more neatly and effectively; he has attained control of his medium and in the octosyllabic couplet has found a form that obviously suits him, one which he was to use in very nearly half his poems.

Swift realised the value of objects in poetry: nouns as well as verbs give an impressive strength to his poems as in the town eclogue 'A Description of the Morning' or in 'A Description of a City Shower', a poem echoing pastorals by Virgil and his follower Dryden, of which Swift rightly thought better:

> Now from all parts the swelling kennels flow,
> And bear their trophies with them as they go;
> Filth of all hues and odours, seem to tell
> What streets they sailed from, by the sight and smell.
> They, as each torrent drives with rapid force
> From Smithfield, or St Pulchre's shape their course;
> And in huge confluent join at Snow Hill ridge,
> Fall from the conduit prone to Holborn Bridge.
> Sweepings from butchers' stalls, dung, guts, and blood,
> Drowned puppies, stinking sprats, all drenched in mud,
> Dead cats and turnip-tops come tumbling down the flood.

This genre was further enriched by 'A Town Eclogue', its Corydon and Phyllis set firmly in London with its Exchange, Lincoln's Inn, Tyburn Road, Fleet Street, St James's and Wapping.

Swift was learning to develop the unexpected, to juxtapose unlikely elements or characters, to blend the high with the low, the refined with the coarse. Thus 'An Excellent New Song being the Intended Speech of a famous Orator against Peace', the speech put in the mouth of Lord Nottingham who went over to the Whig side, is designed to surprise

> The Duke showed me all his fine house; and the Duchess
> From her closet brought out a full purse in her clutches;
> I talked of a peace, and they both gave a start,
> His Grace swore by God, and her Grace let a fart.

The attack here on the Duke of Marlborough, who had encouraged Nottingham, comes from a Swift who in deploying his capacity for satire is obviously enjoying an ability to extend it, to use it for political purposes, to attack prominent people in public office, and, especially, to retaliate. 'The Virtues of Sid Hamet the Magician's Rod', for instance, his lampoon on Lord Godolphin published in October 1710, resulted as much from his resentment at the cold treatment he had received from Godolphin as from a desire to condemn Godolphin's ways of manipulating government by graft, by granting appointments to various public offices – often sinecures – and by involving himself with projectors in such dubious schemes as the opening up of goldmines in Scotland. Swift's dislike of

Godolphin as a politician had been acerbated by Godolphin's responsibility for having brought about the Union of the English and Scottish parliaments in 1707, a measure deeply resented by Swift because it linked England with a Presbyterian country. He thought that his high Anglican royalist grandfather Thomas Swift had been treated abominably by the puritans; had he not described him as 'persecuted and plundered two and fifty times by the barbarity of Cromwell's hellish crew'? Swift himself had not enjoyed living at Kilroot in Antrim, his first parish, where he had been surrounded by Presbyterians. He attacked the Act of Union of 1707 in 'Verses said to be Written on the Union'. He thought that Ireland would have been a better partner for England than Scotland, and the opening of this poem refers to the rejection of proposals for a Union between England and Ireland in 1703.

> The Queen has lately lost a part
> Of her entirely English heart.

Ireland's loss had been Scotland's gain; the poem ends as it began with Ireland, and a Dubliner's comparison of the Act of Union with that famous double-bottomed boat, the catamaran invented by Sir William Petty, which, impressive in its first year, sank in a storm in Dublin Bay in its second.

Swift's satiric exuberance was buoyed up by the political influence his pen achieved. He became a friend of Harley, who had formed the Tory administration in 1710, first as Chancellor of the Exchequer and then as Lord Treasurer, and St John who was Secretary of State in 1710. He wrote *The Examiner* most successfully on behalf of the Tory Ministry from November 1710 to June 1711. His biting attack on the Duke of Marlborough in *The Conduct of the Allies*, published in November 1711, was a uniquely effective piece of political propaganda in favour of the peace the Tories sought; and the assurance Swift had developed, probably as a result of the success of this, led him into a savage and unnecessary poem which was to cost him dear. 'The Windsor Prophecy' tilted at the Duchess of Somerset, who had become a favourite of Queen Anne:

> And dear England, if ought I understand,
> Beware of Carrots from Northumberland.
> Carrots sown Thyn a deep root may get,
> If so be they are in Sommer set:
> Their Conyngs mark thou, for I have been told
> They Assassine when young, and Poison when old.

Root out these Carrots, O Thou, whose Name
Is backwards and forwards always the same;
And keep close to Thee always that Name,
Which backwards and forwards is almost the same.
And England wouldst Thou be happy still,
Bury those Carrots under a Hill.

Here Swift identifies his characters, especially the Duchess, very clearly indeed. 'Carrots', the redheaded Elizabeth Percy, was the daughter of the Earl of Northumberland. In 1679, when twelve years old, she married the Earl of Ogle; widowed within a year, she then married Thomas Thynne of Longleat House, a Whig MP, in 1681. She fled from him, the marriage unconsummated, to Lady Temple (the wife of Swift's erstwhile patron Sir William Temple) in Holland, and he was shot in his coach in Pall Mall in 1682. Swift suggests that she was involved in the deaths of her husbands; Philipp Cristoph, Count Konigsmark, thought to be her suitor or lover, was accused of having arranged Thynne's murder, but was acquitted. The 'Prophecy' advised the Queen, whose name, Anna, is 'backwards and forwards always the same' to get rid of the Duchess and stick to Mrs Masham, that name 'which backwards and forwards is almost the same'. Mrs Masham (née Abigail Hill), always a good friend of Swift, was Bedchamber Woman to the Queen, having supplanted the Duchess of Marlborough as royal favourite. She married Samuel Masham in 1707; he was created a Baron in 1712, as part of the Tory plan to push the Peace of Utrecht through the House of Lords. She sensibly suggested that Swift should suppress the 'Prophesy', but, though he agreed to do so, the poem was printed, and the Queen, having heard of it on 28 January 1712, determined that he should neither become Dean of Wells when the Deanery became vacant nor be preferred to either of the two Irish bishoprics then vacant. There were to be negotiations in 1713 about his obtaining a prebend at Windsor but these came to nothing. The Queen had taken a poor view of *A Tale of a Tub*, being persuaded, according to Abel Boyer, by the Archbishop of York that it would be a scandal to bestow preferment upon a clergyman 'who was hardly suspected of being a christian'. She was not at all pleased at the idea of his becoming Dean of St Patrick's Cathedral in Dublin, and he was only appointed because the Duke of Ormonde, then Lord Lieutenant, had the Deanery in his gift.

Swift was then returned to the land of his birth, 'the land I hate', sent 'like a poisoned rat to die in a hole' as he put it in a mood of despair. He had witnessed the disintegration of the alliance of the

Earl of Oxford and Viscount Bolingbroke (as Harley and St John
had become). A poem, 'The Faggot', records his views about the
need for the Tories to stick together; but he could not achieve the
impossible, and, perforce, took up permanent residence in the
Deanery in Dublin in August 1714. All the court and the Ministry
had done for him, he commented to William Diaper (a clergyman
who wrote the charming *Nereides: or Sea-Eclogues*, in which the per-
sonae were mermen and mermaids beneath the sea), was to let him
choose his station 'in the country where I am banished'.

'The Author upon Himself', probably written before Swift
returned to Ireland, and 'In Sickness', which was written 'soon
after the Author's coming to live in Ireland, upon the Queen's
death, October 1714', show how clear and bleak was his vision of
the failure of his ambitions.

In the first he described the parts played in the frustration of his
hopes for preferment in England or for an Irish bishopric by the
Duchess of Somerset, by John Sharp the Archbishop of York and by
the Queen:

> By an old red-pate, murdering hag pursued,
> A crazy prelate, and a royal prude.
> By dull divines, who look with envious eyes,
> On every genius that attempts to rise;
> And pausing o'er a pipe, with doubtful nod,
> Give hints, that poets ne'er believe in God.

Swift presents himself mockingly as if seen by enemies:

> Swift had the sin of wit, no venial crime;
> Nay, 'twas affirmed, he sometimes dealt in rhyme;
> Humour, and mirth, had place in all he writ:
> He reconciled divinity and wit.

In the guise of envious comment he then describes his achievement, his friendship with the Ministers of State, his coming to the
court at Windsor, and how

> York is from Lambeth sent, to show the Queen
> A dangerous treatise writ against the spleen;
> Which by the style, the matter and the drift,
> 'Tis thought could be the work of none but Swift.

The poem continues to spell it out. Madam Konigsmark vows
vengeance for his remarks in 'The Windsor Prophecy' upon her
murdered husband, and instils venom into the Queen's ear; the
Queen abandons him to the dangers of prosecution for writing *The*

Public Spirit of the Whigs. There is a price on his head; he tries to heal the breach between the Tory leaders; and the poem ends sadly:

> By faction tired, with grief he waits a while,
> His great contending friends to reconcile.
> Performs what friendship, justice, truth require:
> What could he more, but decently retire?

'In Sickness' shows us the effect upon him of Ménière's disease, labryrinthine vertigo, from which he had suffered since before his twentieth birthday. (The symptoms of this syndrome were not recognised until the accounts given of it by Dr Emile Antoine Ménière in the nineteenth century). Debilitating bouts of the illness left him giddy, overcome by nausea and noises in his head.

> My life is now a burden grown
> To others, e'er it be my own.

The gloomy tone of this poem did not persist, though Swift took time to recover from the wounds his selfrespect had suffered, from his disillusionment about the world of politics. What he had experienced at the peak of his period of power is portrayed in 'Horace, Lib 2, Sat. 6":

> 'Tis (let me see) three years and more
> (October next, it will be four)
> Since Harley bid me first attend,
> And chose me for an humble friend.

His sense of exile persisted at first: he wrote to Pope nine months after he had taken up residence in the Deanery to describe his new life in Dublin:

> You are to understand that I live in the corner of a vast unfurnished house; my family consists of a steward, a groom, a helper in the stable, a foot-man, and an old maid, who are all at board-wages, and when I do not dine abroad, or make an entertainment, (which last is very rare) I eat a mutton-pie, and drink half a pint of wine; my amusements are defending my small dominions against the Archbishop, and endeavouring to reduce my rebellious choir.

Swift had a strong sense of duty. He had immediately immersed himself in the affairs of the Deanery, and, after a series of struggles with the Chapter which were to last for nearly seven years, he achieved a position where he could assert his authority, and was regarded as 'a smart dean'. He was increasingly anxious about his friends in England. In 1715 Oxford and Bolingbroke were impeached for high treason and the Duke of Ormonde after them. Oxford was held in the Tower of London, the other two escaped to France. Swift was expecting that he might himself be arrested; his letters were opened and some of his Irish friends were suspected of Jacobitism, among them his most trusted friend, Charles Ford, who had been dismissed from his post as Gazetteer (and was arrested and imprisoned on returning from France in 1715). Swift began to write *An Enquiry into the Behaviour of the Queen's Last Ministry*, a justification of his friends (which was not, however, published in his lifetime). It is no wonder that he had written to Charles Ford in September 1714: 'What do you talk of writing in this country, I can as easily fly'.

To add to his troubles there was the problem of Esther Van Homrigh, whom he called Vanessa. Despite all his anxious advice to her not to come to Ireland, she arrived in Dublin in 1714; after living at first in Turnstile Alley there, she then moved to Celbridge Abbey, a large house and family property on the Liffey, about eleven miles from Dublin. Swift had become an intimate friend of the family in London when Mrs Van Homrigh had moved there with her children in 1707 after the death of her husband Bartholomew Van Homrigh, a successful merchant, of Dutch extraction, who had been Lord Mayor of Dublin. The Van Homrighs lived well in London: as Swift remarked somewhat defensively to Stella in the *Journal* they kept good company there. (Vanessa, however, is only mentioned three times and not by name in the Journal to Stella: it is likely that Stella did not like his friendship with the Van Homrighs and Swift certainly was not very candid about it in the *Journal*.) He had become a constant visitor when he returned to London in 1710, and his friendship with Vanessa, then twenty-two, was close: 'I will .... dine with you thrice a week; and tell you a thousand secrets provided you will have no quarrels with me.' It was a heady mixture: a blend of educative advice, exhortation to take exercise, teasing or raillery, shared joking and appreciation of her as a person that she found delightful: but she was an emotional, highly strung young woman and wanted more than friendship. The poem 'Cadenus and Vanessa' tells us something about the relationship – but only something, for it is primarily a private poem, and an ironic one, to Vanessa, and as such it leaves open the question of how much of it is in earnest, how much in jest:

> But what success Vanessa met,
> Is to the world a secret yet:
> Whether the nymph, to please her swain,

Talks in a high romantic strain;
Or whether he at last descends
To like with less seraphic ends;
Or, to compound the business, whether
They temper love and books together;
Must never to mankind be told,
Nor shall the conscious muse unfold.

Some of the letters between the middle-aged Dean and this lively vivacious girl which survive show his unease at her lack of discretion, for Vanessa was in her own words, 'born with violent passions' and did not take kindly to his caution. He 'ever feared the tattle of this nasty town and told you so', he wrote to her (probably in December 1714). He did not want their relationship in Dublin to be similar to that which they had enjoyed in London, when he had kept his best gown and periwig in the Van Homrigh house, changing into them – as he walked on his way into town to discuss policy and propaganda with the ministers, to meet friends and those who wanted him to use his influence on their behalf – and out of them on the way back. Now he advised her that he thought it inconvenient, for a hundred reasons, that he should make her house a sort of constant dwelling place. (Mrs Van Homrigh had died in London, so had Vanessa's remaining brother by 1715 and her sister Mary (Moll) was to die at Celbridge in February 1721.) He would come when he conveniently could. Vanessa told him 'to alter his behaviour quickly', assuring him that she had too much spirit 'to sit down contented with such treatment'. They did meet at intervals but she suffered 'unexpressable distress' from his 'prodigious neglect' of her. The love she bore him, she wrote, was 'not only seated in my soul for there is not a single action of my frame that is not blended with it.' Separation would not change her sentiments but, she demanded, what had 'caused this prodigious change' in him? Her last known letter to him complains that he had forgotten her, that she had so little joy in life that she didn't care how soon her own life ended. Within a year she died, on 2 June 1723.

Swift, the Irish country clergyman who had persuaded the twenty-year-old Stella and her companion Rebecca Dingley to move to Ireland in 1701, had, not unnaturally, changed after his experiences in London from 1707 to 1714 and particularly as a result of being at the centre of political affairs from 1710 on. And Swift, the influential author, the friend of the Ministers, whom Vanessa had known in London, changed when he became an Irish

Dean. However, despite his warnings to her that all had changed, he was able to write to her in intimate terms: 'Soyez assure que jamais personne du monde a eté aimee honoree estimeè adoree par votre amie [sic] que vous.' But the world of Dublin contained Stella, his 'truest most virtuous and valuable friend'. After they had to come to Dublin the ladies – as Stella and Rebecca became known – were accepted as his friends: conscious of moral rectitude, Swift and they cared nothing for gossip; morally correct, they considered themselves above it. A later poem 'On Censure' (dated 1727 in the 1735 Faulkner edition) conveys something of his attitude:

> Bare innocence is no support,
> When you are tried in Scandal's Court ...
> Alas; they would not do you wrong:
> But, all appearances are strong ...
> The most effectual way to baulk
> Their malice is – to let them talk!

When Swift was away from Dublin the ladies would move into his accommodation; they sometimes stayed at Laracor when he was not there; but when he was in residence in his parish they sometimes stayed nearby. He did not have to defend the unusual arrangements of their friendship – there is the tradition that he never saw Stella alone; he never saw her in the mornings unless the ladies were travelling with him. Vanessa's case, however, was very different: she was a single girl and therefore gossip about her relationship with Swift was likely and had to be avoided. It was, to put it mildly, a difficult situation for all three of them, Swift, Vanessa and Stella.

Swift's close friendship with Stella was celebrated in poems, mainly those he wrote for her birthdays, the first one of which we know being dated 13 March 1718-19. Stella was then thirty-eight, though Swift, perhaps conscious on this occasion of his own casual attitude to dates, begins

> Stella this day is thirty-four,
> (We shan't dispute a year or more)

There are several of these poems, teasing, affectionate, intended to be reassuring. With Vanessa living near Dublin, Stella may have needed to be reassured. In the poem of 1719-20 her appearance is compared to the sign of the true old Angel-Inn, but travellers when a new sign is hung two doors away

> As fine as dauber's hands can make it,
> In hopes that strangers may mistake it;
> We think it both a shame and sin
> To quit the true old Angel Inn.

> Now, this is Stella's case in fact
> An Angel's face, a little cracked;
> (Could poets or could painters fix
> How angels look at thirty-six?)

But can it be of the younger Vanessa that Swift is thinking when he introduces Chloe into the poem?

> Then, Chloe, still go on to prate
> Of thirty-six and thirty-eight;
> Pursue thy trade of scandal-picking,
> Thy hints that Stella is no chicken.

He warns the younger woman that youth alone is not enough

> No bloom of youth can ever blind
> The cracks and wrinkles of your mind,
> All men of sense will pass your door,
> And crowd to Stella's at four-score.

Stella's poem to Swift 'On his Birthday, November 30, 1721' accepts many of Swift's views: he had praised her 'breeding, humour, wit and sense' and in this noble, generous poem she records how he

> taught how I might youth prolong
> By knowing what was right and wrong ...
> How wit and virtue from within
> Send out a smoothness o'er the skin;
> Your lectures could my fancy fix,
> And I can please at thirty-six.

In another poem 'Jealousy' she had recorded her desire to be shielded from the rage of the tyrant Jealousy:

> Ah! Love, you've poorly played the monarch's part,
> You conquered but you can't defend my heart:
> So blessed was I throughout thy happy reign,
> I thought this monster banished from thy train ...

The only direct comment of hers on Vanessa that we know is her remark (when some gentlemen, 'strangers to Stella's situation', visited Ford and one said 'Vanessa must be an extraordinary woman to have inspired the Dean to write so finely upon her') that 'the point was not quite so clear, for it was well known the Dean could write finely upon a broomstick.' In the birthday poem to Swift, however, she reveals herself above pettiness:

> The sigh of Chloe at fifteen
> Coquetting, gives me not the spleen;
> The idol now of every fool
> Till Time shall make their passions cool;
> Then tumbling down Time's steepy hill,
> While Stella holds her station still.

Some words of Yeats, who thought her poem better than any of Swift's to her, could be quoted: 'Heart mysteries there'. The poem with its quiet restraint, its emphasis on dignity, ends memorably, indeed most movingly

> Long be the day that gave you birth
> Sacred to friendship, wit and mirth;
> Late dying may you cast a shred
> Of your rich mantle o'er my head;
> To bear with dignity my sorrow,
> One day alone, then die tomorrow.

Swift complains of his stock of wit decaying in 1721-22; elaborates in a poem of 1722-23 on 'a great bottle of wine, long buried, being that day dug up' which gives a picture of his household staff and their guests present on Stella's birthday, Stella herself, Rebecca Dingley, Charles Ford and the Grattan brothers; and in 1723-4 (three quarters of a year after Vanessa's death) records his illness on her birthday, a time when Stella and Mrs Dingley had moved into the Deanery to nurse him:

> She tends me, like an humble slave;
> And, when indecently I rave,
> When out my brutish passions break,
> With gall in every word I speak,
> She, with soft speech, my anguish cheers,
> Or melts my passions down with tears

The poem of 1724-5 is another where poetic license – or convenience of rhyme – alters their years, he being fifty-eight, she forty-four at the time:

> At fifty-six, if this be true,
> Am I a poet fit for you?

> Or, at the age of forty-three,
> Are you a subject fit for me?

She must be grave; he must be wise. The last poem of 1727 is serious in its tone; he wants to avoid thinking that she is ill and he grown old:

> From not the gravest of divines,
> Accept for once some serious lines.

He seeks comfort for them both: virtue will surely assuage

> Grief, sickness, poverty, and age;
> And strongly shoot a radiant dart,
> To shine through life's declining part

The poem is heartfelt in its ending; he reminds Stella on her 'sickly couch' of past joy, urges her to take pity on her pitying friends:

> Nor let your ills affect your mind,
> To fancy they can be unkind.
> Me, surely me, you ought to spare,
> Who gladly would your sufferings share;
> Or give my scrap of life to you,
> And think it far beneath your due;
> You, to whose care so oft I owe,
> That I'm alive to tell you so.

Swift had not written very much for six years after he settled in Dublin as Dean of St Patrick's. He had determined to keep out of political life. 'I hope', he had written to Charles Ford in September 1714, 'I shall keep my resolution of never meddling with Irish politics'. But by December 1719 he was telling Ford that 'as the world is now turned' no cloister was 'retired enough to keep politics out.' He admitted that 'they raise my passions whenever they come in my way'. And England's treatment of Ireland certainly stirred him. There was the Act passed in March 1720 which removed the jurisdiction of the Irish House of Lords: it provoked universal discontent. They say publicly, Swift told Ford, that 'having been the most loyal submissive complying subjects that ever Prince had, no subjects were ever so ill treated.' Swift was deeply distressed by the poverty he saw everywhere: it prompted him to criticise England's economic policy towards Ireland in *A Proposal for the Universal Use of Irish Manufacture*, a pamphlet declared seditious, its printers brought to trial. Swift then wrote *An Excellent New Song on a*

Seditious Pamphlet, the preamble to the poem recording how 'that infamous wretch' William Whitshed, the Chief Justice of the King's Bench in Ireland, 'prosecuted Waters the printer with so much violence and injustice, that he kept the jury nine hours, and sent them away eleven times, till out of mere weariness they were forced to give a special verdict.' Whitshed came in for further attack in another poem 'Whitshed's Motto on His Coach', but Swift was now largely writing prose.

He was busy with *Gulliver's Travels* in 1721; his Irish patriotism, however, burst out in 1724 with the first of the *Drapier's Letters*, prompted by the award of a patent to William Wood (an ironmaster from the West Midlands of England, a Whig who had smoothed his way with bribery and was involved in various shady enterprises) to coin halfpence for Ireland. Swift's campaign was successful, and the irony which flooded the letters overflowed into poems dealing with Wood and the controversy over his proposed coinage. These include 'A Serious Poem on William Wood', 'An Epigram on Wood's Brass Money', 'Prometheus: on Wood the Patentee's Irish Halfpence', 'Verses on the Upright Judge who condemned the Drapier's Printer', 'Wood, an Insect', 'On Wood the Ironmonger' and 'A Simile'. Swift, despite himself, was becoming an Irish patriot, the first effective anti-colonial author. His sense of public morality was affronted by the poverty he saw around him in 'wretched Dublin, in miserable Ireland'. He resented the effects of England's rule. 'Am I a free man in England', he wrote, 'and do I become a slave in six hours by crossing the channel?'.

Swift was recovering his poetic energy as he built up a new social life for himself in Ireland. Two of his new friends, the Reverend Thomas Sheridan and the Reverend Patrick Delany, shared his delight in the bagatelle, and there are many lively poems to Sheridan, in particular. These squibs are lighthearted, though they come near the bone in their vignettes of Sheridan's scold of a wife. Sheridan's house in County Cavan, Quilca, is depicted in 'To Quilca' but hardly in the terms of an orthodox bread-and-butter letter:

> A rotten cabin, dripping rain;
> Chimneys with scorn rejecting smoke;
> Stools, tables, chairs and bedsteads, broke,
> Here elements have lost their uses
> Air ripens not, nor earth produces....

But then Sheridan obviously enjoyed a joke even when against himself; and there were many of these. The two men exchanged riddles and ridicule. Swift calls Sheridan a goose; then comes in the vein of 'Mrs Harris's Petition' the wonderful breathless outburst of 'Mary the Cook-Maid's Letter to Dr Sheridan'.

Some of the poems to Delany focus on the Epistle that the young clergyman wrote to Carteret, the Lord Lieutenant, with whom Swift was on friendly terms despite the row over Wood's half-pence. 'An Apology to Lady Carteret' shows the easy relationship Swift had with the Carterets. Delany, whose career Swift had aided, was seeking further preferment, and Swift teases him for spending too much on Delville, his villa at Glasnevin to the north of Dublin with its fine view over the Bay. He gives firm advice to the younger man in 'An Epistle upon an Epistle':

> Take this advice then from your friend,
> To your ambition put an end.
> Be frugal, Pat: pay what you owe
> Before you 'build and you bestow'.
> Be modest: nor address your betters
> With begging, vain, familiar letters.

'A Libel on the Reverent Dr Delany and His Excellency John, Lord Carteret' carries on the jesting, but this poem reverts to Swift's London friends, Congreve, Steele (who had quarrelled with him) Gay, Addison and Pope, and then turns, after reminding Delany that he has got a place already

> An office for your talents fit,
> To flatter, carve and show your wit

to Carteret:

> I do the most that friendship can
> I hate the Viceroy, love the man.

This echoes his 'To Dr Delany, on the Libels writ against him' which consoles the younger man:

> 'Tis eminence makes envy rise,
> As fairest fruits attract the flies

And 'To a Friend who had been much abused in many inveterate Libels' points out the need for wit and learning to withstand attack. And there is the serious view put in an earlier poem, 'To Mr Delany':

> Three gifts for conversation fit
> Are humour, raillery and wit.

Swift goes on in this poem to distinguish between raillery and gross abuse, between rudeness and repartee, and then answers Delany's supposed wonder as to why he writes 'So gravely, where the subject's light', and we then realise the poem is an adverse comment on Sheridan's 'illmannered muse', Sheridan having alleged in a poem that Swift's muse was dead.

Swift's circle in Dublin, all of them friends of Stella as well, included the four Grattan brothers, the Reverend Daniel Jackson, whose nose occasioned poems, and the Rochfort brothers. Swift stayed at Gaulstown with George Rochfort in 1721, and the country visit prompted, as many others did, several jesting poems. They included 'George Nim-Dan-Dean Esq to Mr Sheridan', 'George Nim-Dan-Dean's Invitation to Mr Sheridan', 'To Mr Sheridan, upon his Verses Written in Circles'; and 'The Part of a Summer at the House of George Rochfort, Esq', a poem which gives a light-hearted account of the houseparty and its doings.

A bantering poem described how Stella enjoyed Ford's hospitality on a visit to Wood Park in 1723. She obviously liked living in the country, and in 'Stella at Woodpark' Swift teases her about leaving the pastoral scenes for Dublin:

> The winter sky began to frown,
> Poor Stella must pack off to town.
> From purling streams and fountains bubbling,
> To Liffey's stinking tide in Dublin:
> From wholesome exercise and air
> To sossing in an easy chair;
> From stomach sharp and hearty feeding,
> To piddle like a lady breeding:
> From ruling there the household singly,
> To be directed here by Dingley:
> From every day a lordly banquet,
> To half a joint, and God be thank it:
> From every meal Pontac in plenty,
> To half a pint one day in twenty....

Stella's health, however, deteriorated during the seventeen twenties. There were trips to Quilca in search of recovery. Swift prescribed his usual panacea of fresh air and exercise, and she seems to have improved from her visit. Mirth was necessary to recovery also, as 'A Receipt to Restore Stella's Youth' suggests, jokingly urging her to eat more:

> Why, Stella, should you knit your brow,

If I compare you to the cow?
'Tis just the case: for you have fasted
So long till all your flesh is wasted,
And must against the warmer days
Be sent to Quilca down to graze;
Where mirth, and exercise, and air,
Will soon your appetite repair.

Her recovery, however, was not lasting, and Swift's poem, 'Holyhead. September 25, 1727' conveys his frustration when held up at Holyhead, his despair at the delay, knowing that Stella was probably dying in Dublin:

Before, I always found the wind
To me was most malicious kind,
But now the danger of a friend
On whom my hopes and fears depend,
Absent from whom all climes are cursed,
With whom I'm happy in the worst,
With rage impatient makes me wait
A passage to the land I hate.

She was to die four months later on 28 January 1728.

By persuading Stella to live in Ireland in 1701, Swift had created a continuation of some of the enjoyable elements of life at Moor Park; now that she was dead he may have hoped to find some compensation for her loss in the ambience of Market Hill, the seat of Sir Arthur and Lady Acheson, near Armagh; perhaps there could be an Irish echo, however faint, of that earlier orderly life in Sir William Temple's household. He stayed at Market Hill on three occasions, in 1728, 1729 and 1730. He even bought land from Sir Arthur at Drumlack near Market Hill with the idea of building a house there, the purchase recorded in 'To Dean Swift' and 'Drapier's Hill', the name suggested for the purchase by Sir Arthur. The decision to abandon the plan is given in 'The Dean's Reasons for not building at Drapier's Hill':

What'er I promised or intended,
No fault of mine, the scheme is ended.

Were there too many Presbyterians about? Or had the plan of building a house been an over-impulsive expression of lonely bachelor boredom which seemed less sensible on reflection? Did he feel too old for the venture? Or was there a cooling in the friendship with the Achesons? We can but surmise, as in so many happenings of Swift's life. Certainly he must have been an exigent guest in many ways; he may have outstayed his welcome, and been aware or been made aware of it.... if even some of the jesting of 'Lady Acheson weary of the Dean' is to be taken seriously:

> After a week, a month, a quarter,
> And day succeeding after day,
> Says not a word of his departure,
> Though not a soul would have him stay.

He was consistent in his behaviour: poems, penned as if written by others, indulge in complaints about the way he behaved, while Lady Acheson is, like Stella and Vanessa before her, to be educated in 'My Lady's Lamentation and Complaint against the Dean':

> 'What, madam? No walking,
> No reading, nor talking?
> You're now in your prime,
> Make use of your time.'

Lady Acheson, however, does not seem to have minded the mock insults; and he would hardly have been invited back after the first long visit if he had been an unwelcome guest. Like Stella and Vanessa and many others, Lady Acheson was given her nicknames, 'Skinny' and 'Snipe', and her thinness was lamented in 'Death and Daphne' – written 'To an agreeable young Lady, but extremely Lean'. 'Twelve Articles' and 'Daphne' continue with the raillery:

> Lose not time to contradict her,
> Nor endeavour to convict her.
> Never take it in your thought,
> That she'll own, or cure a fault.

'A Panegyric on the Dean in the person of a Lady in the North' puts into Lady Acheson's mouth a matter for which Swift can indeed be praised, his lack of class feeling. Snob he could be on occasion; he had greatly enjoyed his period among the great in London; he respected landed proprietors; but he was always interested in individuals. He had written to Pope on 29 September 1725 'principally I hate and detest that animal called man; although I heartily love John, Peter, Thomas and so forth.' Now he puts this basic attitude into this vignette of his own behaviour, locating it at Market Hill:

> Whene'er you joke, 'tis all a case;
> Whether with Dermot, or his Grace;
> With Teague O'Murphy, or an earl;
> A Duchess or a kitchen girl.

> With such dexterity you fit
> Their several talents to your wit,
> That Moll the chambermaid can smoke.
> And Gaghagan take every joke.

Out of his extended visits to Market Hill came the delightfully comic poem 'On Cutting Down the Old Thorn at Market Hill', a blend of pastoral, mock-epic and mock-romance. The Achesons enjoyed the Dean's jesting in verse; they were, Swift wrote to a clergyman mentioned in the poem, 'Well pleased' with 'The Grand Question Debated', in which he speculated about the likely outcomes of making a bawn, a walled enclosure for cattle, into a barracks or a malt-house, creating a restoration *miles gloriosus* in an imagined captain, and yet again teasing Lady Acheson with being 'skinny and lean'. 'A Pastoral Dialogue' is a cheerful poem, deliberately vulgar in its genial mockery of bucolic poetry, carefully located at Market Hill. Swift's poems include not only neighbours of the Achesons but embrace many members of their staff. 'The Revolution at Market Hill', for instance, brings in Hannah, Lady Acheson's waitingwoman, as other poems had 'Kit, her footman', Darby and Wood 'two of Sir Arthur's managers', Dennis, the butler, Peggy Dixon, the housekeeper and Nick Gahagan, 'Hibernian clown'.

In the midst of poems of particularity, written for his friends' amusement – and his own – were poems of a more general satiric kind. 'The Journal of a Modern Lady', for instance, though written at Market Hill, is probably not to be read as a critical portrayal of Lady Acheson so much as a portrait of any lady enjoying a fashionable life in town, cards and gossip filling not only her days but nights;

> At last they hear the watchman knock,
> 'A frosty morn – past four o'clock.'
> The chairmen are not to be found,
> 'Come let us play another round.'
>
> Now, all in haste they huddle on
> Their hoods and cloaks and get them gone:
> But first, the winner must invite
> The company tomorrow night.
>
> Unlucky madam, left in tears,
> (Who now again quadrille forswears)
> With empty purse and aching head,
> Steals to her sleeping spouse to bed.

There were the more savage portrayals, in true comic vein, of differences between appearance and reality, the so-called 'scatological'
or 'excremental' poems such as 'The Lady's Dressing Room' and 'A
Beautiful Young Nymph going to Bed' or those stressing contrasts,
between dream and reality, as in 'Strephon and Chloe' and
'Cassinus and Peter', with its classical references and imagery slowly leading to the sudden shock effect Swift had carefully planned:

> 'No wonder how I lost my wits;
> Oh! Celia, Celia, Celia shits.'

Apart from Swift's anti-feminine satires being part of a long literary tradition, some of these poems were probably prompted, paradoxically, by personal fastidiousness. Swift's sensitivity to smells
and dirt is obvious; by writing about them he could face their existence: it was a form of exorcism. 'A Description of the Morning'
and 'A City Shower' reveal his horror at some of the sordid scenes
of London, but it is a fascinated horror. His emphasis on the need
for cleanliness was strong. He was obviously disgusted by aspects
of physicality but his poems present this disgust in a complex way,
expressing humour, revulsion and ultimately pity for the human
predicament: the contrast is between ideal and real, between aims
for (and illusions about) spirituality and an animality doomed to
decay. Swift reminds his readers that romantic ideas are based
upon the facts of copulation, that love, so-called but actually lust,
can lead to disease, to pain, to the antithesis of all that christian
love or marriage should mean. It is a moral message; it is
hypocrisy, he insists, to ignore the processes of excretion, urination,
voiding wind: they are, however inelegant, however horrifying to
him, part of human mortality, against which he employed the
defence of examining the worse aspects, of facing them as an inte-
gral part of human behaviour.

Not an 'O altitudo' (though, ironically, perhaps, the Latin word
can also mean the opposite of height), but then that is not what we
expect in Swift's poetry. He is an eighteenth- not a seventeenth-
century poet (and to a twentieth-century reader, affected by nineteenth-century romanticism, he lacks an interest in many things
that might be expected of a poet: in art, for instance, or music, or
landscape, or in introspective analysis). He distrusted imagination,
excessive speculation and mysticism: he wanted to be practical;
and his poetry makes this very clear. Just as faith could be acquired
without, as he put in *A Tale of a Tub*, giving up our senses or contradicting our reason, so the folly of mankind could be laughed out
of countenance. To do this effectively in his poetry – as indeed in

his prose – Swift needed, and had, a basis of morality and the irrepressible imagination to play 'some roguish trick' upon his readers.

While Stella's death in 1728, when Swift was into his sixties, did not cause any diminution in his poetic output, it is perhaps not overfanciful to suggest that she had restrained the expression of some of the excesses of his rage. Though disliking loose talk she was certainly no prude, and the loss of her companionship (and her judgment which he so respected) must have affected his attitudes and poetic reactions not only to contemporary manners, but to public life, to the contradictions between human aspirations and activities, between political professions and performances. For instance, the 'Verses occasioned by the sudden Drying Up of St Patrick's Well near Trinity College, Dublin' of 1729 go back in feeling to 'Ireland', written two years earlier when Swift was at Holyhead, impatiently and despairingly waiting passage to Ireland which he regarded as a

> land of slaves
> Where all are fools, and all are knaves.
> Where every knave and fool is bought
> Yet kindly sells himself for naught.

Swift adopts the persona of Saint Patrick, gives a quick rundown of Irish history up to his time:

> Thou still with tyrants in succession cursed,
> The last invaders trampling on the first

and ends up with a prophecy, attacking, as the notes in the Faulkner edition of 1762 put it, 'Wood's ruinous project against the people of Ireland which was supported by Sir Robert Walpole in 1724' and denouncing 'the absentees who spend the income of their Irish estates, places and pensions in England'.

Walpole himself was the object of attack in 'The Character of Sir Robert Walpole' just as Marlborough had been in 'A Satirical Elegy on the Death of a Late Famous General'. Swift could pursue those of whom he disapproved pertinaciously, and as he grew older his poems became much more powerful: some, such as 'The Place of the Damned', overflow with an exuberant vigour; others face the advance of old age, the inevitability of death, with bravery, an attitude of acceptance irradiated by humour – a heroism in the histrionics to be echoed by Yeats in some of the poems of his old age. 'The Verses on the Death of Dr Swift' avoid self-pity as they picture how the Dean's special friends will herald his approaching end, gradually building up their cumulative effect. The portrayal of age

is devastating: 'that old vertigo', the decay of memory, the old fashioned wit, the search for a younger audience, the inability to find a
rhyme quickly, loss of fancy, failure of appetite, all are listed. Then
comes the fatal day, the bequeathing of all his money to public
uses, and the reactions to the news, of the Queen, of Walpole, of
Curll, of St John:

> Poor Pope will grieve a month; and Gay
> A week; and Arbuthnot a day

After follows the vignette of the

> Female friends, whose tender hearts
> Have better learnt to act their parts

carefully playing their cards while issuing platitudes about the
Dean:

> His time was come, he ran his race;
> We hope he's in a better place

Here the rhymes accentuate contrasts between conventionalities
and concentration on the game of cards:

doleful dumps ...	*What is trumps?*
Mercy on his soul ...	*venture for the vole;*
bear the pall ...	*which King to call;*
I lead a heart ...	friends ... must part.

He envisages his books vanished from the shops; imagines
someone setting out his character impartially. This allows him to
make his own apology: his exposing the fool, lashing the knave; his
being trusted in great affairs and helping individuals. His defence
of liberty is finally summed up in the favourable if not entirely
accurate description of his kind of satire:

> Yet, malice never was his aim;
> He lashed the vice but spared the name.

Then comes the final jest:

> He gave the little wealth he had,
> To build a house for fools and mad:
> And showed by satiric touch,
> No nation wanted it so much.

What he wanted to do in this poem was to justify himself by
giving an accurate account of his character and conduct as he saw
them, of the moral view that, he thought, made his satire objective

and impartial. Being Swift he could not do this without humour, without irony, and without the wit that shaped his very personal brand of raillery.

Two other major poems, 'On Poetry' and 'The Legion Club' demonstrate the continuing strength of Swift's mind, the power of his poetic technique in his sixties. He uses language compellingly, as in this passage from 'On Poetry: a Rhapsody', where the alliteration is forceful in its vigour, the 'b's of the first four lines being a careful preparation in advance for the powerful verb he italicised in the last line:

> Not beggar's brat, on bulk begot;
> Not bastard of a pedlar Scot;
> Not boy brought up to cleaning shoes,
> The spawn of Bridewell, or the stews;
> Not infants dropped, the spurious pledges
> Of gypsies littering under hedges,
> Are so disqualified by fate
> To rise in church, or law, or state,
> As he, whom Phoebus in his ire
> Hath *blasted* with poetic fire.

The picture of ills is repeated with increasing effect, with – a match for Pope's Atticus – its Battus dictating literary fashion:

> Reclining on his elbow-chair,
> Gives judgement with decisive air ...
> He gives directions to the town,
> To cry it up or run it down.

The passage on Grub Street, which begins with the description of Hobbes proving

> that every creature
> Lives in a state of war by nature

gains its force by cumulative energy, by its repetition of examples: the whale eats herrings, the fox geese, the wolf lambs:

> So, naturalists observe, a flea
> Hath smaller fleas that on him prey,
> And these have smaller yet to bite 'em,
> And so proceed *ad infinitum.*

In this poem Swift blends his views on poets and politicians, on princes and potentates, his irony playing powerfully over the prospect of society selected, like some searchlight seeking out the inhabitants in the dark. He is praising in order to blame, employing an inversion of values, a tongue-in-cheek technique designed not only to expose the gimmickry of contemporary authors but the corruption of the chief minister, the contemptibility of the Hanoverian court and, by implication, the general catabasis of the community.

This impressive energy, similar to that employed in outspoken earlier poems such as 'Mad Mullinix and Timothy', 'Tom Mullinex and Dick' and 'Dick, a Maggot', drives 'A Character Panygeric and Description of the Legion Club', an attack aimed at some of the three hundred members of the Irish Parliament, the 'three hundred brutes' of what Swift told Sheridan was 'a very masterly poem'. Himself always a strong support of his church, Swift had been provoked by a committee of the House supporting the protest of a group of freeholders against the pasturage tithes. He describes the House of Commons as a madhouse, obviously thinking of the 'house for fools and mad' that he would endow so generously, the first to be founded in Ireland. (As Maurice James Craig has pointed out 'the apparent flippancy' with which the scheme was treated in a pamphlet of 1733 shows that Swift was in such earnest that he must make a joke of it. Not for nothing had he been a governor of Bedlam; his plans for St Patrick's Hospital, now nearly two hundred and fifty years in existence, were humane and civilised.) His own intellectual energy was now, however, beginning to diminish. The poem 'On his own Deafness' – written in Latin and in English versions, probably in 1734 when Swift was suffering from a severe bout of Ménière's disease – records another depressed mood when he was:

> Deaf, giddy, odious to my friends,
> Now all my consolation ends;

He manages to end the poem, however with a jest

> As thunder now no more I start
> Than at the rumbling of a cart.
> And what's incredible, alack;
> No more I hear a woman's clack.

To alleviate his deafness somewhat Swift had a more than sufficient store of remembered speech – his *Polite Conversation*, published in 1738, running to about 30,000 words in all, including its superbly ironic, fresh and clear introduction, has been judged by Eric Partridge to be by far the best single record of polite English spoken at any given period. We don't know whether Swift, like his supposed author Simon Wagstaff, jotted down in a notebook as soon as he could conversations he had heard. He described the conversations as collected 'with infinite labour, and close application, during the space of thirty-six years'. The speakers reveal themselves in conversations which are completely natural in effect. These conversations, put together as three dialogues, are a culmination of Swift's work on the English language (which included a *Tatler* essay [230], a *Proposal for Correcting the English Tongue, The Letter to a Young Clergyman, A Discourse to prove the Antiquity of the English Tongue*): they are set in Lord Smart's house in St James's Park. His poetry, however, captured sounds of another kind, Dublin sounds which were part of his life, in 'Verses Made for the Women Who Cry Apples, etc.' published a year after his death; they remind us yet again that Swift was interested in the human aspects of life around him, had an ability to find rhymes for them, and was able, too, to put the right word in the right place.

ASPECTS OF SWIFT AS A LETTER WRITER

One of the main delights – and there are many – in reading Swift's letters arises from his writing for the present rather than for posterity. They have a forceful immediacy, for the prose style of his correspondence is generally like that of good talk: unstudied, natural, flowing. Like a good talker aware of his hearers and their reactions Swift obviously kept the recipients of his letters in mind as he wrote. He alters his style to suit the person, the individual whom he is addressing. There is, therefore, great variety of tone: he can be simply descriptive, bringing past or present events sharply into focus, for he could observe skillfully and selectively. Endowed with a great gift for narration, he tells a story well in his letters, just as well as he told the story of *Gulliver's Travels*. He can be witty in his ridicule of pretentiousness, tenderly teasing and flirtatious, friendly, admonitory, jesting, jocose. A man of sharp intelligence and, at times, of immense intellectual energy, he was also moody, driven to deep depression when bouts of Ménière's disease left him deaf, giddy, nauseous, or when he despaired of reconciling the Tory Ministers, or when in pessimistic vein he considered the future of the Church of Ireland. On its behalf he could be aggressive – and also apprehensive: on the state of politics he could be shrewd. Personally proud, prizing his independence, he could be disillusioned by and resentful of broken promises made by the great. But there were, of course, the pleasures of friendship to offset frustrations and failures. Swift liked good company and valued it; he revelled in raillery; he enjoyed the bagatelle. And the letters reveal this engaging element in his personality, both those he wrote and those his friends wrote to him. For some years he was at the centre of power in London, a close friend of the Tory Ministers, an author who played a vital part in 'the Establishment of a European peace'. Later he became an Irish patriot, the first powerful and effective anticolonial writer. All these experiences and the quality of mind that shaped them, all the complexity of his own character, suffuse his letters; they are as varied in nature as were those with whom he exchanged correspondence. And they were many, as a glance at the contents list of the present standard edition of the *Letters* demonstrates, its five volumes amounting to 2377 pages, while the letters written to Stella are also extensive, the standard two volume edition of the *Journal to Stella* containing 801 pages.

Anyone attempting to achieve a selection of the letters that could be contained in a single volume of a reasonable size, say, of three hundred pages or so, the kind of book that might be read comfortably in bed, would find it difficult to do justice to such a rich and varied correspondence. Some broad divisions could be made – though there would obviously be some overlapping – but within them selection would be challenging indeed, for there are so many intrinsically interesting letters demanding inclusion that one volume would seem completely inadequate.

II

Categorising the correspondence leads inevitably to a considera-tion of Swift's life, which is so illuminated by the letters. It would be possible, for instance, to group together letters which relate to his career in the Church of Ireland. He was in orders for fifty years. Ordained as a deacon in 1694, as a priest in January 1694-95, he moved from the remote prebend of Kilroot, (three parishes on the northern shore of Belfast Lough, beyond Carrickfergus) back to England in 1696 (resigning Kilroot in 1698), and thence to Dublin in 1699, to become, in 1700, Vicar of Laracor in County Meath, and Prebendary of Dunlavin in St. Patrick's Cathedral, as Dean of which he was installed in 1713. He was to die in the Deanery thir-ty-two years later, in 1745. Swift was a loyal churchman, seeing himself in the capacity of a clergyman 'to be one appointed by Providence for defending a post assigned me and for gaining over as many enemies as I can'. His letters demonstrate his often con-troversial activity as well as confirming his considerable and con-scientious achievement in the service of the Church of Ireland.

It is not entirely clear why Swift decided to become a clergyman. Living in Sir William Temple's household in England after he left Trinity College, Dublin, had taught him a great deal, but he obvi-ously felt that he could not stay there indefinitely. He would have to make a career. In the *Autobiographical Fragment* he describes him-self as inclined to take orders but as having a scruple of entering the Church 'merely for support'. When Temple offered him a post in the Office of the Rolls in Ireland he told him that this offer meant that, now that he had another means of making a living, he could enter the Church without being driven into it 'for a maintainance', and that he was resolved to go back to Ireland and enter orders. Earlier he had informed his uncle, in late 1692, that Temple had assured him that the King would give him a prebend, but nothing had come of this, Sir William being 'less forward' in the matter than Swift would have wished. By May 1694 he had left Temple to go to Dublin to seek ordination; his departure left Temple extremely angry and refusing to 'promise anything firmly at all.' In Dublin, however, Swift found that the Bishops and particularly Narcissus Marsh, then Archbishop of Dublin, insisted upon his producing a testimonial from Sir William. He had to write the letter that Temple's sister Lady Giffard, who did not like the young man, characterised as his 'penitential letter', asking for some certificate of his behaviour during the period of almost three years he had spent in Temple's family: the certificate was to cover his morals and learning and to make it clear that the reasons of his leaving Temple's service were not 'occasioned by any ill actions'. Temple obliged: whether he also recommended Swift for a benefice we don't know; it seems unlikely. Not being able to make a clean break with Temple at the time of the rift and not to be able to begin his own career through his own efforts must have been disappointing; and to have to write the 'penitential letter' a blow to his pride.

Swift's tenure of Kilroot was hardly encouraging. The Bishop of the diocese, Edward Walkington, thought Swift had obtained his prebend through an error – his predecessor Milne had been deprived of his office for non-residence, intemperance and incontinence, but Walkington argued that he had merely been suspended. Swift's benefice was reduced by twenty pounds a year, allowed to Milne. The diocese of Down and Connor had suffered from scandals and maladministration; many churches were in a state of disrepair or in ruins; there was a lack of manse houses and glebes; and impropriations meant that laymen held Church lands and tithes. All these conditions had led to an increase of dissent. We have no letters recording Swift's immediate reactions to his experiences in what was largely a Presbyterian area of Ireland, though his later letters often deal with Nonconformism and his strong views on the Church's temporalities. He thought a sound financial base essential for the well-being of the Church's activities. Kilroot forcibly brought home to him the weakness of the Church of Ireland. He was soon to play an active part in its defence, couching in the language of struggle the view he formed that Providence had appointed him to defend his post.

After his return from Kilroot to England his hopes of a Prebend there were again disappointed with the resignation from office of the Earl of Sutherland, the death of Temple and the failure of the Earl of Romney to press Swift's claims. He continued to have high expectations: when in Dublin as chaplain to the Earl of Berkeley, a

Lord Justice, he thought he should have been appointed Dean of Derry. When that post went to Bolton, Swift was appointed, in succession to him, as Vicar of Laracor in 1700. He did not, however, receive the neighbouring living of Ratoath which Bolton retained. This was a repetition, on a larger scale, of the disappointment Swift had suffered in Kilroot when Milne had retained part – about a fifth – of the income. Laracor, however, does feature – and generally very happily – in Swift's letters. He retained the living all his life and did much to improve it for his successors. It was his base, if hardly his home, until he took up residency in the Deanery in 1713.

By 1707 the Vicar of Laracor had attained a position of influence in the chapter of St. Patrick's Cathedral. He represented it as proctor in the Lower House of Convocation from July to October 1707; he took part in a controversy over Marsh's library, strongly resisting encroachments of laymen and opposing the higher ranks of the clergy, roles, remarks Professor Landa, that he 'assumed with frequency in later years'. What is more significant, however, is that, during his service, the Lower House pressed the Upper to attempt to gain Remission of the First Fruits and Twentieth Parts. Swift's role in this matter was what brought him prominence in London, and it occupies a significant position in his correspondence.

Remission of the First Fruits was promised to the clergy of the Church of England by Queen Anne in February 1704, and the two Irish Houses had discussed the possibility of obtaining the same benefit for the Irish clergy. The First Fruits was nominally a sum equal to the annual value of a benefice, originally paid to the Pope but after the Reformation to the Crown. The Twentieth Parts, amounting to a twentieth of the of the annual income of a benefice, also came to the Crown at the Reformation. Both levies were in Swift's time based upon a fixed valuation of each benefice, resulting in the payment of a constant sum. There were also the Crown rents, dating to the Reformation; these could amount to about a third of the real value of a living and so were a particularly heavy burden on those who held poorer livings. The Bishop of Cloyne received a gracious answer to the petition which he laid before the Queen. This had been for Remission of the First Fruits and Twentieth Parts only, as it was judged impolitic to ask for more than the English clergy had received.

Swift was entrusted with the task of soliciting for the Remission; he travelled with the Lord Lieutenant, Pembroke, to England. There were delays, but in June 1708 he had a meeting with Godolphin, the Lord Treasurer, and realised that the price to be paid for the Remission was support from the Irish Church for the

Repeal of the Test Act, which would give legal tolerance to Dissent. His correspondence with Archbishop William King, the Archbishop of Dublin, is revealing, both complaining of the Clergy 'who seldom understand their true interest or are able to distinguish their enemies from their friends'.

The account Swift gives King of his interview with the Lord Treasurer is precise and perspicacious. He had sized up the unreliability of the politicians, but thought, erroneously, 'the Thing is done' on November 1708. King, however, wrote to him on 12 March 1708/9 to say it was still on the anvil, something confirmed by Swift in London, who replied that he had only 'the cold amusement' of now and then 'refreshing my Lord Pembroke's memory, or giving the Ministry, as I could find opportunity, good dispositions towards the Thing'. Swift then went to see Lord Wharton, Lord Lieutenant designate, who gave him cautious answers and then 'rose suddenly, turned off the discourse, and seemed in haste', so Swift was forced to take his leave. He was learning even more about the ways – and manners – of politicians: 'It is wonderful a great Minister should make no difference between a grant and the promise of a grant'.

In June 1709 Swift returned to Ireland, but on 8 August 1710 Godolphin was dismissed and Wharton returned to London. Swift travelled on the Lord Lieutenant's yacht to England, the Irish Archbishops and three bishops having given him a commission to assist the Irish Bishops in London, who were to leave matters in his hands if they departed from London. They had done so when Swift arrived, and he wrote to King that he found himself equally caressed by both parties 'by one as a sort of bough for drowning men to lay hold of; and by the other as one discontented, with the late men in power, for not being thorough in their designs and therefore ready to approve present things.' He also told King of the 'short, dry and morose reception' he received from Godolphin. He wrote to Stearne, Dean of St. Patrick's Cathedral, that he was weary of the caresses of men of great place. He did, however, make good progress with the new men in power, a letter of 10 October informing King of his reception by Harley, who received him 'with the greatest marks of kindness and esteem'. Swift sat with him two hours among company and two hours when they were alone. Harley promised to show the Queen the memorial Swift had written on the case for Remission; it was typically clear and cogent. This letter, written 'just as it lies in my memory', shows us Swift as a tactful but forceful negotiator and a sceptical, realistic commentator on public life: he is not convinced access to men in power gives more truth or light than the politics of a coffee house; he had never known one great minister who 'made any scruple to mould the alphabet into whatever words he pleased'. Swift was given further powers from Ireland and was able to report to King on 4 November that Harley had given him leave to 'acquaint my Lord Primate and your Grace that the Queen hath granted the First Fruits and Twentieth Parts to the Clergy of Ireland'.

Swift, however, was enraged by an insensitive letter from King of 2 November (which crossed with his of 4 November) which in effect told him that he might need to exert himself with more vigour, that the Irish Bishops wanted the First Fruits and Twentieth Parts to be negotiated by the new Lord Lieutenant, the Duke of Ormonde. Some social jealousy of Swift must have built up in Ireland. It was known that the Vicar of Laracor had fine friends among the Whig lords and was cutting a dash in London, but the Irish Bishops were not fully *au fait* with Swift's having made such headway, personal as well as political, with the new Tory Ministers, and must have suspected his political attitudes. Swift replied to King with a just and lucid rebuke, and followed this up with a further letter written on 28 November, spelling out how quickly and efficiently he had achieved the Remission and indicating his standing with the new Ministry while pointing out that Ormonde, despite his love for the Church of Ireland, had done nothing about the Remission during the four years he had earlier been Lord Lieutenant. In this letter he described himself as 'a private man whom the Bishops no longer own.' King excused the Bishops' cold behaviour to Swift as caused by their belief that he was too closely associated with the fallen Whigs, 'under the reputation of being a favourite of the late party in power'

III

Though he continued to solicit the speedy Remission of the First Fruits and the Twentieth Parts, Swift no longer regarded himself as a deputed person, and so it must have given him considerable satisfaction to be able to tell King that the Ministry desired him to remain longer in London 'for certain reasons, that I may sometime have the honour to tell you.' He had become Editor of *The Examiner* and embarked on his career as a political propagandist.

Not only did the Ministers find Swift a superb pamphleteer and journalist and author, they liked his company and his wit. He was soon on close and friendly terms with them, as the *Journal to Stella* shows us, telling us of jests he made and in what circumstances.

He was obviously delighted with the way he was appreciated and praised, as this vignette shows: it was written to Stella on the night of 15 October 1710, after Swift had dined with Harley and Prior. Harley had told him that the Queen had agreed to the Remission, and that Swift was not to make it public (he told Stella he hoped to get 'something of greater value,' namely the Remission of the Crown rents); then Lord Peterborough had come in. They began to talk of a paper of verses called *Sid Hamet* (Swift's poem attacking and ridiculing Godolphin, 'The Virtues of Sid Hamet the Magician's Rod', in which he accused Godolphin of buying off opposition by giving places in government). Mr Harley repeated part of them

and then pulled them out, and gave them to a gentleman at the table to read, though they had all read them often: Lord Peterborough would let nobody read them but himself: so he did; and Mr. Harley bobbed me at every line to take notice of the beauties.

Swift was deeply concerned when Harley was stabbed by the Marquis de Guiscard; the account of the incident he wrote to Archbishop King on 8 March 1710/11 is a masterly piece of reporting:

My Lord,

I write to your Grace under the greatest disturbance of mind for the public and for myself. A gentleman came in where I dined this afternoon, and told us Mr Harley was stabbed, and some confused particulars. I immediately ran to Secretary St. John's hard by, but nobody was at home; I met Mrs. St. John in her chair, who could not satisfy me, but was in pain about the Secretary, who as she heard, had killed the murderer. I went straight to Mr. Harley's where abundance of people were to enquire. I got young Mr. Harley to me; he said his Father was asleep and they hoped in no danger, and then he told me the fact, as I shall relate it to your Grace. This day the Marquis de Guiscard was taken up for High Treason, by a warrant of Mr. St. John, and examined before a Committee of Council in Mr. St. John's Office, where were present, the Dukes of Ormonde, Buckingham, Shrewsbury, Earl Poulett, Mr. Harley, Mr. St. John, and others. During examination Mr. Harley observed Guiscard, who stood behind him, but on one side, swearing and looking disrespectfully. He told him he ought to behave himself better, while he was examined for such a crime, Guiscard immediately drew a penknife out of his pocket which he had picked out of some of the offices, and reaching round, stabbed him just under the breast, a little to the right side; but, it pleased God, that the point stopped at one of the ribs, and broke short half an inch.

Immediately Mr. St. John rose, drew his sword, and ran it into Guiscard's breast. Five or six more of the Council drew and stabbed

Guiscard in several places: But, the Earl Poulett called out, for God's sake, to spare Guiscard's life, that he might be made an example; and Mr. St. John's sword was taken from him, and broke; and the footmen without ran in, and bound Guiscard, who begged he might be killed immediately; and, they say, called out three or four times 'my Lord Ormonde, my Lord Ormonde'. They say Guiscard resisted them a while, until the footmen came in. Immediately Buissière the surgeon was sent for, who dressed Mr. Harley: and he was sent home. The wound bled fresh, and they do not apprehend him in danger: he said, when he came home, he thought himself in none; and when I was there he was asleep, and they did not find him at all feverish. He hath been ill this week, and told me last Saturday, he found himself much out of order, and hath been abroad but twice since; so that the only danger is lest his being out of order should, with the wound, put him in a fever; and I shall be in mighty pain 'till tomorrow morning.

I went back to poor Mrs. St. John, who told me, her husband was with My Lord Keeper, at Mr. Attorney's, and she said something very remarkable: that going today to pay her duty to the Queen, when all the men and ladies were dressed to make their appearance, this being the day of the Queen's Accession, the Lady of the bed-chamber in waiting told her the Queen had not been been at church, and saw no company; yet, when she inquired her health they said she was very well, only had a little cold. We conceive, the Queen's reason for not going out, might be something about this seizing of Guiscard for High Treason, and that perhaps there was some plot, or something extraordinary. Your Grace must have heard of this Guiscard: he fled from France for villanies there, and was thought on to head an invasion of that Kingdom, but not liked. I know him well, and think him a fellow of little consequence, although of some cunning, and much villainy. We passed by one another this day in the Mall, at two o'clock, an hour before he was taken up, and I wondered he did not speak to me.

Not only would the country suffer, Swift thought, if Harley died 'when he has all the schemes for the greatest part of the supplies in his head and Parliament cannot stir a step without him', but he himself would lose a person he had 'more obligations to than any other in this Kingdom,' who had always treated him with the tenderness of a parent and never refused him any favour he asked for a friend. Swift had not asked any favours for himself: obviously, however, he hoped for personal preferment. He became more intimate with the Ministers, Harley and St. John. While using his formidable skills to shape public opinion they flattered him; they were resolved, they told him in December 1710, that he should preach before the Queen. He was to be given three weeks' warning, but though he desired to be excused he obviously was pleased, despite the disclaimer to Stella that he hoped they would forget it 'for if it should happen, all the puppies hereabouts will throng to hear me, and expect something wonderful and will be plaguily baulkt; for I shall preach plain and honest stuff.' It did not happen. The Queen was biased against Swift since A *Tale of A Tub* (1707), the 'apology,' in the fifth edition of which she cannot have read or agreed with. In the apology, dated 1709, Swift defended the anonymous *Tale* against the charges of irreligion: it was a satire upon the abuses and corruption of religion itself (the Church of England was the most perfect of all others; Dissenters and Papists got their comeuppance). Swift does not seem to have realised fully what effect his satire would have upon those who could not relish or fathom his irony, nor how that satire would work against him. He does not seem to have understood how his poem 'The Windsor Prophecy' with its savage attack on Queen Anne's favourite, the Duchess of Somerset, would increase the Monarch's distrust and dislike of him, which was to militate against any likelihood of his becoming a Bishop or at least a Dean in England.

IV

Swift seems to have left his work with *The Examiner* with regret in June 1711: he was dubious about the Ministers; 'they think me useful,' he wrote to Stella on 29 June, 'they pretend they were afraid of none but me, and that they resolved to have me; they have often confessed this; yet all makes little impression on me. Pox of these speculations! They give me the spleen; and that is a disease I was not born to.' The Ministers were indeed resolved to have him as their public relations officer, in effect their unofficial spokesman. They offered advice about the pamphlet upon which he had embarked, *The Conduct of the Allies and the Late Ministry, in Beginning and Carrying on the Present War,* and they suggested various alterations after the first edition was published on 26 November 1711. This pamphlet was immensely influential, reaching its sixth edition by the end of January 1711/12.

During August 1711 Swift recorded his disappointment that the Irish Bishops attributed the Remission to the Duke of Ormonde rather than to Harley. In a letter to King of 15 August 1711 (finished on the 21st), he protested at their attitude, telling him of a conversation with Harley in which the Lord Treasurer confirmed Swift's views. He had had hopes of getting remission of the Crown rents but this hindered him from any thoughts of pursuing the matter.

'What can be the matter with those people?' he asks indignantly, 'Do I ask either money or thanks of them? Have I done any hurt to the business?' To Stella he wrote on the 21st to say that the Irish Bishops were angry because he had let the world know that the Lord Treasurer had got the First Fruits before the Duke of Ormonde became Lord Lieutenant.

Swift's comments on the Bishops were tart and he was obviously deeply irritated by a letter from King of 1 September, 1711 advising him to help himself. 'I know,' wrote the Archbishop in a wordly-wise vein, 'you are not ambitious, but it is prudence, not ambition to get into a station, that may make a man easy, and prevent contempt when he grows in years.' He told Swift that he had a good opportunity to provide for himself, and urged him not to neglect it. This was probably well meant, but Swift resented the advice that followed, that he should set himself to some serious and useful subject in his profession and 'to manage it so that it may be of use to the world'. Most subjects of divinity had not been exhausted and Swift should show the world that he had 'patience and comprehension of thought, to go through with such a subject of weight and learning'. Swift's comments to his friend Charles Ford on the advice were not only impatient but acidulous. He had heard that the Archbishop had resolved to provide for him before any man. He sums up the advice and concludes, 'He was afraid, I expected something from him: he had got some other view; and so takes care to undeceive me.' King got a dignified reply dated 1 October: Swift would never be able to make himself believed, as to how indifferent he was about his fortune. Contempt in Ireland would be no sort of mortification. When last there half his time was spent retired to one scurvy acre of ground which he always left with regret. He would never solicit for himself although he often did so for others. As for the advice to be useful to the Church and the public, he would need some settlement which would make him full master of his time: 'to ask a man floating at sea what he designed to do when he gets ashore is too hasty a question: let him get there first, and rest, and dry himself, and then look about him'. King replied in November, telling Swift he should not be indifferent to his own concerns, to making his fortune, and urging him to get a letter from the Lord Treasurer to the Irish government 'for the first good preferment', arguing there could be no immodesty in getting such a recommendation.

What Swift called his 'political letters' to the Archbishop continued, and they and a letter to Stearne – then Dean of St. Patrick's Cathedral, Dublin – recount the political and diplomatic manoeuverings and the suspense before the Peace of Utrecht was finally achieved. As he put it to King, on 3 January 1712/13, some accidents and occasions had put it in his way to know every step of the Treaty better, he thought, than any man in England. After *The Conduct of the Allies* was published Swift's influence increased; he supervised *The Examiner* and *The Postboy*, the main Tory newspaper, he published his own 'penny papers'. He corrected drafts of the Queen's speeches. He was to involve himself in writing a history of the period, to become *The History of the Four Last Years of the Queen*. He was at the centre of affairs though still in an entirely unofficial capacity. As early as April 1711 he had become very concerned about the rift developing between Oxford and Bolingbroke; he had been trying 'to clear up some misunderstanding betwixt them' which he described as a 'plaguy, ticklish piece of work.' But the rift was deepening inexorably.

It seems that Swift took King's advice, for when the Dean of Wells died on 4 February 1711/12 he applied next day to Oxford for the deanery. Two other deaneries, Ely and Lichfield, also became vacant in early 1712. His own future began to occupy him. On 28 February 1711/12 he mentions a large box for books that he has bought; he must buy another for clothes and luggage; this was 'a beginning towards a removal.' Wryly he tells Stella that Dr. Sacheverell's brother was the seventh person he had provided for since he came from Ireland 'and can do nothing for myself.' On 26 March he writes to her that he had hoped the Session would be ended earlier but that he must stay till it was – though he would like to be in Laracor to see the beginning of his willows growing; his heart was set upon the cherry trees by the river. By 31 May a letter to Stella contains his hopes that the Session would soon be over and the Peace made shortly; then there would be no further occasion, nor had he anything to trust to but court gratitude – so he expected to see his willows at Laracor a month after Parliament was up. On 17 June he told her that he did not intend – as she suggested – to stay in England all the summer; he would not stay one minute longer 'than becomes the circumstances I am in.' He was worried about the future, writing to her that 'something or nothing will be done in my own affairs: if the former, I will be a solicitor for your sister [Mrs. Filby] – if the latter, I have done with courts forever.'

He was working hard on *The History of the Four Last Years of the Queen*. After contemplating it in August 1712 he had begun to write it the next month, and the letters report progress. It had gone well by 18 January 1712/13 but was now standing stock still, some people thinking it too dangerous to publish; They would have him 'print only what relates to the Peace.' He was frustrated: he had always had a desire to write history, 'to tell it as it was' and so he writes to Stella 'I can't tell what I shall do.' On 21 January he tells her his large book lies flat. He had undertaken this 'long work' as a justification of the Peace of Utrecht and the proceedings which led to it . He had access to official correspondence and on one occasion insisted on being present – although Bolingbroke had suggested that he should withdraw after dinner – when the first Earl of Oxford (as Harley had become in 1710), Bolingbroke (as St. John had become in 1712) and another person were 'entering on business' – because, he said, it was as fit he should 'know their business as anybody'. for he was to justify it: 'so the rest went and I stayed and it was so important I was like to sleep over it.' Oxford and Bolingbroke were slow in answering his queries; they may well not have wanted him privy to all their activities; and he complains to Stella that he can't finish his work: 'they delay me as if it were a favour I asked of them' . . . and 'these Ministers will not find time to do what I would have them'. By 27 February he tells her he has little to do with his pen for his 'grand business' stops till they are more pressing, and till something or other happens, and 'I believe I shall return with disgust to finish it, it is so very laborious.' But at last he writes to Stella on 16 May 1713 with the news that he had finished it and 'must be ten days correcting it'.

Then came the blow; the gratitude of the court did not exist. On 13 April Swift's friend Erasmus Lewis showed him an order for the three vacant deaneries, 'but none of them to me'. He put a brave face on it. It was what he always had foreseen, he told Stella, and he received the notice of it better, he believed, than Lewis had expected. Swift asked Lewis to tell the Lord Treasurer that he took nothing ill of him 'but his not giving me timely notice, as he promised to do, if he found the Queen would do nothing for me'. At noon Oxford heard that Swift was in Lewis's office and came and 'said many things too long to repeat'. Swift did not beat about the bush with him:

I told him I had nothing to do but go to Ireland immediately for I could not with any reputation stay longer here, unless I had something honourable immediately given to me; we dined together at Duke Ormonde's, he there told me, he had stopped the warrants for the Deans, that what was done for me, might be at the same time, and he hoped to compass it tonight; but I believe him not. I told the Duke of Ormonde my intentions; he is content Stearne should be a Bishop and I have St. Patrick's; but I believe nothing will come of it; for stay I will not.

He told her that he might be be in Dublin before the end of April; he would send his baggage by carrier to Chester. But the suspense continued. On 14 April Oxford informed Lewis it would be determined that night. The next day Bolingbroke 'made' Swift dine with him and he managed to be as good company as ever. Bolingbroke told him the Queen would determine something for him that night; 'the dispute is Windsor or St. Patrick's.' Swift told him he would not stay for their disputes 'and he thought I was in the right'.

The indecision dragged on. On the 16th Lady Masham wept at the thought of his having St. Patrick's; Erasmus Lewis told him the Queen was content Stearne should be Bishop of Dromore and Swift Dean of St. Patrick's, but Oxford would not be satisfied unless Swift was Prebend of Windsor. On the 17th Lady Masham told him the Queen would determine next day. Oxford told Lewis that it would be settled that night. On the 18th Lewis told Swift that the Queen was at last resolved that Stearne should be Bishop of Dromore and Swift Dean of St. Patrick's. Swift was still not sure it would happen. On the 19th Lewis sent a note to say the Queen was waiting to see if the Duke of Ormonde approved of Stearne for the Bishopric. Swift went to the Duke, who made objections – the Deanery was in his gift – he did not like Stearne, Stearne never went to see him, and was influenced by the Archbishop of Dublin. He wished Swift would name any other Deanery. The suspense, Swift wrote, with reason, vexed him worse than anything else. Finally the Duke agreed on the 20th, and said he would speak to the Queen; he did so the next day, and she agreed on the 22nd. But Swift was not sure of her. The Queen, however, did sign the warrants on the 23rd, Stearne being made Bishop. Swift had to wait for the Duke to send over an order making him Dean. The matter was finally settled on 25 April. And Swift hoped 'they will be persuaded here to give me some money to pay off these debts' (the Deanery, the First Fruits and Patent would come to £1000); but it was a vain hope. The Vicar returned to Ireland a Dean.

It had not been easy for an Irish country vicar to keep up with the great men in London. Apart from a legacy of £100 from Temple and the sum he had from the publications of Temple's writing, Swift had to live on his income of about £250 (Laracor brought in about £230, the Prebend of Dunlavin about £15 or £20) out of which he paid a generous salary of £57 to his curate and gave Stella £50 a year. He had horses to buy or hire: he had a servant to pay in England. And he was a most charitable man. In effect he had overspent when he had been in London earlier, courting the Whigs with *A Discourse of the Contests of Dissentions between the Nobles and*

Commons in Athens and Rome, with the Consequences they had upon both those States (1701), which was written in defence of the impeached Whig Lords. These visits, in 1701, 1702 and 1702-4 when he was arranging the publication of *A Tale of a Tub* (1704) had been expensive; on 15 June 1706 he wrote, somewhat ruefully, to John Temple to say his little revenue was sunk 'two parts in three and the third in arrear ' Swift had, however, become friendly with the Earl of Halifax, the Earl of Sunderland and Baron Somers; he obviously enjoyed such acquaintance, though it was not useful to his own career nor to his negotiation on behalf of the Church of Ireland.

His later association with Harley and St. John was on a very different footing. The new Ministers took him up quickly. Addison described him as 'much caressed and invited almost every day to dinner by some or other of the new ministry.' He was soon dining on Saturdays with Harley (what he called their 'Club of the Ministry') and when St. John instituted 'the Society ', a dining club, in the summer of 1711 it was Swift who drew up and systematised its rules, obviously enjoying the fact that its members called each other 'Brother'. It must have given him particular pleasure to invite the Duke of Ormonde to join the club (On 28 December 1711 he and brother Bathurst gave his grace some 'hopes to be one of our Society'; on 7 January 1711/12 he gave the Duke notice 'of the honour done him to make him one of our Society': the Duke accepted 'with the gratitude and humility such a preferment deserves'.) However pleasant the opportunities membership of the group gave Swift to hobnob with its distinguished members (it was intended to bring together writers and powerful politicians) the club was expensive, and he often complained about the cost of the dinners, especially when he presided and had to pay the bill.

There were other expenses, including vails, or tips, for servants, 'half crowns to great men's porters etc.', a crown 'to the rogues of the coffee-house,' or a guinea to the servants of the Earl of Halifax and the coach hire which came to twelve shillings, something which made him curtail such costly visits outside London. There was the careless and exasperatingly wasteful behaviour of his often drunken servant Patrick in stoking up the fire late at night so that Swift plucked the coals off it to save them before going to bed. He put off having a fire in his room till November, though it was 'very cold', and 'cold or not cold' he had no fire after April. Sensibly enough, he economised by putting bricks at the back of his grate which would reduce the fire area and give out stored up heat. He chose rooms at economic rents. Walking, which he enjoyed, saved him a good deal of money on chairs, but when the Mohocks were roaming the streets, attacking pedestrians, he found it prudent to avoid trouble:

Here is the D— and all to do with these Mohocks . . . my man tells me, that one of the lodgers heard in a coffeehouse publicly, that one design of the Mohocks was upon me if [the]y could catch me. And tho' I believe nothing of it yet I forbear walking late, and they have put me to the charge of some shillings already.

He had to count pennies to survive. This is something not always understood by critics. Ehrenpreis, for instance, in his generally percipient biography, alludes to 'the general bleakness of his parsi-mony,' Swift was parsimonious with himself; but to others he was most generous, always, for instance, paying his servants well, and assisting many needy people financially. It is likely that the tone of his comments to Stella is not always understood; he could laugh at himself and indulge in ironic self-parody as well as being proud of what he was able to do on the small amount of money he had; he was sharing his pleasure in his clever London economies with the ladies in Dublin. His pride emerged when Harley sent him fifty pounds:

He gave me al bsadnuk iboinlpl dfaonr ufainfbtoy dpionufnad [a bank bill for fifty pound] which I sent him again by Mr. Lewis, to whom I writ a very complaining letter that was showed him; and so the matter ended. He told he had a quarrel with me; I said I had another with him, and we returned to our friendship and I should think he loves me as well as a great minister can love a man in so short a time. Did not I do right?

He prized his freedom, his independence, above all else. He became extremely annoyed on one occasion when St. John seemed very down and melancholy, on Sunday 1 April: on Tuesday the 3rd, Swift called him 'to see what the D– ailed him on Sunday' and made him 'a very proper speech,' telling him how

I observed he was very much out of temper, that I did not expect he would tell me the cause, but would be glad to see he was better; and one thing I warned him of, Never to appear cold to me, for I would not be treated like a schoolboy; that I expected every great minister, who honoured me with his acquaintance, if he heard or saw any thing to my disadvantage, would let me know it in plain words, and not put me in pain to guess by the change or coldness of his countenance or behaviour; for it was what I would hardly bear from a crowned head, and I thought no subject's favour was worth it, and that I designed to let my Lord Keeper [the Earl of Harcourt] and Mr. Harley know the same thing, that they might use me accordingly.

St. John 'took it all right' and explained his mood as due to work and a hangover; he had been sitting up whole nights at business and one night at drinking. He asked Swift to dine with him 'to make up matters.' But Swift would not: 'I don't know but I would not' (He was, in any case, committed to dine with William Pollinson, a wine merchant, but seems to have stood on his dignity rather than tell St. John that he had a previous engagement for the evening!). The next day he was still brooding over the incident:

> Why, I think what I said to Mr. Secretary was right. Don't you remember how I used to be in pain when Sir William Temple would look cold and out of humour for three or four days, and I used to suspect a hundred reasons? I have pluckt up my spirit since then, faith; he spoiled a fine gentleman.

VI

Swift could write most freely to Stella. He first mentioned writing to 'the ladies' in 1703/4, and his account books from 1708 to 1710 show that he wrote to Stella and her friend Rebecca Dingley during the period from 1 November 1708 to June 1709 fifteen letters and received eleven from them. But what survives is the correspondence between September 1710 and 6 June 1713, sixty-five (extended) letters in all. They are a magnificent story of close friendship, indeed of love.

Hester Johnson, whom Swift called Stella, was born on 13 March 1680/1 and Swift probably first met her when he first stayed in Sir William Temple's household in 1689. Stella lived at Moor Park until Temple's death on 27 January 1698/9, and remained there or with her mother, Mrs. Bridget Mose, at Farnham, for two years after that. She and Rebecca Dingley left England for Ireland in June 1701. Swift recorded how he had 'some share in her education, by directing what books she should read, and perpetually instructing her in the principles of honour and virtue'.

Stella had inherited from Temple a lease of some lands in Morristown, County Wicklow, and her fortune, at the time of Temple's death, was, Swift stated, not in all above fifteen hundred pounds; she had some property at Trim, County Meath, and Temple's sister, Lady Giffard, held £400 for her upon which an annuity was paid. Swift had persuaded the ladies to settle in Ireland where they could get interest at ten per cent and where the cost of living would be lower. They made, as far as we know, only one journey back to England, in 1708. So Swift shared his period of political power and influence with them, talking to them through the *Journal*, but, in effect, to Stella, about his progress, telling them about his health, his friends and his writing, exhorting them to keep well. The *Journal* gives us an evocative picture of Swift's social as well as political and literary life in London.

The tone is teasing – the ladies are addressed as 'saucy rogues,' 'nauti nauti deargirls,' 'sirrahs' – and it is also most tender at times, notably in the 'little language,' probably founded on Stella's speech when young. In this letters are replaced, l replacing r, and vice versa; thus, for example, 'deelest logues' is 'dearest rogues'. There are other less obvious changes: 'ourrichar Gangridge' is 'our little language'; and there are code words and initials, 'MD' or 'Md' standing for 'My dear' or 'My dears' while Swift is 'Pdfr' and 'Presto'. The *Journal is* most affectionate, especially during 1711, and Swift expresses his happiness in Stella's company; his happiest moments are in writing to her; he goes to bed to dream of her; he hopes they may never be apart again ten days together; he yearns for Laracor, and wants to be back where there is peace and quiet; he hopes to see her there after Christmas; he loves her above all things a thousand times.

VII

Other letters show us something of his attitudes to the two other young women with whom he was emotionally involved: Jane Waring, whom he called Varina, and Esther Vanhomrigh, whom he called Vanessa. When he was staying with his mother in Leicester in 1689 he had embarked on several flirtations. He enjoyed the company of women; he described his behaviour then as being 'without any other design than that of entertaining myself when I am very idle'; he had 'no design of anything grave' in this; he thought it 'at worst' a harmless impertinence. But when he possessed his own income, when he was on his own in Kilroot from 1695 to 1696, he became involved with Jane Waring to the extent of proposing marriage to her. A letter of 29 April 1696 indicated he was looking for a cure for his violent desire, something 'little better than a distemper.' He wonders why he was so foolish as to put his hopes and fears into the power or management of another. He tells her she has had time to consider his previous letter, and that he is waiting impatiently for her answer. He has been offered once more (by Sir William Temple) the advantage to have the same acquaintance with greatness that he formerly enjoyed, and 'with better prospect of interest.' He offers to forego it all for her sake; he desires nothing of her fortune; she can live where and with whom she pleases till his affairs are settled to her desire; he, meanwhile, will push his advancement with 'all the eagerness and courage imaginable.' The daughter of an Archdeacon, she presumably had not thought much of his prospects, and had shillyshallied. He reproaches her for this: 'Would not your conduct make one think you were hugely skilled in all the little politic methods of intrigue. The little disguises and affected contradictions of your sex, were all (to say the truth) infinitely beneath persons of your pride and mind; paltry maxims that they are, calculated for the rabble of humanity,' He finally warns her that if she still refuses him, she will 'quickly lose, for ever lose, him that is resolved to die as he had lived.' From Moor Park in January 1698/9 he wrote to his friend the Rev. John Winder who succeeded him at Kilroot, to say he was pleased to have restored a correspondence with him that he feared was declining 'as it requires more *charms and Address in Women* to revive one *fainting Flame* than to kindle a dozen new ones.' The letter deals with various business matters, the disposal of books and sermons – not to mention some 'Letters to Elisa' (probably Betty Jones, for whom he had formed a strong attachment in Leicester, to his mother's alarm) written in his youth which were to be burned – and its final paragraph begins 'You mention a dangerous rival for an absent lover. But I must take my fortune: if the report proceeds pray inform me.'

Various letters passed between Swift and Varina before he wrote to her most sternly from Dublin on 4 May 1770. He had tried to get her away from the company and place she was in, on account of her health and humour. She had been imperious and argumentative; she had asked whether his change of style was due to the thoughts of a new mistress, which he declared, on the word of a Christian and a gentleman, it was not. He had asked what her income was 'in order to consider whether it were sufficient with the help of my poor income, to make one of your humour easy in a married state.' Her income he computed at £100 a year; he had told the 'dismal account' of his livings (at Laracor); since it was dismal even in her opinion she should draw consequences from it.

He had conveyed to her though his uncle, Adam Swift, that if her health and his future were as they ought he would prefer her above all her sex. He went on to some severe questions about her health, since the doctors had advised her against marriage; about her ability to manage domestic affairs on an income of perhaps less than three hundred pounds a year; about the likelihood of her having 'such an inclination to my person and humour, as to comply with my desires and way of living, and endeavour to make us both as happy as you can.' He asked if she would be ready to engage in those methods he would direct for the improvement of her mind, so as to make them entertaining company for each other. And he went on to other questions. If she could answer his questions in the affirmative he would be blessed to have her in his arms 'without regarding whether your person be beautiful or your fortune large. Cleanliness in the first and competency in the other, is all I look for'. He desired a plentiful revenue but would prefer it should be of his own. He expected not to be used like a common lover. This he obviously was not.

VIII

The coming of Stella and Rebecca Dingley to Ireland was hardly a common matter, and of course it provoked comment. Swift told the story of their coming to Dublin in that most moving life of Stella which he began on the night of her death in 1728:

I prevailed with her and her dear friend and companion, the other lady, to draw what money they had into Ireland, a great part of their fortune being in annuities upon funds.... They complied with my advice and soon after came over... but I happening to continue sometime longer in England, they were much discouraged to live in Dublin,where they were wholly strangers. She was at that time about nineteen years old, and her person was soon distinguished. But the adventure looked so like a frolic the censure held for some time as if there were a secret history in such a removal; which, however, soon blew off by her excellent conduct.

The Reverend William Tisdall, appointed a Fellow of Trinity College in 1696, became friendly with the ladies in Dublin. Swift and he were on good terms and Swift wrote to him from London on 16 December 1703 to ask him to inform the ladies he had their letter and would answer it soon; he told Tisdall a way to outwit Mrs. Johnson:

It is a new fashioned way of being witty, and they call it a *bite*. You must ask a bantering question, or tell some damned lie in a serious manner, and then she will answer or speak as if you were in earnest: and then cry you, Madam there's a *bite*.

In the next letter to Tisdall of 3 February 1703-04, he is jocular:

You seem to talk with great security of your establishment near the ladies; though perhaps, if you knew what they say of you in their letters to me, you would change your opinion of them and yourself. A bite!

Then Tisdall wrote to Swift to describe a previous letter as 'unfriendly, unkind and unaccountable'. This was obviously Swift's reply to Tisdall's having told him that he wanted to marry Stella. On April 20 1704 Swift answered with 'the naked truth,' telling Tisdall that he had said to him before that if his own fortunes and humour served him 'to think of that state' [marriage] he would certainly among all persons on earth make her his choice because he never saw that person whose conversion he entirely valued but hers: 'this was the utmost I ever gave way to.' He assured Tisdall that this regard never once entered his head to be an impediment to him, 'but I judged it would, perhaps, be a clog to you rising in the world; and I did not conceive you were then rich enough to make yourself and her happy and easy'. He added that this objection was removed by Tisdall's having got livings in Donegal (which were in the gift of Trinity College); he had no other:

nor shall any consideration of my own misfortune of losing so good a friend and companion as her, prevail on me, against her interest and settlement in the world, since it is held so necessary and convenient a thing for ladies to marry; and that time takes off from the lustre of virgins in all other eyes but mine.... Though it hath come in my way to converse with persons of the first rank, and of that sex,more than is usual to men of my level, and of our function; yet I have nowhere met with a humour, a wit or conversation so agreeable, a better portion of good sense, or a truer judgement of men and things, I mean here in *England*; for as to the ladies of *Ireland* I am a perfect stranger.

The friendship between Tisdall and Swift ended, and Tisdall married a Miss Morgan, becoming vicar of Belfast and Rector of Drumcree (Jane Waring, incidentally, never married).

The letter shows Swift's continuing fear of a marriage without sufficient money to sustain it: it reminds us of how he thought his father had died before he could make a sufficient establishment for his family and how he himself felt 'the consequences of that marriage not only through the whole course of his education, but during the greatest part of his life'. There is more than a hint here of his preoccupation with having enough to live on without worry; it is a poignant awareness of the dangers of marriages with insufficient financial backing. This concern emerges in a letter to Stella of 23 May 1711:

O faith, I should be glad to be in the same Kingdom with MD, however, although you are at Wexford. But I am kept here by a most capricious fate, which I would break through, if I could do it with decency or honour – To return without some mark of distinction would look extremely little; and I

would gladly be somewhat richer than I am. I will say no more, but beg
you to be easy, 'till Fortune take her course, and to believe that MD's felic-
ity is the great I aim at in all my pursuits.

There are very many expressions of his regard for her. On 30 June
he tells her he loves her better than ever 'if possible'; on 19 July
that he loves her above all other things 'ten million of times,' and
on 29 July that he loves her dearly. 'Farewel, dear sirrahs, dearest
lives: there is peace and quiet with MD and nowhere else,' he
writes on 25 August 1711, 'They have not leisure here to think of
small things, which may ruin them; and I have been forward
enough, Farewel again, dearest rogues; I am never happy but when
I write or think of MD.' On 8 September he loves her more than his
life 'a thousand times'. On 17 November he loves her 'infinitely
above all earthly things' and on 15 December above all things 'a
thousand times'. From the end of 1711 there is, as Sir Harold
Williams put it, a 'weakening in the spontaneity and unaffected
naturalness of the expressions of affection.... his greetings [from
February 1711-12] are, though affectionate, more stereotyped and
perfunctory in character'. There are some exceptions, for there are
plenty of instances of tender farewells, and Swift certainly longed
for Laracor in March 1712, while in September of that year he
ended his letter with 'Love pdfr [Swift], who loves Md above all
things – farewell dealest ten thousand times deelest Md Md Md
FW FW Me Me Me Me lele lele lele lele – '

IX

There are several possible reasons for some change in the way that
Swift was writing. In October 1711 he described himself as 'very
busy'; he could 'hardly find time to write, unless it were to MD.'
As the activities listed in the *Journal* show, he was indeed busy. He
was ill as well, with colds in December, with rheumatic pains in
March 1711/12 which turned out to be a most painful attack of
shingles in the first week of April and this continued to trouble
him till beyond the end of May. 'I don't love to write journals while
I am in pain, and above all, not journals to MD.' He still complains
of the pain in his shoulder in June and July, while in mid-
September he was giddy from a bout of labyrinthine vertigo
(Ménière's syndrome, named after the French doctor who first discovered its symptoms in the nineteenth century), the illness which
first afflicted him in his twenties when at Sheen, Sir William
Temple's home in Surrey.

He was still suffering from this in October, taking physic until the end of the month. In December he was giddy with what he hoped was a bad cold that lasted into January; at the end of the month he was giddy again. It has been suggested by Sheridan in his *Life of the Rev. Dr. Jonathan Swift* (1784) and by Scott in his *Memoirs of Swift* (1811) that the reason for the alteration in the tone of the letters was Swift's friendship with Esther Vanhomrigh, mentioned only three times in the *Journal*. Stella must have commented on his friendship with the Vanhomrigh family (where Swift became a constant visitor, changing his clothes there en route to work, and frequently dining there) for he wrote to her on 26 February 1710/11, 'You say they are no consequence; why, they keep as good female company as I keep male.' Mrs. Vanhomrigh was the widow of a wealthy merchant of Dutch extraction who had been Lord Mayor of Dublin. On his death she and her children had moved to London

The early letters to Vanessa and from her to Swift reveal her obvious admiration for him. He enjoyed teaching a receptive and attractive pupil; but his letter to her of 18 December 1711 enclosed a letter to Miss Long which she was to read. This contained a comment on Vanessa's forthright behaviour, which begins by stating that there is not a better girl on earth; he has a mighty friendship for her, he has corrected all her faults, but cannot persuade her to read, though she has 'an understanding memory and taste, that would bear great improvement; but she is incorrigible, idle and lazy; thinks the world made for nothing but pleasure.' He continues to say that she makes him of so little consequence that it almost distracts him; 'She will bid her sister go down stairs, before my face, for she has some private business with the doctor.'

Vanessa, however, did not absorb this delicate cautionary advice about how she should behave more discretely. And he either did not realize the dangers of this friendship or else let the delights of it sway his wisdom. He wrote to her on 1 August 1712 that he would take 'a little Grub Street lodging, pretty near where I did before; and dine with you thrice a week; and will tell you a thousand secrets provided you will have no quarrels to me.' The correspondence took a sour turn after Swift had gone to Ireland in 1713 to be installed as Dean. Vanessa had earlier shown the exigent side of her character: 'Had I a correspondent in China I might have had an answer by now' was how she began a letter to him on 1 September 1712. She writes a self-centred letter in June 1713 enquiring about his health (Erasmus Lewis had told her Swift was ill) and asking him to get his agent Parvisol to tell her how he is. In the next letter she asks why he had not got Parvisol to write to

her if he were ill and how, if he were able to write himself, could
he be so 'cruel to defer telling me the thing of the world I wish
most to know, if you think I write too often your only way is to tell
me so or at least to write to me again that I may know you don't
quite forget me... if you are very happy it is ill natured of you not
to tell me so except 'tis what is inconsistent with mine.' He replied
saying he had her last splenetic letter and reminded her that he
had told her that when he left England he would endeavour to forget everything there and would write as seldom as he could.

But when he returned to England in 1714 and had retired in
June from the political turmoil of London to visit Oxford and then
stay with his friend the Reverend John Geree at Letcombe Bassett,
he could not resist getting in touch with her. She was the first person to whom he wrote, saying he would be glad to hear from her.
He wrote on 8 July offering to lend her money – her mother had
died and she and her sister had incurred various debts. On 1
August he wrote to her explaining forthrightly how he could not
rely on Bolingbroke since he had not responded to Swift's desire to
be Historiographer Royal (actually Bolingbroke had suggested him
for the post); he also praised Harley for his personal kindness. She
must have decided she would visit him unexpectedly, for on 12
August he reproves her for coming to Wantage: 'You used to brag
you were very discrete: Where is it gone?' He tells her he is going
to Ireland. When he is there he will write to her as soon as he can
conveniently do so

but it shall be always under a cover; and if you write to me let some other
direct it, and I beg you will write nothing that is particular, but that may
be seen, for I apprehend letters will be opened and inconveniences will
happen. If you are in Ireland while I am there I shall see you very seldom.
It is not a place for any freedom, but where every thing is known in a week
and magnified a hundred degrees.

These, he added, were rigorous laws; they might meet in London
in the winter, 'or, if not, leave all to fate, that seldom cares to
humour our inclinations'. Vanessa, however, was not to be excluded from his company. She once described herself to him as having
been born with violent passions 'which terminate all in one, that
inexpressible passion I have for you.' Passion was not something
he appreciated or encouraged, and her possessiveness, while obviously flattering him, also made him decidedly apprehensive.
Despite his warnings she followed him to Ireland, taking her
younger sister Mary (Moll) with her.

The next letter that survives is written to her from Phillipstown where Swift was en route to Portarlington to stay with Knightley Chetwode; he had met her servant (who had brought a message to him inviting him to her country house) near Trim. He tells her he would not have gone to Kildrohod (Celbridge, where she had inherited from her father Celbridge Abbey, a fine house on the Liffey about eleven miles inland from Dublin) to see her for all the world: 'I ever told you, you wanted discretion'. He would, however, call on her in Dublin (she had lodgings in Turnstile Place). Other letters indicate meetings in Dublin; then Swift wrote (probably on 27 December 1714) an alarmed letter: 'This morning a woman who does business for me told me she heard I was in – with one naming you and twenty particulars.' He continued that he had ever feared 'the tattle of this nasty town; and I told you so; and that was the reason why I said to you long ago that I would see you seldom when you were in Ireland and I must be easy if for some time I visit you seldomer, and not in so particular a manner.' He reply was both reproachful and appealing:

When I begin to complain then you are angry, and there is some thing in your look so awful that it strikes me dumb. Oh that you may but have so much regard for me left that this complaint may touch your soul with pity....

How much they met each other after Vanessa came to Ireland is not clear. Her emotional blackmail, no doubt, induced guilt in Swift. And in Dublin there also lived Stella, whom he loved, whose friendship was untroubling, whereas Vanessa was demanding in the extreme, and would not accept the kind of role he prescribed. The letters that remain convey his reply of 12 May 1719 to one of hers (possibly also written in French) advising her to take care of her health, to spend part of the summer in her country house and to make excursions on horseback. The letter praises her merits:

Il n'y a rien a redire dans l'orthographie, la proprietè, l'elegance, le douceur et l'esprit, et que je suis sot moy, de vous repondre en meme langage; vous qui estes incapable d'aucune sottise si ce n'est l'estime qu'il vous plaist d'avoir pour moy, car il n'y a point de merite, ni aucune preuve de mon bon goût de trouver en vous tout ce que la Nature a donnee à un mortel, je veux dire l'honneur, la vertue, le bon sens, l'esprit, la douceur, l'agrement, et la firmitè d'ame, mais en vous cachant commes vous faites, le monde ne vous connoit pas, et vous perdez l'eloge des millions de gens. Depuis que j'avois l'honneur de vous connoitre j'ay toujours remarquè que ni en conversation particuliere, ni general aucun mot a echappè de votre bouche, qui pouvoit etre mieux exprimè; et je vous jure qu'en faisant souvent la plus severe Critique, je ne pouvois jamais trouver aucun defaut ni en vos Actions ni en vos parolles. La Coquetrie, l'affectation, la pruderie, sont des imperfections que vous n'avois jamais connu. Et avec tout cela, croyez vous qu'il est possible de ne vous estimer au dessus du reste du genre humain. Quelles bestes en juppes sont les plus excellentes de celles que je vois semeès dans le monde au prix de vous; en les voyant, en les entendant je dis cent fois le jour – ne parle, ne regarde, ne pense, ne fait rien comme ces miserables, sont ce du meme Sexe – du meme espece de Creatures? quel cruautè de faire mepriser autant de gens qui sans songer de vous, seroient assès supportable – Mais il est tems de vous delasser, et dire adieu avec tous le respecte, la sincerite et l'estime du monde. Je suis et seray toujours –

There is here something of a tutor praising a pupil; and that was the role Swift had enjoyed playing in London, something made clear in the poem *Cadenus and Vanessa*, written to her but not intended for others; Vanessa's misfortune was to want to be more than a pupil, more than a friend. And indeed there was something more than a tutor's sentiment in Swift's letter. He simply could not cut her off: he obviously found her very attractive. The letters, apart from some raillery – she was addressed as Governor Huff when she reproached him for neglecting her – convey his concern for her: on 5 July 1721 he advised her against becoming depressed; company and exercise would protect her against the spleen, 'than which there is not a more foolish or troublesome disease.' He also advises her to settle her affairs 'and quit this scoundrel Island, and things will be as you desire'. Here he had to break off, being called away, and ended the letter 'mais soyez assurè que jamais personne du monde a etè aimèe honorèe estimèe adoreè par votre amie [sic] que vous, I drank no coffee since I left you nor intend till I see you again, there is none worth drinking but yours, if my self may be the judge – adieu.'

Vanessa's last surviving letter (of June 1722) pleads with him to write to her soon; in his absence his letters are all the joy she has on earth – 'Cad [Cadenus, an anagram of Decanus, Latin for Dean] think of me and pity me.' He did write to her in July and August that year, the latter letter bidding her go over past scenes in their lives. He often thinks of them, he tells her, and exclaims 'What a foolish thing is time and how foolish is Man, who would be as angry if time stopped as if it passed.' He had not wanted the permanent relationship of marriage with her; she had been an amusement, an alleviation of anxiety in England, a cause of it in Ireland. Their rules were tragically different. Life must have seemed easier for him, and certainly less complicated, after she died on 2 June 1732.

XI

There succeeded the problem of Stella's increasing ill health. On 12 February 1723 Swift describes her as eating 'an ounce a week'; in poems he bothers about her lack of appetite. She obviously enjoyed the visit she and Rebecca Dingley made to Charles Ford at Wood Park from April to October 1723 (it is celebrated in the poem 'Stella at Wood Park') while Swift toured the south and west of Ireland from June to September. All three spent Christmas 1723 at Quilca, Thomas Sheridan's house in County Cavan, and Stella was 'much better in the country... not so ill as usual'; but she was ill again in some weeks' time. He was deeply worried about her 'weak stomach' in March 1725, and the next month he accompanied the ladies on an extended visit to Quilca, in search of Stella's health. His letters describe the shortcomings of the household amusingly, but Stella's condition did improve there, and so did Swift's spirits – he was working on *Gulliver's Travels*.

During the visit to England begun in March 1725, made largely to arrange the publication of *Gulliver's Travels*, Swift heard from friends that Stella's health was deteriorating: it had 'given her friends bad apprehensions.' He wrote to Sheridan to say he feared the worst, and doubted all good accounts. He could not bear the thought of being in Ireland were she to die. He wrote to the Reverend John Worrall that what he had told him of Stella's condition he had long expected 'with great oppression and heaviness of heart': he and Stella have been perfect friends for thirty five years; since she and Rebecca Dingley came to Ireland they have been his constant companions, and the remainder of his life will be a very melancholy scene 'when one of them is gone whom I most esteemed on the score of every good quality that can possibly recommend a human creature.' Ever since he had left Dublin his heart had been so sunk, he continues, that he has not been the same man nor ever shall be again 'but drag on a wretched life' until it shall please God to call him away. He tells Worrall if he has reason to think Stella cannot hold out till his return he will not himself think of coming back to Ireland till he can be 'in a disposition of appearing after an accident' that must be so fatal to his quiet. After suggesting that Stella should make her will he explains this decision:

I would not for the universe be present at such a trial of seeing her depart. She will be among friends that upon her own account and great worth will tend her with all possible care, where I should be a trouble to her and the greatest torment to myself.

He was determined not to go to Ireland to find her just dead or dying:

Let her know I have bought her a repeating gold watch for her ease on winter nights. I designed to have surprised her with it, but now I would have her know it, that she may see how my thoughts were always to make her easy – I am of opinion that there is not a greater folly than to contract too great and intimate a friendship, which must always leave the survivor miserable.

Every post he expected to hear of her death and in writing to the Reverend James Stopford on 20 July 1726 he praised Worrall for telling him the truth about Stella's condition; however racking this news it was better than being struck on the sudden. He broke off with a heartfelt statement: 'Dear Jim, pardon me, I know not what I am saying; but believe me that violent friendship is much more lasting, and as much engaging, as violent love. Adieu'. To Sheridan he wrote next day, on receiving worse news from him, that he looked upon this as the greatest event that could ever happen to him but

All my preparations will not suffice to make me bear it like a philosopher, nor altogether like a Christian.... Nay, if I were now near her I would not see her; I could not behave myself tolerably, and should redouble her sorrow. Judge in what a temper of mind I write this. The very time I am writing, I conclude the fairest soul in the world hath left its body.

Swift did, however, return to Ireland, leaving London on 1 August and arriving seven days later in Dublin where he, now the popular patriot, the author of the *Drapier's Letters,* was greeted with public acclaim, wherries adorned with streamers and flags meeting his ship, among them a boat containing Sheridan and other friends who brought him the news that Stella was out of immediate danger. He returned to the Deanery to the ringing of the bells of St. Patrick's Cathedral and adjacent churches; bonfires were lit in the streets and flaming torches on top of the cathedral steeple illuminated the whole town.

In October, though Stella was 'much recovered' she was 'very lean and low'; he described her as never having had 'a day's health' in her last year. Swift installed the ladies in the Deanery and set out on what he expected to be his last crossing to England in early April 1727. He wanted to meet the second Earl of Oxford to get some materials for the memoir he was writing of the first Earl; he also wanted him to read *The History of the Four Last Years of the Queen.* And there was a new corrected edition of *Gulliver's Travels* to be arranged. He had an idea of going to Aix la Chapelle where, he was advised, his own health might improve. He was very ill during this last stay in England, his nerves exacerbated by the strain imposed by his anxiety about Stella. On 29 August he described his giddiness and deafness to Sheridan and on 2 September returned to the subject:

If I had any tolerable health, I would go this moment to Ireland; yet I think I would not, considering the news I daily expect to hear from you. I have just received yours of August 24; I kept it an hour in my pocket, with all the suspense of a man who expected to hear the worst news that fortune could give him; and at the same time was not able to hold up my head. These are the perquisites of living long: The last act of life is always a tragedy at best; but it is a bitter aggravation to have one's best friend go before one.... I long knew that our dear friend had not the *stamina vitae;* but my friendship could not arm me against this accident although I foresaw it.... I know not whether it be an addition to my grief or no, that I am now extremely ill; for it would have been a reproach to me to be in perfect health, when such a friend is desperate. I do profess, upon my salvation, that the distressed and desperate condition of our friend, makes life indifferent to me, who by course of nature have so little left, that I do not think it worth the time to struggle; yet I should think, according to what hath been formerly, that I may happen to overcome this present disorder; and to what advantage? Why, to see the loss of that person for whose sake life was only worth preserving. I brought both those friends over, that we might be happy together as long as God should please; the knot is broken, and the remaining person you know, has ill answered the end; and the other who is now to be lost, was all that is valuable.

There was, however, some alleviation in his condition in mid-September, and he left London on the 18th, arriving at Holyhead on the 24th. What frustration he experienced, having missed the packet boat by a day, was recorded in a journal, as the Captain waited for more passengers, then put out to sea, only to return because of an adverse wind, not to get out again for three or four days, and then to arrive at Carlingford, not Dublin. The poem 'Holyhead 1727' sums up his despair:

> the danger of a friend
> On whom my fears and hopes depend
> Absent from whom all climes are curst
> With whom I'm happy in the worst
> With rage impatient makes me wait
> A passage to a land I hate.

When he returned to Ireland he had to endure nearly four months of her illness before Stella died on 28 January 1728: during them he composed prayers for her which were also for himself; they are hauntingly eloquent. But far more moving is the memoir he wrote of her life the night she died, and the night after, and the night after that when, ill and wretched, he was unable to bear looking from his window at the light in the Cathedral where she was being buried. It had indeed been a violent and engaging friendship. One of his prayers asked for her forgiveness for those who sank under the grief and terror of losing so dear and useful a friend.

XII

There were, of course, other less violent but close friendships, and the letters convey Swift's capacity for friendship convincingly. Perhaps his letters to Charles Ford are the best of them. Ford was described as gay and sprightly; he was scholarly, as well, and Swift trusted his literary judgement. He found him 'an easy companion' and had been responsible for his being appointed Gazeteer in 1712, 'the prettiest employment in England of its bigness'. Ford got two hundred pounds a year besides the perquisites. He had, in Swift's view, little to do for it: 'He has a pretty office, with coals, candles, papers, etc; if he takes care, maybe worth one hundred pounds more'. Swift trusted him, and the letters bear this out, for he wrote to him with obvious ease, with a sense of intimacy; was he not a friend both of Stella and Vanessa, to the one 'Don Carlos,' to the other 'Glassheel'?. Ford was privy to the writing of *Gulliver's Travels,* a secret he divulged to Bolingbroke probably late in 1723; letters from Swift to him refer to the work from 1721 onwards and include the triumphant sentence of 14 August 1725 written from Quilca: 'I have finished my travels, and I am now transcribing them; they are admirable things, and will wonderfully mend the world'. These are not, in the words of their distinguished editor, David Nichol Smith, great letters,

but their distinction is that much better than any series of letters to any other friend, they give us Swift in undress. We know him the better for seeing him in undress.

Whether formal or informal, Swift is inevitably worth knowing. Despite intermittent tensions between himself and Archbishop King their letters offer us unique insights into the political affairs of the time: both protagonists of the Church whose interests they defended so stoutly, they did not see eye to eye over many matters, and Swift obviously resented King's thinking he was privy to Bolingbroke's Jacobitism. Misguided in his loyalty to the two Ministers he may have been, but he emerges well in the generosity of spirit which marks his comments on Oxford, while his appreciation of Bolingbroke was the more impressive for his having to tolerate faults in him of which he strongly disapproved.

Swift's capacity for affection emerges in his letters to John Arbuthnot, for anger in those to Richard Steele, and for the appreciation of intellectual agility in his letters to his younger Irish friends, particularly the Reverend Thomas Sheridan. His women correspondents enjoyed his wit, notably Lady Betty Germain, Mrs. Howard, the Countess of Orkney and Lady Acheson. His letters to Pope are literary and lively. What emerges from the richness of his writings to his friends is the Swift who was such good company, the engine of whose formidable mind fired so quickly into life, who did not like the company of bores, and who stimulated so many others into lively intellectual exchanges. Novelist, journalist, propagandist, supreme satirist and poet, he remains one of the best letter writers in English.

FARQUHAR'S FINAL COMEDIES

In 1705 George Farquhar, commissioned as a Lieutenant of Grenadiers the year before in Lord Orrery's regiment of foot, was sent on a recruiting trip to Lichfield and Shrewsbury. The Irish playwright had, reputedly, at the age of thirteen, taken part in the Battle of the Boyne in 1690 'under Colonel Hamilton', so he may have had a predilection for military life. He certainly enjoyed his recruiting experiences, and Lord Orrery commented on his great diligence in this occupation, regarding him as 'very Serviceable both in Raising and Recruiting ye sd. Reigmt'.[1] Out of memories of his stay in Lichfield Farquhar was to create *The Beaux Stratagem* when he was dying in 1706 at the age of thirty, but he began *The Recruiting Officer* when he was still in Shrewsbury in 1705, completing at least the draft and probably the whole of the play there. He dedicated it 'To all Friends round the Wrekin', a steep hill outside Shrewsbury. It was approved by the Duke of Ormonde and by Lord Orrery, who were both engaged in exercises in the area. Farquhar had finished the comedy by 12 February 1706 and gave the manuscript to Bernard Lintot in Fleet Street, receiving £16 2s. 6d. as an advance. It was first performed at Drury Lane on 8 April 1706 and was enormously successful, seven further performances being given that April, three of them, on 10, 15 and 20 April, for the author's benefit. The cast included Wilks as Captain Plume, Cibber as Captain Brazen, and Estcourt as Serjeant Kite, while Anne Oldfield played Silvia. The play was repeated in June; a gala performance took place in Bath in October; and the Drury Lane Company played it for their re-opening at Dorset Gardens on 24 October. After most of the Drury Lane actors had gone over to the Haymarket in the autumn of 1706 the play was staged there by Swiney on the same nights in November that Rich played it with the remains of his company now back in Drury Lane.[2]

Lintot published the first quarto of the play on 12 April 1706, four days after the highly successful first performance. In the Dedication of the play, Farquhar remarked that the entertainment he found in Shropshire commanded him to be grateful. His period of recruiting had gone pleasantly and well there, though he probably spent too much of his money on it in the hope of promotion. He had made friendships with the local Justices and country gentry, and he liked the people and the place. Both provided much of the material for his play, 'some little turns of humour', he remarked, that he met with 'almost within the shade of that famous hill', the Wrekin, gave rise to his comedy. Some of the Salopians were anxious lest he should ridicule the country gentlemen when back in London, but he reassured them that he was writing a comedy not a libel, and that no one from that area could suffer from being exposed while he 'held to nature'. He had found that recruiting in Shrewsbury was the greatest pleasure in the world to him: 'The Kingdom could not show better bodies of men, better inclinations for the service, more generosity, more good understanding, nor more politeness than is to be found at the foot of the Wrekin.'

The characters were based on living originals. E. Blakeway wrote to Bishop Percy, on 4 July 1765, that an old lady in Shrewsbury remembered that Farquhar remained on his recruiting tour in the town long enough to write his play, and she identified the characters as follows:

Justice Balance is Mr Berkley then Deputy Recorder of the town – One of the other Justices, a Mr Hill, an inhabitant of Shrewsbury – Mr Worthy is Mr Owen of Rusason on the borders of Shropshire, Captn Plume is Farquhar himself – Brazen unknown – Melinda is Miss [Dorothy] Harnage of Belsadine near the Wrekin – Sylvia, Miss [Laconia] Berkley Daughter of the Recorder above mentioned. The story I suppose the Poets invention.[3]

Jones, who accompanied Farquhar on his recruiting tour, provided a model for Sergeant Kite, while Farquhar obviously put a great deal of his own personality into Captain Plume, dashing, lively, impressionable and, ultimately, serious. Plume explains himself to the supposed Jack Wilful:

No, Faith, I am not that Rake that the World imagines, I have got an Air of Freedom which People mistake for Lewdness in me as they mistake Formality in others for Religion; the World is all a Cheat, only I take mine which is undesign'd to be more excusable than theirs, which is hypocritical; I hurt nobody but my self, but they abuse all Mankind.

Brazen was probably a mixture of the stock *miles gloriosus* character, of aspects of Farquhar's fellow-officers, and of various foppish characters in Restoration drama. He does, however, gain Plume's recruits at the end of the play, and so may be regarded as an efficient recruiting officer.

There were, of course, literary sources. Farquhar's own play *The Stage-Coach* (1704), founded on Jean de la Chapelle's *Les Carosses d'Orleans,* had shown him the dramatic benefits of observing the unities, and had also taught him the advantages of placing his action in the country rather than the town, and of avoiding the stereotyped plots of the Restoration wits. In his own *The Twin Rivals* he had used the idea of two couples. And he owed much to his study of Ben Jonson, to whom he paid tribute in the preface to *The Stage-Coach.* Willard Connely has argued[4] that Kite's haranguing manner came from the opening scene of the second act of *Volpone* (where Volpone, disguised as a mountebank doctor, sets up to sell his remedies to the crowd), though Farquhar, who particularly appreciated the 'rich gifts of Nature' in Jonson, made Kite's speeches more natural.

The plot revolves around the recruiting of rustics and the love affairs of Captain Plume, Captain Brazen, Worthy and the two girls Silvia and Melinda. Sergeant Kite, masquerading as an astrologer, and possibly based on Congreve's character Foresight in *Love for Love,* becomes a king-pin in the action, and the Justices aid the recruiting and, less wittingly, one of the love affairs.

The main lines of the plot are not very complex. The first act opens with Sergeant Kite trying to recruit grenadiers. The local bumpkins are suspicious of him, but learn to take advantage of his offer of ale. Kite confers with Plume and thus we learn, in a dialogue which is highly amusing on stage, of the birth of Plume's bastard, of Kite's five marriages, and of the enlisting of Plume's child. This establishes the play's parallels between military and civilian life; for war, as Ballance later points out, is the soldier's mistress; begetting bastards is another form of recruiting. We also hear of Kite's fortune-telling disguise, and next, on Worthy's entry, we learn of his so far unsuccessful pursuit of Melinda, who has inherited twenty thousand pounds and become affected. Plume, for his part, loves Silvia but remarks that he is resolved never to bind himself to a woman for his whole life till he knows whether he will like her company for half an hour:

if People wou'd but try one another's Constitutions before they engag'd, it would prevent all these Elopements, Divorces and the Devil knows what.

Silvia's character is then explained. She would have the wedding before consummation while Plume was for consummation before the wedding: yet he admires her frank, generous disposition. Indeed Silvia has given money to the mother of Plume's child and sent word to her that the child will be taken care of; she has also sent a message that her father, Justice Ballance, would like to see Plume. Silvia is unlike Melinda, who is inclined to coquet with everyone she sees, and Worthy fears that Captain Brazen, the other recruiting captain, may be his rival for her affections. Both Silvia and Worthy are wholehearted lovers, and Silvia's viewpoint rather than Melinda's is the one with which we are meant to sympathise.

The play continues to develop the differences between Silvia and Melinda in the second scene of the first Act. Silvia is a 'natural' woman with the constitution of a horse: able to 'gallop all the Morning after the Hunting Horn and all the Evening after a Fiddle', she is troubled by 'neither Spleen, Cholick nor Vapours'. Melinda, however, is affected in her treatment of Worthy, for whereas Silvia does not like a man with confirmed thoughts and regards constancy as but a dull sleepy quality at best, Melinda thinks the worse of Worthy for associating with Plume.

Plume's character, however, is not as depraved as Melinda's words might suggest. In the opening of the second act there is a frank discussion between Justice Ballance and Plume, in which Plume assures him he has no designs on Silvia. He tells Silvia herself that he has made her his heir and in her generosity and determination not to be possessive or censorious she remarks that he should have left something to his child. Later in the fourth act Plume explains to Silvia (then disguised as Mr Wilful) that he is 'not that Rake that the World imagines'. He has an air of freedom which people mistake for lewdness. Unlike those who mistake formality for religion, he is no hypocrite. He talks briefly about his recruiting methods.

These we have seen in action earlier in the play. Plume and Kite work well together. When Kite has planted his gold pieces (he was only paying the equivalent of twenty three shillings and sixpence, whereas according to the relevant Acts of Parliament the sum should have been twenty shillings for each person recruited. Plume's two guineas was more correct, as volunteers were paid forty shillings) Plume affects to drive him off and the men enlist in admiration of Plume's apparent championing of their cause. Again, he works very successfully through the agency of Rose. And Kite, as supposed astrologer and fortune-teller, sets up situations through which Plume will be able to recruit the credulous visitors to the astrologer. (In this role Kite also continues to bring Melissa and Worthy together.) Plume's generosity appears later in the play when Justice Ballance, realising Silvia's disguise as Wilful and suspecting this is a plot of Plume's, offers to buy the supposed young man out of the army. He is freely given the discharge by Plume who, ignorant of Wilful's true identity, values the Justice's friendship too much to make money out of him. Plume is not, of course, committed to his recruiting trade, and at the play's end is happily ready to settle down to the life of a country gentleman, offering Brazen the twenty recruits he has collected.

The court scene where dishonesty reigns, offers the audience, beyond its pure comedy, the chance to realise that some of those who are impressed do not deserve its pity. For instance, the man who pretends to support five children is enlisted because he is a poacher. The collier who pretends to be married is accused by Kite of having no visible means of livelihood because he works underground: but his supposed wife clinches this dubious argument in favour of his enlistment by revealing that they had agreed she should call him husband to avoid passing for a whore and that he should call her wife 'to shun going for a soldier'. The dishonesty of the constable is shown when Silvia is brought into court; and he is then taken into custody by Kite, to be held until his friends have ransomed him with four recruits.

A bald account of the plot of *The Recruiting Officer* could hardly convey the speed of its action, the involved interweaving of the recruiting and the three love affairs. Indeed Farquhar probably wrote the play quickly, and was himself entangled enough in it to have made some mistakes.[5] For instance, Silvia calls herself Jack Wilful in III, ii when Plume enlists her, and she is known by this name in IV, ii, but in V, ii when she is first brought into court she calls herself Captain Pinch. When she is brought in again, she is called Pinch by her father and Plume, who is now present, makes no objection when she is enlisted as Pinch. We might argue that Plume would tolerate a pseudonym, as he tolerated Silvia's supposed conquest of Rose, but it seems that Farquhar either didn't develop this idea or else forgot that Plume knew her previously only by the name of Wilful. The latter seems probable since in V, vii Ballance sends for Silvia as Mr Wilful though previously he has only known her in court as Pinch. Another inconsistency is that Lucy has been writing in her own hand to Captain Brazen (in the hopes of marrying him) but signing her letters Melinda. But she uses Melinda's signature (which she steals – 'I'll secure one copy for my own Affairs' – at the fortune-teller's in IV, ii) when she writes to Brazen to arrange a place of meeting whence they can elope. She runs a risk, and for no apparent reason, as Brazen may realise that the signature has changed. The dramatic purpose behind this is, of course, that Plume shall recognise this signature as genuinely Melinda's when Brazen shows it to him and report this to Worthy, who will regard the elopement of Brazen and Melinda as genuine, rush to interrupt it and thus ruin Lucy's plot of trap-

ping Brazen into marrying her. Again, the first and second bumpkins are Costar and Thummas respectively when they appear in
the second act; but at the end of the act they give their names as
Thummas Appletree and Costar Pearmain.[6]

The main action of the play centres on the recruiting drive.
Farquhar presents recruiting as it was. In the process we learn how
soldiers were recruited for the war of the Spanish Succession.
There were many ways of using and abusing the Mutiny and
Impressment Acts of 1703, 1704, and 1706, and the Justices of the
Peace could put able-bodied men into the armed forces if they were
deemed to have no lawful calling or occupation, or no employment, or no visible means of support. The court scene in the play,
the antics of Kite and the pressure exerted by Plume illustrate the
power of the Justices, as well as the dishonesty of both recruiters
and those unwilling to be recruited. Plume is successful in his
operation. Farquhar is not concerned to sermonise about Plume's
methods (no doubt he acted similarly on his own campaign in
Lichfield and Shrewsbury), nor does he provide socio-political
comment on them. He is out to amuse, and he does this with a mixture of gaiety and tolerance; indeed Professor Rothstein has called
the play 'almost a comic documentary'.[7]

Farquhar made use of Restoration devices in his comedy. There
are echoes of Restoration bawdiness in plenty in the dialogue. The
love affairs revolve around the finances of marriage and the choice
of a socially suitable partner, as in most Restoration comedies.
Kite's bogus-astrology reminds us of Congreve's *Love for Love,* and
both Lucy's wearing a mask in her vain attempt to deceive Captain
Brazen and her use of false letters, and even Silvia's pretending to
be a young man have their models. The 'breeches' part appealed to
Farquhar; he had used it earlier, for Leanthe in *Love and a Bottle
(1698)* and for Oriana in *The Inconstant* (1702). But he gave it a new
turn with Silvia's pursuit of Plume, for she is a tolerant heroine;
not unlike Sophia Western, she has grown up in the country, no
milk and water Miss, but rather a new type of heroine, just as the
play itself is a new kind of comedy. She can act the part of a gallant, she can be pert and witty; but she is lacking in feminine jealousy, in pride and in affectation, and is a 'natural' woman.

The treatment of the rustics also reveals some natural kindness
at work – in Bullock's clumsy protectiveness of his sister Rose, for
instance. The same easiness appears in Plume's relationships with
Ballance – the two men genuinely like each other – and Silvia
wants to be brought to court so that her father will commit her (as
'Jack Wilful') to Plume's care and thus authorise her escapade.

Melinda is frightened by Kite into caring for Worthy – both Silvia
and Lucy had urged her to this earlier – and it seems likely that she
and Worthy, who lives up to his name, will make a success of marriage. Plume, of course, is not the gay libertine he might at first
seem. He and Silvia have a liking for each other which is based on
a tolerant attitude to life.

There is, then, a benignity in the drawing of the characters
which marks the play off from other Restoration comedies, as well
as a liveliness which came from Farquhar's portrayal of new
themes: recruitment and country life. He is concerned to wed army
and country together, and Silvia is the necessary link. Kenneth
Tynan reports William Gaskill when producing the play as seeing
three main actions or objectives in it: (1) Silvia's determination to
get Plume (2) Plume's and Kite's determination to get recruits and
(3) Worthy's determination to get Melinda. Gaskill saw (1) and (2)
brought together by Silvia's male impersonation, while Brazen's
designs on Melinda linked (1) and (3).

There is no censorious attitude to the army, which reduces all
matters to military parlance and situations. But civilian life provides analogies and sex is seen in martial terms. The two worlds
need each other: the army defends the social order represented by
Justice Ballance. The virtually stock characters illustrate Farquhar's
view of what a harmonious, stable society could be, and he regarded the army as an essential part of it. The rustics have an energetic
patriotic capacity, so have the Justices, especially Ballance, who is
one of Farquhar's best creations. Both he and Plume play their
parts in seeing that the army is supplied with recruits. The role of
the army in society is underlined by Silvia's love for both her
father and Plume: that she successfully deceives both is in the best
traditions of comedy, and leads to an ideal solution in which
Ballance regains a son and heir in the person of Plume, while
Plume is deceived in order, ultimately, to win his wife. Silvia's
actions lead also to the marriage of Melinda and Worthy, and to
Brazen's success in recruiting.

The Beaux Stratagem, Farquhar's last and best play, was written
at the instigation of his friend Robert Wilks the actor, who called on
him at his lodgings in York Buildings about the middle of
December 1706 only to find Farquhar had moved to a cheaper gar-
ret in St Martin's Lane. At the time the young Irish playwright was
in debt, miserable – 'heart-broken' in his own words – and
extremely ill. Wilks gave him twenty guineas, urged him to write
another play, and promised to call in a week to see its framework.
Within six weeks Farquhar had finished the comedy, though he

rewrote parts of it up to its production. It is likely that his illness was tuberculosis; before he had finished the second act he is said to have 'felt death upon him': he managed, however, to resume work and *The Beaux Stratagem*, with all its lively gaiety, is a monument to his courage and determination as well as to his sense of humour and his ability to innovate. He died in his thirtieth year, in May 1707, and was buried on 23 May.[8]

The sources for the play are several and are both literary and autobiographical. Cervantes probably provided the basic idea of an inn in *Don Quixote*, but via Jean de la Chapelle's *Les Carosses d'Orleans*, which Farquhar, in collaboration with Peter Motteaux, had adapted as *The Stage Coach* (1704). Some of the ideas in *The Stage Coach* are developed in *The Beaux Stratagem*. Farquhar's recruiting tour of 1705, during which he visited Lichfield and Shrewsbury, provided him with other material for the scenes of the play and its characters. Just as he had written *The Recruiting Officer* (1706) out of his experience of Shrewsbury, now he turned to his memories of Lichfield. He had stayed at the George Inn there, and its landlord, John Harrison, gave him ideas for Bonniface the innkeeper. Harrison's daughter perhaps served as a model for Cherry, Bonniface's daughter, though she may also be founded upon Dolly in *The Stage Coach*.[9]

Farquhar became friendly with Sir Michael Biddulph on his recruiting tour and frequently visited him and his family at Elmhurst. This was a large and charming country house outside Lichfield, which was probably a model for Lady Bountiful's house, just as Sir Michael's humorous servant, Thomas Bond, inspired the creation of Scrub, Sullen's servant. Farquhar enjoyed the company of Sir Michael's family: two of his children, the daughters of his first marriage, were just out of their teens; and there were three others by his second wife, who may herself have provided material for the character of Lady Bountiful. Lichfield also contained French officers who were prisoners of war and presumably lent themselves to the portrait of Count Bellair. Foigard, the Irish character, a type Farquhar had drawn before in Macahone in *The Stage Coach*, and earlier in Teague in *The Twin – Rivals* (1703), was founded upon an actual Father Fogarty or 'Fogourdy' mentioned by Pepys in February 1664.

The play owed something to Vanbrugh's work. The concept of an ill-assorted husband and wife in *The Provok'd Wife* is developed in *The Beaux Stratagem*. Sir John Brute, who comes home roaring drunk and disturbs his wife when she is asleep,[10] seems a mild rehearsal for Farquhar's Squire Sullen who returns at four in the morning to 'flounce into Bed, dead as a Salmon into a Fishmonger's Basket; his Feet cold as Ice, his Breath hot as a Furnace, and his Hands and his Face as greasy as his Flanel Night-cap' [II. I. 65-7]. Vanbrugh also depicts the situation of an ill-assort-ed pair in *The Relapse,* where Berinthia makes a speech[11], in which she describes the differences between her late husband's interests and her own. She is, however, a different kind of woman from Farquhar's Mrs Sullen. In *The Relapse* when Loveless enters Berinthia's chamber her protests are mild and he ravishes her off stage. But, when this situation of the lover concealed in the lady's bedroom is repeated in *The Beaux Stratagem,* Mrs Sullen, though greatly taken with Archer, shrieks violently, and the seduction does not occur.

This is symptomatic of the change which occurs between the drama of Vanbrugh and Farquhar. Farquhar reflects a shift in sen-sibility. He has an Elizabethan vitality: but though he moves away from the Restoration comedy of manners he is not moving com-pletely into sentimental comedy. Just as he places his plays in the country, just as he turns from the wit and repartee of Restoration court drama towards an easier eighteenth-century dialogue, so he tackles, head on, a moral situation new in the drama: the question of divorce. His own unsatisfactory marriage, which took place in 1703, may well have prompted his reading of Milton's *Doctrine and Discipline of Divorce* when he wrote *The Beaux Stratagem.* Margaret Parnell, a thirty-five year old widow with two children, had deceived him by pretending she had an income of £500 a year. Farquhar had been in debt when he married her, but even the good fortune of the Lieutenant's commission which he gained in 1704 was not enough to keep him and his new family, to which he had speedily added two daughters. His illness depressed him and despite the success of *The Recruiting Officer* in 1706, he was deeply worried about the future of his children, for he was still in debt, possibly as a result of spending his own money on the recruiting expedition. It is possible that his own marital situation lent greater intensity to his dramatic investigation of a situation where an illas-sorted husband and wife dislike each other and wish to separate. As in his other plays, he put a good deal of himself into the main character, Aimwell, though Archer, the other young man in search of money through marriage, is also reminiscent of some aspects of Farquhar's own personality. (There is only one passage of bitter-ness in the play – that in which they discuss Jack Generous who is avoided 'for no Crime upon Earth but the want of Money' [I. I. 147-8].) But though his own energy and his regard for the ladies inform the young men, he is also deeply influenced by Milton. Archer, for instance, describes his flirtation with Cherry in Miltonic tones:

> The Nymph that with her twice ten hundred Pounds
> With brazen Engine hot, and Quoif clear starch'd
> Can fire the Guest in warming of the Bed . . .

There's a Touch of Sublime *Milton* for you, and the Subject but an Inn-keeper's Daughter. [III. II. 22-6]

Milton was a direct influence on the situation between Sullen and his wife. This passage between them is one of economical hatred:

SULLEN. You're impertinent.
MRS SULLEN. I was ever so, since I became one Flesh with you.
SULLEN. One Flesh! rather two Carcasses join'd unnaturally together.
MRS SULLEN. Or rather a living Soul coupled to a dead Body.

[III. III. 276-281].

It derives from the second book of Milton's *Doctrine and Discipline of Divorce:*

Nay, instead of being one flesh, they will be rather two carcasses chained unnaturally together; or, as it may happen, a living soul bound to a dead corpse.[12]

And when Dorinda tells Mrs Sullen that the divisions between her husband and herself don't come within reach of the law for a divorce Mrs Sullen bursts into heartfelt speech:

Law! what Law can search into the remote Abyss of Nature, what Evidence can prove the unaccountable Disaffections of Wedlock – can a Jury sum up the endless Aversions that are rooted in our Souls, or can a Bench give Judgment upon Antipathies. [III. III. 414-8]

She appeals to Nature, the first lawgiver, who when she has 'set Tempers opposite, not all the golden Links of Wedlock, nor Iron Manacles of law can keep 'um fast'. This dialogue, with its appeal to Nature, echoes Milton's general account of the evils of natural hatred and has taken over his phrases, as, for instance, in this sentence:

To couple hatred, therefore, though wedlock try all her golden links, and borrow to her aid all the iron manacles and fetters of the law, it does but seek to twist a rope of sand.[13]

Again, when Sullen accidentally meets his wife's brother, Sir Charles Freeman, for the first time in the Inn, their discussion contains further echoes of Milton on the subject. Milton's views – that the greatest breach of marriage is unfitness of mind, that thère is no true marriage between those who agree not in true consent of mind and that the unity of mind is nearer and greater than the union of bodies – are formulated in compressed form by Sir Charles in answer to a query of Bonniface's when the Innkeeper asks "Are not Man and Wife one Flesh?':

SIR CHARLES. You and your Wife, Mr. Guts, may be one Flesh, because ye are nothing else – but rational Creatures have minds that must be united.

SULLEN. Minds.

SIR CHARLES. Ay, minds, Sir, don't you think that the Mind takes place of the Body? [V. I. 58-63]

This attitude to divorce as a subject for drama was new, and so was Farquhar's picture of the unhappy yet loyal wife. Mrs Sullen's view of Archer is honest:

I do love that Fellow; – And if I met him drest as he shou'd be, and I undrest as I shou'd be – Look'ye, Sister, I have no supernatural Gifts; – I can't swear I cou'd resist the Temptation, – tho' I can safely promise to avoid it; and that's as much as the best of us can do.

[IV. I. 447-451]

And yet she does resist. This marks a departure from the libertinism of the Restoration court dramatists, but it is a realistic one. The characters are not what they seem; neither she nor her husband see each other as they are; and some of the other characters surprise us too: even Scrub, for instance, has an abundant simplicity with which to conceal his cunning.

The names of the characters indicate something of their nature. The name of Count Bellair suggests how different his manner will be from that of Sullen, a name which so suits the squire. His wife's maiden name was Freeman, and freedom from the sullen temper of her husband is what she seeks. Lady Bountiful has given her name to the phrase 'to play Lady Bountiful': it was well conceived as a name for a countrywoman who is 'one of the best of Women', laying out half her income 'in charitable Uses for the Good of her Neighbours', and curing people of illness.

Cherry's name suggests her bright manner, and Gipsey's her wild one, while Dorinda is a suitable name (this is an early use of it) for the young woman who is a stock heroine. Aimwell, her lover, is well named for the effect Farquhar wanted to create, of a wild young man who none the less intends well, is generous, and honest. Archer, his friend, is more of a Restoration rogue-hero: his name is stressed twice in the play: in II. II. 40 he remarks 'Let me alone, for I am a Mark'sman' and in III. II. 1. Archer takes up the point 'Well, *Tom*, I find you're a Marksman'. The imagery is that of military aggression and amorous attack. No scruples restrain his pursuit of maid or matron; he is more apt to deceive; he is quiverful of amorous energy:

> I can be charm'd with *Sappho's* singing without falling in Love with her Face; I love Hunting, but wou'd not, like *Acteon*, be eaten up by my own Dogs; I love a fine House, but let another keep it; and just so I love a fine Woman. [I. I. 219-222]

The stock villains are likewise indicated by their names. Gibbet is clear enough: the names of Hounslow and Bagshot are perhaps suggested by the heaths which were infested by highwaymen. Bonniface's name suits his trade as innkeeper: his duplicity is part of the deceiving which goes on; the name soon appears ironic and contributes to the stratagem of the play, where appearances are specious.

Surprise is one of the elements that Farquhar built into *The Beaux Stratagem:* its construction is skilful. He is again contrasting city and country, contrasting life in the inn and in the house, the honest lover and the less scrupulous, the sottish Sullen and the polished Count Bellair, the innocent Dorinda and realistic Mrs Sullen. The plot revolves around deception. In the first act we learn about the designs of Aimwell and Archer, a fortune-hunting and flirting pair of impoverished young men. The next act tells us clearly that Mrs Sullen's marriage is intolerable: she is flirting with Count Bellair – to revenge herself upon her husband; this is her stratagem, but one set within wishful limits. We learn that Bonniface and his highwaymen friends are deceivers also and plan to rob Lady Bountiful. The third Act gives us the lovers' views of each other; Mrs Sullen and Dorinda have observed Archer and Aimwell in church with some interest, and Aimwell has fallen in love with Dorinda. The plot becomes more complex and the action livens up with the introduction of Foigard. Scrub fears Foigard's relations with Gipsey the maid; Mrs Sullen has begun to think of Archer rather than Count Bellair; and Dorinda becomes interested in Aimwell. The tempo of the action accelerates sharply as Count Bellair's wooing of Mrs Sullen is interrupted: she draws a pistol on him – and on Sullen who bursts in on them and ruthlessly expresses his indifference as to how she behaves provided she does not misbehave with a Frenchman. The third act moves from a gay picture of love and intrigue to an examination of the intolerable nature of unhappy marriage.

The fourth act speeds up the action even more with Aimwell, who is pretending to be his brother Lord Aimwell, feigning illness in Lady Bountiful's house, and thus managing to propose to Dorinda while Archer makes propositions to Mrs Sullen. The plot is complicated further by Foigard's bribing Gipsey to hide Count Bellair in Mrs Sullen's closet. Archer replaces him, having blackmailed Foigard by threatening to reveal him as an Irishman serving with the French army. The highwaymen arrive to rob the house at midnight.

The final act resolves the situation, though not as simply as might have been expected. Mrs Sullen's brother, Sir Charles Freeman, meets Sullen at the Inn; their frank discussion prepares us for the subsequent solution of the situation between the Sullens. Aimwell is told by Cherry of the plot and he arrives to fight two of the thieves while Archer, foiled in his attempt on Mrs Sullen by the entry of Scrub when she shrieked, has overcome another of them in Mrs Sullen's room. He aids Aimwell and urges him – once the highwaymen are consigned to the cellar – to marry Dorinda at once, with Foigard at hand to conduct the service. Archer himself attempts to trade on his wound in order to resume his advances to Mrs Sullen. But then all this stratagem seems likely to fail, for Sir Charles Freeman, who knows Archer in London, is announced.

The complications continue. Aimwell tells Dorinda he is not Lord Aimwell. But Dorinda hears from Sir Charles that Aimwell's brother is dead; he is Lord Aimwell. Archer now demands half Dorinda's fortune in view of his earlier arrangement with Aimwell; but Aimwell offers him it all because of his own new wealth. Sir Charles enters; he intends to arrange for his sister to part from Sullen and all agree to aid him. Then Sullen comes on the scene; and he and Mrs Sullen, after their doxology of hatred, agree to part. Sullen, however, will not give up her dowry, whereupon Count Bellair offers to pay a dowry and take Mrs Sullen away. But the total sum involved (£10,000) appals him. Then Archer offers to pay it. He can resolve the situation since he has taken from one of the highwaymen all the contents of Sullen's escritoire, 'all the Writings of your Estate, all the Articles of Marriage with his Lady, Bills, Bonds, Leases, Receipts to an infinite Value'. Cherry becomes maid to Dorinda, and Archer and Mrs Sullen round off the play by leading a dance. The play echoes Milton to the end, extolling divorce by mutual consent in the name of freedom:

Both happy in their several States we find,

Those parted by consent, and those conjoin'd,
Consent, if mutual, sayes the Lawyer's Fee,
Consent is Law enough to set you free, [V. IV. 288-291].

GOOD-NATURED GOLDSMITH

Carlyle was taken by William Allingham to Goldsmith's grave in the Temple. They stood beside what Allingham described as the simple but sufficient monument, a stone about coffin length and eighteen inches high. Allingham read the inscription aloud, Carlyle took off his broad-flapped black hat and said 'A salute' ... after they had replaced their hats and turned away Carlyle remarked, 'Poor Oliver, he said on his deathbed, "I am not at ease in my mind".'

There have been many biographies – Carlyle complained later to Allingham that Black's gave no creditable Goldsmith – and many explanations of Goldsmith's deathbed remark. Dr Johnson who knew, and, in his way, loved him, told Boswell that Goldsmith had died of a fever made more violent by uneasiness of mind. 'His debts began to be heavy, and all his resources were exhausted. Sir Joshua [Reynolds] is of opinion that he owed not less than two thousand pounds. Was ever poet so trusted before?' And the next day he wrote to Bennet Langton that Goldsmith had 'died of a fever, exasperated, as I believe, by the fear of distress. He had raised money and squandered it, by every artifice of acquisition and folly of expense. But let not his frailties be remembered; he was a very great man'. Johnson's famous Latin epitaph for the monument in Westminster Abbey included the phrase that there was almost no form of literature Goldsmith had not put his hand to, and that whatever he had attempted he had made elegant.

To Johnson, then, as to many of Goldsmith's biographers it was a matter of the contrast between greatness and frailty. By the time Goldsmith died in London on 4 April 1774, he had composed two of the eighteenth century's best known poems, 'The Traveller' and 'The Deserted Village' – and there are other good poems too, notably the 'Stanzas on Woman', 'When lovely Woman stoops to folly', 'Retaliation' and the 'Elegy on the Death of a Mad Dog'. He had also written *The Vicar of Wakefield* which was probably at its most popular in the nineteenth century but is still read for its gentle irony, and for its wisdom as well as its sense of absurdity. He had created two comedies, *The Good Natur'd Man* and the ever-amusing *She Stoops to Conquer*, which have been seen by vast audiences on television, and are still standing up nobly to the onslaughts of amateur dramatic groups. He had written histories of England, of Greece and of Rome which survived in school syllabuses up to this century. He had written the *Letters from a Citizen of the World* in which he viewed his London world from the point of view of a Chinese visitor. He had written a sensitive biography of Richard Nash as well as one of Voltaire. He had provided much information, still giving pleasure to those who enjoy description – and humour – in his *History of the Earth and Animated Nature*. And, of course, there was his hack writing: Introductions, Prefaces, biographies, criticism, and compilations.

His output of writing was very large indeed, impressively so, and he may well have been temporarily written out when he died. Unlike Johnson he had received no State pension. He had outrun the constable. His life as a writer went through a cycle, indeed a series of cycles, of over-spending (very often in charity to others, for he was generous to the point of absurdity), of over-borrowing and then of overworking in vain efforts to catch up.

The strain was very great, and his London friends were not perceptive; they did not realise at the end how ill he was. He must have reached the point of asking himself what the value of it all was. But that does not fully answer his final mental unease. And yet there are many passages in his writings which indicate more of his nature than may have been obvious to his friends in London. He suffered from *maladie du pays*. Indeed he can be explained in terms of equations which describe the lives of many Irish writers. In one equation poverty, ambition and ability equal achievement; in another achievement is the sum of compulsion to write and sacrifice of happiness. Goldsmith was ambitious, but his father gave him no training for fending off poverty. Here is how Goldsmith's character, the Man in Black – who is very like his author – described his father the country clergyman:

As his fortune was but small he lived up to the very extent of it; he had no intention of leaving his children money, for that was dross; he was resolved they should have learning; for learning, he used to observe, was better than silver or gold. For this purpose he undertook to instruct us himself; and took as much pains to form our morals as to improve our understanding. We were told that universal benevolence was what first cemented society; we were taught to consider all the wants of mankind as our own, to regard the human face divine with affection and esteem; he wound us up to be mere machines of pity, and rendered us incapable of withstanding the slightest impulse made either by real or fictitious distress; in a word, we were perfectly instructed in the art of giving away thousands before we were taught the more necessary qualifications of getting a far-thing.

And this father was disappointed in his expectations by the mid-dling figure made in the university by his son:

He had flattered himself that he should soon see me rising into the fore-most rank in literary reputation, but was mortified to find me utterly unno-ticed and unknown. His disappointment might have been partly ascribed to his having overrated my talents, and partly to my dislike of mathemat-ical reasonings, at a time when my imagination and memory, yet unsatis-fied were more eager after new objects than desirous of reasoning upon those I knew. This, however, did not please my tutors, who observed indeed that I was a little dull; but at the same time allowed, that I seemed to be very good natured, and had no harm in me.

Here is the *leitmotif* which runs through many of Goldsmith's self-portraits. He was indeed very goodnatured and there was no harm in him – the latter a very Irish phrase, the meaning and overtones of which are no doubt well known, certainly to many in Ireland.

Like Swift before him, Goldsmith disliked the mathematics of the Trinity College syllabus. Like Swift he got involved in distur-bances – Swift cut his lectures and joined in starting a tumult in college, and had to beg the Dean's pardon publicly on bended knees. Goldsmith, too, got involved in a tumult, a more serious one which went beyond the walls of the College. A bailiff arrested an undergraduate in debt, was himself hunted by the debtor's fellows in the streets and brought to the College pump to be ducked. There was an irruption into the streets, the Trinity students storming the Black Dog prison with the idea of freeing its prisoners, and in the ensuing riot lives were lost. Five undergraduates were struck off the books and Goldsmith was one of five others publicly admon-ished.

Worse followed – he began to cram, and so successfully that he won a money prize. He promptly spent the money on that famous party in his rooms – to which he had invited women. His tutor, Theaker Wilder, burst into the middle of this party and knocked his pupil down. Goldsmith left College, hung about Dublin till his money was exhausted, then walked towards Cork for three days before heading for home in Lissoy, Co.Westmeath. Eventually all was sorted out by his brother and he returned to College. Like Swift before him he must have realised he was neither exhibiting brilliance nor the application displayed by those worthy if dull pupils who found it easy to fit into the orthodox university pattern of the day. In his admirable *Enquiry into the State of Polite Learning in Europe* he criticised British universities for using their magnificent endowments to 'more frequently enrich the prudent than reward the ingenious':

A lad whose passions are not strong enough in youth to mislead him from that path of science which his tutors and not his inclinations, have chalked out, by four or five years' perseverance may probably obtain every advantage and honour his college can bestow. I forget whether the simile has been used before but I would compare the man whose youth has been thus passed in the tranquillity of dispassionate prudence, to liquors which never ferment, and consequently continue always muddy. Passions may raise a commotion in the youthful breast, but they disturb only to refine it. However this may be, mean talents are often rewarded in colleges with an easy subsistence. The candidates for preferments of this kind often regard their admission as a patent for future indolence; so that a life begun in studious labour, is often continued in luxurious laziness.

Goldsmith had come to college with reluctance. He belonged to the middle rank of the Anglo-Irish, the professional class. Shaw has described this particular level of Irish society well. Discussing his family in the preface he wrote in 1879 to his first novel *Immaturity*, he said the Shaws were younger sons from the beginning. 'I was', he said 'a downstart, and the son of a downstart: I sing my own class: the shabby Genteel, the Poor Relations, the Gentlemen who are No Gentlemen ...' He described his family in terms that would apply to Swifts, or Congreves, or Farquhars, or Goldsmiths, or Sheridans, or Wildes or Yeatses or Synges:

On the whole, they held their cherished respectability in the world in spite of their lack of opportunity. They owed something, perhaps to the confidence given them by their sense of family. In Irish fashion they talked of themselves as the Shaws, as who should say the Valois, the Bourbons, the Hohenzollerns, the Hapsburgs, or the Romanoffs, and their world conceded the point to them. I had an enormous contempt for this family snobbery, as I called it, until I was completely reconciled to it by a certain Mr Alexander Mackintosh Shaw, a clansman who, instead of taking his pedigree for granted in the usual Shaw manner, hunted it up, and published one hundred copies privately in 1877. Somebody sent me a copy, and my gratification was unbounded when I read the first sentence of the first chapter, which ran: 'It is the general tradition, says the Rev. Lachlan Shaw [bless him!], that the Shaws are descended of McDuff, Earl of Fife.' I hastily skipped to the chapter about the Irish Shaws to make sure that they were my people; and there they were, baronet and all, duly traced to the third son of that immortalized yet unborn Thane of Fife who, invulnerable to

normally accouched swordsmen, laid on and slew Macbeth. It was as good
as being descended from Shakespeare, whom I had been unconsciously
resolved to reincarnate from my cradle.

Goldsmith's father had behaved within this tradition. When he
was tutoring a wealthy neighbour's son this lad fell in love with
the clergyman's daughter and married her. Out of pride, self-
respect, in short out of an awareness that the Goldsmiths were
somebodies, Mr Goldsmith entered into a bond to pay £400, twice
his total income, in order to match the young man's position. Land
and tithes were sacrificed to this sense of family pride or self-
respect and so, in a way, was Oliver, for there was no money now
to send him to Trinity as his brother Harry had gone. The only way
for him to obtain a university education was to become a sizar.
And even before he was awarded a sizarship Goldsmith viewed
the prospect of becoming one with loathing. His brother had told
him enough about it to make it seem humiliating to him, ambitious
as he was, to have as a sizar to undertake menial tasks in return for
his free education, rooms and commons.

In his Enquiry into the *Present State of Polite Learning in Europe*
Goldsmith had ended his chapter on the universities with a heartfelt echo of the humiliation he had experienced because, as a sizar,
he had been in a different category from that of the average undergraduate:

Surely pride itself had dictated to the fellows of our colleges the absurd
passion of being attended at meals, and on other public occasions by those
poor men who, willing to be scholars, come in upon some charitable foundation. It implies a contradiction, for men to be at once learning the liberal arts and at the same time treated as slaves; at once studying freedom and
practising servitude.

And later he advised his brother when the clergyman was thinking
of sending his son to Trinity that the boy, if assiduous and divest-
ed of strong passion, might do well in college, for, he said, it must
be owned that the industrious poor have perhaps better encouragement there than in any other university in Europe. But, he
added, if he 'has ambition, strong passions, and an exquisite sensibility of contempt, do not send him there unless you have no trade
for him but your own.'

However little Goldsmith liked being a sizar, however dull he
thought the curriculum, and however unpleasant he found Theaker
Wilder as a tutor, he discovered some compensation: playing the
flute and composing ballads which he sold at five shillings a piece
to the printer Hicks. The first stanza of one of his compositions,

'The March of Intellect' clearly conveys his attitude to academic life.

> Oh, learning's a very fine thing,
> As also is wisdom and knowledge,
> For a man is as great as a king,
> If he has but the airs of a college.
> And now-a-days all must admit
> In learning we're wonderful favoured,
> For you scarce o'er your window can spit,
> But some learned man is beslavered.
> Sing, tol de rol, lay.

He was certainly very happy to be back at home in 1749 once he had obtained his B.A. His father had died in 1747, his own future could be left to its own devices and an essay in *The Bee*, written when he was thirty and beginning his career as a writer looks back on these halcyon days:

When I reflect on the unambitious retirement in which I passed the earlier part of my life in the country, I cannot avoid feeling some pain in thinking that those happy days are never to return. In that retreat all nature seemed capable of affording pleasure; I then made no refinements on happiness, but could be pleased with the most awkward efforts of rustic mirth; thought cross-purposes the highest stretch of human wit, and questions and commands the most rational amusement for spending the evening. Happy could so charming an illusion still continue! I find that age and knowledge only contribute to sour our dispositions. My present enjoyments may be more refined, but they are infinitely less pleasing. The pleasure Garrick gives can no way compare to that I had received from a country wag, who imitated a Quaker's sermon. The music of Mattei is dissonance to what I felt when our old dairy-maid sung me into tears with Johnny Armstrong's Last Good Night, or the Cruelty of Barbara Allen.

But the cares of the world had crept into this Irish midland paradise and there is a likely explanation in *The History of the Man in Black*:

In order to settle in life my friends advised (for they always advise when they begin to despise us), they advised me, I say, to go into orders.

To be obliged to wear a long wig when I liked a short one, or a black coat when I generally dressed in bright, I thought was such a restraint upon my liberty, that I absolutely rejected the proposal. A priest in England is not the same mortified creature with a bonze in China: with us, not he that fasts best, but eats best, is reckoned the best liver; yet I rejected a life of luxury, indolence, and ease, from no other consideration but that

boyish one of dress. So that my friends were now perfectly satisfied I was
undone; and yet they thought it a pity for one who had not then the least
harm in him, and was so very good-natured.

The *leitmotif* is there again; he was good natured, with no harm in
him. There was no harm in appearing before the local Bishop as a
candidate for ordination in scarlet breeches; and he took his dismissal in a good natured way. There were various efforts to make
a living, and he tried tutoring. Was there autobiographical experience behind the Man in Black's description of a period in his life
when poverty begot dependence, when he was admitted as flatter-
er to a great man, and at first found the situation agreeable?

I found, however, too soon, that his lordship was a greater dunce than
myself; and from that very moment my power of flattery was an
end. . . . Every time I now opened my lips in praise, my falsehood went to
my conscience; his lordship soon perceived me to be unfit for service; I was
therefore discharged; my patron at the same time being graciously pleased
to observe, that he believed I was tolerably good-natured, and had not the
least harm in me.

There was an expedition to Cork with a very vague idea of emigrating to America, with his own horse under him and thirty
pounds in his pocket from a year's tutoring. He was soon back
minus his horse and his money, but with a very good story about
his adventures. Next time, off he went with fifty pounds from an
uncle to enter the Inns of Court in London. Soon he was back, penniless and with yet another good story about his misadventures.
Then the idea of medicine arose and in 1752 he left Ireland for ever.
His letters from Edinburgh where he was studying medicine – in
his way – are delightful. On 8 May 1753 he told his uncle Contarine
that he had left behind in Ireland everything he thought worth possessing – friends that he loved and a society that pleased while it
instructed. He had left home, where he was somebody. He
described himself in Edinburgh 'almost unknown to everybody,
except some few who attend the professors of physic as I do.' He
was, of course, having a lot of social life, and dressing well – his
great weakness – in rich sky blue satin, white allopeen, blue
dinant, fine sky blue shaloon, and high claret coloured cloth. He
hoped to return a skilled physician, to find his friends standing in
need of his medical assistance. Two winter sessions at Edinburgh
and then he was off again, to the University of Leyden first – after
another absurd adventure on the way involving shipwreck and
imprisonment at Newcastle when he was thought to be associated

with 'six agreeable companions', Scots in the French service who
had been in Scotland recruiting for the French forces. In Leyden, he
said, necessaries were so extremely dear and the professors so very
lazy. In February 1753 he was off on his grand tour of Europe, a
guinea in his pocket, one shirt to his back and his flute in his hand.
It was the last year of his education.

He arrived in London in February 1756, at the bottom of fortune's wheel, confident that every new revolution might lift but
could not depress him, cheerful as the birds that carolled by the
road, heading to the mart where abilities of every kind were sure
of meeting distinction and reward. He worked as a dispenser for
the apothecaries, as a proof reader for Samuel Richardson, as an
usher, and even during this period as a physician, something for
which he was not very suited. (A later anecdote tells us that when
a patient called in her apothecary instead of Goldsmith he swore
he would leave off prescribing for his friends and Topham
Beauclerk replied 'Do so, my dear Dr. – whenever you undertake
to kill, let it only be your enemies'.) Then for six months he worked
as Griffith's assistant on the *Monthly Review*, reviewing amongst
other books *A Philosopical Enquiry into the Origin of our Ideas of the
Sublime and Beautiful* by Edmund Burke, his fellow countryman
(indeed fellow midlander) and contemporary in College. After two
years in London he wrote a letter to his brother Henry, telling him
how, without friends, recommendations, money or impudence, he
had had difficulties to encounter. He described them and returned
to his imaginary picture of Lissoy, his fondness for Ireland:

I suppose you desire to know my present situation. As there is nothing in
it at which I should blush, or which mankind could censure, I see no reason for making it a secret. In short, by a very little practice as a physician,
and a very little reputation as a poet, I make a shift to live. Nothing is more
apt to introduce us to the gates of the Muses than poverty; but it were well
if they only left us at the door. The mischief is, they sometimes choose to
give us their company at the entertainment; and want, instead of being
gentleman-usher, often turns master of ceremonies.

Thus, upon learning I write, no doubt you imagine I starve; and the
name of an author naturally reminds you of a garrett. In this particular I
do not think proper to undeceive my friends. But whether I eat or starve,
live in a first-floor, or four pair of stairs high, I still remember them with
ardour; nay, my very country comes in for a share of my affection.
Unaccountable fondness for country, this *maladie du pays*, as the French call
it! Unaccountable that he should still have an affection for a place who
never, when in it, received above common civility; who never brought any-

thing out of it except his brogue and his blunders. Surely my affection for it is equally ridiculous with the Scotchman's, who refused to be cured of the itch, because it made him unco' thoughtful of his wife and bonny Inverary.

But now to be serious, – let me ask myself what gives me a wish to see Ireland again? The country is a fine one, perhaps? No. There are good company in Ireland? No. The conversation there is generally made up of a smutty toast or a bawdy song; the vivacity supported by some humble cousin, who has just folly enough to earn his dinner. Then perhaps there's more wit and learning among the Irish? Oh, lord, no! There has been more money spent in the encouragement of the Padareen mare there one season, than given in rewards to learned men since the times of Usher. All their productions in learning amount to perhaps, a translation, or a few tracts in divinity, and all their productions in wit, to just nothing at all. Why the plague then so fond of Ireland? Then, all at once, – because you, my dear friend, and a few more who are exceptions to the general picture, have a residence there. This it is that gives me all the pangs I feel in separation. I confess I carry this spirit sometimes to the souring the pleasures I at present possess. If I go to the opera where Signora Columba pours out all the mazes of melody, I sit and sigh for Lishoy's fireside and 'Johnny Armstrong's Last Good night,' from Peggy Golden. If I climb Hampstead Hill, than where Nature never exhibited a more magnificent prospect, I confess it fine; but then I had rather be placed on the little mount before Lishoy gate, and there take in – to me -the most pleasing horizon in nature.

There were several letters in this vein: Bob Bryanton his friend had not written to him, and a letter to his cousin records the fact that he himself had written from Leyden, Louvain and Rouen but received no answer. He wrote to his brother-in-law and to his brother Charles whom he advises on his son's future education – 'Take the word of a man who has seen the world, and who has studied human nature more by experience than precept; take my word for it, that books teach us very little of the world.' The paradox was that he had both attitudes of mind in him. He was deeply read in French literature, as his prose continually shows us: his reflections in the *Present State of Polite Learning in Europe* were highly intelligent and based on an unusual experience and observation of European intellectual life which he had gained on his grand tour (in which he is reputed to have paid his way by debating in universities as well as playing his flute in less intellectual societies). Though this long essay lacks the flow and ease of his later prose, he had realised the virtues of directness and simplicity: 'Let us instead of writing finely try to write naturally'. Poetry, however, seemed to him, as he wrote to his brother, 'a much easier and more agreeable species of composition than prose, and could a man live by it, it were not unpleasant employment to be a poet'.

The first work he published – on 19 December 1764 – under his own name was *The Traveller*. He had proudly added after the title 'by Oliver Goldsmith, M.B.' He dedicated the book to his brother – thus giving up a possibility of advancing his own career in an accepted way by dedicating it to some patron. It is a model of dignity and self-respect, and was a sign that Goldsmith (who, as author of *The Traveller*, became famous in London, once people got over their shocked unbelief that the man who laughed at himself and made a butt of himself to amuse company could have written it) in writing this poem and inscribing it to his brother had shown he was his own man; he was somebody good-natured, and there was no harm in him. And Goldsmith praised his brother, in explaining that

It will also throw a light upon many parts of it [the poem] when the reader understands that it is addressed to a man, who, despising Fame and Fortune, has retired early to Happiness and Obscurity, with an income of forty pounds a year.

The Traveller is an unusual poem for its time, just as its author was an unusual man. And his tour had indeed been unusual. In the Enquiry he remarks:

Countries wear very different appearances to travellers of different circumstances. A man who is whirled through Europe in a post chaise, and the pilgrim who walks the grand tour on foot, will form very different conclusions.

He records his *maladie du pays* in a manner which shows how personal emotion can ring through the formality of the couplet, extending its force through the poem's narrative:

Remote, unfriended, melancholy, slow,
Or by the lazy Scheld, or wandering Po;
Or onwards, where the rude Carinthian boor
Against the houseless stranger shuts the door;
Or where Campania's plain forsaken lies,
A weary waste expanding to the skies.
Where'er I roam, whatever realms to see,
My heart untravell'd fondly turns to thee;
Still to my brother turns, with ceaseless pain,
And drags at each remove a lengthening chain.

He is like the traveller in his essay in the first number of *The Bee*:

When will my wanderings be at an end? When will my restless disposition

give me leave to enjoy the present hour? When at Lyons, I thought all happiness lay beyond the Alps; when in Italy, I found myself still in want of
something, and expected to leave solitude behind me by going into
Romelia, and now you find me turning back, still expecting ease everywhere but where I am.

And in verse that moves beyond the confines of the couplet he
records his travelling:

> But me, not destin'd such delights to share,
> My prime of life in wand'ring spent and care:
> Impell'd, with steps unceasing, to pursue
> Some fleeting good, that mocks me with the view;
> That, like the circle bounding earth and skies,
> Allures from far, yet, as I follow, flies;
> My fortune leads to traverse realms alone,
> And find no spot of all the world my own.

The *maladie du pays* emerges strongly:

> But where to find that happiest spot below,
> Who can direct, when all pretend to know?
> The shudd'ring tenant of the frigid zone
> Boldly proclaims that happiest spot his own,
> Extols the treasures of his stormy seas,
> And his long nights of revelry and ease;
> The naked Negro, panting at the line,
> Boasts of his golden sands and palmy wine,
> Basks in the glare, or stems the tepid wave,
> And thanks his Gods for all the good they gave.
> Such is the patriot's boast, where'er we roam,
> His first best country ever is at home.

There is praise of Italy's scenery, 'Bright as the summer', in the
generalised terms so beloved of the eighteenth century, with reflections on the pastoral revival, the peasants building sheds out of
and in vast ruins; there is a realisation that the Swiss are cheerful
despite or because of their rigorous climate. France is a 'gay
sprightly land of mirth and social ease' where Goldsmith's tuneless
pipe led the sportive choir

> And haply, tho' my harsh touch faltering still
> But mock'd all time, and marr'd the dancer's skill
> Yet would the village praise my wondrous power
> And dance, forgetful of the noontide hour

Holland is described in a few compressed lines, the land won from the ocean:

> The slow canal, the yellow blossom'd vale
> The willow tufted bank, the gliding sail,
> The crowded mart, the cultivated plain,
> A new creation rescued from his reign.

But liberty is bartered there, and there are equal dangers in Britain where the English exercise the consequence of freedom, which was, as he put it in an essay entitled 'A Comparative view of Races and Nations', the power of reason:

> Stern o'er each bosom reason holds her state.
> With daring aims, irregularly great,
> Pride in their port, defiance in their eye,
> I see the lords of human kind pass by
> Intent on high designs, a thoughtful band,
> By forms unfashion'd, fresh from Nature's hand;

'The Traveller' ended with a summing up as 'vain, very vain' his search for final bliss. In *The Deserted Village* he took up the subject matter of a couplet in *The Traveller*:

> Have we not seen at pleasure's lordly call
> The smiling long-frequented village fall?

The second poem, which took two years to write, combined Goldsmith's overflowing affection for homely simplicity as well as his indignation at its destruction. He could present a generalised picture, assembling detail generously: he conveyed the settled nature of the society he depicts with the effective repetition of 'How often':

> Dear lovely bowers of innocence and ease,
> Seats of my youth, when every sport could please,
> How often have I loitered o'er thy green,
> Where humble happiness endeared each scene!
> How often have I paused on every charm,
> The sheltered cot, the cultivated farm,
> The never-failing brook, the busy mill,
> The decent church that topt the neighbouring hill,
> The hawthorn bush, with seats beneath the shade,
> For talking age and whispering lovers made.
> How often have I blest the coming day,
> When toil remitting lent its turn to play,
> And all the village train, from labour free,

> Led up their sports beneath the spreading tree,
> While many a pastime circled in the shade,
> The young contending as the old surveyed;
> And many a gambol frolicked o'er the ground,
> And sleights of art and feats of strength went round.

He is excellent in his emphasis on the continuity of country life:

> Sweet was the sound, when oft at evening's close,
> Up yonder hill the village murmur rose.
> There, as I past with careless steps and slow,
> The mingling notes came softened from below;
> The swain responsive as the milk-maid sung,
> The sober herd that lowed to meet their young,
> The noisy geese that gabbled o'er the pool,
> The playful children just let loose from school,
> The watch-dog's voice that bayed the whispering wind,
> And the loud laugh that spoke the vacant mind;-
> These all in sweet confusion sought the shade,
> And filled each pause the nightingale had made.

He drew vignettes of the country parson, who is usually presented through quotation of the couplet detailing the richness of forty pounds a year. The sketch, however, deserves to be considered at greater length for its full effect to emerge:

> Near yonder copse, where once the garden smiled,
> And still where many a garden flower grows wild;
> There, where a few torn shrubs the place disclose,
> The village preacher's modest mansion rose.
> A man he was to all the country dear,
> And passing rich with forty pounds a year;
> Remote from towns he ran his godly race,
> Nor e'er had changed, nor wished to change, his place;
> Unpractised he to fawn, or seek for power,
> By doctrines fashioned to the varying hour;
> Far other aims his heart had learned to prize,
> More skilled to raise the wretched than to rise.
> His house was known to all the vagrant train;
> He chid their wanderings, but relieved their pain:
> The long-remembered beggar was his guest,
> Whose beard descending swept his aged breast;
> The ruined spendthrift, now no longer proud,
> Claimed kindred there, and had his claims allowed:
> The broken soldier, kindly bade to stay,

Sat by his fire, and talked the night away,
Wept o'er his wounds or tales of sorrow done,
Shouldered his crutch, and showed how fields were won.
Pleased with his guests, the good man learned to glow,
And quite forgot their vices in their woe;
Careless their merits or their faults to scan,
His pity gave ere charity began.

Throughout his pictures – and they are pictures, as John Montague has pointed out in his essay 'Exile and Prophecy'[1] – there runs a gentle vein of humour, as in the description of the village schoolmaster:

Beside yon straggling fence that skirts the way,
With blossomed furze unprofitably gay,
There, in his noisy mansion, skilled to rule
The village master taught his little school.
A man severe he was, and stern to view;
I knew him well, and every truant knew;
Well had the boding tremblers learned to trace
The day's disasters in his morning face;
Full well they laughed with counterfeited glee
At all his jokes, for many a joke had he;
Full well the busy whisper circling round
Conveyed the dismal tidings when he frowned.
Yet he was kind, or, if severe in aught,
The love he bore to learning was in fault;
The village all declared how much he knew'
'Twas certain he could write, and cypher too;
Lands he could measure, terms and tides presage,
And e'en the story ran that he could gauge:
In arguing, too, the parson owned his skill;
For e'en though vanquished, he could argue still;
While words of learned length and thundering sound
Amazed the gazing rustics ranged around;
And still they gazed, and still the wonder grew,
That one small head could carry all he knew.

Into this rustic happiness had come the tyrant, and Goldsmith describes the change; he laments the disappearance of a way of living, a vanishing of traditional ways, of virtues associated with rural life, which are being destroyed by an emerging commercialism.

Sweet smiling village, loveliest of the lawn,

Thy sports are fled, and all thy charms withdrawn;
Amidst thy bowers the tyrant's hand is seen,
And desolation saddens all thy green:
One only master grasps the whole domain,
And half a tillage stints thy smiling plain.
No more thy glassy brook reflects the day,
But, choked with sedges, works its weedy way;
Along thy glades, a solitary guest,
The hollow-sounding bittern guards its nest:
Amidst thy desert walks the lapwing flies,
And tires their echoes with unvaried cries;
Sunk are thy bowers in shapeless ruin all,
And the long grass o'ertops the mouldering wall;
And, trembling, shrinking from the spoiler's hand,
Far, far away thy children leave the land.

There is a pensive note woven through the contrapuntal composition of the poem; there follows a sonorous outburst of thundering rhetoric:

Ill fares the land, to hastening ills a prey,
Where wealth accumulates, and men decay:
Princes and lords may flourish, or may fade;
A breath can make them, as a breath has made:
But a bold peasantry, their country's pride,
When once destroyed, can never be supplied.

In turn this declamation gives way to a quieter, generalised picture of what has gone. T.S.Eliot rightly praised Goldsmith's 'art of transition', the shift 'just at the right moment' and this transition is most effective here in the poem's change of tone; it becomes elegiac:

But times are altered; trade's unfeeling train
Usurp the land and dispossess the swain;
Along the lawn, where scattered hamlets rose,
Unwieldy wealth and cumbrous pomp repose,
And every want to opulence allied,
And every pang that folly pays to pride.
Those gentle hours that plenty bade to bloom,
Those calm desires that asked but little room,
Those healthful sports that graced the peaceful scene,
Lived in each look, and brightened all the green;
These, far departing, seek a kinder shore,
And rural mirth and manners are no more.

There is a passage in the poem which is the real key to Goldsmith, the man, the exile. The poet's memories of a former communal life, an established social order, jostle with those of desertion. His poem has gained intensity by constant contrast, constant awareness of the past in its view of the present. Memories of country living, of home, crowd in upon the solitude of the city dweller. Goldsmith was living as a solitary guest in England, but in Ireland his brother was dead, the man he had loved better than most men. And once his brother was dead any imagined retreat from loneliness was cut completely. No future existed in terms of the past for the traveller, that lost past, that timeless past, spent in the peaceful Irish midlands:

> In all my wanderings round this world of care,
> In all my griefs – and God has given my share -
> I still had hopes, my latest hours to crown,
> Amidst these humble bowers to lay me down;
> To husband out life's taper at the close,
> And keep the flame from wasting by repose:
> I still had hopes, for pride attends us still,
> Amidst the swains to show my book-learned skill,
> Around my fire an evening group to draw,
> And tell of all I felt, and all I saw;
> And, as a hare whom hounds and horns pursue
> Pants to the place from whence at first he flew,
> I still had hopes, my long vexations past,
> Here to return – and die at home at last.

The hope was vain. But Goldsmith seldom permitted himself to complain and then not for long. He had not wanted to be an exile: but he was by nature a citizen of the world. His financial gener-osity to his ever-needy contemporaries continued on its para-doxically self-destructive yet harmless good-natured way. It was matched by his generosity to his readers, then and now. We taken into this writer's confidence; he is patient, gentle, kind, and amusing. He wishes to please us; he makes his moral points with ease; he disguises his personal melancholia and his loneliness with public laughter. He shows his good nature throughout his writings; he was indeed a gentle and magnanimous man. It is most fitting that he and his friend and contemporary, Edmund Burke, civilised sons of their university, stand, in Foley's fine statues, in front of the walls of Trinity College to welcome those who enter its doors. Both of them enriched its humane traditions and those of the world outside.

THE VICAR OF WAKEFIELD

There is something compelling about *The Vicar of Wakefield*. You go on reading it. And you can reread it – and that's a very good test of a novel. The strange thing is that *The Vicar of Wakefield* seems unlikely to attract a modern reader. It is a moral story. It is didactic. It skirts the sentimental. All these aspects of it might seem off-putting to a generation suckled on James Bond and weaned with a clockwork orange. And yet it goes on selling. Many publishers keep it on their lists. Enlightened educational authorities still prescribe it on school syllabuses when others have given way to setting more gimicky modern texts, such as, say *Lord of the Flies* or *The Catcher in the Rye* or something by Alice Walker. And *The Vicar of Wakefield* will probably still be set long after such fashionable novels have had their day on the examination syllabus. Why? I suppose because, above all else, Goldsmith could tell a story. His narrative art is such that you go on reading him. There are many other reasons, of course. But perhaps he had this particular ability to tell a story because he grew up in eighteenth century Ireland – still largely a country where oral traditions prevailed. Do you remember how Goldsmith described village life in his poem *The Deserted Village*? There is a vignette of the schoolmaster here which is germane; it shows how rare writing was, indeed how rare was education as we know it today:

> 'Twas certain he could write, and cypher too;
> Lands he could measure, terms and tides presage,
> and een the story ran that he could gauge:
> In arguing, too, the parson owned his skill;
> For een though vanquished, he could argue still;
> nile words of learned length and thundering sound
> Amazed the gazing rustics ranged around;
> And still they gazed, and stil; the wonder grew
> That one small head could carry all he knew.

And in *The Deserted Village* Goldsmith also describes his ideal retirement:

> I still had hopes, for pride attends us still,
> Amidst the swains to show my book-learned skill,

> Around my fire an evening group to draw,
> And tell of all I felt, and all I saw

He was used to a situation where people talked rather than read, told of all they felt and saw, and told stories too, of course, for entertainment. But stories, founded as they are upon basic problems and situations inevitably raise moral issues – think of the basic European stories, the *Iliad* and the *Odyssey*, or think of the *Taín* in the Irish legends. They exist, they still exist for our entertainment, and they revolve upon moral issues. The Greeks besieged Troy because Paris of Troy stole off from Sparta with Menelaus's wife Helen. After that long war, after many wanderings, Odysseus returned to Ithaca and exacted a terrible punishment upon the wooers who had plagued his wife Penelope in his absence, and he hanged all the maid servants in the household who had been the wooers' girl friends. And we know how the Gaelic story of the *Taín* revolved around the stealing of Cooley's bull.

Like the poets who composed the *Iliad* and the *Odyssey* and the *Taín*, Goldsmith knew very well that a good story draws upon basic human responses. And his novel *The Vicar of Wakefield* does that very effectively. we read about a family living a peaceful, idyllic life in the country. Misfortunes overwhelm them, and particularly the Vicar himself, who ends up in prison thinking that his eldest daughter, whom the local Squire has ruined, is dead. His eldest son George is also thrown into prison, accused of attacking the Squire's servants. It is a severe test of the Vicar's Christian principles, but he remains staunch to them. And then, suddenly, everything is put right – the ending is happy, the Vicar and his son are released, the eldest daughter Olivia is not dead, she *is* married to the Squire, the other daughter, Sophia, makes a magnificent match with Sir William Thornhill, the eldest son George marries his true love Arabella, and the other son, Moses, is likely to be married as well. And the Vicar's fortune is restored.

We enjoy this happy ending, however contrived the critics rightly tell us it is, because Goldsmith has engaged our sympathy for the Primrose family. And a family is decidedly a European unit. Paris's great fault was that he broke up Menelaus's family, and the fall of Troy destroyed the closely knit family of Priam and Hecuba and Odysseus wanted to get home to his family, despite all the temptations he met on his wanderings after the Fall of Troy. We are all deeply aware of this idea of a family, and Goldsmith, in focussing his story upon one, draws upon our natural interest, and sympathy.

The story is told by the Vicar himself, and so we see the

Primrose family through his eyes. He has a strong belief in the merits of large families, and describes his own very clearly in the first chapter. His wife, whom he chose, as she did her wedding gown, not for a glossy surface but such qualities as would wear well, could 'read any English book without much spelling, but for pickling, preserving, and cookery, none could excel her'. And there – in the first paragraph – we come across the ironic, detached turn of the vicar's mind when he goes on: 'She prided herself also upon being an excellent contriver in housekeeping, though I never could find that we grew richer with all her contrivances'. And he describes himself as being somewhat less than innocent, for he says, for if one of the numerous relations who visited them turned out to be 'a person of very bad character, a troublesome guest, or one we desired to get rid of', the vicar 'even took care to lend him a riding-coat, or a pair of boots, or sometimes a horse of small value', and remarks that he 'always had the satisfaction of finding the guest never came back to return them'.

We get this very neat and convincing account of the family's life, and then the catastrophes begin, just as George is to marry Arabella. The match is broken off by Arabella's father when he learns from the Vicar that the merchant who held their money has vanished. Now the Vicar exhorts his family to adjust themselves to their new circumstances, and they move to another part of the country. Here Goldsmith offers us a brilliant miniaturisation of their new way of living:

The little republic to which I gave laws was regulated in the following manner: by sunrise we all assembled in our common apartment, the fire being previously kindled by the servant. After we had saluted each other with proper ceremony – for I always thought fit to keep up some mechanical forms of good-breeding, without which freedom ever destroys friendship —we all bent in gratitude to that Being who gave us another day. This duty being performed, my son and I went to pursue our usual industry abroad, while my wife and daughters employed themselves in providing breakfast, which was always ready at a certain time. I allowed half an hour for this meal, and an hour for dinner; which time was taken up in innocent mirth between my wife and daughters, and in philosophical arguments between my son and me.

As we rose with the sun, so we never pursued our labours after it was gone down, but returned home to the expecting family, where smiling looks, a neat hearth, and pleasant fire, were prepared for our reception. Nor were we without guests, sometimes Farmer Flamborough, our talkative neighbour, and often the blind piper, would pay us a visit, and taste our gooseberry wine, for the making of which we had lost neither receipt nor the reputation. These harmless people has several ways of being good company; while one played, the other would sing some soothing ballad, – Johnny Armstrong's Last Good-night, or The Cruelty of Barbara Allen. The night was concluded in the manner we began the morning, my youngest boys being appointed to read the lessons of the day; and he that read loudest, distinctest, and best, was to have a halfpenny on Sunday to put into the poor's box.

This passage establishes the new peaceful routine – it is as if Goldsmith was using the Irish present habitual tense

The place of our retreat was in a little neigbourhood, consisting of farmers who tilled their own grounds, and were equal strangers to opulence and poverty. As they had almost all the conveniences of life within themselves, they seldom visited towns or cities in search of superfluity. Remote from the polite, they still retained the primeval simplicity of manners; and, frugal by habit, they scarce knew that temperance was a virtue. They wrought with cheerfulness on days of labour; but observed festivals as intervals of idleness and pleasure. They kept up the Christmas carol, sent true loveknots on Valentine's morning, ate pancakes on Shrovetide, showed their wit on the first of April, and religiously cracked nuts on Michaelmas eve.

This picture is built up with great economy; but Goldsmith establishes it most effectively through its almost ritualistic calendar approach based on the Church's festivals, only to destroy it with a speedy disruption.

The destruction comes about partially through the character of the Vicar's wife. She wants to get her daughters well married at all costs. For instance, on the way to their new farm the family meet Mr Burchell, who makes a strong impression on the younger daughter, Sophia, whom he rescues from drowning. When Mr Burchell leaves, Mrs Primrose observes that she likes him extremely, protesting that 'if he had birth and fortune to entitle him to match into such a family as ours she knew no man she would sooner fix upon'. The Vicar 'could not but smile to hear her talk in this lofty strain' but, he says, 'I was never much displeased with those harmless delusions that tend to make us more happy'.

He probably should have been more critical of this strain in his wife, for she soon begins to form a hope that the Squire, Mr Thornhill, may marry one of her daughters. The episode of his calling and tasting a glass of Mrs Primrose's famous gooseberry wine is brilliantly recounted. And when the Squire has gone the Vicar begins to tell his family that fortune-hunting women are contemptible,but he is interrupted by a servant bringing them a side of venison from the Squire and his promise to dine with them some days later. This well-timed gesture pleaded more powerfully in his favour, says the Vicar, 'than anything I had to say could obviate? He adds, 'I therefore continued silent, satisfied with just having pointed out danger and leaving it to their own discretion to avoid it.' And he makes one of his sententious but sensible comments on life: 'that virtue which requires to be ever guarded is scarce worth the sentiment'. The Vicar continues silent, satisfied with having pointed out danger. But the irony is that it is a very real danger indeed which he has pointed out; and the vicar knows it. When he finds his daughters preparing some cosmetic wash for their faces he tells us how he had a natural antipathy to such washes, for he knew that instead of mending the complexion they spoiled it.

I therefore approached my chair by sly degrees to the fire, and grasping the poker, as if it wanted mending, seemingly by accident overturned the whole composition and it was too late to begin another.

Goldsmith contrasts the Vicar's daughters with two apparently fashionable ladies from town, Lady Blarney and Miss Carolina Wilelmina Amelia Skeggs, and provides us with the comedy of his wife and daughters going to church on the farm horses, the Vicar not displeased when this scheme goes astray, as it would teach his daughters humility. There are many such scenes, these mini-comedies built into the texture of the story, such as the classic gulling of the younger son Moses, who is taken in by a sharper at the fair and sells the horse for a packet of worthless spectacles. There are also the very human episodes which make the story realistic. The Vicar is pleased that Mr Burchell goes off in a huff when Mrs Primrose is all for her daughters going to town, and does not want to listen to Mr Burchell's advice against the plan. The possibility of Mr Burchell marrying Sophia frightened him. The misfortunes multiply, the Vicar himself is taken in by the same man who cheated Moses; the trip to town is off because Mr Burchell interferes, and then the family toy with the idea of Olivia's marrying Farmer Williams, to see if this will stir the Squire into a proposal.

The story begins to darken. After Olivia runs off with the Squire the Vicar's essential decency of character emerges very clearly; he searches for her – and in the process finds his son George who has become a strolling player – and once he does meet Olivia by chance, in dire straits, he assures her that she will never see any change in his affection for her. When Mrs Primrose does not seem to be completely reconciled to Olivia on her return he becomes severe with his wife, and firmly re-establishes Olivia in the family. His courage, too, emerges when the house is burnt down, and

when Mr Thornhill has the effrontery to ask the Primroses to his
wedding with Arabella Wilmot. This defiance and denunciation of
the Squire lead to the Vicar's imprisonment, since he is unable to
pay the Squire the annual rent for the farm. And then he persuades
his parishioners not to rescue him from the officers of justice who
are conveying him to the prison. In the prison he shows his fortitude; and Goldsmith uses him to put forward his own theories
about reforming the criminal code. They were very advanced ideas
for the time. Goldsmith preferred the aim of reformation rather
than severity of punishment. He was strongly against capital punishment for petty crime. In the prison the Vicar busies himself with
good works, with remarkably rapid results, and he preaches a sermon, the truth of which he is demonstrating by his own fortitude
and his submission to a succession of appalling reversals of fortune.
But then the tide turns and everything eventually falls into place.

Things have not been what they seemed. *The Vicar of Wakefield* is
a novel full of disguises. Mr Burchell turns out to be the wealthy
Sir William Thornhill, an archetypal eccentric, who acts as a *deus ex
machina* in dealing with the Squire, his nephew. Lady Blarney and
Miss Carolina Wilelmina Amelia Scraggs are revealed to have been
low women suborned by the Squire. Mr Jenkinson, too, has played
several roles. And so the revelations explain the problems in the
plot. This is the stuff of romance: disasters overcome, mysteries
explained, good fortune emerging out of bad; and Goldsmith has
mixed with the elements of romance the idea of the journey, the
vicar's various travels, and the adventures of change in circumstance and place – and indeed the seventy miles which the
Primrose family travelled meant a major journey in the eighteenth
century, a complete change of life and scene.

To these changes and adventures, these rapid shifts in fortune,
Goldsmith added a series of philosophical reflections. And for
variety he built in the ballad of Edwin and Angelina, and the
melancholic lines of

> 'When lovely woman stoops to folly,
> And finds too late that men betray,
> What charm can soothe her melancholy,
> What art can wash her guilt away?

And there is humour in 'An Elegy on the death of a mad dog' with
its final ironic lines

> The man recovered of the bite
> The dog it was that died.

To this variety of material Goldsmith also added the story of George Primrose's adventures, which surely echo his own experiences as he wandered the continent on his grand tour with 'a guinea in his pocket, one shirt to his back and a flute in his hand'. George Primrose is philosophical, indeed optimistic: 'the less kind I found fortune at one time, the more I expected from another; and being now at the bottom of her wheel every new revolution might lift, but could not depress me'. He gives us his experience of the prospect of teaching in England, of becoming a Grub Street writer in London, of going to Amsterdam to teach Dutchmen English, without knowing any Dutch himself, of vainly offering to teach Greek in Louvain, and then of making a vagabondish living by his knowledge of music:

> I passed among the harmless peasants of Flanders, and among such of the French as were poor enough to be very merry; for I ever found them sprightly in proportion to their wants. Whenever I approached a peasant's house towards nightfall, I played one of my most merry tunes, and that procured me not only a lodging, but subsistence for the next day.

George Primrose was like his creator; there was no harm in him. And there is no harm in the *Vicar of Wakefield* as a novel; it is full of Goldsmith's essential decency, his sanity and commonsense. There is a simplicity, a virtual naivety, in the Vicar and his son; for instance, when Mr Thornhill offers to get George a commission in a regiment going to the West Indies neither father nor son see that this is merely a device to get George out of the way and thus to advance the squire's designs of marrying Arabella.

This unworldliness perhaps came from Goldsmith's memories of his own father, whom he described as having 'wound his children up to be mere machines of pity before they were taught the more necessary qualifications of getting a farthing'. Goldsmith's father, who was an Irish country clergyman, had a contempt for money, and gave away his land and titles in a vain attempt to match the marriage portion of one of his daughters to the wealth of her young husband, a pupil of his son Henry. It is likely that the match-making propensities of Mrs Primrose were founded upon Goldsmith's own mother's activities. The Goldsmith family's situation must have resembled the situation in *The Vicar of Wakefield*: here is how Mrs Primrose eggs on the flirtation between her daughter and the Squire:

> It must be owned, that my wife laid a thousand schemes to entrap him; or, to speak it more tenderly, used every art to magnify the merit of her daughter. If the cakes at tea ate short and crisp, they were made by Olivia;

if the gooseberry-wine was well knit, the gooseberries were of her gathering; it was her fingers which gave the pickles their peculiar green; and in the composition of a pudding it was her judgement that mixed the ingredients. Then the poor woman would sometimes tell the squire, that she thought him and Olivia extremely of a size, and would bid both to stand up to see which was the-tallest.

The scene of the lovers being put back to back by the girl's ambitious mother is repeated in Goldsmith's play, *She Stoops to Conquer.* He presumably thought that this was an effective match-making device. And in *She Stoops to Conquer* he makes it a funny device as well. Fun is ever present in the *Vicar of Wakefield* too. At the end of the novel the Vicar says 'I can't say whether we had more wit among us now than usual, but I am certain we had more laughing, which answered the end as well'.

There is Goldsmith's own capacity in a nutshell: a sense of fun, a peculiarly Irish capacity. Where he is neither creating obvious fun, nor sharing the ludicrous with us, he is getting another aspect of amusement out of his characters by his use of deadpan irony. This is how he avoids the melodramatic – despite all the tricks of the novelist's trade, such as coincidence, the misunderstood letter, the literary parallels, the disguises, the reversals of fortune, all the differences between appearance and reality. He creates the irony by providing a factual, a completely matter of fact tone for the Vicar's speech. Here is how the Vicar describes – his own reactions to the Squire, and the very different ones of his wife and daughters:

This gentlemen he described as one who desired to know little more of the world than its pleasures, being particularly remarkable for his-attachment to the fair sex. observed, that no virtue was able to resist his arts and assiduity, and that there was scarcely a farmer's daughter within ten miles round, but what had found him successful and faithless. Though this account gave me some pain, it had a very different effect upon my daughters, whose features seemed to brighten with the expectation of an approaching triumph; nor was my wife less pleased and confident of their allurements and virtue.

In this novel, which, as he said in his advertisement or foreword, had a hundred faults (and, as he added, 'a hundred things might be said to prove them beauties') he is giving us an apologia for his own gentleness. Mr Burchell, for instance, treats the young children as equals, sings them ballads and stories and, at intervals, talks with great good sense. Goldsmith himself loved children and they loved him; and he also loved anticlimax, he liked saying droll things with a serious face; and as a result he was often misunder-

stood. But he talked good sense, and the difficult thing that he succeeded in doing in this novel was showing us a good man. The
Vicar's sermon is given in prison; he seeks happiness in heaven, for
philosophy can bring the miserable no comfort. His moralizing –
even if it may sometimes seem unsound – is thoroughly tested by
calamity and becomes the more convincing. The Vicar has a faith in
humanity, and, as Goldsmith said firmly in the advertisement to
the book, his chief stores of comfort were drawn from futurity. Let
us leave the last word with his Vicar:

As we grow older the days seem to grow shorter, and our intimacy with
time ever lessens the perception of his stay. Then let us take comfort now,
for we shall soon be at our journey's end.

THE WILD IRISH GIRL

The Wild Irish Girl is often described as a novel by Lady Morgan, but it is better considered as the work which made Sydney Owenson famous when it was published in 1806. She married Sir Charles Morgan six years later. *The Wild Irish Girl* was not her first novel. She began with *St. Clair; or, The Heiress of Desmond*, published in Dublin in 1802 and re-issued in London in 1803. This was an epistolary novel, showing the effect on her of Macpherson's *Ossian*, Rousseau's *Nouvelle Heloise* and Goethe's *Werther*; it describes the growth of love between Olivia and St. Clair as they lend each other books, exchange poems and discuss literature, music, scenery and their own romantic feelings. There is virtually no action until the end of the novel when a rival kills St. Clair and Olivia dies of a broken heart.

Olivia was partly a self-portrait, as might have been expected from the volume of Sydney Owenson's *Poems* published in 1801. Among these often apparently orthodox verses are many signs of an unusually exuberant, restless vitality and self-confident ambition. In the novel Olivia exhibits a similar vivaciousness; she has also a similar interest in Irish scenery, in the legends of the countryside, and in what may be called Irish antiquarianism; and she shares her creator's liking for translating and singing Irish songs. Olivia, however, endeavours to conceal her intellectualism; and the novel also carries an implicit condemnation of self-indulgent sentimentality. Despite this lofty moral purpose *St. Clair* is little more than a fashionable romance, couched in terms of highly-strung sensibility. The intense introspection and self-pity of the hero are well conveyed, but the main virtue of the book lies in its description of the scenery of Sligo 'where you find the character, the manner, the language, and the music of the ancient Irish in all their primitive originality, and the names Ossian and Fingal are as well known among these old Milesians as in the Hebrides: to this remote province whose shores are washed by the 'steep Atlantic' were the native Irish driven by political and religious persecution'. The heroine's grandfather is 'the true type' of an old Irish chieftain: he owns a ruined castle and Irish manuscripts; he has an Irish harper and is deeply interested in Irish literature.

All this Irish material was, however, subordinated to the

Platonic relationship which develops into love, and the next novel Sydney Owenson wrote, *The Novice of St. Dominick*, was an historical romance set in sixteenth century France. This was issued in 1805 by the London publisher Richard Phillips, who, sensibly insisted on its being cut from seven volumes to four. It is still a long novel, blending historical and imagined characters with an often pedantic insistence upon the author's knowledge of the background. The heroine again closely reflects the nature of the authoress: she enjoys a social success but she also sees through the superficiality of society. The account of Provence's culture, its music and language, the sufferings of its poor and the destructive forces of religious struggle, was, of course, easily applicable to Ireland.

Sydney Owenson was praised by Tom Moore for her patriotic genius, when he wrote the advertisement for the first number of his *Irish Melodies;* he was alluding to her *Twelve Original Hibernian Melodies*, issued by Preston, a London musical publisher, in 1805. This collection proved very popular, and the Dedication to her father was properly enthusiastic: he had played the melodies on his fiddle for her, and sung them 'in the *true attic* style of Conomarra'. She believed Ireland had a music more original, 'more purely its own, more characteristic and possessing more the soul of melody, than any other country in Europe'.

A visit to London to meet publishers showed her how others regarded Ireland. It was in the course of one of the many conversations which occurred 'on the subject of my (always termed) "unhappy" country that a hint casually here suggested, formed the origin of a little work which has since appeared under the title of *The Wild Irish Girl*'. She decided that she wanted to write a national novel blending ancient and modern Irish history, manners and culture:

To blend the imaginary through probable incident with the interesting fact, to authenticate the questioned refinement of ancient habits, by the testimony of living modes,faithfully to deliniate what I had intimately observed, and to found my opinions on that medium which ever vibrates between the partial delineation of national prejudice, on one side, and the exaggerated details of foreign antipathy on the other; such was the prospectus my wishes dared to draw.

Her publisher, Phillips, was not convinced that a matter of fact didactic novel would do; it would suit no class of readers, he told her; but while she realised that – as she put it many years later in the prefatory address to the 1846 edition of *The Wild Irish Girl* – it was 'dangerous to write on Ireland, Hazardous to praise her, and difficult to find a publisher for an Irish tale which had a political tendency', she nonetheless determined to pursue her patriotic purpose in writing a novel about Ireland. A visit to Connaught, where she stayed with her maternal grandmother's family, Sir Malby and Lady Crofton of Longford Hall in County Sligo, gave her a renewed sense of the scenery and atmosphere of the west. The Croftons were of Elizabethan English origin, and had married into a distinguished Irish family. She now read Irish history and archaeology with zest and was helped by Joseph Cooper Walker, the antiquary and author of *Memoirs of the Irish Bards*, who was an expert on Irish dress and armour.

The new novel, then, was designed, in part, to alter English views of Ireland. It followed upon Maria Edgeworth's aim in *Castle Rackrent* (1800) of representing to English readers 'manners and characters perhaps unknown to them in their island'; but it goes deeper, as Sydney Owenson's Preface to *Patriotic Sketches of Ireland, Written in Connaught* (1807) tells us. Maria Edgeworth had remarked that 'the domestic habits of no nation in Europe were less known to the English than those of their sister Country, till within these few years', but Sydney tells us that her experience was that not only did the English know very little about Ireland, but it seemed

Requisite therefore that I should leave my native country to learn the turpitude, degradation, ferocity and inconsequence of her offspring; the miseries of her present and the falsity of the recorded splendours of her ancient state.

Both Sydney Owenson and Maria Edgeworth had a desire to educate the English about Ireland and both of them used the same device as they wrote novels which were both published in 1806, for Maria Edgeworth's *Ennui*, like *The Wild Irish Girl*, introduces an Englishman into Ireland. Miss Edgeworth was attacking laziness and allowing her jaded sophisticate to redeem himself in the course of the novel. Miss Owenson, however, was using the framework of her love story to show something of Ireland's history and the ancient culture, remnants of which survived mainly in the west; she was also making clear the problems of Irish poverty and the need for mutual understanding on the part of Protestants and Catholics in Ireland.

Sydney Owenson drew upon herself for the heroine Glorvina, who sings, dances and plays the harp; though deprived of the advantages of society, she is none the less elegant in manner, self-possessed, witty but profoundly serious: in short an unusual and vivacious heroine with whom the English hero cannot but fall in love. Glorvina's father calls himself the Prince of Inismore and was modelled upon the MacDermott of Coolavin in Sligo, descendant of the MacDermotts of Moylurg. Father John, the Prince's chaplain, was founded upon Dr. Flynn, the Roman Catholic Dean of Sligo, who later became Bishop of Achonry. However, the real source for the Prince of Inismore's character was Sydney Owenson's father, the actor Robert Owenson.

Owenson was a handsome man of great physical energy, an actor and an outgoing personality who deserves a biography in his own right. He was born in the barony of Tyrawley in 1744, the son of Walter MacOwen, a farmer who had persuaded Sydney Bell into a runaway marriage with him. She was the orphan granddaughter of a George Crofton (not of an early Sir Malby Crofton as the Owensons supposed) and a fourth cousin of Oliver Goldsmith. The Croftons disowned her, and the couple remained poor, the handsome young husband a frequenter of fairs and generally a neer-do-well, the wife known for her singing of Irish songs and playing the harp. Their only son, Robert, learned French and Latin from the local priest and rector, and his music from his mother. He was taken up by a rich gentleman named Blake, a landlord at Ardfry, who brought him to London to learn music from Dr. Worgan, the Vauxhall Gardens organist, and to be generally educated at an academy run by a clergyman named Eyle. He became the lover of the singer Madame Weichsel, and, in Blake's absence, left his duties in Blake's house to partner her at Vauxhall. Blake returned and dismissed his protégé, leaving him a letter and a draft for £300. Refuge was sought with Oliver Goldsmith and the draft returned to Blake.

Through Goldsmith came an introduction to Garrick in 1771 and minor roles at Covent Garden ensued, MacOwen having anglicised his name to Owenson. Acting with provincial companies added to his experience and he was so well received at the Theatre Royal in Dublin in 1776 at the age of thirty-two that he decided to stay in Ireland, his success being perhaps due to his habit of uttering interjections in Irish as well as to his physical attractiveness, his fine voice and sense of comedy.

In England he had persuaded Jane Hill to elope with him; she was the daughter of a well-to-do Shrewsbury merchant, and was brought up a methodist. Disliking the idea of Ireland, she nonetheless followed her husband, giving birth to Sydney on 25 December 1776, reputedly in the middle of the crossing of the Irish Sea. She hated both potatoes and Papists, her daughter recorded, 'with

Christian inveteracy and culinary prejudice', and she provided a
calm counterbalance to her husband's vivid exuberance. A second
daughter, Olivia, was born several years after Sydney, and the
Owenson household spent half the year in Dublin and half in
Drumcondra, then a village north of the city. Owenson's acting in
Irish parts and his singing of Irish songs brought him great popularity. He quarrelled with Richard Daly over the producer's
approaches to the sixteen year old Mrs Billington (who was reputed to be Owenson's child by Madame Weichsel) whose salary Daly
then suspended. Owenson left the Smock Alley Company in a
rage, and leased the Fishamble Street Music Hall, hoping to outdo
Daly, and to build up the repute of Irish drama. His attempt
aroused political controversy, for his opening night on 20
December 1784 coincided with the Congress of the Irish
Volunteers, and he spoke his prologue in Irish Volunteer uniform.
Eventually he was paid compensation (an annual grant of £300 a
year for ten years) when the Irish House of Commons decided that
only one theatre should be licensed in Dublin.

Owenson's generosity led him to offer a home to Thomas
Dermody, a highly talented boy, who had left Ennis at the age of
eleven or twelve because of his schoolmaster father's drunkenness
and because he had been influenced by reading *Tom Jones* (it is possible that Maria Edgeworth used this as a starting point for the
early behaviour of the hero of her novel *Ormond*.) Dermody translated Greek and Latin into English verse, he wrote poetry, and he
was extremely well-read. He taught Sydney and Olivia,and himself
attended Dr. Austin's school for a time until he quarrelled with
him; having refused to compose a complimentary ode on one of
Mrs Austin's guests, he subsequently wrote an epigram on her
which Austin was given. The happy days enjoyed by the Owenson
children and Dermody came to an end with Mrs Owenson's death
in June 1789. The actor now began to appear in other cities, having
put his daughters into an academy run by Madame Terson, a
Huguenot. Dermody studied in the country with the Rev. Boyd,
having been supported by the Countess of Moira, until he declined
her offer to place him as an apprentice with a London bookseller.
Owenson helped him again and got his poems (written between
his 13th and 16th years) published by subscription.

The annual compensation paid to Owenson had been given on
condition that no paid performer should appear at his Music Hall,
and when some amateurs who had hired the hall also hired pro-
fessionals to aid their productions, this grant was withdrawn,
which was a severe blow. By way of compensation some of the

amateurs then encouraged Owenson to build a theatre in Kilkenny
and form a company to act there. He brought his two girls to
Kilkenny – after they had been three years in Madame Terson's
school she retired and they were placed in another school in
Dublin run by Mrs Anderson: they also learned music and dancing
from Owenson's friends, Tomaso Giordani (whom he had known
at Covent Garden and who was his musical director in Dublin) and
Fontaine, his *maître de ballet* at the theatre. The sisters greatly
enjoyed the change afforded by the social life of Kilkenny, where
they met county society and, particularly, officers of the Irish
Brigade who had left France because of the Revolution. The whole
Kilkenny enterprise, however, failed in a few months, and
Owenson moved to Sligo, where he was encouraged by the
Croftons. This theatrical venture flourished until audiences diminished during the 1798 rebellion and Owenson's costumes and
scenery were seized by his landlord. In dire financial straights he
was helped by a wealthy Sligo merchant, Ignatius Everard. At this
point in her father's career Sydney decided – against his wishes
but with the help of his friend Dr. Alphonse Pelligrini, Professor of
Italian at Trinity College, Dublin – to become a governess. This
marked a turning point in their relationship, for Sydney now
began to make decisions for herself and though, as we can see from
her poems, she had a deep and lasting affection, even an emotional
dependence upon her father, who encouraged her to write, she was
now launched into making her own way in life. He was running a
theatrical company in northern Ireland, but after her experiences of
life in the Featherstone family, at Bracklin Castle in Westmeath and
at their Dublin town house in Dominick Street, she found sharing
her father's life in poor lodgings in Coleraine in 1801 and in a hotel
in Londonderry, where Owenson managed the theatre in 1805, was
not attractive, despite the pleasure she always took in his company.
His return to the Dublin stage after ten years' absence came with
Sydney's comic opera *The First Attempt, or the Whim of a Moment*, in
which he played the role of an Irish servant, and sang 'This Twig
in my Hand'. He then reappeared in *Midas* and finally on 27 May
1807 made his last appearance, in a benefit night, demanding vast
physical stamina, in which he sang songs, gave a comic address,
played Major O'Flaherty in *The West Indian* and acted in *The First
Attempt*. He lived till May 1812, having seen both his daughters
married, titled ladies who ameliorated the sufferings and illness of
the last years of his life by their affectionate attention: he lived in
conflict with Olivia and her husband, the successful doctor Sir
Arthur Clarke, in Great George Street, Dublin.

We can return to the sources of other characters in *The Wild Irish Girl* by way of Owenson's merchant benefactor in Sligo, Ignatius Everard. He had a son Richard, who fell in love with Sydney when she returned to Sligo in 1805. His father opposed any idea of marriage since his son was not yet established in any profession and was in any case indolent; he called on Sydney to make his views clear to her. She fully concurred with them and the young man's father then fell in love with her himself and proposed to her frequently. Here is the germ of the idea of Horatio M., the Englishman and his father Lord M...(who was also modelled upon Mr. Blake of Ardfry) both in love with Glorvina, which enlivens the melodramatic end of the novel.

Characters, plot, and copious information were duly assembled, and Sydney Owenson offered the novel to Phillips early in 1806. He proposed a sum to her, and was then amazed to be told that she was offering the novel to Johnston, another London publisher. After several letters in April, Phillips then offered her £250 on the publication of the second and third editions respectively. He was more amazed still to be told that Johnston had offered her £300 – 'so monstrous a price' he commented on 26 April. But by 12 May he capitulated, agreeing to pay her £300. The novel was immediately popular in Ireland, and it gained from the publicity stirred up by 'M.T.'s (John Wilson Croker) adverse criticism of her work in the *Freeman's Journal*. These were probably prompted by personal feelings as well as being political propaganda, for Sydney seems to have written one of the replies to Croker's anonymous satire of 1804, *Familiar Epistles on the Present State of the Irish Stage*. There was, however, a reaction to the anti-nationalist line of these attacks on Miss Owenson as the Whig government began to adopt a policy of conciliation. The Duke of Bedford, then Lord-Lieutenant, became patron of Sydney Owenson's comic opera, and the ladies of the Viceregal Court took her up. She became widely sought after in Dublin society, and the golden bodkins worn by the Princess of Inismore became fashionable as 'Glorvina ornaments' to act as hairpins, and 'Glorvina Mantles' were widely worn.

The success of *The Wild Irish Girl* is easy to understand. After the traumatic experiences of the 1798 revolution and the disappearance of the Irish Parliament from Dublin as a result of the Act of Union in 1800 this novel reminded Irish readers, in particular, that Ireland had its own culture, that the peasantry were badly treated, that landowners should spend some of the year on their estates, that national unity needed Protestant and Catholic alike to attempt to overcome their differences.

English readers found the material entertaining, just as they welcomed Sydney Owenson – and Tom Moore – to their drawing rooms as entertainers: they were, some of them, prepared to follow Horatio M's example and be educated as well as entertained. And so the novel's flaws, clearly realised by Sydney herself in later life, did not mar its effect. There are indeed many obvious flaws in it; and modern readers, who may well find the excessive information heavy going, must remember that it was innovative in its day, that it even verged on the daring at that time to write so patriotically in Ireland about Ireland. Such stylistic habits as the excessive use of French phrases now seem mannered – but then Sydney Owenson had spent three years speaking nothing but French in her Hugenot school. The romantic sensibilities displayed are part of her desire to add genius and the graces to virtue: she, bright, lively, intelligent, flirtatious, creative creature that she was, disliked stupid heroines; she was tired of morality that did not influence the imagination in the way that heartfelt emotion could sway her and many of her readers. From her father's side came music and speech, the emotive inheritance of an oral tradition; from her mother's came the written word with that faint dash of puritanism, that ultimate seriousness, that let the authoress see the dangers of excesses of sentimental emotion. When the novel was re-issued she recognised 'the over-charged style, and exaggerated and very youthful opinions'. The palliation she offered can still stand, for she did love Ireland, as she put it, not always wisely and sometimes perhaps too well, while being full of an 'earnestness of purpose and desire to serve' which continued through her career as a writer. This novel was, in her words, the first instalment of a very small capital of talent, paid into the account of her country's wrongs.

LADY MORGAN'S *O'DONNEL*

When *O'Donnel* was published by Henry Coburn in 1814 Lady Morgan had been married for two years to Sir Charles Morgan. Born Sydney Owenson, the daughter of an Irish actor-manager, who was well-known for his Irish songs, and an English methodist mother, she had been well-educated before becoming a governess. Her literary career then blossomed with the publication of her novel *The Wild Irish Girl* in 1806; this had followed upon a volume of poetry of 1801, and two novels, *St Clair; or the Heiress of Desmond* (1803) and *The Novice of St Dominick* (1805), and *Twelve Original Hibernian Melodies* (1805). *The Wild Irish Girl* brought her wide popularity and she was launched upon a successful social life in both Ireland and England.

Her ebullient personality, her lively conversation, her ability to sing, dance and play the harp attracted the Marquis and Marchioness of Abercorn, who also admired her books greatly; they asked her to live with them as a companion, arranging opportunities for her to continue her writing and her frequent rounds of visits. At the time she had her own lodgings in Dublin, and was near her father, now living with her sister Olivia who was married to Dr Arthur Clarke, a Dublin doctor and wit. But the offer was tempting and she accepted it: it was to bring her into the heart of aristocratic society, for the Abercorns, who had an Irish place, Baronscourt in County Tyrone, entertained the English fashionable and political world lavishly when they were in residence at Bentley Priory in Stanmore.

Sydney Owenson had many suitors and admirers. She liked the company of men, and was highly flirtatious. After she left school there had been platonic – and highly romantic – friendships in Sligo, where her father was running the theatre, with sentimental army officers. On one occasion, when the family were in Kilkenny, Sydney's sister Olivia came in from a ramble to find Sydney and two officers, Captain White Benson and his friend Captain Earle, 'sitting in the parlour talking high sentiment and all the three shedding tears'. Molly the maid, come in to lay the table for dinner, thought the officers had stayed long enough and said, 'Come, be off with yiz – an the master will be coming in to his dinner, and what will he say to find you fandangoing with Miss Sydney?'

Olivia, who had no patience with sentiment, fell on them with her stick and pelted them with the apples she had picked up on her ramble, and Sydney burst out laughing, sensibility completely overcome by comedy.

Robert Owenson, too, thought these officers of the 61st Foot were indeed indulging their sensibilities over-freely, and had little patience with them. The officers moved to England, Earle died, but letters from White Benson survived: one of them recorded how Sydney had laid down the sacred rule of friendship, and he had prescribed to himself in fine sentimental style 'limits of affection over whose boundaries it were wrong to pass'. He continued in this letter of 8 June 1798 written from York – much as St Clair might have:

You conceive, perhaps, it is imprudent in you to continue a correspondence with a man who has said that he once loved you. Be it so, I pledge to you my word of honour to mention the subject no more; I pledge you my promise never to violate that friendship I have so repeatedly professed for you, and to remember only the sister of my heart.

The sister of his heart endorsed the letter thus: 'This elegant-minded and highly-gifted young man drowned himself near York a few months after I received this letter!'

Later she inspired love in Thomas Dermody, the brilliant run-away boy her father had befriended when he was eleven or twelve. Dermody had taught Sydney and her sister for a time; but he was erratic and proud and fell out with the Dublin families who tried to help him. He became, like the schoolmaster father he had left behind in Kerry, a hopeless drunkard who continually disappoint-ed his patrons; his 'little span' was spent 'twixt poetry and ale-house/Twixt quill and can'. He joined the army as a private, became a Second Lieutenant, was twice wounded and then, on half pay in London, burnt out the rest of his brief life in drinking and dissipation. But his letters to Sydney Owenson were buoyant, even boastful, giving no hint of his destitution. Memories of happy youthful days in Dublin recurred to them both; he hoped to see her again in Ireland; and his letters exposed his feelings for her as did some of his poems:-

> Why, though the tender rows recall another
> May not my rapt imagination rove
> Beyond the solemn softness of a brother,
> And live upon thy radiant looks of love?

She did not realise that he was seriously ill; he was twenty-

seven when he died in 1802; and she obviously cared for him, as
her own elegy on him makes clear:

His bud of life was then but in its spring,
Mine scarce a germ in Nature's bloomy wreath;
He taught my timid muse t'expand her wing,
I taught his head its first fond sighs to breathe.

When her father's dramatic company was in Lisburn a youth
called Francis Crossley proposed marriage to her. She was then
writing *The Novice of St Dominick*. Crossley was sixteen, and had no
prospects; he spent much time transcribing the manuscript of the
long novel for her, and she 'by over-refining his taste' made the
girls of Lisburn intolerable for him. He kept her poems along with
copies of *Ossian* and *Werther*; she advised him to become a cadet in
the East India Company. He duly went to India and is probably
depicted in *Woman, or, Ida of Athens*, in which the heroine is
attracted by two lovers, the younger ardent and honourable in his
intentions, but away in foreign parts, the old, cynical and a roué
who wanted to make her his mistress. The model for the latter was
probably Sir Charles Ormsby, a witty Dublin barrister, whose relationship with Sydney was a difficult if flattering one; she did not
succumb to his advances despite their seeing a great deal of each
other. She described him as 'one of the most brilliant wits, determined roués, agreeable persons and ugliest men of his day'.

Woman, or Ida of Athens was attacked by Gifford in the first number of the new *Quarterly Review* in 1809. He described the sentiments of the authoress as 'mischevious in tendency, and profligate in principle, licentious and irreverent in the highest degree'.
She respected Nature, which was to be honoured 'by libertinism in
the women, disloyalty in the men, and atheism in both'. So much
for exposing the heart in an address to the readers, in which she
told them, *inter alia*, that she has been necessitated to compose with
great rapidity, and that her little works

have always been printed (from an illegible MS.) in one country while their
author was the resident of another – *Woman* though I had long resolved its
plan and tendency in my mind, and frequently mentioned it in society, was
not begun until the 20th of last July. It was written at intervals, in England,
Wales and Ireland, and almost always in the midst of what is called the
world. It was finished on the 18th of October and is now printed from the
first copy. It is a fact that can be attested by my publishers that I never corrected a proof sheet of any one of my works, nor even resided in England
during their printing or publication.

This address was full of over-confidence based, no doubt, upon the success of *The Wild Irish Girl*, and Gifford joyously seized on the point of illegibility:

The printer, having to produce from volumes from a MS. of which he could not read a word performed his task to the best of his power; and fabricated the requisite number of lines, by shaking the types out of the boxes at a venture.

Gifford also advised her to drop idle raptures for commonsense, to practise a little self-denial and gather precepts from an old fashioned book so that she might then hope to become 'not a good writer of novels but a useful friend, a faithful wife, a tender mother, and a respectable and happy mistress of a family'.

The review came at a difficult period in her life. She broke with Sir Charles Ormsby; *Woman, or, Ida of Athens* had been published by Longman, but the terms Phillips offered her for her next novel, *The Missionary, an Indian Tale*, did not seem sufficient, and she withdrew it from him – even though he had sent the first volume to the printer. It was at the instigation of Lord Castlereagh that Stockdale agreed to publish the novel and pay her £400 for it.

The magnificent social round of the Abercorns, however, continued; it was gaily described by Sydney in a letter to her friend Mrs Lefanu:

I am surrounded by six Lord-Lieutenants, unpopular princesses and 'deposed potentates' (for in the present state of things we here are in the wrong box); on either side of me I find chatting Lords Westmorland and Handwicke (poor dears!) pop, then comes the Princess of Wales, with 'quips and cranks and wreathed smiles,' and 'anon stalks by in royal sadness' the 'exiled majesty of Sweden' .... It were vain to tell you the names of our numerous and fluctuating visitors, as they include those of more than half the nobility of England, and of the first class; add to which, many of the wits, authors and existing ministers (poor dears!). The house is no house at all, for it looks like a little town, which you will believe when I tell you that a hundred and twenty people slept under the roof during the Christmas holidays without including the under-servants.

This social life, however, did not compensate for moods of depression. She had other admirers besides the discarded Sir Charles Ormsby; her 'army of martyrs', as her sister called them, were assiduous, but the gibe of the *Quarterly* about her need to settle down may have struck home. Though she concealed her age, and her letters described her as young, she was, after all, thirty-six. She could appreciate her sister's happy domesticity and, besides, her brother-in-law had been knighted. She described her heart as disappointed, her imagination as exhausted, when she wrote to console her close friend the barrister Thomas Wallace on the death of his invalid wife; and she told Mrs Lefanu that she wished that he might get a star or garter that she might smile on him. She wanted to be married, but she also wanted to be married well.

Through the Abercorns she had met Dr Charles Morgan, a thirty-one year old widower with a small daughter who became their family physician, and seemed to them a most suitable match for Sydney. She admired his linguistic and musical gifts: he was good-looking and witty, and despite initial reluctance he fell deeply in love with her. The Abercorns 'hurried on the business', and she wrote to ask her father's advice. Morgan had £500 a year of his own apart from what he earned by his practice; the Abercorns offered the couple a year with them, or two years if they stayed in Ireland so that they could lay up their income during that time 'to begin the world' while he remained their physician. It was not, however, a match Sydney Owenson could embark upon with alacrity: 'I have refused and denied him over and over again because if it is not in worldly circumstances a very good match for me, it is still worse for him'.

They became engaged; she was impressed by his outspokenness though she feared he would harm his worldly interests: but she was in a state of agitation at the thought of being parted from 'a country and friends I love and a family I adore'. The Abercorns persuaded the Lord-Lieutenant, on a visit to Baronscourt, to knight Dr Morgan, which should have encouraged her, but Sydney, on a fortnight's visit to Dublin to bid her family good-bye, stayed on for three months, to Morgan's chagrin. She pleaded her father's ill health; Morgan accused her of leaving him for the invitations of her other admirers, Charles Parkhurst and Sir Charles Ormsby. Another excuse was that she was collecting material for a new Irish novel; she told Morgan that he had met with a more formidable rival in O'Donnel of Tyrconnel 'than all your jealous brain ever fancied in Generals, Aides-de-Camp, and Dublin Lawyers'. She returned to Baronscourt, was firmly told one morning by the Marchioness that there must be no more trifling, and was led upstairs to the waiting chaplain and bridegroom. She afterwards said that it was on that day she had received a letter from Francis Crossley, newly promoted in India, and now in a position to marry her.

The Morgans' marriage seems to have been highly successful, for in her husband Sydney found an intellectual companion whose patience had more than proved his love for her; he certainly knew her foibles. They balanced each other: she had the energy to get him away from the ease of living in the Abercorn *ménage* which she had found so useful. It was, however, a *milieu* in which she could clearly see dangers for them both. Her father's death occurred in May 1812 and this seems to have strengthened her resolve to settle in Dublin: a plan that came to fruition a year after their marriage. After a stay with the Clarkes they settled in 35 Kildare Street, a small house in the centre of Dublin, where they lived till 1837, then moving to London.

The novel on which she had been working before her marriage was not moving fast. Research into the background of Elizabethan Ireland presented the problems which historical novels inevitably pose to authors; she found many difficulties as to the domestic regime of the Irish noblesse – whether they burnt lamps, or flambeaux, whether they had any liquors besides Spanish wines, or whether they had glass in their castle windows; these are the kind of trifles that puzzle and retard one.

There was, however, one larger problem. The more she read of the period the more horrible history seemed; it was better to get away from such bitterness. So she abandoned the idea of a historical novel and shifted to the present without, however, entirely jettisoning what she had read in her source-books. By inventing a descendant of the O'Donnels she was able to use much of the information she had collected. But she did not draw her material from books so much as she had earlier in her career, for now she could draw upon her own extensive experience of contemporary life. She was no doubt influenced by her husband's balanced attitude of mind, and she may have sensed a coming change in taste as she laid aside sentimental romance in favour of an ironic realism. Satire and seriousness march hand in hand in a novel that seemed to Sir Walter Scott when it was published to have nature and reality for its foundation.

The story is built around the misadventures of an Irish aristocrat who has taken service with the Austrian and later the French army: after the Revolution he volunteers to serve in the British Army in Flanders, then, after being wounded, he fights in St Domingo. On his return to Ireland he applies for a majority, a company, a lieutenancy, but he has no interest, no kinsman high in the service and his letters of nobility which served him abroad would here, he says, be ridiculous. He may owe something to Count O'Halloran, a former officer in the Austrian service whom Maria Edgeworth introduced into *The Absentee* (1812) as a dignified representative of the old Gaelic aristocracy; he provides a dignified contrast to the pretentious vulgarity, the *nouveau riche* nature of Dublin suburban life after the Act of Union.

Colonel O'Donnel is a new development in Lady Morgan's fiction, and so is Mr Glenthorn, an Englishman and Liberal landlord, who dies early in the novel's progress. She had learned how to present her male characters more convincingly, and in O'Donnel's servant M'Rory she provided a talkative idiomatic Irishman, loyal and lively. The heroine does not dominate the action of the novel, though she does echo Lady Morgan. This time she is Miss O'Halloran, the daughter of an artist, who after a spell as governess becomes a portrait painter. As a governess she pretends to stupidity but cannot always restrain herself from making shrewd comments, despite the dismissive treatment she often receives from the fashionable world about her. As an artist she captures an aged Duke, who proposes marriage to her: she laughs at this idea, but he is made the more determined by this treatment and marries her, to die a few months later, leaving her everything he possessed unentailed. She reappears about halfway through the novel as the Duchess of Belmont, and is welcomed in society. Here is how she is described by Lady Llanberis:

She has the gift *de raconter* in great perfection; makes a good story out of nothing at all; and mimics in a manner which is nothing short of miraculous. Then you know her voice alone would *faire fortune:* what sort of a brogue which some of you Irish have, so soft and so *caressante;* the 'ah! do,' and the 'ah! don't'; besides her laugh is quite charming.

Needless to say, the Duchess, like her creator, plays the harp 'with a light and brilliant finger', and, like her, chooses a fine and ancient Irish melody to entertain her listeners. And, like Lady Morgan again, she has seen through the pretences and hypocrisies of fashionable life.

Fashionable life in England is well-drawn; satire excels in the portraits of Lady Llanberis, with her inconsequential and amiable chatter, and of Lady Singleton with her self confident and interfering insensitivity: these characters were founded upon real people, Lady Llanberis on the Marchioness of Abercorn, Lady Singleton on Lady Cahir.

The first part of the novel is set in northern Ireland, and its scenery is well described; here and there throughout the novel are injections of Irish history, and the situation of Roman Catholics under the penal laws is made clear. The fact that the hero is an Irish Catholic aristocrat was, in itself, an innovation, a political gesture. The gentlemanly nature of Colonel O'Donnel is perhaps over-

stressed, but then Lady Morgan was writing the novel as 'a national tale', and wanted to demonstrate how unjust, how divisive the
penal laws had been in their effect upon people who could be
respected by her English readers. The restoration of O'Donnel to
his property, achieved largely by the cleverness of the heroine, is
conciliatory, and the general tone of the novel optimistic. It is better written than Lady Morgan's earlier novels: the information is
now more successfully incorporated into the action. There is still
an over-abundance of French phrases but adjectives are less in evidence, and the dialogue which is less high-faluting can, at times, be
notably sharp and witty.

Henry Colbourn recognised the marketable value of the story;
he paid Lady Morgan five hundred and fifty pounds for it and sold
two thousand copies of it after its publication in March 1814, an
impressive figure for the time. It was generally well received both
in Ireland and England and a third edition was printed by 1817,
though not without argument between authoress and publisher
over the royalties she was to receive. This was finally settled by a
bonus on the royalties of fifty pounds on the third edition.

It can still be read with pleasure and it is a landmark in the
process towards undoing the Penal Laws, a continuation of Henry
Grattan's views of what Ireland ought to be.

MATURIN THE INNOVATOR

(Written in collaboration with H.W. Piper)

Charles Robert Maturin (1782-1824) is chiefly remembered as one of the followers of 'Monk' Lewis and Mrs. Radcliffe, and he deserves his place in the history of the Gothic novel, for his *Melmoth the Wanderer* (1820) is an impressive example of the kind. Nevertheless, this reputation obscures his equally important place as a serious novelist of interest to the student of cultural history.[1] It is the purpose of this article to show him as one of the earliest distillers of that blend of nationalism and romanticism which was to be so potent in the nineteenth century.

He is not the less interesting because his blend was of Irish nationalism and Wordsworthian romanticism. Certainly Scott's poetry and Irish ballads played their part in Maturin's development, but his first novel, *Fatal Revenge; or, The Family of Montorio* (1807), makes it clear that the *Lyrical Ballads* and its preface gave his variety of romantic nationalism its foundation. It is perhaps unusual to think of that volume as a special incitement to nationalism, but it led Maturin to see Irish resistance to English rule as part of a clash between two cultures, one nationalistic and romantic, based on a Gaelic folk tradition and the 'natural' emotions of a native population living in close contact with nature, and the other cosmopolitan and neoclassical, making nature conform to the habits and tastes of society.

When this theme appears in *Fatal Revenge,* it is only incidental to a very Gothic plot. It is, however, introduced through one of the two heroines, who, under the name of Cyprian, has disguised herself as a young man in order to be near the object of her affections, Ippolito. The two soon discuss poetry, and when Ippolito says, 'Nature must indeed be the object of poetical representation but it must be nature modified and conformed to the existing habits and tastes of society,' Cyprian replies to this in romantic terms, 'I would invert your rule, and admit the influence of prevailing manners into my strains, so far as they were conformable to nature'. When she has discoursed for a time in this way, Ippolito suggests that she should study 'the poesy of the heretic English which has a spirit of simple appeal to the strong and common feelings of our nature,

131 of the bottom

often made in such language as the speakers of common life clothe their conceptions in'. The subjects of English poetry, says Ippolito, are 'the indigent peasant weeping over her famished babes – the maniac who shrieks on the nightly waste age – pining in lonely misery – honest toil crushed in the sore and fruitless struggle with oppression and adversity'.

Maturin linked this spirit with that of the native Irish, for he makes Ippolito move from these obvious references to *Lyrical Ballads* to ballads in general and the claim that Irish poetry is richer in its harmony and more melting than English. As an example, and perhaps not a very happy one, Ippolito quotes a ballad of Maturin's own composition, 'Bruno-Lin, the Irish Outlaw'. The poem itself is not particularly nationalist in spirit, but the strength of Maturin's national feeling is shown by a curious piece of sarcasm, perhaps directed at the Union. Ippolito cannot even recall the name of Ireland, and remarks, 'I have forgot their name, but of a people so endowed the name will not always be obscure'.

Before Maturin began his career, two women novelists had started their exploration of Irish subjects, Maria Edgeworth in *Castle Rackrent* (1800) and Lady Morgan (Sydney Owenson) in *St. Clair; or, The Heiress of Desmond* (1803) and in *The Wild Irish Girl* (1806).[2] Maria Edgeworth was virtually the creator of the regional novel. *Castle Rackrent*, she thought, might convey a specimen of manners and characters perhaps unknown in England. Her story is told by an old peasant, whose speech she created with a skill anticipating the later work of Lady Gregory and Synge; but the subject is the lively life of the landed proprietors in Ireland before the Union. Her motives in capturing and echoing peasant speech were based more upon a genuine delight in its turns, locutions, and vocabulary, in its sense of exaggeration and of anticlimax, and in its sheer liveliness, than upon any wish to demonstrate any superiority of past or present Gaelic culture. The peasants were incidental to the squirearchy; she saw them through no Wordsworthian belief in the intrinsic significance primitive people should possess for civilized people; she was, after all, an eighteenth-century rationalist in spirit, and could not envisage primitive people possessing any superiority over those who were civilized.[3]

Lady Morgan, however, seized on the romantic possibilities of Ireland. The priggish hero of her first novel arrives in a 'castle in Connaught where you find the character, the manner, the language, and the music of the native Irish in all their primitive originality.' This locale led her hero to expect to find literary traditions, because the native Irish had been driven to this area by religious and political persecution and secluded there until after the Restoration. But *St. Clair's* series of letters busy themselves mainly with recording the minutiae of the hero's platonic affair with Olivia, an Irish girl, modelled not a little on Lady Morgan's own character. The two exchange poems, lend and give each other books, including the inevitable Goethe and Rousseau, and read Guarini together. But in the midst of *St. Clair*, supposedly written to illustrate the dangers of rhapsodies upon passionate love, of contempt for self-restraint, the heroine sings Irish songs to her own harp accompaniment, discusses the birthplace of Ossian, and introduces the hero to her grandfather, 'the only gentleman in these parts who cultivates Irish wit, or appears anxious to rescue from total oblivion the poetry and music of his country: he is in every respect the true type of the old Irish chieftain, implacable in his resentments, making decision the criterion of his wisdom'. Irish manuscripts, his harper, and his ruins hold the next place in his heart to his family.

Most of the Irish material in *St. Clair* was incidental to the exploration of the lovers' sensibilities. After Lady Morgan had been to England and realized the attitude of people there toward Ireland, she wrote *The Wild Irish Girl* as a patriotic gesture, as an essay in propaganda, more self-conscious than *Castle Rackrent* or, probably, than any other novels that preceded it, excepting those of Godwin. *The Wild Irish Girl* contains developed versions of the previous heroine and the chieftain, this time attended by a cultivated priest as chaplain. Many passages of the earlier novel are simply recapitulated, but the hero is a vast improvement on the priggish nonentity who romanticized his way through platonic mazes in *St. Clair*. This one has a Byronic touch; he has 'lived too fast in a moral as well as a physical sense'. However, he is reclaimed from his enervation by the attraction of everything Irish, aided by Glorvina's charms. The novel is packed with information upon many and diverse aspects of Irish life: language and literature, legends and antiquities, music and dancing, topography and modes of life in both peasant's hut and chieftain's castle.[4] Indeed, footnotes frequently occupy far more space than does the text.

Maturin had these three novels by his two countrywomen to use as examples when he began writing. He must also have been affected by the rapidly increasing interest in Irish music (as well as in the customs and manners of the Irish), which was occurring in Ireland at the end of the eighteenth century, a probable concomitant of the successful bloodless revolution of 1782 and the establishment of the short-lived yet brilliant Irish parliament in Dublin.

Joseph Cooper Walker had published his *Historical Memoirs of the Irish Bards* in 1786;[5] Charlotte Brooke, her *Reliques of Irish Poetry* in 1789; and Edward Bunting, his *General Collection of the Ancient Irish Music* in 1796. the last work resulted from the famous festival arranged in Belfast in 1792 by Dr. James McDonnell at which the last ten harpers met and played.[6] The vogue for Irish music spread to England when Lady Morgan's *Twelve Original Hibernian Melodies, with English Words, Imitated and Translated, from the Works of the Ancient Irish Bards* appeared in 1805, a work that Thomas Moore thought of using in the preparation of his *Irish Melodies*, the first collection of which was published three years later. These melodies were partly due to Moore's work with Edward Hudson, a fellow undergraduate at Trinity College Dublin, condemned to exile for his part in the 1798 rebellion.

Sylvester O'Halloran's *Introduction to the Study of the History and Antiquities of Ireland* of 1772 was followed by his *General History of Ireland from the earliest accounts to the close of the twelfth century* in 1778. His work had an effect upon the growing national self-consciousness of Irish writers after the Union. Another sphere of writing which helped to create a climate of interest in the Gaelic-speaking world outside the neoclassical culture of Dublin and the country houses was the work of travellers[7] such as Arthur Young[8] and Charles Topham Bowden,[9] not to mention the illiberal reflections of Richard Twiss, whose effigy afterward appeared on the bottoms of a popular line of chamber pots.[10] The most likely and obvious influence upon Maturin must have been his own experience of the 'hidden Ireland,' to borrow Professor Daniel Corkery's phrase, which he obtained sometime during 1804-1806 when acting as a curate in Loughrea, a market town in the west of Ireland.[11] He visited the seat of the O'Moore family, Cloghan Castle, during this time and thus came in contact with an ancient Irish family's mode of life.

What distinguished Maturin from the two novelists who preceded him was that his interest in Irish subjects, such as folk song and harp music, was so affected by Wordsworth's romanticism. Maria Edgeworth was anti-romantic in tone; Lady Morgan owed more to continental than English sources. Though Maturin's own ballad in *Fatal Revenge* acknowledged Scott's influence, which was certainly neither 'democratic' nor revolutionary, his romanticism, like Wordsworth's, looked to the present and the future. Indeed, he had absorbed from Wordsworth not only a faith in the strong 'natural' feelings common to all men, but also a belief in the power of Nature herself. When the dialogue in *Fatal Revenge* between Cyprian and Ippolito ends, Ippolito, who is given to fashionable dissipation, is reassured by Cyprian: 'Be assured that these cool and healthful moments of reproving thought snatched from the fevering turmoils of the world, will have an effect that shall not be unfelt or forgotten there.'[12]

It is interesting, for reasons which will appear, that Maturin should have introduced these ideas through his love story. But they are only an interlude in this novel, for, despite a misleading assurance, an 'adieu to dungeons and poisons and monks,' the rest of the story is a creaking display of the Gothic paraphernalia, its scenery, unlike that in his other novels, glowing with colors borrowed from Mrs. Radcliffe's palette.

These passages between Cyprian and Ippolito constitute the only originality in the novel, and it is not surprising that they should reappear in various forms as the themes of the works which give Maturin his place as a regional novelist: *The Wild Irish Boy; The Milesian Chief; Women;* and, to a certain extent, *Melmoth the Wanderer.* But before we leave *Fatal Revenge,* there is a further passage which casts a good deal of light on the importance of these ideas to Maturin, and on why he laid so much stress on emotion. At one point the plot of the novel called for poems written by a nun to express her forbidden love for a man. Maturin, as we have seen, was in the habit of using up his own poetry, but, of course, he would hardly have on hand poems written from a woman's point of view. What he did use were his own poems describing a man's guilty love for a woman:

> Enough for me the joy to view
> Thy purer beauties glow,
> Bid unrestrained those odours rise
> Whose sweets I ne'er must know

The second poem makes the nature of the relationship clearer:

> I wish I were a blushing flower,
> Within thy breast one hour to reign,
> Then I might live without a crime,
> Then I might die without a pain.

The third is most explicit:

> And I'll quench in the nectar that bathes thy red lip
> The fever that's burning in mine.
> And lapt in a dream, I'll forget that a voice
> Would recall, that a fear would reprove –
> Till I start as the lightning is lanced at my head
> And wonder there's guilt in our love. (p. 131)

There is no suggestion in any of the biographies of Maturin of any guilty passion which might have given birth to these poems. Though young, he was in Holy Orders when he married, but there seems nothing in his marriage with Miss Henrietta Kingsbury, the daughter of the Archdeacon of Killala, which would call down lightning from heaven. He always stressed domestic bliss as the highest attainable human happiness, and his marriage was spoken of as very happy. His wife, a pupil of Madame Catalini, was one of Dublin's best singers, and had an appetite for social life the equal of his own. The poems suggest either a fresh attraction felt by an affianced young man (such as he depicts in *Women)* or one already bound by marriage vows (as in *The Wild Irish Boy).* Certainly he wrote in the preface to *The Milesian Chief,* 'If I possess any talent, it is that of darkening the gloomy, and of deepening the sad; of painting life in extremes, and of representing those struggles of passion when the soul trembles on the verge of the unlawful and the unhallowed.'[13]

In his novels Maturin usually contrasts two heroines, one cultivated and intellectual, the other simple in her emotions. For the first heroine love nearly always ends in tragedy, though only in his play *Bertram,* a story of adultery, can the love between men and women be described as guilty. All this, with the poems, makes it a reasonable conjecture that some important personal experience reinforced Maturin's interest in romantic passion and his interest in what may be called the spiritual differences between Ireland and England. Be that as it may, Maturin's power of emotional analysis and his ability to contrast Irish and English types of nationalism, as revealed by the new values which romanticism was finding in popular tradition, give his novels a peculiar confidence and strength.

His second work, *The Wild Irish Boy* (1808), was written primarily out of a desire and a need to make money, which it signally failed to do. Its title suggests at once its affinities with Lady Morgan's *The Wild Irish Girl,* published two years earlier. Maturin obviously hoped that the similarity of title and, to a certain degree, of subject, would push his novel into the slipstream of Lady Morgan's successful work. From her he had learned several useful things: that a regional novel based on Ireland could be romantically coloured in the style of the Gothic romances upon which he had greedily fed his youthful and impressionable imagination; that a good plot could be made by bringing a sophisticated and *ennuyé* stranger into suitably romantic Irish surroundings and then hurling this character into a love affair (more passionate than that used by Maria Edgeworth in *Ennui)* with a natural and individualistic

Irish person; and that an Irish (or Milesian) chieftain complete with chaplain could prove a dignified and unusual character, and a further means of using the almost anthropological lore about the Irish which was to his hand.

He used some of these ideas in *The Wild Irish Boy*. Unsuccessful potboiler though this is, it does demonstrate Maturin experimenting with various approaches to a regional Irish novel and continuing to develop the relationship between Wordsworthianism and other phases of romanticism already suggested in *Fatal Revenge*. The wild Irish boy, Ormsby Bethel, has spent three years as the pupil of an indolent clergyman amid 'the most wild and aerial scenery of the lakes,' and the effect of this scenery on his character has been 'powerful and almost creative'; his three years in the lake district, 'a species of romantic intoxication.' He traversed the solitude of the lakes and mountains in the day and read the books his tutor had brought with him from Oxford, which had never been opened since, amid 'the evening murmur of winds and dashing of waterfalls.' He became 'an incurable visionary.'

After experiencing *Ossian*, his infatuation was complete; but he had an 'exercise of mind' which blended all this Wordsworthianism directly, and curiously, with Irish nationalism:

Amid the spots of quiet clouds that lay scattered over the evening sky, like islands on the great deep; I have imagined some fortunate spot, some abode peopled by fair forms, human in their affections, their habits, in every thing but vice and weakness; to these I have imagined myself giving laws, and becoming their sovereign and their benefactor.

The idea was sufficiently chimerical, for in a state of innocence there was no occasion for restraint; and in the equality produced by universal excellence, there was no room for sovereign or superior. I was therefore compelled to admit some shades into the character of my imaginary community; but I resolved they should be such as held a latent affinity with virtue, or could be easily reconciled to it by legislative discipline and cultivation. I therefore imagined them possessed of the most shining qualities that can enter into the human character, glowing with untaught affections, and luxuriant with uncultivated virtue; but proud, irritable, impetuous, indolent, and superstitious; conscious of claims they knew not how to support, burning with excellencies, which, because they wanted regulation, wanted both dignity and utility; and disgraced by crimes which the moment after their commission they lamented, as a man laments the involuntary outrages of drunkenness. I imagined a people that seemed to stretch out its helpless hands, like the infant Moses from the ark, and promise its preserver to bless and dignify the species.

When I had conceived this character, such was its consistency, its *vraisemblance*, that I immediately concluded it to be real. I was satisfied

there existed such a people – with the hesitation of one who fears his purpose is suspected, I mentioned the character I had conceived to my tutor,
and asked if he thought it possible that any people were distinguished by
such features. He answered immediately, that I had accurately described
the Irish nation.[14]

After a time spent in Trinity College Dublin, where he falls
under the spell of Calvinistic society, Ormsby is summoned by his
mysterious father to the west of Ireland, and there he meets the old
Irish chieftain De Lacy, becoming 'acquainted with modes of life
which appear to the inmates of England like the visions of
romance'. Around the chieftain's castle are sallow, meagre, and ill
clad people; but even the faces of the meanest indicate the
influence of the chief whom they love and who loves them. The
castle in which he lives is surrounded by bogs, its gate out of
repair, access to its kitchen is by means of a cart laid across a gap,
and the kitchen itself is thronged with a horde of idle followers.

De Lacy himself is modelled upon Inismore of *The Wild Irish
Girl*, but he is toned down. He does not wear native costume but
an out-of-fashion English dress covered with a scarlet cloak. He is
dignified 'in a wild and original way,' speaks French, Italian, and
Spanish, and is acquainted with continental literature and politics.
He keeps to the customs of his fathers, thinks in Irish, and when he
speaks in English uses 'strong and peculiar phrases.' He is a puritanical nationalist, a *laudator temporis acti* who declares: 'He who
shakes my belief in the antiquity of my country, must first shake
my belief in the beatitude of the immaculate Virgin Mary' (p. 194).
What is more important, he is made to denounce England: 'Is it for
those who have desolated the country, and razed every mark of
power or of resistance from the face of it, to demand where is the
proof of power, or of resistance, and after beating down with the
savageness of conquerors, the monuments of our strength and
greatness, to ask with the insolence of conquerors, what monuments of strength and greatness are left to us?' (p. 193)

Maturin also tried his hand at a piece of Edgeworthian material,
not even thinly disguised:

a castle-rack-rent, an house of disorder and riot, where a bad dinner, vile-
ly dressed, and attended by careless servants, was washed down by floods
of wine, that were swallowed with the precipitation of men who were in
haste to forget themselves. His mistress sat at the table, some of his illegitimate children by his servants attended at it; the company were some vulgar and worthless wretches, who were permitted to live there to excite
laughter, and to swallow wine. The conversation was such as not even
young Hammond could give a colouring of decency to, and the jests such

as buffoons or schoolboys would substitute for wit. (p. 221)

This type of treatment of Irish material is unique in Maturin's work, for in this lighter vein he handles the peasantry with a touch of the lively farce which marks the novels of Lover and Lever. The hero passes by Montrevor House when the family arrives from London. A sound arises that he can compare to 'nothing human', and a crowd of peasants surrounds the carriages. Ormsby prevents one from being pushed over the verge of a hill by the terrified horses, and is shot by an outrider in the confusion. Later he gets an explanation of what happened from one of the tenants: they had decided to go out and give the new lord a shout of joy on his arrival. They had come too early, stepped into Paddy Donnellan's and taken a drop of whiskey, emerged, fallen in the ditch, fought, and then heard the carriages approaching:

And we all rolled out as bad as we could, and when we all began to shout, hell to the soul of us that could open our mouths, and my lord's servants knocked down some of us, and the rest of us knocked down ourselves . . . (p. 287)

After the melee, the tenant and his friends had explained to Lady Montrevor the reasons for what they had done, the servants had pushed them away, and a gentleman had given them

a power of money in her ladyship's own sweet name, and then we gave a shout in earnest, that would have brought her in from the other world if we had murdered her. But may I never die in sin, if when I heard of you, and of that blundering rogue that put a bullet in your arm, if I did not determine to go drown myself in the bog, and never come out of it again till I heard you were well and alive. (p. 288)

Well as the last passages catch the Synge-song of the peasants, the rapid flow of their exaggerated speech, it was not what Maturin wanted to get across to his readers. He sought something much more dignified than what verges upon the stage Irish character of the eighteenth century, the blundering Paddy. He wanted to impress the rulers of England with the reliability of the Anglo-Irish and their ability to run Ireland, however much he disapproved of their apparent desertion of it after the Union.

Ormsby is therefore translated from the country to the dissipations of Dublin, thence to London, having inherited De Lacy's fortune (an unusual touch, that the old chieftain was wealthy), and being ambitious 'to show that Irishmen were not the degraded beings that Englishmen have a right of concluding from their scandalous desertion of their duties and their country.' He is filled with an intense nationalism; he speaks of Ireland's depressed trade, a sign perhaps of the increasingly middle-class nature of Dublin after the Union, her neglected populace, her renegade nobility, her dissipated, careless, and 'unnational' gentry; and he is made anxious by the country's being 'deteriorated by a religion, which, in every country where it had prevailed, had extinguished all spirit but the spirit of superstition.' The need was for national education. He attacks the Union, the fatal measure which 'could not probably be recalled but might certainly be alleviated.' The Union had not even given the internal security from commotion and danger which had been promised by its sponsors, for in July 1803 'a troop of rebels had marched within half a furlong of the Castle of Dublin, the seat of a Military Governor.'

This reference to the enormity of rebellion makes it clear that Maturin is placing respectable arguments in the mouth of his hero. There is no question of independence from the crown (Maturin was a protestant clergyman, a member of the Established Church of Ireland); this is a plea for a return of the Irish parliament, or, failing that, some degree of what might be called home rule. The English statesman to whom he addresses these remarks makes use of the information but does nothing, and Ormsby continues to squander his substance in the fashionable world of London. He is emerging from a passionate devotion to his wife's mother when he becomes ensnared and ruined by the gently insinuating Lady Delphina Orberry.

Once Ormsby has rejected this lady's advances, she contrives his financial ruin along with the loss of his reputation. During his attempts to pull himself out of the ensuing morass, he regards Ireland as an antithesis to London's profligate world of fashion. He can escape there and recover. Here is the implicit doctrine Cyprian had advanced in *Fatal Revenge*, that Nature can refresh and restore the jaded or debauched sophisticate. Lady Montrevor, Ormsby's mother-in-law, promises to go back with him and her daughter. Her sophistication appears not utterly sunk into puritanical gloom; that would be altogether too sudden and unconvincing a transformation: '*Allons donc a l'Ireland, you* know, it is the *Island of Saints, so* we shall be quite in character, by being out of all *human* character.' But she does make it clear to the youth that this artificiality is but a mask:

I protest I only fear we shall be too perfect; so lest I should rise too rapidly in my own estimation, I will go talk nonsense to all the world for another hour – once more let's, 'mock the midnight bell.' Oh, my dear Ormsby, don't despise me for this levity – it is not levity – a glow of natural feeling pervades my whole heart and soul, and if I don't laugh, I must certainly cry. (p. 367)

We are now back, most obviously, to the conversations of Cyprian and Ippolito in *Fatal Revenge.* Lady Montrevor is subtly indicating her change from one type of character to the other. She is beginning to turn to the world of natural feeling, to leave the cosmopolitan world of neo-classical convention. Her return from London to the west of Ireland is symbolic of the change. Once more Ireland has conquered spiritually.

All this use of Irish material in *The Wild Irish Boy is* not tightly integrated with the structure of the novel. It indicates what Maturin meant when he wrote in the preface, 'He who is capable of writing a good novel ought to feel that he was born for a higher purpose than writing novels.' He wanted, obviously, to write about Ireland. He wrote better about it than about a fashionable London of which he knew nothing. He felt that a fashionable novel would sell better, and its materials should be 'a lounge in Bond Street, a phaeton tour in the park, a masquerade with appropriate scenery, and a birth-day or birth-night, with dresses and decorations, accurately copied from the newspapers.' This cynicism about the making of a novel did not suit him – though it is possible that he thought he might combine the Irish material of Lady Morgan with the social satire of Maria Edgeworth's *Belinda,* which Ormsby Bethel praises fulsomely. He was too romantic for satire. He lamented he had not time to write more about Ireland; his heart was full of it. His head was apparently full of London newspaper reports. But he was compelled, he asserted, to consult the pleasures of his readers, not his own.

The Milesian Chief, written four years later, was a more conscious attempt to gain literary laurels. In it he was being truer to his inclinations and the result is a far better novel. He was now much more skilled in his method of contrasting English and Irish national character (for that, ultimately, is what Cyprian and Ippolito were also rehearsing in *Fatal Revenge,* though no reader but an Irishman might have suspected it at the time) as well as comparing 'natural' with sophisticated characters. In *The Wild Irish Boy* he had merely produced the commonplace Irish remarks about the difference between the English and the Irish character. The Irish were formed to give more delight, the English to give more tranquil and rational happiness; the Irish were more ardent as lovers, the English better as husbands; and, a detached piece of generalization, the Irish, while better acquainted with the modes of pleasing, attained their success by some sacrifice; they have less dignity, stability, and force

142 Images of Invention

of character than those who live for other purposes. But Maturin, despite his apparent detachment, contrived, like Dr. Johnson with the Whig dogs, that the English did not get the best of it.

The contrast is achieved more subtly in *The Milesian Chief* by means of opposing characters. Here Maturin uses Lady Morgan's device of placing a sophisticated stranger in Ireland. He gives the idea a twist by making the stranger a beautiful talented girl, Armida Fitzalban, who has had a *succès d'estime* in Europe, and is engaged to Wandesforth, an English officer. Her father, Lord Montclare, brings her to Ireland. Her sensibility has previously been affected by the 'sombrous imagery and luxurious melancholy' of Ossian, yet she trembles at the thought of the savage country she is to visit, and her heart is desolated by the 'bleak waste of bog, scarce seen through the rain that beat heavily against the carriage windows' as she travels across the flatness of the central plain toward the west.

Once arrived, she falls violently in love with Connal O'Riordan, the Milesian chief, a member of an old and once powerful Irish family, who lives with his old grandfather in a ruined watchtower, the castle proper and the estates having been sold to Lord Montclare. This is another vestigial idea probably taken from *The Wild Irish Girl*, where the Milesian chieftain's lands had been confiscated by the Saxon hero's family in Cromwellian times. Both writers realize that the possession of land is the basic element in the racial antagonisms of Irish and English. The old grandfather plans a rebellion to free Ireland, with Connal as its leader. Connal, however, thinks the venture is impossible, endeavours to check it, but is foiled in his attempts by the treachery of Wandesforth (who has arrived in Ireland with his regiment), and is furious that Armida has rejected him. After various agonizing misunderstandings, jealousies, and suspicions which lead to a renewal of her engagement with Wandesforth, Armida eventually throws in her lot with Connal and goes to an island off the coast with the retreating rebels. She later returns to the castle, where her mother tricks her into agreeing to a marriage with Connal's brother Desmond, and she dies through a self-administered poison. Connal, meanwhile, has surrendered, been mercilessly flogged at Wandesforth's command and released. He shoots Wandesforth and is finally executed by a firing squad.[15]

Maturin is, in part, investigating the reasons why an intelligent young Irishman would consider rebellion against English rule, and discovering reasons why such an attempt was bound to fail without adequate assistance from continental Europe. Maturin was not only a post-revolutionary romantic, he was a post-'98-rebellion, post-Robert-Emmet-rebellion romantic. He had none of the earlier Wordsworthian idealism about the virtues of the lowly born. He said in one of his sermons: 'God knows, and all the world knows, that there is more evil among the lower classes than among any other in society, and that, not because they are *lower*, but because they are more destitute of the benefits of knowledge, and the blessings of religion – because they are more ignorant – and of ignorance the almost certain companion is vice.' [16]

On the whole, *The Milesian Chief* depicts the unsuitability of the peasantry as revolutionary troops. They are not amenable to any discipline, though they fight courageously against hopeless odds; they are brutal, the people are terrified of them, and their leader's heart 'swelled with agony at the thought of the high born Armida being seen by the eyes of rebel peasantry.' He is himself murderously attacked by some of his own men, one of whom later informs against him. He thinks gloomily of what would happen to his forces if they were to survive victorious: they would receive the curses of their countrymen; they would see the desolation of their own native land. He had himself decided, before the rebellion was forced into being by Wandesforth's breach of faith, that it would be impossible for Ireland to subsist as an independent country, to exist without dependence upon continental powers or a connection with England. These views are reinforced when he returns from a vain journey to Dublin to explore the possibilities of obtaining pardon for his troops and discovers that the 'few brave men penitent for their crime' he had left behind are now transformed into a 'ferocious band, mutinous to their leader, hostile to Government, and formidable to the country' and with the 'inflamed passions and unruly habits of a rabble mad for rapine.' Connal's experience and disillusionment are sadly akin to those of Beauchamp Bagenal Harvey, one of the gentlemen who led the Wexford rebels in 1798.

But the rebellion is only part of Maturin's design to portray his native country to the world; he had a larger plan in mind: 'I have chosen my own country for the scene, because I believe it the only country on earth, where, from the strange existing opposition of religion, politics and manners, the extremes of refinement and barbarism are united, and the most wild and incredible situations of romantic story are hourly passing before modern eyes.' [17] He fulfilled that larger plan by creating an intense drama out of the tragic and passionate love of Armida and Connal, and that of Connal's brother Desmond and Armida's half-sister Endymion, or Ines. Desmond is introduced as a contrast to Connal. He is no nationalist, joins Wandesforth's regiment, but finally deserts to the rebels and dies with Connal.

Armida's ostensible tragedy is that she is overcome by love for this proud savage, Connal. He rescues her from death three times but resists her attraction for him. His is a masochistic love doomed to despair, just as his love of his country leads him to what he knows will be ultimate defeat. She fails fully to understand or appreciate his world, and he tells her he will never be happy out of it. He despises her spiritual home, Italy, which, characteristically, he has never seen, in comparison with his western world. She understands nothing of the history of, or the political situation in, Ireland. And because of both history and politics he hates her presence in the castle of his ancestors, hates all she stands for; yet despite these differences, or because of them, Armida and Connal become infatuated, incompatible in every way as they are. The blind harper's burst of song foretelling death symbolizes the future course of their relations, a series of constant misunderstandings and misinterpretations of each other's actions. Yet their passion is genuine, as genuine as Connal's passion for the antiquities of his race and for Irish music, on which he lectures Armida constantly.

Maturin's insistence upon bringing Irish culture before his readers derives (though he uses less footnoting) from Lady Morgan's informative technique, but he contrives to weld his material to the story more neatly. Connal's proud character would be insupportable if he did not have this lofty love of a Gaelic culture utterly unknown to Armida's world. As Niilo Idman has pointed out, *The Milesian Chief* ultimately records the triumph of a weaker country, since Armida, standing as a symbol of the civilized world, abandons it for the product of this wild, romantic, ancient race, who has, for all his barbarism, a dynamic attraction lacking in the more stolid (if more convincingly drawn) Wandesforth.[17a]

The lesser love affair is curiously like that of Cyprian and Ippolito in *Fatal Revenge*. In each case Maturin has thrown two ostensible males together and they develop feelings of what almost amounts to homosexual attachment for each other, before one of the two is conveniently discovered to be female.[18] To give Desmond his due, he runs away from Endymion because he is afraid of the possibility of an unnatural relationship, while Endymion regards him as an elder brother and can't understand her feelings for him, as she thinks herself a boy. He has, besides, been renowned for 'local gallantry' before he meets her, and after escaping from what he regards as an intolerable situation he lives in sin in Dublin with Gabriella, a well-born young lady who has

unsuccessfully pursued Connal. The preface to *The Milesian Chief*
already alluded to may indeed refer to such struggles of passion as
these, 'when the soul trembles on the verge of the unlawful and the
unhallowed.'

The other two spheres in which Maturin thought his talents
might lie, darkening the gloomy and painting life in extremes, are
amply explored in *The Milesian Chief*, the best portions of which are
the descriptions of Irish scenery. He uses nature to reinforce the
novel's mood of impending disaster throughout; rain, storm, tem-
pest add to the wildness of the western scenery. Seascapes, solitary
islands, ruins, bogs, barren mountains, all play their part in creating the atmosphere of wildness and brooding melancholy, which
informs his interpretation of Irish nationalism.

Maturin's next novel, *Women, is* a study of inner life, a novel too
advanced for its age,[19] and a sensitive portrayal of young love. In
it Maturin continues his exploration of regionalism. He sets the
novel in Dublin and exposes the life of one of its Methodist circles.
De Courcy, a young Trinity College undergraduate of excessive
sensibility, falls in love with Eva, whom he has rescued from mysterious assailants; she is a passively lovely girl in a theologically-
minded and dreary household. After becoming engaged to her, he
is attracted by a woman who is her opposite, Zaira, an opera
singer, a development of Lady Montrevor and Armida Fitzalban.[20]
Though overflowing with the conversational gush of the blue-
stocking, she is less fantastic than her dilettante predecessors. De
Courcy runs away with her; she teaches him too much, and too
obviously, and as a result he has a typical young man's flirtation
with another woman, Eulalie. The logical result of all this is his
return to Eva. When he leaves Zaira, her passion increases, and the
second half of the novel is a protracted though penetrating analysis of her mental state. When De Courcy returns to Eva, she is
dying of consumption brought on by his earlier desertion of her;
his declination into death follows on hers; and then Zaira discovers that she has been responsible for bringing about the death of
her own daughter. A mysterious old peasant woman, who has
been moving in and out of the story with some of the omniscience
of Meg Merrilies, turns out to be Zaira's mother, Eva's grandmother. This, then, is another anatomy of romantic love; but it is
also, paradoxically, an advanced piece of realistic psychology.

Women takes up and gives fuller treatment to several of the
ideas of *The Wild Irish Boy*. The Methodist home of the Wentworths,
which De Courcy visits and endures for Eva's sake, corresponds to
the Calvinist circles in which Ormsby Bethel found himself as a

student, with the absurd Macowen's ranting thrown in for good measure. De Courcy's vacillations between an intellectually brilliant mother and a religiously respectable daughter develop the situation in which Ormsby had found himself: married to a pale, delicate daughter while enraptured by the brilliance of her mother. In each case the obvious discrepancies of age assert themselves and the hero eventually realizes he is really in love with the daughter.

Women has fewer of the improbabilities that marred the earlier novel. For instance, Hammond, the worthy counsellor of *The Wild Irish Boy*, lacked life, whereas the dour Northern Montgomery, himself in love with Eva, is convincing: he is too human to resist the temptation of telling Zaira that De Courcy is engaged to Eva or of commenting sourly upon Zaira's failings to De Courcy. The realism can be measured by Maturin's dwelling upon an apparently unpromising milieu. It was, however, one which he knew and understood. He describes the social life of Dublin with a satiric eye, and a much more satisfactory picture he makes of it, too, than of fashionable London at fifth hand. For his *mise en scène* he selects the immediate neighborhood of Dublin. He is not looking for the wilder effects of the west that he had used in *The Milesian Chief*, but he is none the less determined to use nature for his purposes. As the story develops, the mad old peasant woman's wild appearances, her speeches, and songs in Irish add their mystery; and her entrances are led up to by the changing aspects of nature. The Gothic spirit raises its head in a description of a city fire, an anticipation of Lady Morgan's tranference of that type of romantic treatment into urban scenes in *The O'Briens and the O'Flahertys* (1827). Zaira displays 'the theology of the heart' in her raptures over the beauties of nature. And for them Dublin had suitable scenery near at hand. There is a description of an equestrian picnic which Zaira arranges in Wicklow, in which the picnickers explore the wild and mountainous scenery of Luggelaw. A storm breaks out and this allows De Courcy to contrast Eva's earlier terrified, almost superstitious, behaviour under the same conditions with Zaira's intellectually stimulated fortitude. Montgomery, with a surly ungraciousness, points her out as 'quite a female Plato lecturing on the promontory of Sunium, lecturing away amid a storm that terrifies every other female.'

This storm[21] is a means of building up the tension, which discharges with the sinister utterances of the mad old woman:

The clouds, rising slowly above the Killina hills, soon spread far south; Bray-Head was enveloped from its summit to its base; and the long sweeping folds of leaden-coloured vapour passed from hill to hill southward, like giant spectres gliding over their summits, and leaving the folds of their mysterious mantles lingering and darkening on the track of their progress.[22]

But the scenery's effect upon the soul could also be described in Wordsworth's tones (adapted, admittedly, to the purposes of romances):

Beneath them, to right and left, lay the bays of Dublin and Killina, still as if in the first moment of their creation, before they had felt the rush of the breeze, or the ripple of the tide. The low murmur of the waves, that scarce reached their ears, seemed to send a voice of deep, lonely tranquillity to the heart, where its tones were addressed. It seemed to say – 'Listen to us, and be at peace.' The grey hill, smooth to its summit, the rude obelisk against which they leaned, and which appeared rather like a thing placed there by Nature than by man, all around them seemed to mark the boundary between the world of Nature and of man. They felt themselves alone, and they felt, what those who love alone can feel, that such moments of abstraction are moments of the most exquisite enjoyment. (pp. 62-63)

Scott's novels as well as his poetry had their effect on Maturin. Not only does the old peasant woman remind us of Meg Merrilies, with her uncanny ability to arrive on the scene of action, but the supernatural is also present. The appearance of the figure of Eva upon Killina Hill is a symbolical warning incident parallel to but more intense (because of its occurrence in a 'natural' setting) than the earlier melodramatic occasion on which De Courcy clasped Eva to his bosom:

Her long, light hair (of a different colour from Zaira's) diffused its golden luxuriance over his bosom; her white slender fingers grasped his with the fondling helplessness of infancy, and twined their waxen softness round and round them; her pure hyacinth breath[23] trembled over his cheeks and lips. In clasping her closer to his heart, he felt something within his vest; he drew it out; it was the flower Zaira had given him the night before, and which he had placed there; it was *withered;* he flung it away. (pp. 22-23)

There was only one peasant character in *Women.* Paradoxically, in his next novel, *Melmoth the Wanderer,* which is the quintessence of the tale of terror and a return to his earlier and lasting delight in the Gothic phenomena, Maturin begins the introductory tale with his most realistic characterizations of peasants. This first unit of the novel's sixfold plot, with its Chinese-box continuity, is a superb piece of storytelling. There is a steady increase in suspense achieved in two ways, through the realistic rendering of the peasant character which keeps the imaginative soaring of the story firmly rooted, and through the use of emotive descriptions of nature which set a suitable scene wherein Maturin's brooding eerie imagination could display its power.

Young John Melmoth, yet another undergraduate from Trinity College Dublin, travels to the house of his dying miserly uncle in County Wicklow; the atmosphere of the place gets on his nerves and prepares us for the horrors to follow:

The weather was cold and gloomy; heavy clouds betokened a long and dreary continuance of autumnal rains; cloud after cloud came sweeping on like the dark banners of an approaching host, whose march is for desolation. As Melmoth leaned against the window, whose dismantled frame, and pieced and shattered panes, shook with every gust of wind, his eye encountered nothing but that most cheerless of all prospects, a miser's garden – walls broken down, grass-grown walks whose grass was not even green, dwarfish, doddered, leafless trees, and a luxuriant crop of nettles and weeds rearing their unlovely heads where there had once been flowers, all waving and bending in capricious and unsightly forms, as the wind sighed over them. It was the verdure of the church-yard the garden of death.[24]

Maturin's last novel, *The Albigenses,* was to form part of a trilogy dealing with ancient, medieval, and modern manners in Europe. It owed its inception to the popularity of Scott's historical novels. And it might be argued that Maturin was using as a basis Irish material translated into another place and time. Lady Morgan had done this in her novel of Provence, *The Novice of St. Dominick* (1805).[25] Maturin was using for background the situation of a religious community under the threat of attempted domination by superior power, which brought out the heroic qualities of the oppressed. The novel was highly praised by contemporary critics, but cannot be thought successful in comparison to some of his earlier work. It has two dissimilar heroines, Isabelle, a nobly-born lady, and Genevieve, probably modeled upon Rebecca in *Ivanhoe,* who is modest, self-denying, and not of exalted origin. But there is no sensitive yet proud hero torn between these two ladies, who experience Radcliffean escapes through secret passages, doors, and vaults, all for the sake of two of the most unrelentingly dull paragons ever wished upon fiction. Whereas in *The Milesian Chief* Armida and Connal addressed each other histrionically, struck attitudes, and often seemed stilted, they were full of life in comparison to all the characters of this novel. *The Albigenses is* ruined by its melodramatic style which not even the descriptions can overcome. And the best of the descriptions derive from Maturin's Gothic rather than his Wordsworthian genre.

It is easy to find faults in Maturin's novels. They are full of them: sometimes excessively complicated in structure, usually brought to a hasty finish, with frequent errors in syntax and grammar, containing manifest absurdities in character and plot, and overflowing with melodramatic excesses. Throughout them, however, Maturin showed his ability to make innovations in the novel such as those suggested in this essay. That these remained unnoticed was part of his tragedy, a tragedy much akin to that of another Irish eccentric and writer, James Clarence Mangan, who wrote of Maturin with sympathy. Maturin could write compellingly- indeed, language occasionally took on a plastic quality in his hands; he invested the least likely of situations with a passionate intensity and a comprehension of human emotions, particularly those of young lovers, which stemmed from the conviction he expressed in one of his sermons: 'Man is unhappy, not because the world is hostile to his happiness, but because he is a guilty creature and no guilty creature can be happy while he remains in that state.'[26]

READING LEVER

Scott was the model. He generally begins a novel with a description of the scenery, often in blank verse, a kind of easement of the reader into the story: are you sitting comfortably? Here is an example of how it is done: .

The mountains, rugged and broken, are singularly fanciful in their outline; their sides a mingled mass of granite and straggling herbage, where the deepest green and the red purple of the heath-bell are blended harmoniously together. The valley beneath, alternately widening and narrowing, presents one rich meadow tract, watered by a deep and rapid stream, fed by a thousand rills that come tumbling, and foaming down the mountain sides, and to the traveller are seen like white streaks marking the dark surface of the precipice. Scarcely a hut is to be seen for miles of this lonely glen, and save for the herds of cattle and the flocks of sheep here and there to be descried, it would seem as if the spot had been forgotten by man, and left to sleep in its own gloomy desolation. The river itself has a character of wildness all its own – now, brawling over rugged rocks – now foaming between high and narrow sides, abrupt as walls, sometimes, flowing over a ledge of granite, without a ripple on the surface – then plunging madly into some dark abyss, to emerge again, lower down the valley, in one troubled sea of foam and spray: its dull roar the only voice that echoes in the mountain gorged.[1]

I have cheated a little here by omitting the first sentence of this particular novel which shows this is not a highland scene described by the Wizard of the North. Charles Lever places his reader precisely in the opening sentence of his novel:

In that wild and picturesque valley which winds its way between the town of Macroom and Bantry Bay, and goes by the names of Glenflesk, the character of Irish scenery is perhaps more perfectly displayed than in any other tract of the same extent in the island.

Like Scott, Lever peoples his places. You put moving figures into the landscape you have described, you sometimes have another stationary figure observing them so that the dimensions are naturally extended. The following passage could well have been written by Scott:

The sun was just setting on a mellow evening, late in the autumn of a year towards the close of the last century, as a solitary traveller sat down to rest himself on one of the large rocks by the road-side; divesting himself of his gun and shot-pouch he lay carelessly at his length, and seemed to be enjoying the light breeze which came up the valley. (*Ibid.* p. 2)

There follows a description of the young man: he is strong, his face attractive except for a discontented mouth, his clothing classless: 'a shooting jacket of some coarse stuff, stained and washed by many a mountain streamlet; loose trousers of grey cloth and heavy shoes' (*Ibid.* p. 3). Indeed he reminds us not only of Yeats's ideal, the freckled fisherman going to a grey place on a hill in his grey Connemara clothes at dawn to cast his flies, but also of Michael Robartes and Owen Aherne, who had trod the southern roads, their boots soiled, their Connemara cloth worn out of shape. Lever's young man is listless, but he becomes alert when he hears a carriage. Into his view comes, ahead of it, a man advanced in years but hale and vigorous, his features expressing the habitual character of one accustomed to exert a degree of command and influence over others. He is accompanied by a girl of about sixteen, obviously his daughter. She asks her father what the fire that she sees can mean.

It is a thin wreath of smoke that curled its way upwards from what appeared a low mound of earth, in the valley below the road; some branches of trees, covered with sods of earth, grassgrown and still green, were heaped up together, and through these the vapour found a passage and floated through the air. (*Ibid.* p. 4)

We have had description, now we move into dialogue. The old man says to his daughter that there is someone who will explain it and addresses the youth, who is studiedly ignoring them, with: 'I say my good fellow, what does that smoke mean we see yonder?' The young man is galvanized into action, he leaps to his feet, his features are convulsed, dark with blood: ' "Was it to me you spoke?" said he, in a low guttural tone, which his passion actually made tremulous.' Before the old man can reply, his daughter, 'with the quick tact of womanhood', seeing the mistake her father has fallen into, interrupts him by saying 'Yes, sir, we were asking you the cause of the fire at the foot of that cliff'. The young man explains it as a cabin; he goes on to say that the people are not so poor as she thinks, when she weeps at the thought of people actually living there. When the old man asks whose estate this is, the young man stares at him before replying:

'This belongs to an Englishman – a certain Sir Marmaduke Travers – It is
the estate of O'Donoghue'.

    Was, you mean, once, answered the old man quickly.

    'I mean what I say', replied the other rudely, 'Confiscation cannot take
away a right, it can at most . . . (*Ibid*. p. 5)

Now, having had description and dialogue, we are into narrative, into action. While the young man was speaking 'his quick
glance detected a dark object soaring above his head'. In a second
he had seized his gun, and taking a steady aim, he fired: 'The loud
report was heard repeated in many a far-off glen, and ere its last
echo died away, a heavy object fell upon the road, not many yards
from where they stood'. Now comes the theme: that the English do
not understand the Irish, for, as you will have guessed, the young
man is Irish; he is, in fact, Mark, the elder son of the O'Donoghue,
and the old man is English; he is Sir Marmaduke Travers himself.

'This fellow', said the youth, as he lifted the body of a large black eagle
from the ground – 'This fellow was a confiscator too, and see what he has
come to. You'd not tell me that our lambs were his, would you?'

    Into narrative, into action, into allegorical symbolism, into
theme? Well, nearly . . . *The O'Donoghue* (1845) is a novel in which
Lever moves away from the roistering, rattling stories with which
he began his career.

    There are other similarities to Scott's work in *The O'Donoghue*.
The early stages of a Lever story, for instance, can move at too
leisurely a pace (I used to advise my students to skip the first six
chapters of a Scott novel, and then return to them after they had
read the rest; and this advice might be useful to those beginning a
Lever novel who are unused to leisurely nineteenth century introductions to action).

    Another parallel is the use of two heroes and two heroines. Did
Scott get this idea from Shakespeare's comedies, or from more
recent Restoration and eighteenth-century comedies? Think of
Goldsmith, for instance, who has two heroes in *She Stoops to
Conquer*, Marlow and Hastings, two heroines, Miss Hardcastle and
Miss Neville; or consider Sheridan, who, in *The Rivals*, has Jack
Absolute in love with Lydia Languish and Faulkland with Julia
Melville. Earlier, Farquhar used the technique in *The Recruiting
Officer*, where Captain Plume pursues Silvia, the lively girl who
dresses up as a man and enlists in his company, and where Worthy
– a fore-runner of Sheridan's Faulkland – almost proves himself
unworthy of Melinda. In *The Beaux' Stratagem* there are two young
men on the make, Aimwell and Archer, who pursue two young

women, Dorinda, Lady Bountiful's daughter, and Mrs. Sullen, her unhappily-married daughter-in-law.

The idea probably goes back far further than Shakespeare, back to the Latin comedies of Plautus and Terence, some of whose plays would have been known to these Irish authors writing in English, who, like Scott, had been educated in the classics. Scott, however, often had a blonde and a brunette as heroines and was careful to delineate the different natures of his two heroes also. This is something Lever developed finally to the pitch of having eight young people to pair off in *Lord Kilgobbin* (1872). In his middle period he was less ambitious and rang the changes upon two heroines, though they are, admittedly, pursued by four men in *The O'Donoghue*.

Lever is a nineteenth-century author, Scott his most obvious exemplar. Now Scott's career as a writer of fiction ran from *Waverley* of 1814 to 1826, Lever's from *Harry Lorrequer* of 1837 to *Lord Kilgobbin* of 1872. How then does Lever fit into the general pattern of the nineteenth century novel? In the decade when he began writing, 1830 – 1840, the established novelists were Peacock, Bulwer Lytton, Susan Ferrier and Frances Trollope. New novelists to appear in the period were Harrison Ainsworth, Disraeli and Dickens. They were finding their feet. Disraeli, for instance, wrote *The Young Duke* in 1831 – 'What', asked his father in amazement, 'does Ben know of Dukes?' *Contarini Fleming* (1832) was, to be polite, highflown, whereas *Alroy* (1833) demands to be read for its sheer ludicrosity: Alroy has escaped from the city of Hanmadar; his horse dies from exhaustion when they reach a well and Alroy falls asleep from exhaustion:

The lion advanced to the fountain to drink. He beheld a man. His mane rose, his tail was wildly agitated, he bent over the sleeping prince, he uttered an awful roar, which awoke Alroy.

The narrative now seems unwittingly absurd in its superbly pretentious style:

He awoke; his gaze met the flaming eyes of the enormous beast fixed upon him with a blended feeling of desire and surprise. He awoke, and from a swoon; but the dreamless trance had refreshed the exhausted energies of the desolate wanderer; in an instant he collected his senses, remembered all that had passed, and comprehended his present situation. He returned the lion a glance as imperious, and fierce, and scrutinising, as his own. For a moment, their flashing orbs vied in regal rivalry; but at length the spirit of the mere animal yielded to the genius of the man. The lion, cowed, slunk away, stalked with haughty timidity through the rocks, and then sprang into the forest.[2]

Henrietta Temple (1837), highly strung romantic reflection of an intense love affair, then followed. Disraeli had not yet found his subject, nor yet got into his stride. *Coningsby* (1844), *Sybil* (1845) and *Tancred* (1847), novels of the hungry 'forties, made his reputation – the first two for their political content, the third for its bravery in plugging mysticism while its author was digging himself into the Tory party – but I believe that, as in Lever's case, Disraeli's best novels, *Lothair* (1870) and *Endymion* (1880), came at the end of his life. In him Lever may have found further sanction beyond that of Scott for involving his heroes and heroines in politics.

Dickens, too, was beginning his career, and it developed fast – in five years, between 1835 and 1840, he had to his credit *Sketches by Boz* (1835), *Pickwick Papers* (1836), *Oliver Twist* (1837), *Nicholas Nickleby* (1838) and *Master Humphrey's Clock, Barnaby Rudge,* and *The Old Curiosity Shop* – all of 1840. In this decade Thackeray had only *The Professor* and *The Yellowplush Papers* published by 1837. And Surtees's *Jorrocks' Jaunts and Jollities* of 1838 ran a little parallel to Lever's boisterousness.

There are not many close linkages to be discovered there, then. And the English novel from 1800 to 1830, apart from Scott, was graced by Jane Austen and Peacock, whose works cannot particularly have affected Lever. He did not like the Gothic, so Monk Lewis and Mary Shelley were not influential, nor, presumably, was the gushing nonsense of Lady Caroline Lamb, while Galt, writing in the 1820s, was probably somewhat dour for Lever's liking.

Some other influences should be considered. Scott is the obvious inspiration, Lever sharing his nineteenth-century ability to parade a large cast of characters, to invent unusual, idiosyncratic ones, and to place them not only against the background of history but in an evocative regional atmosphere. But to mention regional fiction is to demand that we trace the links back to the first year of the nineteenth century, for Scott's exemplar in regional fiction was Maria Edgeworth. Her *Castle Rackrent* was published in 1800, and when he began writing the *Waverley* novels Scott said he wanted to do for Scotland what Maria Edgeworth had done for Ireland. It is time, then, to think of Charles Lever as an Irish novelist. How does he continue the work of his earliest predecessors, Maria Edgeworth, Lady Morgan and Charles Robert Maturin? They had various aims, but they shared a desire to present Ireland to English readers. They did this, at times, by the device of bringing a stranger into Ireland, whose fresh impressions would be likely to make an English reader empathise with the stranger's reactions to the new scenery, new

attitudes, new views of history and politics, in short, to a new way
of life. Thus Lord Glenthorn a bored young man in Maria
Edgeworth's tale *Ennui*, returns to Ireland, and his reactions to it
give the story its dramatic force. Thus Lord Colambre returns, in
The Absentee (1812), to see vulgar suburban life in Dublin and the
poverty of the west. *Castle Rackrent* had deliberately gone back to
the manners of the squirearchy in pre-1782 days, but both these
later tales deal with a contemporary problem: the evils of bad land
agents – increasingly a problem in the nineteenth century after
many landlords had left their Irish estates to the tender mercies of
agents as a result of the Act of Union which had eliminated the
Parliament in Dublin and made it a less attractive centre for them.
Carleton's *Valentine McClutchy* of 1845 was a darker study – and
we remember that the main villain in *The O'Donoghue*, also of 1845,
is an agent. There were many hints in Maria Edgeworth for Lever.
In *Ennui* the English Lord Craglethrope thinks he understands
Ireland and, like Lever's Sir Marmaduke Travers, he doesn't even
begin to do so. The, tension of potential rebellion is there in *Ennui*,
and Lever is writing about this in *The O'Donoghue*. Maria
Edgeworth's views about the problem of Ireland are ones Lever
began to adopt: equality, not colonial status; prosperity, not poverty; education, not ignorance. In *The Absentee* Maria Edgeworth portrays the decline in Dublin's life after the Act of Union (1800) with
the loss of the Dublin Parliament; Lever was to draw the same
deterioration of life when the Capital became a provincial city even
more poignantly in his *Barrington* (1862).

Much of Maria Edgeworth's *Ormond* (1817) could have come out
of a Lever novel. In this novel the alcoholic hospitality of Sir Ulick
Shane is overgenerous to the point of excess. The shooting of
Moriarty is almost paralleled by the behaviour of Mark to Kerry
O'Leary in *The O'Donoghue*; it is the sort of thing we find in
Barrington's *Recollections of the Later Eighteenth Century:*

As Mark spoke he turned his eyes to the corner of the room, where Kerry,
in a state of the most abject fear, was endeavouring to extract a cork from
a bottle by means of a very impracticable screw.

'Ah! you there,' cried he, as his eyes flashed fire. Hold the bottle up –
hold it steady, you old fool,' and with a savage grin he drew a pistol from
his breast pocket and levelled it at the mark.

Kerry was on his knees, one hand on the floor and in the other the bottle, which, despite all his efforts, he swayed backwards and forwards.

O master, darlin' – O Sir Archy, dear -- O Joseph and Mary!'

'I've drank too much wine to hit it flying,' said Mark, with a half drunk-
en laugh, 'and the fool won't be steady. There': and as he spoke, the crash

of the report resounded through the room, and the neck of the bottle was snapped off about half an inch below the cork.

'Neatly done, Mark – not a doubt of it,' said the O'Donoghue, as he took the bottle from Kerry's hand, who, with a pace a kangaroo might have envied, approached the table, actually dreading to stand up straight in Mark's presence.

'At the risk of being thought an epicure,' said M'Nab, 'I maun say I'd like my wine handled more tenderly.'

'It was cleverly done though,' said Talbot, helping himself to a bumper from the broken flask. 'I remember a trick we used to have at St. Cyr, which was,.to place a bullet on a cork, and then, at fifteen paces cut away the cork and drop the bullet into the bottle.'

'No man ever did that twice, cried Mark, rudely.

'I'll wager a hundred guineas I do it twice, within five shots,' said Talbot, with the most perfect coolness. (*The O'Donoghue*, ed.cit. p. 217)

It may be that Maria Edgeworth's portrayal of Cornelius O'Shane, King Corny of the Black Isles, a development of her earlier character Count O'Halloran, who presided over hunting, shooting and an independent mode of life in the west, paved the way for the kind of life Mark O'Donoghue inherits from his aged and improvident father.

Lever, however, learned other things from Lady Morgan and from Charles Robert Maturin. The former's first novel *St. Clair, or the Heiress of Desmond* shows us the west of Ireland as seen by a young English officer who finds the local heiress able, like her creator, to sing and play the harp – and her father has a ruined castle, a cromlech, Irish manuscripts and a harper. This novel is overcome by romantic sensibility of a kind Lever would never have countenanced, but its successor, *The Wild Irish Girl*, got down to a didactic purpose of expounding the Gaelic culture that formerly flourished in Ireland. Irish scenery is emotively expressed in terms of Salvator Rosa, and the English hero finally falls for and marries his wild Irish girl, having had a preparatory series of lectures upon the flora, fauna and cultural history of Ireland.

Maturin, after trying to cash in on Lady Morgan's *The Wild Irish Girl* with his own *The Wild Irish Boy*, did achieve an original novel in *The Milesian Chief* (1812) which may have affected some of Lever's *The O'Donoghue*. In this novel there are two brothers, and Connal, the patriot, could, in his moodiness and recklessness, have been a novel for the Byronic aspects of Mark O'Donoghue, sulky, proud, rude and aggressive. Why Connal should have considered rebelling is one of Maturin's questions, which Lever faces when dealing with his character Mark; and Maturin had read the past as

Lever did later: without massive support from the continent any Irish rebellion was bound to fail. Maturin drew upon his experiences as a curate in the west of Ireland in Loughrea; he disliked flat country, he thought Loughrea boring, he depicted damp with great feeling as part of his doomladen atmosphere, something Lever was to do very effectively indeed in *Lord Kilgobbin* though he had already begun to explore decay in the damp of the O'Donoghue's castle.

While we do get pictures of Dublin in the seventeen-nineties in *The O'Donoghue,* it is perhaps fairer to compare Lady Morgan's best novel, *The O'Briens and the O'Flahertys,* with Lever's *Tom Burke of 'Ours'* (1844) for effective portrayal of the conspiratorial element in the city.

To return to *The O'Donoghue* at this point is to enquire how Lever treated the politico-military situation in the novel. He had moved from his three early novels in his attitude to the differences between Irish and English. The well-meaning intentions of Sir Marmaduke, because they are based upon ignorance of Ireland and the Irish character, are bound to fail. Sir Marmaduke's son, who is a Guards Officer, is equally ignorant of matters Irish at first but later becomes involved in the repression of revolutionary movements. He emerges well from the confusion of misunderstanding. Though he fails to win the hand of the beautiful and intelligent niece of The O'Donoghue, he gains the reader's respect because he is a generous man, and the reader's sympathy for failing to win the attractive Kate. We can clear off his somewhat insipid sister and Mark's scholarly brother fairly quickly from the scene, and while Mark's eventual pairing with Kate has a certain credibility we are left, ultimately, with the question of what is memorable about the novel. What are its merits?

Bearing in mind that the title of my essay is *Reading Lever* this is the point where the matter should be discussed in general terms. There is a lot of Lever to read: 33 novels, a lot of squibs, literary journalism and some letters. If you mention Lever those who recognise the name will probably give a knee-jerk reaction to it: *Harry Lorrequer;* a smaller number might add *Charles O'Malley.* It is odd, though explicable, that he should largely be remembered for his first two novels, whereas his novelistic skills improved with practice, his attitudes to life deepened with experience; he became more ready to write thoughtfully of the tragedies of life than to create rollicking comedy. I have suggested in the following essay[3] that he has received less attention than he is due because critics fastened upon the farcical elements in his two early novels and attacked him for portraying Ireland in terms of the comedy of the stage Irishman. Carleton wrote a vicious unsigned review in *The Nation* in October 1843, accusing Lever of 'selling us for pounds, shillings and pence'. Daniel O'Connell and Thomas Davis also joined the fray. Some of this may have come not so much from their reaction to Lever's fiction as to his editorship of the *Dublin University Magazine* from 1842 to 1845. And his Irish way of living at Bridge House, Templeogue, where hospitality was generous indeed, may well have caused jealousy.

In 1888, however, Yeats re-activated this Irish hostility to Lever, linking him with Lover and accusing them the next year (in 'Popular Ballad Poetry of Ireland', *The Leisure Hour*, November 1889) of writing ever with one eye on London. He argued that because they never wrote for the people they never wrote faithfully of the people. In 1891 he hedged by calling Lever's books 'quite sufficiently truthful', but said the vices and virtues of his characters were those of the gentry, and turned his attack on the gentry instead. The same year he included (in 'The Young Ireland League', *United Ireland*, 3 October 1891) 'the best novels' of Lever in a list of books Young Ireland Libraries should include; in a letter to the Editor, *Daily Express* (Dublin), 27 February 1895, he put *Charles O'Malley* as eleventh out of thirteen in the *Novels and Romances* section of his list of thirty books necessary to the understanding of Ireland; and he placed Lever in the same position in the eighteen titles of *Novels and Romances* given later in an article in the *Bookman* of October 1895. Then in 1908, attacking the English influence running through nineteenth-century Irish novels, he did find a 'rightful Irish gaiety in him'; but in *Autobiographies* he says the Wildes would have fed Lever's imagination – (Lever was, in fact, a friend of Sir William Wilde, Oscar's father) – for being dirty, untidy and daring. He might not, he added, have valued their imaginative and learned qualities so highly. He lumped Lever in with Daniel O'Connell and Tom Moore later on in the pre-Young Ireland tradition of 'con- vivial Ireland with the tear and the smile'. Lady Gregory adopted Yeats's attitude to Lever, and his bias was also followed by that of E. A. Boyd and Daniel Corkery. I am convinced that Yeats could not have read the later novels *Barrington*, (1863) *Sir Brook Fossbrooke*, (1866) and *Lord Kilgobbin*, (1872). But did he read *Jack Hinton* of 1843? This uses the stranger-in-Ireland technique of Maria Edgeworth, Lady Morgan and Charles Robert Maturin (who varied the pattern by creating an English woman character, Lady Armida Fitzalban, as his visitor to Ireland). Lever used a young English A.D.C. to show English misjudgment of Ireland, and also to explore the individuality, the essentially Irish qualities of life in Ireland, while attacking the degeneracy of the Viceregal court. In this novel Lever echoes the great past of Dublin, at the end of the eighteenth century when the names of Burke, Sheridan, Grattan and Curran start up. Or did Yeats read *St Patrick's Eve* of 1845, Lever's account of the cholera epidemic that he had himself experienced as a country doctor? Or did Yeats choose to ignore another novel of 1845, *Tom Burke of 'Ours'* with its fourteen-year old witnessing the brutality of the Yeomanry after 1798, leading a mob on the night of voting for the Union, then escaping to France and joining Napoleon's army, only to resign his commission and be arrested later in Ireland with experience of the *agents provocateurs* and informers before returning to fight for Napoleon again? The novel had, in Lever's words, rebellion enough 'to make Daniel O'Connell recant his judgement of me'. *The O'Donoghue* discusses the system of land tenure, and the attitudes of the Ascendancy, as well as English ignorance of Ireland.

There are so many other novels Yeats and Lever's other Irish detractors simply cannot have read. *Roland Cashel* (1848) attacks middle class vulgarity in a way Yeats would surely have approved had he read it. *Maurice Tierney* (1850) showed the way to *The Year of the French*, though Professor Flanagan does not discuss Lever – nor Maturin either – in his study of the *Irish Novel* (1959). *In Sir Jasper Carew* (1852) Lever digs back to the Cromwellian period. But it is *The Martins of Cro Martin* (1854) that brings home to us Lever's bitter despair about Irish politics. He shows the stupidity of romanticising the Ascendancy in *Barrington* (1863), and in *Luttrell of Arran* (1865) he has his main character withdraw from an uncongenial society. *Sir Brook Fossbrooke*, published in 1866, the year after Yeats's birth, provides us with a searching analysis of the Anglo-Irish decline as well as of English misrule, both to be developed even further in his final novel *Lord Kilgobbin* (1872).

The scope of Lever is wide indeed; his attitude to Ireland and her political and social situation changed and developed. He gives us a generously broad picture of nineteenth-century Ireland. This achievement was well praised by the late Professor Roger McHugh in an article in *Studies* in 1939.[4]

I have rushed through Lever's significant Irish writings, because the merits of *The O'Donoghue* are the sort of achievement much past criticism ignored or was not prepared to examine dispassionately. I have asked myself what are its merits, and digressed generally before coming down to particulars. Now I should like to give both a personal and a general answer to my query.

My personal pleasure in rereading the novel is akin to that
which I find in reading many nineteenth-century Irish novels:
imagining them as scripts for film or T.V. One's own view of the
characters is not affected by Phiz's splendid drawings. They were
less caricatured than earlier (in 1841 he had gone to Brussels along
with Lover and the publisher McGlashan; Lever, Lover and Phiz
drank 108 bottles of champagne in six days – half-a-dozen bottles
a day each). There are superbly dramatic scenes in so many nineteenth century Irish novels: the novelists of that period had to
appeal in that way to *their* captive audience. For instance,
Meredith, largely unread, like Lever, has in *Vittoria* a T.V. script for
the taking. What of *The O'Donoghue?* We have episodes where the
characters express themselves with vigour through their actions.
Mark, for instance, undisciplined creature of impulse that he is,
sells a horse to Lanty Lawler for fifty-five pounds, tries to buy her
back and then suddenly gallops off with her, jumping a ditch,
dashing madly through a gate before finally handing the mare over
to Lanty. His younger brother, Herbert, saves Sybella from a sudden flood with the loss of this mare, which Lanty had sold on for
£100 profit. But though this is a photogenic scene, of 'young man
to the rescue of helpless maiden', more violent matters ensure. A
band of French smugglers attack Sir Marmaduke's lodge and fire
the ricks when their captain is detected as he tries to force an
entrance to pay his respects to Sybella. Then the servant, Kerry
O'Leary, thinking the doctor is the sheriff, fires a carbine at him
through a small window in the castle; this prompts the doctor's
pony to bolt and destroy the doctor's gig. And into the masculine
citadel of the O'Donoghue's castle comes the convent-educated
niece, Kitty, and later Sir Marmaduke's son Frederick, a captain in
the Guards.

These events are obvious enough. Lever can vary his pace and
tone. There follows a piece of Jane Austenesque comedy of manners when he brings together the Travers family with the
O'Donoghue household. Mark, who has been rude to Frederick,
the Guards captain, the day before, and committed himself to the
United Irishmen in the local shebeen, is not there; all is sweetness
and light until Kerry O'Leary comes in to tell of Mark's treatment
of a process server. The incident is being glossed over when Kate
declares Mark should have horsewhipped the fellow within an
inch of his life – a startling speech which attracts the young Guards
officer. She is torn between Mark and Travers and there are two
encounters – once while she is with Travers, and then when she is
with Mark.

Suspense is also kept up through the earlier introduction of Talbot, the emissary sent by the Irish party in France to report on the state of the insurgents in Ireland, of Hemsworth, the agent who gets Mark's compromising letters to revolutionary leaders from Lanty, who turns out to be an establishment spy, himself black-mailed by Hemsworth, whose complete duplicity matches that of Talbot, with whom Mark has gatecrashed a castle gathering. Mark goes on the run, returns home, then goes into hiding again, and sees the French ships arrive in Bantry Bay. There follows another dramatic episode at the castle, when Mark fights with Hemsworth, who fires twice at him and faints when Mark wrestles with him and presses a pistol on his forehead – it misfires and Mark throws him out of the window: 'the heavy mass was heard as it fell crash-ing among the bushwood that covered the precipice'. Hearing can-non in the bay, Mark vanishes, hoping the French landing is at last taking place. It is not. The storms are too much for the ships and the order to sail is given. Hemsworth recovers; he goes to the she-been with his men, determined to burn it to the ground. But before that he drinks a great deal of wine, cursed by Mary who leaves her home; then they fire the thatch, and Hemsworth fires at the door where the French arms have been stored and blows the whole place skyhigh, himself and his three men with it. Meanwhile Mark is surrounded by the dragoons, but Travers allows him to escape. The final episode is tense, as Mark is rowed out when the French fleet stands out to sea in the gale, and he just manages to get to a ship.

All of this balances the somewhat contrived business of how Sir Archy, The O'Donoghue's Scottish brother-in-law, outwits Hemsworth's plans to obtain the estate by marrying Kate. We have been given enough hints to realise that Mark will mature in the French service and marry her, that Herbert will marry Sybella. But Lever had not himself, by the way, intended this.

When editing *The Dublin University Magazine* he was extremely sensitive to critical reception of his work, and 'an impertinent para-graph or some malicious sneer' could make him throw his manu-script aside, to doodle caricatures instead of writing. He found the strain of editing considerable. He took a holiday – sleeping twenty hours a day and yawning through four had begun to alarm him. Despite his doctor's warnings against railways and steamboats he travelled from New Ross to Waterford on a start to recovery; thence he went to Cork and eventually finished *Tom Burke* in Killarney. He began to plan *The O'Donoghue;* his wife and he hav-ing had so much salmon and so many chickens to eat in the inns en route that they found it difficult, he wrote, to prevent themselves from swimming and flying. 'Climbing mountains, fording rivers, crossing bays, tramping along roads' in Clare and Galway, he then went up to Mayo, where the scenery reminded him with delight of his friend Maxwell's *Wild Sports* of *the West* (1832), the main influence which had led him to write fiction. Now he had recovered, had got a second wind. Back in Dublin, he began to wonder whether he was getting too serious. He consulted his publisher, McGlashan, while thinking *The O'Donoghue* should have a tragic ending: would he wind it up amid the lightning and thunder which scattered the French fleet in Bantry Bay? Or would he end it in Colburn and Bentley fashion with love and marriage licences? McGlashan wouldn't have tragedy – 'the ladies wouldn't like it' – and this view prevailed.

After Lever got away from Dublin in February 1845 – the victim of vile headaches – and had arrived in Karlsruhe, he wrote to his friend Alexander Spencer about his pleasure in Maria Edgeworth's praise and criticism of *The O'Donoghue* which she was reading to her nephews and nieces. He had an immense respect for her and valued her judgement highly. In a letter of 1847 – she was then in her eighties – she probably dissuaded him from writing a novel about the priest in politics. Now he recorded in 1846 his pleasure in her comment that the early chapters augured well. He felt that she had repaid him for all the bitterness and injustice of his Irish critics: 'I never made such an effort as in this book'.[5]

Effort is a suitable word on which to draw to a conclusion, for we need to make an effort to approach Lever in a new way. Modern critics are not programmed to assess him, educated as most of them are in specialised factories prepackaging literary problems and solutions for their consumers, their customers, their students. Students come to treat literature as if they were scientists mastering one abstruse page of concentrated formulae a day. They are reared upon the metaphysical metaphors of Donne, the wave patterns of Virginia Woolf's subconscious, the sophisticated symbolism of Yeats, the pastiche puzzles of Pound, the jaunty maunderings of Joyce, the structure of Wallace Stevens's reality, even the crying of Thomas Pynchon about his lot. Weaned on these authors, students seem to avoid reading fast. Their long books tend to be their set books and some of these, like *Middlemarch,* can sap their vitality. There are obvious distractions, such as television, which hinder the enjoyment of wide reading of long novels. There tends to be a canon beyond which many university indoctrinators do not stray; Lever is on no syllabus! Indoctrinators do not stimulate their students to pursue their own tastes but to echo their own admired and fashionable critics, and they tend to pepperpot in the fashionable names – but these are usually the names of other critics. The serpent bites its own tail.

Where, then, do we direct our efforts? To overcome these difficulties we have firstly to adjust to length. This is probably why people read *Castle Rackrent* and *The Absentee* rather than Maria Edgeworth's much longer and in many ways more fascinating *Ormond*. The length of Lever's novel is, however, not a disadvantage when you become used to it. And there is the noble art of skipping to be developed.

Secondly, it is difficult for us to assess Lever and allow for a lot of the somewhat dated mechanisms he uses unless we have an idea of what his contemporaries were writing. If, for instance, we find Lever's love affairs conducted with, by modern standards, a good deal of delicacy, we must remember how inhibited Scott was in such matters. We need to look at Lever comparatively not only in relation to his English but his Scottish and, especially, his Irish contemporaries.

Thirdly – the crucial point – we have to get texts. Alas, there are no easily accessible, attractively produced, modern texts. Lever, like George Moore, suffers from small type, from a slabby setting of pages; in short from looking old-fashioned in an age when fashion affects us more than we fully realise or are willing to admit. Even up to two years ago you could get even first editions of Lever for one or two pounds. The attractive ones have Phiz drawings. I was looking for some particular texts recently – having had to dispose of a large collection of Lever texts (they are briefly described in 'Yeats and the Wrong Lever') because of shortage of shelf space in a new, smaller study – and I could find nothing in Dublin – except that at the last moment, a complete set appeared on a bookseller's shelves. I thought, well, maybe I could go to £50 – or perhaps even £75 – for it. I asked the price: £750. The market has obviously taken off. But support systems do not exist in the form of readily available, attractive texts. Perhaps current critical studies will encourage their production and bring about a wider appreciation of an unduly neglected and most impressive novelist.

YEATS AND THE WRONG LEVER

I

If one grows up in a university where one's teacher or supervisor or professor has, very properly, a book-lined room – not, please, an office, that hideous term applied to the concrete box occupied by an academic careerist, usually distinguished by only the texts set him as a student and the few extra texts he or she has set to the students they 'teach' – or, alas, often indoctrinate under this term – if, as I say, one grows up in the company of scholars who enjoy literature, and enjoy having books about them, then some emulation is stirred and the tyro academic naturally wants to fill his or her own shelves.

Today it is a costly operation, and one which becomes costlier. No longer, for instance, are there the barrows on the Dublin quays – there even in my youth – where for 6d (d not p) there were bargains galore. The banks of the Seine are very nearly as bare as those of the Liffey. The paradox is that sometimes the bargains can now be found in the centres of wealth, in New York, say, or by the banks of the cold green river that leads off the Lake in Geneva. But when beginning an academic career what seems very, indeed horribly metaphysically obvious to oneself are the gaps in one's knowledge – the yawning unplumbed deeps of ignorance (with which one later learns to live!) – but what may be more physically obvious, particularly to others, are the empty shelves, the unbooklined room. Mental and physical furniture are needed urgently. And so there are the temptations – shelf-filling temptations of sets of out-of-fashion authors: on the one hand, Donn Byrne at 20p a copy (dear at the price), and, on the other, George Moore, still a superb bargain in 1st editions at one or two pounds each, and not a writer to cull once the shelves, eventually, get filled. Sets of Charles Lever could be bought relatively cheaply some years ago, but they are now becoming very expensive, though a single volume can still be got reasonably.

With that remark it is time for personal reminiscence. As an undergraduate in Dublin I used to buy some 18th century editions of classical texts – for a shilling or so – largely for the sake of their

superb leather binding, for they were often excellent examples of
that Irish craftsmanship, so well, so lovingly, described by Maurice
James Craig. I treasure, for instance, two of Mahaffy's books, simply but elegantly bound Tauchnitz editions of 1854, of Horace and
of Virgil, the latter used by John Pentland Mahaffy in 38 Trinity
College, Dublin in 1862, and then by Arthur Mahaffy in iii Cloisters
at Magdalen College, Oxford in 1888. And at about the time I got
these, I fell for some equally attractively bound copies of some of
Lever's novels, *Roland Cashel*, *Tom Burke of 'Ours'* and *Davenport
Dunn*: all first editions, illustrated by Phiz. The total costs respectively were 15/-, 17/6 and 15/-, in all, less than £2.50 now. There
they sat on my shelves, in Holland, in Edinburgh, in Adelaide, in
Leeds and then in my study at Rumbling Bridge. At first I never
read them, of course: but I liked the look of them, and told myself
that, one day, of course, I would read them, when there was leisure,
or need. And naturally I couldn't resist adding to my Lever texts –
and I got 20 more volumes – none of them, alas, leather bound, and
some of them foxed and mouldy – but for only some £3 apiece.
When a complete set of his 33 novels came to my notice I never had
sufficient spare cash to buy it. Anyway there they sat, my Levers,
in a row, making me feel like some Yukon prospector, who had
staked a claim to an area of the potentially gold-bearing soil of the
Irish novel.

Lever, however, was not an author whom I had an immediate
impulse to read. But why? I suppose there was an instinctive
reaction against my parents' enjoyment of him, notably of *Harry
Lorrequer*. (I did, however, enjoy Carleton's *Traits and Stories of the
Peasantry* which they thought unfit for my tender years when I was
seven or eight, since, to our Protestant household, frequent excla-
mations like 'My soul to the devil' and 'Glory be to God' could
only encourage taking the names of the Lord and the leader of His
disloyal Opposition in vain.) I also found, you might say, sanction
for my abstention when I came to read Yeats – indeed I suppose for
a long time I was unduly influenced by his lumping Lever together with Lover, whose *Handy Andy* did seem to me to be stage-
Irish in an offensive way and dated, at that.

What did Yeats say about Lever, then? An early oblique reference came in an article published in the *Providence Sunday Journal*
of 2 September 1888.[1] This piece, 'The poet of Ballyshannon', was
based upon William Allingham's *Irish Songs and Poems* (1887) and
Yeats claimed that one needed to have been born and bred in a
western Irish seaboard town to understand these poems. Originally he had an ambition of writing about Sligo as Allingham had

about Ballyshannon. But he had his reservations about Allingham. Though he is always Irish, he said, he is no way national, and 'this widely effects [*sic*] his work'.[2] Allingham created isolated artistic moments; he had a need of central seriousness: 'Like Lever and Lover he does not take the people quite seriously.'[3] This damaging description, the yoking together of Lever and Lover was repeated later in this piece, with even more damaging comments:

What a sad business this non-nationalism has been! It gave to Lever and Lover their shallowness, and still gives to a section of Dublin Society its cynicism! Lever and Lover and Allingham alike, it has deprived of their true audience. Many much less endowed writers than they have more influence in Ireland. Political doctrine was not demanded of them, merely nationalism. They would not take the people seriously – these writers of the Ascendancy – and had to go to England for their audience. To Lever and Lover Ireland became merely a property shop and to Allingham a half serious memory.[4]

Yeats continued his incidental sniping in an essay in 'Popular Ballad Poetry of Ireland'[5] published the following year, but written in 1887:

Lever and Lover, kept apart by opinion from the body of the nation, wrote ever with one eye on London. They never wrote for the people, and neither have they ever, therefore, in prose or verse, written faithfully of the people. Ireland was a metaphor to [Thomas] Moore, to Lever and Lover a merry harlequin, sometimes even pathetic, to be patted and pitied and laughed at so long as he said 'Your honour', and presumed in nowise to be considered a serious or tragic person.[6]

Yeats did not discuss the poetry of Moore, Lever or Lover in this piece; he thought the English reader might be surprised that there was no mention of them. But 'they were never poets of the people'.[7]

In his Introduction to *Representative Irish Tales* Yeats spelt out this idea more clearly:

Charles Lever, unlike Lover and Croker, wrote mainly for his own class. His books are quite sufficiently truthful, but more than any other Irish writer has he caught the ear of the world and come to stand for the entire nation. The vices and virtues of his characters are alike those of the gentry – a gentry such as Ireland has had, with no more sense of responsibility, as a class, than have the dullahans, thrivishes, sowlths, bowas and water sheries of the spirit-ridden peasantry.[8]

In view of his admission that Lever's books were 'quite sufficiently truthful', it is perhaps not quite so surprising that Yeats, in
an article, 'The Young Ireland League', printed in *United Ireland* on
3 October 1891, recommended that reading-rooms should be established by the Young Ireland Societies to be stocked with libraries
containing 'not only the best Irish books, but the masterpieces of
other countries as well'.[9] And he recommended that the libraries
should include:

Mitchel, Mangan, Davis, both prose and verse, all the Irish ballad collection, the radiant and romantic histories of Standish O'Grady, the 'Celtic
Romances' of P W Joyce, the poems of Sir Samuel Ferguson, the poems of
William Allingham, the best novels of Carleton, Banim, Griffin and Lever,
three or four of the Irish stories of Miss Edgeworth, the folk-lore writing of
Hyde, Croker, and Lady Wilde, Moore's Melodies, and some of the best
translations from the old Celtic epics.[10]

In passing, Yeats attacked a list of the 'hundred best Irish books'
which had appeared in *The Freeman's Journal*, and then been published in pamphlet form in 1886. He made his own list of thirty
books, included in a letter to the Editor of the *Daily Express*
(Dublin) of 27 February 1895; these books were ones which seemed
to him 'necessary to the understanding of the imagination of
Ireland.'[11] He had excluded every book in which there was strong
political feeling. In the section 'Novels and Romances' he included,
as the eleventh item out of thirteen in this section of his Lever's
Charles O'Malley, and described it – along with 'Father Tom and the
Pope', 'Barney O'Reirdan' and Carleton's *Traits and Stories of the
Irish Peasantry* – as being

Also in a sense true records but need no recommendation, for the public
has always given a gracious welcome to every book which amuses it and
does not bid it take Ireland seriously.....[12]

This business of the list arose out of Yeats's controversy with
Professor Edward Dowden over 'Irish National Literature'. In *The
Bookman* Yeats pursued the matter further. Four articles appeared
in July, August, September and October 1895. In the last article he
gave another list, now composed of forty titles, and this time
Lever's *Charles O'Malley* again appeared eleventh in the section
'Novels and Romances', which now included eighteen titles.

He then seems to have left Lever alone until 1908, when, in the
course of attacking nineteenth century Irish novelists for having
an English influence running through them, he makes a slight
exception for Lever:

Here and there, of course, one finds Irish elements. In Lever, for instance, even after one has put aside all that is second-hand, there is a rightful Irish gaiety, but one finds these elements only just in so far as the writers had come to know themselves in the socratic sense.[13]

Two more remarks about Lever are to be found, both in the section of *Autobiographies* entitled 'The Trembling of the Veil'. The first contrasted Lever with the Wildes: 'The Wilde family was clearly of the sort that fed the imagination of Charles Lever, dirty, untidy, daring, and what Charles Lever, who loved more normal activities, might not have valued so highly, very imaginative and learned.'[14] The second described some of the youthful Yeats's Dublin enemies: 'There were others with followers of their own, and too old or indifferent to join our Society. Old men who had never accepted Young Ireland, or middle-aged men kept by some family tradition to the school of thought before it arose, to the Ireland of Daniel O'Connell and of Lever and of Thomas Moore, convivial Ireland with the traditional tear and smile.'[15]

There are problems here. How many of Lever's thirty novels had Yeats actually read? And how right was he in his critical view of Lever? (It was shared by Lady Gregory: how many of the novels had she read?) We could argue that, since he put *Charles O'Malley* into his reading list, he regarded that as 'the best of Lever'. But what was the nature, the range of Lever's novels from which he could select? I began to read my Lever texts. But who was Lever, anyway?

II

Charles James Lever was born in Dublin in 1806. His father James Lever, a builder's apprentice who came to Dublin from Manchester, became a successful builder and contractor, who built the Custom House, the General Post Office, the Round Church and St George's Church. He adapted the Parliament building when it became a bank after the Act of Union. He married a Miss Chandler, from County Kilkenny, of Cromwellian stock. Lever sent his two sons to Trinity College, remarking that they could not live the lives of idle gentlemen. He gave them 'a fair start in life but nothing to deprive them of the pleasure of making their fortunes.'[16] John, the elder brother, entered the Church of Ireland, and Charles drew his early knowledge of the West from visits to him to Portumna in County Galway.

Tutored by his brother, Charles went to various small schools in Dublin. His schooldays were not uneventful as W. J. Fitzpatrick points out in his *Life of Charles Lever*:

The north side of Dublin was then noted for the escapades of vagabonds who played malign tricks on unoffending citizens. Party feeling ran high in those days. Lever's schoolfellows, who all represented families with unpopular sympathies, were more than once pelted as they passed. The roughs found allies in the pupils of another school in Grenville Street – one of inferior social caste. These boys were under the able generalship of a stripling not undistinguished in after life. Skirmishes took place, and at last it was agreed that a regular pitched battle should be fought in Mountjoy Fields, then a piece of waste ground on which Gardiner Street Church and Convent have since been built. Lever helped to organise the tiny troops. The little army had its companies, commander-in-chief, its outlying pickets, reserves, and even its sappers and miners. Mr Robert Mallet, a subsequent eminent engineer and FRS, first showed his talents by mining the ground on which the enemy were to be next day engaged. A small mine was worked, and some pounds of blasting powder laid. The opposite faction mustered at length in great force, and opened the fight by a brisk discharge of sharp stones, which was returned by Mr Wright's boys with shouts of defiance, and a fire of miniature cannon. A charge forward was then made by the roughs, some of whom were provided with black thorns, which, if applied to the skulls of the juvenile army, would have inflicted serious subsequent loss on letters, law, science, physic, and divinity. Dr Biggar is now almost the only survivor who took part in this conflict. He held a high rank in the command, and just as the enemy was about to fall upon them like an avalanche, word was given to fire the mine, which a lighted cigar promptly accomplished. The explosion scattered dismay, and inflicted some slight bodily wounds. Lever's company suffered quite as much as the enemy; the faces on both sides were scorched and scratched. The army of the north retreated in disorder, leaving Mr Wright's pupils in possession of the field – only to be scared, however, by the rapid approach of the police, who, with their glazed caps and side arms, the uniform of that day, entered Mountjoy Fields at every point. Marlborough Street Police Office exhibited a scene of some excitement when the case came on next day. Hanging was still the penalty for incendiarism; and terrible forebodings of the gibbet or Botany Bay smote the small prisoners brought up before Mr Magrath, who, in his occasional ebullitions of temper, resembled Mr Fang, Oliver Twist's stern judge: and Fang, we know, was a veritable portrait. Some fussy matrons were in attendance to testify that the north side had been all but blown into the southern division by the shock, while the weak police seem to have regarded the whole affair very much as a god-send. The boy-prisoners, including Edward Dix, afterwards police magistrate, are described by Dr Biggar as tongue-tied. Mr Magrath said it was a bad case, and scowled. The police shook their heads, and a pin might be heard to drop. At last a boy came forward as spokesman, and appealed to the bench. The magistrate declared that they were before him on a charge of riot and outrage, which it behoved him to suppress with a firm hand. Lever submitted that the provocation they received from a lawless gang justified them in inflicting condign punishment: that the vagabonds were the first aggressors; that self-defence was the first law of nature, and that a war of juveniles was not worse in principle than war waged by wiser heads.

MR MAGRATH. – 'But you are not to take the law into your own hands. Moreover, you use firearms and introduce gunpowder into a mine previously prepared, and with malice prepense.'

MASTER LEVER. – 'All sound and smoke, sir; our cannon were only toy-guns, and the mine a mimic mine. Most of us may take up arms yet in defence of our king and country; and might we not be worse employed than in learning the science at the most susceptible period of our lives?'

Mr Magrath's attitude of hostility relaxed: without complimenting Lever on his eloquence, he certainly seemed struck by it; and he brought the case to a close by imposing sundry small fines, which would suffice, he said, to satisfy offended justice.

This magistrate was himself soon after arraigned for much graver offences. He was proved guilty of embezzlement and banished. As for Master Biggar – the juvenile commander-in-chief – he was flogged five successive days because of the determination with which he refused to divulge the spot where Mallet had concealed his mining powder.

Charles Lever entered Trinity in 1822. Here he had a full life, of parties, riding, sailing, drinking, and hoaxing; he also read widely, enjoying Terence, Molière, Shakespeare, Cervantes, Le Sage and the classic Anglo-Irish writers, Swift, Sterne, Goldsmith, Sheridan. A graduate in 1827, he set off for the wilds of Canada and New York state. He was held captive by an Indian tribe, rescued by a squaw, and walked the streets of Quebec 'in the moccasins and with the head feathers'. (His novels *Con Cregan* and *Arthur O'Leary* draw on his North American experiences.) He brought back an Indian canoe with which he cut a dash on the Grand Canal on his return to Dublin.

From Dublin to Paris and to Germany, where he studied at Gottingen, and then to Louvain. He was destined for medicine; he graduated MB in 1831, but failed the College of Surgeons' Fellowship and so gave up his brief attempts to become a successful Dublin doctor and instead accepted the post of dispensary doctor in Country Clare, experiencing the horrors of a cholera epidemic there for four months. Next he spent five years in Derry, at Portstewart, again as a dispensary doctor. While here he married Kate Baker with whom he had fallen in love as a schoolboy in Dublin and whom he loved all his life. It was a secret marriage because her father, a schoolmaster who had moved to Navan, and Lever's own father disapproved thoroughly, James Lever because Kate had no money.

Provincial life – and the tiresome nature of his employers, the Poor-Law guardians – bored him. He went to Brussels where he built up a promising practice and had a highly enjoyable social life. But in 1842 he gave this up and returned to Dublin: he had decided to live by his pen. He was offered the editorship of the *Dublin University Magazine* on condition he contributed part of a story each month, and he was given what was then a very good salary of £1,200 a year. He lived at Templeogue House (in our times Austin Clarke lived in Bridge House, Templeogue) and entertained lavishly there.

What had led to this change? Largely the success of *The Confessions of Harry Lorrequer*, the first instalment of which had appeared in the *Dublin University Magazine* in 1837. Here was the episodic story of a hero whose life was an energetic round of dining, drinking, dancing, riding, steeplechasing, pigeon shooting and tandem driving; this active, hearty life of a property owner was matched to a curiously dreamy character who plays a mock Hamlet-like role, his doings translated into superb farce against the comic background of the garrison's social life. Lever had begun writing in imitation of William Hamilton Maxwell, the Scottish cleric and author of *Wild Sports of the West* and *Tales of the Peninsula War*. Maxwell had encouraged Lever to write, and Lever was surprised by his success, *Harry Lorrequer* being published in book form in three volumes, and his future work being sought by rival Dublin and London publishers.

There followed *Charles O'Malley*, written in Brussels, when Lever was

very low with fortune, and the success of a new venture was pretty much as eventful to me as the turn of the right colour at rouge et noir. At the same time I had then an amount of spring in my temperament, and a power of enjoying life, which I can honestly say I never found surpassed. The world had for me all the interest of an admirable comedy.[17]

This novel, obviously considered Lever's best by Yeats, was strung together somewhat more effectively than the picaresque *Harry Lorrequer*. There is a picture of ascendancy life, of government corruption, of electoral malpractice, of riotous undergraduate behaviour in Trinity College personified by Frank Webber, a character founded on the man who had shared rooms in college with Lever. The hero leaves the university for the army and having had more than his share of the Peninsula War, returns to his uncle's estate, which he runs efficiently, only to come back to the army when Napoleon escapes from Elba. Finally he marries one of the heroines and settles down in the West. Lever describes the topography of the battles superbly; he inserts comic situations and anecdotes freely; and he conveys, notably in the excellent account of Waterloo, his disgust at the waste of war. There are lively characterisations, emphasised by a caricaturist's sense of dominant humours, and Lever casts a sharply satiric look over landlords, undergraduates, military man, and servants alike. The whole story, punctuated by vivacious songs, rattles along at a lively speed, and was enormously successful. *Harry Lorrequer* had been written to amuse but *Charles O'Malley* deliberately showed what pre-union Ireland was like in one of its aspects. For three years Lever edited the *Dublin University Magazine*, finishing *Jack Hinton* and writing several novels, among them *Tom Burke of 'Ours'* and *The O'Donoghue*, which not only described military life but set it in a historico-political background.

When he left Ireland again, in 1845, Lever moved from Brussels to Bonn; then he rented a castle in the Tyrol; after this he tried Zurich and Lake Constance, moving thence to Florence. He lived high in Florence, his horses and equipage being notably showy, his expenses vast. In Hood's phrase, he said he was 'sipping champagne on a tight rope'[18] for his royalties were declining. In the 1850s he tried to get some public post but his hopes vanished with the fall of Lord Derby's ministry. In 1854 he visited Ireland and was depressed by his reception, writing that he received as much ridicule as was consistent with viceregal politeness to bestow, and the small wit of ADC's to inflict. *The Martins of Cro' Martin* of 1854 shows an increasing awareness of Ireland's political problems, illustrating the effects of rapid social change and the emergence of a new middle class. He saw English rule of Ireland as tragic in its consequences and resented his role of jester rather than tragedian as his view of life deepened. He was appointed Vice-Consul at La Spezia in 1858. His spendthrift son died in 1863 and with him died the remains of Lever's social ambitions. He had escaped from his middle class situation in Ireland only to find English high society empty, vain, and selfish. Depressed by what he now knew of government politics and diplomacy, a visit to London in 1856 led him to dislike also the literary world there, 'a self perpetuating clique passing promissory notes on one another'.[19]. He was promoted to the post of Consul at Trieste in 1867. It did not greatly please him to be in this Dalmatian exile, and his depression deepened when his wife became ill in 1869 and died in 1870. He himself died two years later.

His last novel, *Lord Kilgobbin*, was dedicated to her and the dedication shows us something of the fierce affection he had for her, and the equally fierce dislike of English rule he had come to hold. His novels from the 'forties onward show this increasingly critical spirit, a sense of impending disaster no less acute than Yeats's own. And yet Yeats and most Irish critics have labelled him a mere creator of the stage Irishman, a hearty, a garrison writer. The only conclusion one is forced to is that they accepted the fashionable labels and read no further than *Harry Lorrequer* and *Charles O'Malley*. They got hold of the wrong Lever.

Let me now sketch very briefly indeed something of what they missed. I shall be very selective, bearing in mind that there are thirty-three novels, but I want to suggest that Lever gives us a fascinating insight into eighteenth and nineteenth century Irish life. By this I mean an insight into history and politics as well as social, economic, military and sporting details, as well as interpretations of Irish character in speech and action, for Lever like all Irishmen was deeply conscious of the different ways Irish and English speak and think. These novels were written by a man who travelled, who was well read and highly intelligent, who knew Ireland's poverty and bravery as perhaps only a dispensary doctor could, who came to know how government or, rather, British party politics worked, who increasingly wanted to air his own point of view, who provided a rich range of character as well as historical background and physical locale in his writings, who could provide examples of both the dashing feckless Ascendancy and the self-deluding romantic, being himself a subtle blend of romantic and realist.

It will be clear to any contemporary reader who approaches *Charles O'Malley* that Lever ran into unduly sensitive nationalist attitudes. Even Shaw, who has paid tribute to Lever most handsomely, whose criticism ought to be taken as an antidote to Yeats's, has recorded some misgivings or reservations about Micky Free, O'Malley's servant. But is the stage Irishry of this character so different from the stage cockney of, say, Sam Weller? It is possible that the excessive nationalist bias of critics neglected the harsh criticism of Irish political life and social life dropped, incidentally at it were, in this novel. While the faked death of Charles O'Malley's uncle is primarily amusing it also reflects upon the attitudes of landowners to debt and mortgages, as an incidental passage shows the casual attitude young officers adopted to the bills they ran up with tradespeople.

The first signs of direct criticism of English attitudes to Ireland come in *Jack Hinton* (1840), where Lever placed a young Englishman in Ireland as an ADC. This device of seeing Ireland through a stranger's eyes was originally developed by Maria Edgeworth, from whose novels – and whose encouragement and advice – Lever learned much. Jack Hinton is shown the wretchedness of Ireland, and told that it is caused by English misrule. The English, argues Father Tom Loftus, do not know, or will not know the Irish: 'More prone to punish than prevent, you are satisfied with the working of the law, and not shocked by the accumulation of crime; and, when broken by poverty and paralysed by famine, a gloomy desolation spreads over the land, you meet in terms of congratulations to talk over tranquillised Ireland'.[20] The priest argues that English laws and institutions are inadequate and unsuitable for Irish conditions; he maintains that the Irish see them as sources of their misery and instruments of tyranny. And the picture is Swiftian in its analysis, because the Irish do not help themselves. Dublin is shown as it was after the Union, with a nostalgic look at the glories of the late eighteenth century 'when the names of Burke, Sheridan, Grattan and Curran start up'.[21] The heroine's father, Sir William Bellew, deals with 'the brightest period in Ireland's history – when wealth and genius were rife in the land, and when the joyous traits of Irish character were elicited in all their force by prosperity and happiness. It was then shone forth in all their brilliancy the great spirits whose flashing wit and glittering fancy have cast a sunlight over their native country, that even now in the twilight of the past, continues to illuminate it. Alas! they have no heritors to their fame – they have left no successors behind them'.[22]

The Viceregal court is degenerate – the Viceroy when drunk knights O'Grady's servant Corny Delany – this was based on a real incident; the social life of Dublin is being invaded by *nouveaux riches*. But there is a larger aim behind the novel, which Lever described later. He had been provoked by characteristically disparaging remarks on Ireland and Irishmen in the London press and he decided not only to show an Englishman misjudging Irish people but also to demonstrate that the Irish squire, priest and peasant were not like anything in the larger island, that the Dublin professional men, officials and shopkeepers had traits and distinctions entirely their own. He saw Irish habits of quizzical speech playing on the credulity of visitors[23]; he stressed the virtues of Irishwomen who were not overcome by 'the fatigues of fashionable life' and retained an enjoyment of society. Lever, whose youth had been coloured by the loss of Dublin's former vitality as a capital which was caused by the Union (and the consequent removal of Parliament and aristocracy to London), had come to see that Dublin had not necessarily lost a great deal. His hero speaks of 'the supercilious cant and unimpassioned coldness of London manners'.[24]

Jack Hinton is, relatively speaking, an early novel, begun in Brussels. What of those that Lever wrote while in Dublin editing the *Dublin University Magazine*? If we read *Tom Burke of Ours* – and I have now reaped the rewards of my 15/- expenditure: after all these years I have enjoyed reading the two leather bound volumes – we find the so-called 'garrison writer' taking as his hero a fourteen-year-old orphan who is caught up with the loathing for British rule in Ireland – witnesses the savagery of the yeomanry after 1798 – and escapes from trial in Dublin to arrive in France, join the Polytechnique and become an officer in Napoleon's army. Disgusted by the arrogance of the French in victory and the suspicion attaching to him personally, he resigns his commission and returns to Ireland, is again arrested, and is lucky to be acquitted. His trial reveals the duplicity and the degradation of informers and *agents provocateurs*. He returns to France to fight for Napoleon and the romantic ends of what is largely a military-historical novel are tied up. This is an anti-Dublin Castle, anti-British novel, though the hero is befriended at several points in the story by an eccentric English officer – but even he is shown to misunderstand the Irish utterly.

In 1845 Lever also published *St Patrick's Eve* which deals with the cholera epidemic of 1832, as it effected the population around Lough Corrib. Here we find him dealing with the poverty, 'the same dull routine of toil and privation', of small farmers and peasants, with faction fights, and with the relations between landlords and their agents and the tenantry. Here is both sympathy for those in adversity and a stern warning that prosperity has duties.

In the 1872 Introduction to *The O'Donoghue* (1845) Lever doubted whether it had been right to extinguish the old feudalism which bound peasant to landlord before preparing for the new relationship of gain and loss which was coming into being. And he wrote a superb account in this same preface of this feudal aristocracy, wondering whether it could change its nature:

Between the great families – the old houses of the land and the present race of proprietors – there lay a couple of generations of men, who with all the traditions and many of the pretensions of birth and fortune, had really become in ideas, modes of life, and habits, very little above the peasantry around them. They inhabited, it is true, 'the great house', and they were in name the owners of the soil, but crippled by debt and overborne by mortgages, they subsisted in a shifty conflict with their creditors, rack-renting their miserable tenants to maintain it. Survivors of everything but pride of family, they stood there like the stumps, blackened and charred, the last remnants of a burnt forest, their proportions attesting the noble growth that had preceded them. What would the descendants of these men prove when, destitute of fortune and helpless, they were thrown upon a world that actually regarded them as blameable for the unhappy condition of Ireland?[25]

Here Lever attacks 'duty work',[26] and the enaction of 'gifts' by unscrupulous agents which led to 'the great man of the great house' being felt to be an oppressor.[27]

This novel shows Lever's increasing contempt for 'Castle' society[28] and for the administration in Ireland.[29] In *The Knight of Gwynne* (1846) he showed how the Union and the destruction of the Irish Parliament in Dublin, once decided upon in England, had been pushed through by 'gross corruption' and 'trafficking for title and place'. Here Lever picked out the reasons for the fall of the Ascendancy, a 'fatal taste for prodigality'. The gentry were 'reckless, wasteful, extravagant'; they lived beyond their means; they were without foresight or prudence (which they would have regarded as meanness) – while believing they were sustaining the honour of the country they were sapping the foundations of its prosperity. The English in England, however, were also to blame. For instance, they simply had not faced the reasons for the disastrous famine of the mid-century. In *The Dodd Family Abroad* (1854) one of Lever's characters attacks the English view that the peasantry's laziness had caused the famine:

Ask him, did he ever try to cut turf with two meals of wet potatoes per diem....

The whole ingenuity of mankind would seem devoted to ascertaining how much a bullock can eat, and how little will feed a labourer. Stuff one and starve the other, and you may be the President of an Agricultural Society and Chairman of your Union [workhouse].

Lever continued his analysis of the Ascendancy's situation in *The Martins of Cro' Martin* (1854), where he again dealt with the cholera epidemic of 1832, giving affectionate praise to the 'poor famished and forgotten people' of Clare. In this novel he pictured the old relationship between landlords and tenants collapsing and estrangement between the two classes deepening. Despite mistakes, however, he thought more generosity and forbearance on both sides was emerging.[30] Later he saw the post-famine period as one of transition, and in his preface to the 1872 edition he wrote that.

There was not at that time the armed resistance to rents, nor the threatening letter system to which we were afterwards to become accustomed, still less was there the thought that the Legislature would interfere to legalise the demands by which the tenant was able to his landlord; and for the brief interval there did seem a possibility of reuniting once again, by the ties of benefit and gratitude, the two 'classes whose real welfare depends on concord and harmony.'[31]

In *Barrington* (1862) Lever further explored the Ascendancy in decline. Barrington, a former pre-Union Dublin parliamentarian, and his sister, a former belle in Castle society, try to manage an inn in the country, she apparently realistically, accepting her role as that of the hostess of a little wayside inn, he romantically pretending the clients were guests and pouring the remnants of the family's money into useless law suits. The return of brother and sister to the once fashionable and now decaying Reynolds Hotel in Dominick Street in Dublin echoes Maria Edgeworth's picture of the faded glories of the former capital in *The Absentee*. Lever, however, treats this Anglo-Irish nostalgia for the past with detachment.

His increasing dislike of English administrators and Dublin Castle Society emerges here and there in *Sir Brook Fossbrooke* (1865), a novel with a complex plot and increased depth in portrayal of character. Here there are attacks on jobbery, police spying, the use of informers, the invention of 'treason-felony'. Lever had developed some Swiftian irony; and he also speculated on the differences in English and Irish character.

Plodding unadorned ability, even of a high order, meets little favour in Ireland, while on the other side of the Channel Irish quickness is accounted as levity, and the rapid appreciation of a question without the detail of long labour and thought, is set down as the lucky hit of a lively but very idle intelligence[32].

And he had direct scorn for those English officials in Ireland from whose rudeness he had himself suffered:

Is it fancy, or am I right in supposing that English officials have a manner specially assumed for Ireland and the Irish – a thing like the fur cloak a man wears in Russia, or the snowshoes he puts on in Lapland not intended for other latitudes, but admirably adapted for the locality it is made for?.... I do not say it is a bad manner – a presuming manner – a manner of depreciation towards those it is used to, or a manner indicative of indifference in him who uses it. I simply say that they who employ it keep it as especially for Ireland as they keep their Macintosh capes for wet weather, and would no more think of displaying it in England than they would go to her Majesty's levee in a shooting-jacket.[33]

Lever's last novel – and the best of them – *Lord Kilgobbin* (1870) provides a sombre story, illustrating how Ireland was misgoverned and ready to explode, in his words 'uneasy, disquieted and angry'. Here are the views of Molyneux and Swift given fresh life: here is fierce indignation at the ineptitude of English politicians who vacillated between repression and submission to terrorism, here is a vacuum, for he thought that the Anglo-Irish had lost their power, indeed their will to govern the country. The landlords were decadent, the Fenians inefficient, and he disliked the new citified commercial class that was emerging out of the poverty of the country people, weakened by the effects of famine and by continuing emigration. However, despite this anger and despair, despite his feeling of unpending catastrophe Lever loved his country; he surveyed its politics sardonically, at time detachedly; he was Anglo-Irish in his enjoyment of scenery, in his analysis of the complexity of character, in his sharp awareness of the perennial differences between Irish and English sensibilities. How could Yeats and Lady Gregory and a horde of lesser writers have got hold of the wrong Lever? I suggest to you that they read the wrong labels, and accepted them as true, without testing the truth by reading the novels that they too readily wrote off.

LEVER'S *LORD KILGOBBIN*

Charles Lever has been unreasonably treated by most critics of Anglo-Irish literature. He wrote thirty-three novels in thirty-five years, between 1837 and 1872, and these are not at all the same in tone. Lever, however, has been generally dismissed by Irish critics as a novelist who dealt in stage Irish characters or merely gave a picture of the lighter side of garrison life in Ireland. The labels rightly attached to his earlier novels *Harry Lorrequer* (1837), *Charles O'Malley* (1841) and *Arthur O'Leary* (1844) were also applied to his subsequent and very different novels. The earlier novels, light-hearted and full of lively incident, were rollicking tomes of nine-teenth-century gaiety, akin most of all perhaps in their ebullience to the farcical elements in Farquhar's earlier comedies. Carleton attacked Lever, notably in an unsigned review it in *The Nation*, October 1843, in which he accused Lever of 'selling us for pounds, shillings and pence', and regarded him as not unlike a common informer 'receiving good pay from England for bearing false witness against his country'. Political leaders also criticized him adversely, Daniel O'Connell with some savagery and Thomas Davis with a dislike of his 'Donnybrook school' depictions of Irishmen. When Lever left Ireland in 1845, the attacks largely ceased. Lever himself had begun to write historical rather than military novels, to examine the social milieu outside Ireland in European novels, to take in the political scene and to comment critically on life itself

This deepening in Lever's understanding, accompanied as it was by corresponding developments in style and technique, seems not to have been acknowledged by critics in Ireland. It was as if the earlier nationalistic commentators had precluded any subsequent detachment of viewpoint, any objective analysis of what Lever was actually writing from the middle of the 'forties to the middle 'fifties, or indeed as if they had created a climate in which barely any comment at all was made on his writings after 1845. From the middle eighteen-fifties to his last novel *Lord Kilgobbin* (1872) Lever wrote several novels which might well have appealed even to extremely nationalistic critics: but the labels had been printed in the 'thirties and 'forties and continued to be attached. There was one perceptive article in *Blackwood's Magazine*, April 1862, which,

while it mourned the departure of the earlier heroes, did recognize
Lever's increased novelistic skill and deeper human sympathy.

Yeats, however, continued the denigration. Intent on rooting out
from Irish literature the image of the stage Irishman, he entirely
failed to do justice to Lever's later novels, let alone the earlier.
E. A. Boyd followed Yeats's example, stressing the stage Irish element in Lever in *Ireland's Literary Renaissance* (1968). Stephen Gwynn
and Hugh Law, however, realized that Lever had been unreasonably denigrated, but Daniel Corkery naturally enough found Lever
unacceptable in his view of Anglo-Irish literature. Contemporary
critics tend to follow these traditional views, Benedict Kiely, for
instance, stressing the rollicking aspect of Lever's work in *Modern
Irish Fiction* while Vivian Mercier in *The Irish Comic Tradition* (1962)
concentrates on Lever's small development of the grotesque. There
are some exceptions. For instance, Roger McHugh in 'Charles
Lever', an article in *Studies* XXVII, 1938, argued that Lever gave a
full picture of various aspects of political and social life in nineteenth-century Ireland, and it is significant that Shaw had earlier
acknowledged his debt to Lever in the preface to *Major Barbara*
(1905). He found Lever poignant, and Lever's tragi-comic treatment of the irony of the conflict between real life and the romantic
imagination as well as the earlier writer's impartiality impressed
him deeply.

This detached impartiality grew steadily in Lever and reached
its fullest development in his last novel *Lord Kilgobbin*. This novel,
written between 1870 and 1872, was dedicated to the memory of
his wife, and written 'in breaking health and broken spirits'. In it
Lever casts a cold eye on political life in both Ireland and England;
analytically aware of the interactions between the two countries, he
shows that he had learned – probably from Maria Edgeworth and
from Disraeli's political novels – the attraction of blending political
affairs with those of the heart. His novel is no romance; the common sense materialism of marriage looms large in the thoughts if
not always the emotions of its younger as well as its older characters.

Lord Kilgobbin is a long novel, of about 220,000 words, and it
moves, at first, at a leisurely pace. Its tempo, however, quickens
considerably as the story progresses, its complications develop and
its interest intensifies. This is a sombre book. Lever sets most of the
action in the flat midland country of Ireland, Kilgobbin Castle
being situated in King's County (modern Offaly) and near to
Moate, in present-day Westmeath. The rain is early described as
falling steadily on the bogland and through its pervading presence

Lever evokes the smell of damp decay which invests the whole Irish situation in his day. The landlords were decadent – indeed the Kilgobbin estate is no model of management, and evictions, inevitably the cause of much human suffering, take place on a neighbouring estate – yet while Lever dislikes the manner in which the British government is ruling Ireland he is equally distrustful of the apparent alternative of mob rule which a successful Fenian rising might introduce. The future is unsettled and decidedly disturbing.

Against this background Lever gives us the drama of his plot. He owed much to Scott. Like Scott he can lapse into blank verse in his narrative descriptions; like Scott he can prolong the earlier stages of a story to what becomes, for modern readers, a tediously drawn out length; but like Scott he can create unusual characters and create an evocative regional atmosphere. He also owed much to Balzac, and he presents us in this novel with a Balzacian view of life. Confidently in control of his canvas, he writes with the skill and control of experience, and he has an eye for significant detail, for dialogue, and for the general Irish social scene.

Lever focuses interest on the eight younger characters. To a certain extent he may have been influenced by Maria Edgeworth's novel *Patronage* (1814), in which she discussed the problem of how members of an Anglo-Irish family were to make their way in the world – a matter obviously discussed frequently and fully in the talkative Edgeworth family, for Maria's father Richard Lovell Edgeworth had had twenty-two children by his four wives. Lever shows us two undergraduates at Trinity College who have not yet settled on suitable careers. Dick Kearney, the son of the owner of Kilgobbin Castle, echoes his father's earlier extravagances. He is slow, plodding, self-satisfied and dull: in short not a very attractive young man. Lever contrasts him with Joseph Atlee, who shares his rooms in college. The son of a Presbyterian minister in Northern Ireland, Atlee is indolent, discursive, superficial and decidedly sharp-witted. Irresistibly attracted by the fraudulent in literature, he himself writes anonymously for journals of different political beliefs as well as secretly writing nationalist ballads. Something of his ambitious nature appears in the soliloquies which Lever supplies as an occasional change from his own role as omniscient narrator, and in an early piece of self-communing Atlee also ponders on the contrast between his intellectual powers and his penniless state. During the course of the novel we trace Dick's emergence from self satisfaction into annoyance at his father's idea of a career in law for him; he has no interest in the estate and forms a plan of emigrating to Australia: finally he is given a place in the police, through Atlee's not entirely disinterested efforts. Atlee's own career is pursued with energy and skill, once he has seen a way into the world of affairs through making himself useful to the Viceroy's aide-de-camp, Cecil Walpole, and later to the Viceroy himself, Lord Danesbury.

Dick Kearney and Joseph Atlee are young Irishmen in search of a career. It is perhaps significant that they are contrasted with two practical and pragmatic young Englishmen both already successfully launched into theirs. Cecil Walpole, a gifted dilettante, greater in promise than performance, has done a little of almost everything and likes to display 'the scores of things he might be, instead of that mild very ordinary young gentleman' that he is. A promising Whig, he is summed up by Lever as a political animal, who coquets with Radical views but fastidiously avoids contact with the mob. (Lever had been disillusioned by Whiggery, and his dislike of Gladstone shines through at times, not least in the matter of the weaker clarets.) We meet him in the Blue Goat at Moate, where he and his companion have come on a fishing trip from Dublin. His friend, Major Henry Lockwood, another aide-de-camp, takes a Wellingtonian view of the need for 'putting down': a good soldier, a 'very safe' character, his dullness is similar to Dick Kearney's, though we discover later that he is unlike Dick in being proud of his estate in England, which, though small, is very successfully run. Something of Scott's puzzlement at how the English are more successful than the Scots underlies Lever's presentation of these four young men: why are the English more *au fait* with the ways of the world than the Irishmen; why should they possess power while the equally intelligent, more lively and imaginative Irish do not? He concentrates attention on the two more intelligent young men: the successful English politician and the Irish would-be politician; we see Atlee's fortunes rising as Walpole's fall. Both men pursue the same two women with some calculation and these involvements form a lively part of the latter stages of the novel.

Lever often gave his women characters more life and energy, more force of personality than his men, and in *Lord Kilgobbin* he drew yet another contrast: between Kate Kearney, who managed her father's estate, insofar as it could be managed, with the Stewart, Peter Gill, as a kind of Grand Vizier. Her 'fine temper and genial disposition' offset Gill's craft and subtlety in dealing with the tenants, who are wretchedly poor (but, as Lever is careful to point out, far from unhappy). Kate is unambitious and unpretentious; an open-air girl, she likes living at Kilgobbin. This is a difficult experience for her cousin Nina Kostalergi, who has recently arrived at the Castle and finds its lack of social life very different from the fashionable world she has known in Italy. Her mother, Matthew Kearney's sister, had married the Secretary of the Greek legation at Naples, Spiridion Kostalergi, a compulsive gambler who lost his post after a duel. This was a romantic marriage – the Irish girl having earlier refused 'sensible offers' – but after Nina's mother had died in poverty in Palermo Spiridion brought Nina to Rome intending to make her a *prima donna*. She has escaped this fate by fleeing to Ireland and appealing to Matthew who takes her into the family. She sings superbly, she paints, she converses well and she is highly temperamental and flirtatious. Lever provides a steady view of the realities of marriage both in his own comments and in the conversations of the characters throughout the novel: social position and financial standing are carefully considered by the characters though emotion will keep breaking through!

The two girls receive Walpole at the Castle in Matthew's absence – Lockwood has disapproved of the visit once he hears Walpole had known Nina in Italy, for Walpole is engaged to his cousin Lady Maude Bickerstaffe – and Walpole anticipates some romantic episode as he is driven across the wet bogland from Moate to the Castle. A very different kind of episode, however, ensues, for the Castle is attacked by an armed band in search of weapons. Kate is largely responsible for a successful defence of the Castle against them, and in this affray Walpole is wounded. Nina teases him about his declaration to her in Italy, and she quickly sees through Atlee's ambitions (he and Dick have arrived at the Castle after the affray) and tells him that he and she are both Bohemians.

Lever varies the action and skilfully threads his characters in and out of the plot. Matthew Kearney has been described as an indolent and impoverished landlord. He is known locally as Lord Kilgobbin (James the Second had created an ancestor a viscount; he had sheltered the fleeing king after the Battle of the Boyne, but the title was largely concealed during the Williamite period). His eccentric neighbour Betty O'Shea visits him and reveals that Peter Gill who has resigned will become her Stewart at Shea's Barn. She is no respecter of persons, her direct speech is overbearing, and she is unreasonable, indeed, unfair, in her treatment of Kate. She is determined her nephew Gorman O'Shea, now serving in the Austrian army, shall form no connection with the improvident Kearneys. Nina, with justification, calls her 'an insufferable old woman.'

Two more men enter the story. While Atlee is making himself

agreeable to Walpole and later to the Viceroy in Wales, Dick
Kearney finds Atlee's friend Dan Donoghan in his rooms at Trinity,
and invites him to stay *incognito* at the Castle. He persuades Dick
to stand as a candidate for King's County. Donoghan is a Fenian
leader who has escaped from Dartmoor. Gorman O'Shea returns on
leave from Austria to visit his aunt. His return coincides with a
political meeting at Moate. Lever gives us an acute analysis of the
political situation from Donoghan's point of view as well as the
line pursued by the local Whig candidate, who dines with Miss
O'Shea and enlists support from the Catholic Church.

Lever's earlier novels favoured military heroes and in *Lord
Kilgobbin* the two more dashing characters win the ladies, after
overcoming apparently insuperable difficulties. Gorman O'Shea is
cut off by his aunt, and given hospitality by Matthew while he
makes up his mind what to do. He has not sufficient funds to sup-
plement his pay in the Austrian army. He becomes involved in a
misunderstanding with Peter Gill which leads to both of them
falling out of a balcony at Shea's Barn, whereupon Gill's support-
ers beat up O'Shea savagely. Though he eventually recovers, he has
to be hurried from the gaol to Kilgobbin Castle (a nice piece of co-
operation between Matthew Kearney and the Tory magistrates)
only to face the threat of charges of burglary and assault – O'Shea
not having realized his aunt had virtually handed over her estate
to Gill. Donoghan meanwhile has declared his romantic interest in
Nina, but he is on the run, and she is likely to marry Walpole who,
after Lady Maude has broken with him, proposes to Nina and is
accepted on condition his family receive her. By this time his plans
to avoid confrontation with the Fenians have become public property whereupon Lord Danesbury has resigned as Viceroy. Walpole
has been appointed Ambassador to Guatemala – an undistinguished and dangerous post – Lord Danesbury taking up his old
post as Ambassador to the Porte.

Atlee, whose insinuations have helped to increase the breach
between Walpole and Lady Maude, himself makes a declaration to
this cold English beauty and, repulsed, thinks of marrying Nina.
He has gone to Turkey and Greece on Lord Danesbury's business
and has almost negotiated a payment of £10,000 from Lord
Danesbury to Spiridion Kostalergi (for the return of indiscreet letters) which is to be Nina's dowry. But he fails in virtually all his
plans. Nina, who has been conveying information to Donoghan
about the measures taken against him and also telling him that
some of those through whom, he had told her, messages could be
secretly conveyed to him, were informers, finally runs away with

him, being married in Maryborough on their way to a new life in America. Donoghan has ordered Peter Gill and other witnesses to leave Ireland, so the case against O'Shea collapses. His aunt, moved by his illness, returns to arrange his becoming master of Shea's Barn and the estate on condition he marries Kate, who has earlier refused a lamely put proposal from Lockwood. Atlee conveys the news of Nina's marriage to Walpole who – not unreasonably, given his nature – finds it all very Irish.

Any résumé of the plot of this novel hardly reveals the total effect of its portrayal of a county torn with unrest. Lever mocks the Viceregal system, officialdom's government of Ireland from Dublin Castle. Lord Danesbury (who is a Disraelian character) is appointed because he knows nothing of Ireland, and, once he has performed some official duties, retreats to his family place in Wales, still interested in the affairs of Turkey where he had previously been ambassador. He leaves everything in Ireland to subordinates whose methods are to divide and rule. Lever's satiric exposé of Castle policies follows on the earlier attack in *Sir Brook Fossbrooke* (1866) where he expressed his unease at the methods of government. He is, of course, equally ready to reveal the inefficiencies and unreliability of the Fenian movement, notoriously riddled by intelligence agents and informers paid by Dublin Castle. Donoghan realizes that he is out of step with the times and has the intelligence to leave Ireland.

The movement from the corruption or the decadence of the landlord to the emergence into power of a new commercial middle-class from the peasantry is hinted at in the career of Peter Gill. This is yet another echo, perhaps, of Maria Edgeworth. In *Castle Rackrent* the process takes place with four generations of Rackrents and two of the Quirkes, for Thady, the apparently loyal stewart of the Rackrent family, tells the story of how the estate is finally taken over by his son Jason. Peter Gill goes through the whole cycle himself, for he begins as an apparently loyal stewart to the Kearneys, then reveals his tougher nature in arranging the evictions on the Shea's Barn estate, next becomes an unscrupulous user of the law in trying to retain his hold on Shea's Barn (which has only been leased to him by Betty O'Shea for a year for a nominal sum) and then is ready to give false evidence against Gorman O'Shea before he is banished by Donoghan's decree.

So Gorman O'Shea inherits his estate, and marries Kate, and Donoghan heads for success in America with Nina as his wife. The would-be politicians, Walpole and Atlee, do not receive the rewards for which they schemed, Dick Kearney and Henry

Lockwood will remain dull (Betty O'Shea's Irish denunciation of the latter's English dullness being an intensification of Atlee's earlier musings), Lady Maude will no doubt continue on her cold-blooded courses, and the problem of Ireland will certainly remain.

Lever reveals himself as truly Anglo-Irish in this novel. He enjoys character – the minor episodes, such as Matthew Kearney's row with the Goat Club and the visit of the Dublin specialists to Kilgobbin to treat Gorman O'Shea, are well done – and he analyses the differences between English and Irish sensibilities well, not least in his disquisition on Irish chaffing or teasing. He likes Ireland itself, rain and all, and he despairs of extreme solutions. He has come a long way from his early establishment views. The British party system was at fault. Westminster, he concludes, is no substitute for a parliament in College Green. Indeed Lever had finally moved to a desire for home rule, and *Lord Kilgobbin* explains why he thought it necessary. His political comments throughout the novel are shrewd and they carry weight because he conveys them with the appearance of a certain sardonic detachment. His social comments are often warmer: he can capture a lively conversation; he conveys the atmosphere of a drawing room or a dining room with skill. One of the pleasantest of the novel's incidents is the meeting between Kearney and the Tory magistrate and the local rector where orange and green unite in order to achieve the humane purpose of getting Gorman O'Shea out of danger (Lever's penchant for describing good food and wine pervades most of his novels). He has, however, few illusions about Ireland: he paints the incompetence of the Fenians clearly and he shows the venal informers at their work, and he cannot resist some comic scenes at the expense of the local Chief Constable whose men seize Walpole's luggage and papers, with grave results, when searching the Castle for traces of Donoghan.

He records vanity and wit and he also succeeds in conveying a natural and likeable virtue in Kate. His range of characters is wide: here he particularly shows the influence of Balzac, whom he greatly admired. As always he is shrewd in observing national characteristics. Thus we have frequent illustrations of Irish persiflage; we have Irish comment on such aberrations of English rule as the famine relief works – Walpole finds a road ends in the midst of the Bog of Allen and is told:

It's one of their tricks the English played on us in the year of the famine. They got two millions of money to make roads in Ireland, but they were so afraid it would make us prosperous and richer than themselves, that they

set about making roads that go nowhere. Sometimes to the top of a mountain, or down to the sea, where there was no harbour, and sometimes like
this one, into the heart of a bog.

Here are the views of Molynéux and Swift all over again about
English economic exploitation of Ireland, and Lever, too, felt fierce
indignation at the English politicians who vacillated between
repression and submission to terrorism, with the result that
Ireland's problems multiplied, the secret societies flourished and
divided a population weakened by the effects of the famine and
subsequent emigration. Ireland was in his view uneasy, disquieted
and angry. He described himself, in April 1871, during his last visit
to England and Ireland from Trieste where he was British Consul,
as half mad between gout and indignation. But Gladstone at
Whitby was worse than his swollen ankle, and he had come to dislike and distrust English rule while realising that the Anglo-Irish
Ascendancy's power had long vanished. No wonder his last days
were haunted, as a reviewer wrote of *Lord Kilgobbin* in the *Dublin
University Magazine*, July 1872, 'with a melancholy and over-true
foreboding of great catastrophe'. He had moved from comedy
through elements of tragi-comedy to a tragic view of life in the
Ireland he loved.

TORRENS: AN IRISHMAN IN SOUTH AUSTRALIA

South Australia arose out of theory, the theory that arises from the premise: sales of land to individuals should pay for the passages of emigrants who would be available as a labour force to work the land. The theory was Edward Gibbon Wakefield's; but the practice, putting the theory into action, was largely carried out by an Irishman, Colonel Robert Torrens.

Torrens was an interesting man. Born in Derry in 1780, a son of an Irish rector who was himself the son of a rector, he distinguished himself as a soldier, then turned to the study of politics and economics – his theories were quoted with approval by Lord Robbins in our own time – and developed advanced liberal views. Deeply moved by peasant poverty in the poorer parts of Ireland, he saw in emigration a means of alleviating it.[1] He held decided views upon emancipation, expressing them strongly in 1807.[2] Indeed, he refused a Treasury borough because he would not abandon his views about the need to introduce unconditional emancipation. He won a seat in parliament and that year gave his strong and energetic support for the proposed colony in South Australia.[3] As he wrote himself, 'the colony devised by Mr Wakefield was planted by me'.[4] His exertions moved 15,000 people there and he believed wholeheartedly in the self-supporting system on which the colony was to run.[5]

The Colonel was loquacious and had a quick tongue. Though he made some mistakes himself, he disliked inefficiency. This was recognised by James Stephen who, as Counsel to the Colonial Office, virtually ran its affairs from 1825 to 1845. The early board of nine commissioners, meeting in the Albany in London, was chaotic, amateurish. Stephen remarked that 'a board of nine commissioners sitting in London to send emigrants to South Australia is as ill-imagined an institution as could be conceived'. He added:

Col. Torrens tells me that the result has been to produce a lamentable waste of time and to convert the board into a sort of debating club discussing for days together the most frivolous and unmeaning objects .[6]

Lord John Russell revoked the commission of the South Australian Board on 23 December 1839.[7] Torrens was appointed one of three commissioners who replaced it. They were paid £800 per annum each and £200 from the South Australian Land Fund; they were to safeguard the revenues from the sale of land and devote it to 'a well regulated emigration'. Torrens organised the departure of a hundred Irish families a month.[8] One hundred and five vessels were engaged and, by 1840, 13,842 people were in the colony. Torrens authorised a good deal of the Land Fund to pay for ancillary items as well as passages. Costs of steerage passengers began at £14 in 1836 and rose to £18 in 1840. By 1840, the commission, without knowing it, had become insolvent, partially because of delays in surveying the land, partially because the land sales did not cover the expenses of the administration in South Australia.

A parliamentary enquiry into the affairs of South Australia was therefore instituted in 1841. The Governor, George Gawler, was made the scapegoat. Two of the commissioners, Thomas Frederick Elliot and Ernest Villiers, were whitewashed on the grounds that the causes of the colony's financial collapse had been in operation before they entered on their duties in 1840. Torrens was forced to resign. He pointed out that Gawler had no friend at court and that Lord John Russell was engaged to marry Elliot's sister, Frances, remarking that there was a mark upon the forehead of Lord John Russell which can never be erased'.[9] The South Australian Commission was revoked by Lord Stanley when Russell lost office in September 1841 and the colony then came under the control of the Board of Colonisation Commissioners for Land and Emigration. It took three years to adjust the debts of the colony in England, about a generation in South Australia.

Despite losing his commissionership, Torrens became a director of the Australian Mining Company in 1843, a leading figure in the Society for the Promotion of Colonisation in 1847, and a director of the City and Port Railway of Adelaide in 1849. His interest in getting Irish emigrants to Australia. intensified by the effects of the Famine, was successful and the St Patrick's Society, 'formed to cheer every voluntary exile of Erin in the colony', sent cheerful reports back to Ireland. It is noted, for example, in a letter of 14 July 1849, from the Governor, Sir Henry Fox Young, to the Colonial Secretary, Earl Gray:

Here the man who on his native soil was a careworn, toilworn being . . . ill clad, hungry and hopeless, finds for the first time in his life the luxury of feeling that he can earn something to save and that he occupies a higher position in the social scale and unfolds qualities that never seemed to belong to the national character. The reckless and the turbulent finds it in his interest to become thrifty and peaceful and gets a foretaste of the dignity of independence.

The society cheered itself so well at its first dinner in Adelaide that the landlord had to bring it to an end by using his sword on the revellers.[10]

Colonel Torrens did more than send out emigrants: he had wanted to get unused waste land and labour together, and thought redundant capital would bring them into active co-operation.[11] Emigration would cost less than maintaining paupers at home.[12] As time passed, he shifted to the aim of getting out the largest possible number of emigrants with the largest possible amount of capital.[13] 'Concentration and couples' was the early watchword of the colony.

In South Australia, Torrens declared, 'there would be no solitary hearts.... They had all heard of the demoralising doctrine that working classes ought to delay their marriages, but by their plan, that doctrine would be blown to the winds. In South Australia a large family would be a large source of wealth, and happy is a man who has his quiver full of them'. Promises of free passages led many emigrants to marry before embarking. As Colonel Napier put it, 'the colonists would consist of young married people married about a year before they land in Australia so the ladies will be either a little above or a little below or just at par!'[14]

The first Colonial Secretary, Robert Gouger, said to one enquirer about marrying: 'I can only answer by saying that being now a single man I intend to marry before leaving England.'[15] But he could not marry for months after his appointment, as no salaries were paid till the colony was reached. He got a 5 per cent commission on land he had sold to his own family and with £286 could manage marriage. Another to marry before going to South Australia was Colonel Torrens's son, Robert Richard Torrens, who married a niece of Mungo Park, the explorer, two years before he and his wife embarked on the barque *Brightman* on 15 August 1840. They arrived in Adelaide over four months later with three other cabin passengers and one hundred and sixty-nine emigrants.

Born in Cork in 1814, Robert Richard Torrens was the oldest son of Colonel Torrens, who had married Charity Herbert Chute.[16] Robert Torrens grew up in an Irish-speaking Kerry, where he formed a love of hunting and mountain climbing and became a friend of Daniel O'Connell's son, who was a contemporary of his at Trinity College Dublin .

Torrens came up to Trinity in 1830 and was soon known as 'Radical Torrens'. He gained an easy self-assurance through social life in Kerry, Dublin and then in London, where he was a tide-waiter in the Customs Service. When Governor Gawler requested that an instructed officer of customs should go to Adelaide, the junior Torrens was nominated. He went to Cork without pay to learn the duties of a collector and thus arrived in the colony to take up his duties as Collector of Customs for South Australia on 1 January 1841. Although only twenty-six, he was not worried by his new responsibilities:

I detest that mawkish affectation of humility which leads some men to talk loudly of their fears lest they should be found incompetent to fulfil their duties which they know well they are able to fill. I do understand my duties both in theory and in practice.[17]

Torrens certainly carried out his duties with vigour, being involved within a few weeks of his arrival in the affair of the *Ville de Bordeaux*. This was a French ship, which put into Holdfast Bay to take on some sheep. Torrens ordered her to be seized and transferred to Port Adelaide,[18] but the ship put out to sea with a customs officer on board. Torrens manned a boat but failed to catch up with the French ship, so he galloped to Port Adelaide and commandeered an old paddle steamer, the *Courier*. There was little or no coal on board; fence posts were thrown into her firebox, steam raised and off she went, only to break down in mid-stream with the customs men, to the amusement of the onlookers, working her paddles with their feet. Torrens hunted the *Ville de Bordeaux* for five days in the gulf, only to find she had sailed up the river in his absence, the crew having decided to disobey their captain and to follow Torrens's instructions to berth her in Port Adelaide.

The *South Australian Register* took a poor view of what it called 'this mad steamboat excursion' in the gulf at a cost, the paper alleged, of £600 and at the likely cost of £14,000 compensation to the owners of the *Ville de Bordeaux*. Torrens replied in a trenchant letter of 11 February 1841 to the signatories of a paper calling a meeting of the merchants of Adelaide to discuss the affair. He assured them that he knew his duty, 'both its theory and its practice'. He explained why he found their conduct unprecedented, impolitic and insulting and he gave them some lessons about interfering too much with the executive, accusing them of acting as if they were collectors of customs themselves, lacking courtesy, neither giving him any notice of their intention to hold their meeting nor enquiring from him about the legality of the proceedings of the *Ville de Bordeaux*.[19] He was later proved right.

The judge declared the vessel forfeited to the Crown in November 1841. She had been sold illegally in Sydney; her original captain had gone to India with part of the proceeds and an agreeable actress. The trade in which the ship had been subsequently engaged was illegal. The British treasury eventually paid £4,000 compensation to the owner, who had been swindled out of his ship in Sydney. The ship never sailed again and was finally forgotten, broken up after serving as a lightship for some years. But Torrens was never allowed to forget his 'mad steamboat excursion'.

He was frequently attacked by the *South Australian Register*. For instance, there is an early comment on 3 May 1841 on the extraordinary officer 'who . . . obliges the public of South Australia by condescending to collect the custom`s revenue at the cheap rate of twenty-five per cent or thereabouts'. He was empowered to pay the costs of his department out of revenue. The costs, like the duties he levied, seemed too high to the merchants. There were constant controversies.[20] The *South Australian Register* sneered at Torrens's parade of 'a few schoolboy scraps of Latin' during the libel actions that ensued after the affair of the *Emma Sherratt* in 1848.[21] There was squabbling over whether or not this ship's cargo should be discharged pending a decision on her ownership. The police, on Torrens's orders, forcibly removed the captain of this ship when he and his crew had, in a brief but bloody battle, recaptured the *Emma Sherratt* from the agent who had unmoored her, at Torrens's orders, to stop further discharge of the cargo.

In 1849, Torrens suspended his senior clerk and the Treasury Commissioners sent out a Mr Cassell from London to make a report on the running of the customs, which cleared Torrens of all criticism. But the former attacks[22] on Torrens made by George Stevenson continued. Stevenson, who had been joint editor in England of the *Globe and Traveller*, a paper of which Colonel Torrens became part proprietor in 1836, was possessed of an unceasing hatred of the Torrens family. He was a liberal Whig who went out to work for the first governor, Hindmarsh. He was, all at once, Private Secretary, Clerk of the Court, editor of the *South Australian Register*, Justice of the Peace, Protector of Aborigines, Registrar of Shipping, Agent for Lloyds, Postmaster and customs officer. This last post explains his dislike of Torrens's arrival as Collector of Customs, properly trained and appointed from London.

Stevenson did not publish[23] all the facts about Watson's dismissal by Torrens from the Customs Service in Adelaide and, worse, when Cassell came to carry out his inquiry into the South Australian Customs, he wrote a lampoon on the whole affair in the style of *Private Eye*, accusing Torrens of offering hospitality to Cassell to ensure a favourable report. This lampoon[24] played on Torrens's pet phrase in a dialogue between himself and Cassell in Scene IV:

COLLECTOR: I learnt my business theoretically and practically at Cork.
CASSELL: Yes – I heard you were there a few days...

In Scene V, the jibing continues:

CASSELL: Well, I must say, Torrens, you are a trump.
COLLECTOR: No doubt of it. When I was at Cork –
CASSELL: Oh, never mind Cork, except to uncork another of the same.
COLLECTOR: Good – ha! ha! – very fair indeed! Capital! Another of the same
   – oh! *(aside)* my best beeswing.
CASSELL: Well, Torrens, as I was saying, you are a pattern of Collectors, and
   so I shall report you – attentive, able, zealous, never absent from duty,
   on all occasion – always – ever – *(hesitates)*
COLLECTOR: Practically and theoretically acquainted with my duty!
CASSELL: Certainly. The many weeks my family and I have spent under
   your roof – the admirable dinners you give – the wine – Come Torrens,
   there is no mistake here *(filling a bumper and passing the bottle)* – enable
   me to speak conscientiously. I have had opportunities of watching you
   closely and I say sincerely, I could never desire a more comfortable
   billet.
COLLECTOR: Oh, Cassell, you flatter.
CASSELL: By no means my kind friend – how can I? With a pitiful allowance
   of three guineas a day, what should I have made here but for your hospitality: or how should I show my gratitude otherwise than by giving
   you a lift?
COLLECTOR: True – true – as Paddy O'Rafferty sings: Be to his virtues very
   kind And to his faults a little blind.
CASSELL: Of course. But I say, Collector, was it not a lucky thing you asked
   me at first to stay at Irish Town?
COLLECTOR: Why? *(aside)* He smells the trap!
CASSELL: Because, suppose when I first saw the jerquing ships' Blue Book I
   had reported you, what a devil of a mess you would have been in
   today!
COLLECTOR: Oh, don't mention it.
CASSELL: Or before I had known of the bin where that (pointing to the
   decanter) came from, I had inscribed you in the Account Book of
   Officers' ages and capacities.
COLLECTOR: My dear sir, pray drop unpleasant reminiscences. Here are dev-
   illed biscuits and the left leg of the goose broiled.
CASSELL: Oh, that alters the case!

It was all too much for Torrens. He was walking to an auction mart
with a friend, Captain Bagot, when he saw Stevenson talking to
one of his friends. He went up to him and beat him over the head

with his walking stick, exclaiming, 'I have an account to settle with you, sir!' Stevenson preferred an indictment for felonious assault, and a Bench warrant for Torrens's arrest was issued. Bail for £200 was put up; and the public interest grew. Here is a contributor to the *South Australian Register* of 21 March 1849:

Picture to yourself Mr Torrens like another David, armed not with sling and stone, but with a stick of half an inch in diameter, in editorial parlance a bludgeon, marching forth to slay this new Goliath.... The blow, which if it had taken its intended effect, would probably have occasioned death, was rendered comparatively innocuous; and, instead of breaking the skull, it barely broke the skin .

The case was opened next day. Damages of £250 were paid out of court and all seemed to be settled.[25] When the criminal case was brought forward, the Attorney General suggested that the jury find for common assault, but Stevenson said from the witness box that he did not wish the trial to proceed.

The case had its comic moments. A merchant, Mr Vaiben Solomon, gave evidence that Torrens had struck Stevenson with a stick as thick as 'that'. indicating a bludgeon 'of formidable dimensions', a stick which he alleged could knock down a bullock. He himself had purchased a similar stick to show the jury the size of Torrens's weapon. In answer to some pointed questions by counsel, he admitted that he had some personal grievances over Customs matters, but these, of course, had nothing to do with his appearance in court as a witness. Further evidence received from a wine merchant established that Mr Torrens looked wild about the eye and seemed highly excited.

Captain Bagot emerged rather badly from the affair, for when he had seen Torrens's stick raised above Stevenson's head, 'not wishing to be in a street row', he had passed on and taken no further notice. Torrens's counsel made the best he could of his brief:

It was not until his hearth was invaded, his household goods desecrated, his hospitality misrepresented and his friend, his guest, traduced that he stepped forward to punish the calumniator.... Some men, especially Irishmen, considered it a sacred duty to avenge an insult offered to a guest whom they honoured with their hospitality.

The jury fell in with the Attorney General's suggestion. It was then that Torrens brought an action for libel, alleging that Stevenson had charged him with a deliberate intention to commit murder, 'the fact being that he only gave the defendant an Irish horsewhipping'. Torrens won a farthing damages and it was generally agreed,

even by the *South Australian Register,* that Torrens had been a target
for the 'barbed aims and bitter jibes of the press' and had suffered
injuries enough to have harmed a saint. His views of the press
were not unlike those some politicians have of the media today.

Torrens entered upon a second career in 1851, when he was
nominated to the Legislative Council, becoming Registrar General
and Colonial Treasurer the following year. His ten years of controversy had toughened him and tempered some of his early radicalism. Tempered, too, was his instinctive unradical distrust of full
democracy, no doubt because he had himself headed the poll in the
first election held by ballot in Adelaide in 1857. He was now a figure in the community: trustee of the Port Adelaide Mechanics'
Institute, Vice-President of the Savings Bank of South Australia,
Lieutenant Colonel, then Colonel of the Volunteer Artillery – no
doubt a good outlet for his explosive temperament. He was ready
for the great constructive period of his life in South Australia.

The province, remarked Douglas Pike, had 'a few men with university degrees, mostly from Trinity College Dublin'.[26] It was natural that they should help each other. For instance, the judge, Sir
John Jeffcot, whose judgments favoured Torrens, was an Irishman
and a Trinity graduate. After a brief but distinguished career as
Chief Justice in Sierra Leone, he had returned to England and had
killed a doctor in a duel. He applied in April 1836 for a post in
South Australia, saying with understandable urgency that he must
have 'a speedy appointment'. Half his salary had to go to creditors
before he was allowed to sail. Governor Hindmarsh commented
gloomily[27] that a pauper had been placed on the bench: 'He will
probably be sued in his own Court by his English creditors and
will appear in the list of insolvent debtors.'

Jeffcot settled down and enjoyed the company he found in the
colony, unlike George Stevenson, who called the colonists 'the ver-
iest set of buggers he had ever met'.[28] Jeffcot was drowned on his
way to visit his fiancée in Hobart in 1857, without having made
much impact on the life of the colony. A man of tougher calibre
was the governor, Sir Richard Graves MacDonnell, another
Irishman from Trinity, whose father had been appointed Provost of
the college shortly before the governor's arrival in Adelaide in
1855, after a successful period in Gambia.

MacDonnell, described as 'a fine powerful masculine fellow, full
of life, vigour and animal spirits' was, like Torrens, 'hospitable and
devoted to outdoor sports'.[29] But the grudging attitudes which had
greeted Torrens, characterised sourly as 'brilliant as a rocket' by his
contemporary B. T. Finniss, also embraced the governor, who was

spoken of as being 'rather too clever for his position'. MacDonnell
was an able man faced with unusual difficulties. Many of the
immigrants, who were meant to work on the land, obstinately
stayed in or returned to Adelaide. The ratios of the sexes added to
the problem. In 1853, the colony had 679 more women than men,
the next year 1,604 and the year after that 2,829. That year, 1855,
incidentally, saw 2,921 Irish immigrants arrive, compared to 851
English and 217 Scottish. There seem to have been 2,047 single Irish
women unemployed that year, out of 2,800 in the colony as a
whole.

MacDonnell, when retired and back in Europe, gave a lively
paper about the situation at the Royal Colonial Institute. In one
year, 12,000 emigrants were sent out by the commissioner and of
these, 4,004 were able-bodied single ladies. The governor did what
he could for them: he built barracks for them and offered to pay
their fare and all expenses to any employers willing to take them
off his hands, for he was sorry to have to add that they were occasionally very unruly. Now as women in a state of rebellion are not
so easily dealt with as men, he thought that he might mention that,
by a happy thought, they were on one occasion reduced to obedi-
ence by the cooling effects of water from a fire engine.[30]

This was obviously an early water cannon in action. The governor, like Torrens, liked action. He was 'rather inclined to chafe
under the restraints inherent to the condition of the strictly constitutional governor', we are told. Torrens wrote to MacDonnell in 1856
to say that he wanted to amend the law relating to conveyancing;
the reply was to press on with the Bill as quickly as possible.
Heading the new government was to give him the opportunity.

The Times maintained a smugly insular English attitude to the
establishment of this local government. Here was a state three
times the area of England and Ireland, with by now a population
of 109,000, but the 'Thunderer' remarked:

It must be confessed that it is rather an odd position for a new community
of rising tradesmen, farmers, cattle breeders, builders, mechanics, with a
sprinkling of doctors and attorneys to find Prime Ministers, Cabinets, a
Ministerial side, an opposition side and all the apparatus of a
Parliamentary government, to awake one morning and discover that this is
no longer a colony but a nation saddled with all the rules and traditions of
the political life of the mother country.[31]

Torrens broke one tradition very quickly once elected. He
objected to the fact that land could be sold several times over, to
the expense involved in transferring land and to what Anthony

Forster, the editor of the *South Australian Register,* had called the 'absurd and apparently unfair practice of charging heavy fees for retrospective investigations in every separate transaction where the same title had been investigated a dozen times before'.[32]

Torrens told an audience in 1858 that the lawyers to whom he had shown his scheme had laughed at it, that the judge had advised him to confine his attention to the routine duties of his office and not to meddle with it, for the lawyers would be too powerful for him. But the Real Property Act was passed in January 1858. It happened to be parallel to the findings of an English Commission of 1854, but news of that act had not reached Australia[33] before the second reading of the Torrens Act. This act abolished retrospective titles: land could be transferred by Registration of title alone; the documents involved were to be so simple that no solicitor would be needed by any man of ordinary sense and education.

Torrens was delighted. His victory would gladden the declining days of his father, whose name had been impressed upon the lakes, mountains and rivers of the colony. He went off on a missionary tour to New Zealand to extol the virtues of his system and was warmly received in Wellington and Aukland.[34] Torrens had accepted the post of Registrar General to get the system going. He visited other Australian states which subsequently passed similar legislation.[35]

In November 1862, Torrens left South Australia, sent off to martial music, processions of wagons in the villages, speeches, banquets and torchlight processions in his honour, with the firm intention of returning from his unpaid leave in November 1864.[36] He badly needed a rest and spoke of the strain caused by 'great responsibilities and continuous effort in a public cause'.

Tired though he had been in South Australia, he became more so when back in Ireland and England, attacking the evils of the transportation of convicts,[37] busily pushing his system of land registration, the benefits of which he thought should be available to the British and Irish public as well as to South Australia. He spoke in Edinburgh, in London and in Dublin, where he was strongly supported by Sir Richard MacDonnell, who testified to the efficient operation of the scheme in South Australia. But then he seems to have had a breakdown; he was ordered to keep in the open air and to avoid pen and ink, indeed any mental activity at all. He looked forward to the return voyage to Adelaide as likely to provide a period of relaxation.

Torrens's friends urged him to enter the House of Commons. He was not afraid of work, but he began to feel that recognition and reward had not followed his work in South Australia. What should he do? His only real tie to the colony was his property in the Adelaide foothills, Torrens Park, with its ornamental lake and its six hundred orange trees that would in a few years yield enough income for him. But all he had was his salary as Registrar General and Torrens Park: he would have to sell it if he were to live in England and immerse himself in Westminster politics. He put off his return; he put off the decision.

On July 24 1865, Torrens wrote to say that he would sail for Adelaide in September yet the next day he wrote to resign his Registrar Generalship. He had been nominated as a candidate for the Borough of Cambridge and probably had decided to accept the nomination because his activities in Ireland had been successful – sixteen grand juries, Dublin Corporation and several boards of guardians had agreed to petition in favour of his South Australian Bill being adopted for Ireland. The decision had obviously not been an easy one to reach. In October 1865, he wrote to South Australia to justify his decision:

My affection for that charming spot, Torrens Park, is so great that I have felt a sort of remorse ever since I parted with it. Yet when I look around me here I find that in addition to my immediate relatives I am surrounded by a very agreeable circle of literary and political men with whom I am associated. I have really at this moment in England a far greater number of old and valuable Australian friends than I should have in Australia.[38]

In November 1865, Torrens admitted that he had felt so grieved once he had agreed to the sale of Torrens Park, that he wrote immediately to Mr Hughes, the purchaser, and offered to buy it back, paying seven hundred and fifty pounds as a forfeit. After no reply had come in four months, he had to assume the original contract stood. It was a muddled transaction for a Registrar General to be involved in. In January 1866, Torrens wrote to his agents that Hughes had agreed to give up the original agreement because conveyances had been lost, but that he was to be given first refusal of the new arrangement. In May 1866, notes were exchanged between himself and Hughes, but by June, Hughes was still, reasonably, making his purchase conditional on the titles being perfect.

Losing his estate was depressing, but shooting ptarmigan in Norway in the summer of 1865 had meant that Torrens had walked himself into health. Then it appeared his wife's health was affected by the English climate. Would he return to Australia? The die was finally cast in July 1866: the agents got a letter telling them to complete the sale of Torrens Park as quickly as possible. He had taken a long lease on a property in Devonshire; he had to furnish a town-house in Gloucester Place. He needed the money.[39] For a second time, Torrens had to put down roots.

Torrens stood twice before being elected as Member of Parliament for Cambridge. The elections seemed to him to be dominated by the intimidation practised by the heads of colleges and by plain bribery. Once elected, he was able to continue in his wish to reform. From seeming a cast-iron Tory in Adelaide, he was now a Liberal – and surprisingly willing to admit that some of his opinions had been wrong, notably about the ballot which he now supported strongly. The Reform Bill of 1867 was good, he thought, but more reform was needed to protect the people against coercion. But reform had to be achieved cautiously: he would oppose universal suffrage until universal education was established.

Torrens was sympathetic to the poor, notably to the agricultural labourers hit by the economic situation of 1870. His father's views in support of emigration were restated by him, but his proposal to create public assistance for emigration by raising local rates was rejected: 'My firm belief,' said Gladstone, 'is that the English people desire to stay at home.'[40] So was another proposal of his designed to strengthen ties between Westminster and the colonial governments. He resented the 'assumption of superiority' at the centre; he wanted representatives from the colonies present in London to be regarded as *chargés d'affaires*. He had a firm belief in the value of personal contact. His speech was easily outflanked by Gladstone, but is still worth reading for its largeness of vision, as is a speech on the need for an island which had to import food to guard its supply lines. His knighthood, awarded in 1872, marked the peak of his progress in public life.

After a financial crisis over falling interest rates there in 1872, Torrens was finally to sever his connections with South Australia, by withdrawing the residue of his capital from the colony in 1875. Though living in England, he had become a director of the Bank of South Australia. He found, with relief, that he could invest his money at favourable rates there and so could, after all, maintain his new life in England.

Torrens failed to gain re-election in 1874. That year, he built himself Hannaford, near Holman Vicarage in Devonshire, where he spent the last ten years of his life, largely living the life of a country gentleman, though he was obsessed by his latest enthusiasm, fish farming. At sixty-eight, he rowed his way from Oxford to London. At seventy, he was still active, delighted at being asked to initiate the Torrens system in Algiers. He died of a chill caught on the return from a trip to the Scilly Isles. His funeral service was thronged, not only by his friends and the country gentry, but by many labourers and their families. He had, typically, been the first landowner in Devonshire to raise his labourers' wages by twenty-five per cent.

The physical energy that carried Torrens so effectively through life was matched by strong emotions and equally strong expressions of them. Torrens had a warm heart and his heart was in the right place. He believed in improvement. He had lived up to his concept of serving others not only theoretically, but very practically indeed.

BLUNT: ALMOST AN HONORARY IRISHMAN

There are several illustrations of Wilfrid Scawen Blunt which bring us nearer to the nature of this romantic poet and revolutionary propagandist, this traveller, this lover of women and horses, this Englishman who hated the idea of Imperialism and delighted in both the space of the desert and the serenity of Sussex. English of the English, he tried to convince his countrymen that their treatment of the Egyptians, the Irish and the Indians was wrong. He was ahead of his time, and thus seemed to many to be an eccentric. A photograph of Blunt when he was in his late teens shows us finely chiselled, almost feminine features crowned by luxuriant hair, and it conveys the intensity of a Byronic stare. Although the young man is leaning on a chair, an orthodox pose no doubt suggested by some photographer, the unorthodoxy and magnetism of his personality is already clear. Another side of him appears when dressed for amateur theatricals at Petworth in the 1860s, where the elegance of some Restoration gallant, some blasé fashionable young man-about-town, permeates the photograph. Intensity and the forceful impact of his individualism are there in another portrait of Blunt the traveller surveying horizons of memory, matched by a defiant lack of compromise in a smuggled photograph of Blunt the revolutionary wearing prison garb in Galway Gaol in 1888. And then there is the haunting face of the Elliot and Fry photograph, that of Blunt the poet, quill pen poised above the paper. But of all the images the best is the painting by Lady Anne Blunt of her husband on his Arab stallion Pharaoh in flowing Arab robes, for this conveys his interest in Islam, in Egypt, in Arab horses, and suggests an element of the solitary in this most sociable man, his proud and dignified detachment and his capacity to see beyond the conventions of his contemporaries.

Blunt is beginning to be better understood: our age is more sympathetic to his ideas than his own was. Edith Finch's admirable pioneering biography *Wilfrid Scawen Blunt 1840-1922*, published in 1938, suffered from the hostility of Blunt's daughter Judith, and from the fact that many of Blunt's unpublished memoirs, contained 'in a secret box' in the Fitzwilliam Museum in Cambridge were embargoed until 1972. Other 'Secret counter-boxes' were left by Blunt's daughter, and when his grandson the Earl of Lytton was writing his *Memoir*[1] of Blunt he had access to neither his grandfather's nor his mother's secret material. Lady Longford, in completing her recent fine biography[2] had access to the material in the Fitzwilliam Museum which makes her biography a much fuller, more definitive work than the earlier Finch biography, the Lytton *Memoirs* and various essays dealing with Blunt. From what has already been written about him, and from his own *Diaries*, letters and poems, we can form some idea of this man whose romantic life was independent, courageous, and richly varied in activity.

Some pattern emerges from a consideration of the course of his eighty-two energetic years. He ended where his family had lived for at least 300 years, in Sussex; he was of the squirearchy, of a family which sat on the bench, rode to hounds, professed Tory politics and increased its acreage by judicious marriages. The estates of Crabbet (Blunt's home for twenty-five years was the handsome house of Crabbet Park) and Newbuildings (to which he had moved after his marriage and in which he again lived after his separation) both came into the family by the marriage of a Samuel Blunt with Sarah Gale in 1762; his second marriage was with Winifred Scawen of Molenick, and this brought into the family an adventurous Cornish strain, possible increased by Samuel's son William marrying into another west country family, that of the Glanvilles. The son of this marriage, Francis Scawen Blunt (1790-1842) was the father of Wilfrid Scawen Blunt.

Francis Blunt fought in the Peninsula War, was wounded in the Battle of Corunna, returned to England on the *Victory*, and after the Peace made his Grand Tour of Europe, speaking French, Italian and Spanish. He settled down to life as a squire, administering four thousand acres of land efficiently as proprietor and landlord. He married Mary Chandler in 1838 and there were three children of the marriage, Francis Scawen (1839-72), Alice (1842-72), and Wilfrid, who was born on 17 August 1840 at Petworth. Petworth belonged to George Wyndham, later the first Lord Leconfield, who had married Francis Blunt's sister Mary in 1815. When Francis Blunt died in 1842 his widow and the three children spent a year at Petworth Rectory House, on which Wilfrid's earliest memories centred. He played with his Wyndham cousins from the big house; a continuity of life existed there that was lacking in his own situation, for his widowed mother moved her family frequently, taking them to the continent in 1846.

The two boys were sent to a bad school at Twyford; then when the school's failings were eventually recognised after several years, they travelled to the continent again; instead of going to Harrow, as their father had, they were told by their mother that they were to travel in Italy with a tutor, and, a more serious matter, that she had, under the influence of Henry Manning, the rector of Lavington, later to become the famous Cardinal, been received into the Roman Catholic church. The boys themselves were similarly received at Aix-en-Provence in 1852, and then, in 1853, were sent to Stonyhurst, the Jesuit School. Wilfrid was shortly afterwards taken away from the school, to become an artist, but his mother's death in June 1853 meant another change, because their guardians decided to leave both boys at Oscott, a Catholic school they had attended during their mother's illness. Oscott had been at a low ebb but when Charles Meynell was appointed to its staff Wilfrid was intellectually stimulated by him; he learned to think and reason for himself, to read poetry critically and to develop an ambition of romance. He left the school in 1857 and read with a tutor in London with the aim of taking an examination for the Indian Civil Service. He formed friendships with several girls, moved, to a mild degree, in London society under the guidance of his aunt Mrs Wyndham, and then was sent off to France for a while, to prepare for the Foreign Office, since Mrs Wyndham was able to get him nominated. He passed the examination and entered the service as an unpaid attaché in December 1850.

The second period of his education began. He served at Athens, became obsessed with Byron; he had fallen in love with Helen Leutwein who was a Protestant; she died during his second year in Athens, and raised a religious problem for him; would she inevitably burn in Hell Fire as a heretic? He visited Constantinople en route to a new post in Germany, meeting on a Danube steamer, and forming a strong friendship with Lord Stanley, who was a Mohammedan and pro-Turkish. At Frankfurt Blunt's religious feelings were disturbed by discussions of Darwin's *Origin of Species* and Jowett's *Essays and Reviews*. He disobeyed his confessor in reading these books, and then, in 1862, rushed back to England to persuade his sister not to enter a convent for at least two years. His religious doubts increased and when he was transferred to Madrid he made a retreat on the way there at the Redemptorist Convent at Clapham to try to regain his faith. The result was negative; he decided to enjoy life, even to risk it by bull fighting in Madrid.

After the negativity of his spiritual retreat came the success of his advance into sexual adventure. Transferred to Paris in 1863, he promptly fell in love with 'Skittles', Catherine Walters, the famous courtesan. Intelligent, entertaining, wild, generous, volatile, and untamed, she was the inspiration of many of Blunt's *Sonnets and*

204   *Images of Invention*

Songs of Proteus (1875); she was Manon in the *Love Sonnets of Proteus*
(1881) and Esther in *Esther, Love Lyrics and Natalia's Resurrection*
(1892). With her Blunt experienced ecstasy, lived through his 'term
of glory': he seemed, he wrote later, 'for days together to be walking some cubits high above the ground'; indeed, after Skittles no
other woman could rekindle the grand passion that burnt through
him in those three years of bliss – and despair, as other suitors took
the place of this

>   pensioner and bondsman
>   Doing a fool's service thus for love of thee.

Blunt, exhausted, and depressed, was posted to Lisbon, where he
became a friend of Robert Lytton; then he had a second spell at
Frankfurt; next he left in late 1867 for Buenos Aires, meeting there
Richard Burton, whose wild drunken tales of travel and amorous
escapades had their influence on him; his last posting was in
Switzerland before he resigned from the diplomatic service in 1869.
He had moved in the great world without wishing to be fully
engaged in its diplomatic affairs; he had experienced a grand passion; he was ready for marriage.

He married a wealthy woman, Lady Anne Isabella King-Noel.
She was the daughter of the Earl of Lovelace and Byron's daughter
Ada. Lady Byron had brought her up, and she was in many ways
like her grandmother. She was a good and generous wife. She had
a sweet voice, though her playing the piano was mechanical and
ran to little more than scales. She could draw and paint well; she
was an excellent linguist, notably in Arabic. But though she had
her grandmother's intellect, indeed was intellectually curious, she
lacked a sense of proportion, and could be insensitive. As she
became older she was to develop eccentricities – notably in dress –
she wore a fishing hat and mackintosh in bed in lieu of a night-
dress. Although frail in physique she was fearlessly energetic and
helped Blunt in all his activities.

They lived in Paris from 1869-1870; then they moved to the family property of Newbuildings, near Horsham in Sussex. Francis
Scawen Blunt, their only son, born in 1870, died after a few days,
as did twin daughters, born in 1872. Two other deaths, those of
Blunt's elder brother Francis Scawen and his sister Alice made 1872
a sad year for him. After his brother's death Blunt inherited
Crabbet Park and he and his wife set about remodelling the house:
the concept was Blunt's, the plans were drawn by Lady Anne, and
the local builder was employed by contract for each stage. Blunt
himself designed a fine alabaster figure of Francis in his Friar's

habit for the tomb at the Franciscan Friary at Crawley in Sussex. The Blunts' only surviving child, Judith, was born in 1873 and lived until 1957.

In 1873 they travelled to Constantinople, where Blunt was told he was suffering from galloping consumption and had but a few weeks to live. One of his lungs collapsed, but this didn't stop the Blunts from travelling in the wild country round Scutari. Their trip, well off the beaten track, marked the beginning of their interest in politics. Blunt praised the 'honest goodness' of the inhabitants while recognising the badness of their government. There was, however, a paradox in that there existed, despite this misgovernment, great personal freedom. The following year the Blunts pushed their political education further by visiting Algeria, realising how much better conditions were for the nomads living in the deserts with their camel herds and horses than for those living in urban poverty. And Blunt thought that western civilisation – 'the ignoble squalor of the Frank settlers' – had a corrupting effect, realising also the contrast, the incongruity, between the lords of the land and their servants. There followed an interlude of travel in France and Italy, before the Blunts went to Egypt in the winter of 1875. The poems in *Songs and Sonnets by Proteus* published in that year show us something of Blunt's hedonistic temperament, his desire to experience the joys of life and of love to the full, but they also illustrate the bitterness of his passion, his resentment at Death's incursions and his growing awareness that he needed a life of action and of service, as well as of pleasure.

The Blunts approached Cairo from Suez, began to learn Arabic, and to discuss living conditions with the fellahin. There was a situation of wretched poverty in this part of the Ottoman Empire. It was ruled by the Khedive Ismail, a hereditary viceroy, who had succeeded to a situation of economic well-being which his own extravagance and borrowing had destroyed by 1876. The Khedive's refusal to pay interest on his bonds led to British and French governmental interference in Egypt, and Blunt met members of the British financial mission in Cairo, from whom he learned about the economic situation of Egyptian life. The extremes were emphasised by the Khedive's lavish entertainment of the head of the British mission at a banquet while the peasants were starving.

In the spring of 1876 the Blunts left Cairo and travelled through the Sinai peninsula via Akaba to Jerusalem, a perilous and risky journey undertaken with only two boys as camel drivers: it whetted their appetite for a deeper knowledge of Arabia, of its language and its people.

In 1877 they went to Aleppo where they met the British Consul, James Henry Skene, a courageous traveller himself, who gave them useful advice and help. They were less foolhardy now, and better prepared for desert travel. They bought horses at Deyr, where the Turkish Governor delayed them until they agreed to go to Baghdad rather than join Jedaan, a sheik, whose romantic reputation had attracted them. In Baghdad, with the aid of the dispossessed King of Oude, a distinguished Indian Nawab, they managed to evade the Valy, who, like the Pasha at Deyr, did not want them to visit the desert tribes; this time they had letters of introduction to various Bedouin sheiks and were glad to be camping again. As they met the Bedouin, they experienced Arab hospitality and courtesy, and Blunt became a brother of Sheik Faris, of the Shanmax tribe. Finally they met Jedaan but did not take to him. Mashur Ibn Meshid of the Gomussa tribe also became a brother to Blunt as did Mohammed Ibn Arûk. When they reached Damascus they sent to England half a dozen Arab mares to begin their stud of Arab horses at Crabbet, an idea probably suggested by their having brought a stallion from Asia Minor to England four years earlier. Skene had helped them in their purchases for the stud, notably of the filly Dajanieh; and he shipped the horses back to England for them. He knew the tribes' rules for breeding, and supplied material for the *Bedouin Tribes of the Euphrates* (1879), a joint two-volume account of the Blunts' travels in the Arabian desert. The second volume dealt with the geography of the region, gave an account of the Bedouins, and supplied much information about Arab horses and their breeding. Her account of their travels was illustrated by Lady Anne's sketches and a map.

Their next journey brought them to Nejd, the story of which is told in *A Pilgrimage to Nejd, The Cradle of the Arab Race* (2 vols, 1881). They were lucky to escape with their lives from the charge of a raiding party who turned out to be of the tribe of Sheik Ibn Shaalan who had been their host the previous year, and, therefore, once they had established their identity, they were under his protection. They arranged the marriage contract of Blunt's brother Mohammed Ibn Arûk who accompanied them when they crossed the Nefûd, a ten days' journey of about two hundred miles, with only two wells on the way, the first on the second day's travel, but the other on the eighth day. At Hail they missed meeting another distinguished traveller and writer, Charles Doughty. Here Mohammed Ibn Rashid received them with courtesy and they saw his horses, the most famous in Arabia. In Nejd the Blunts found an 'ancient system of free government' with no taxes, no police, and no compulsions. They liked what they found in this unique society, and it confirmed their liking of the Bedouin life. They decided to accompany the Persian pilgrims, the Haj, returning from their visit to Mecca, and they were the first Europeans to travel this route to Baghdad, an exhausting journey via Mershid and Kerbela.

From Baghdad they left for India. Their lives were at risk when they were guided beyond the Tigris by some members of the Beni Laam tribe, but they eventually got to Persia, travelled through superb though difficult country, and finally – despite Blunt falling seriously ill, and recovering miraculously on a wild gallop into Ram Hormuz – reached the Persian Gulf after travelling two thousand miles. They arrived at Bushire exhausted after this foolhardy but splendid journey through wild country and wild people, travelling mainly by night and suffering greatly from the heat and flies by day.

In India Blunt stayed with his friend Robert Lytton, who had become viceroy in 1876 and met his main officials, discussing his visit to Arabia and Indian conditions. About these Blunt was radical in his views; he wrote that he believed that the Indians were capable of governing themselves 'far better than we can do it, and at about a tenth part of the expense'. He had begun to formulate his views on political matters, and when he returned to England in 1879 he began to express them with confidence. This was the busiest period of his life. He was energetically developing the Arab stud at Crabbet, meeting many of the racing fraternity at Newmarket and elsewhere, arranging for a race for Arab horses to be run there in 1844 under the auspices of the Jockey Club. Through his interest in horses he entered into correspondence with Gladstone (who was interested in the kind of horses bred by the Greeks and Trojans), one of whose secretaries, Edward Hamilton, was a close friend of Blunt's. Then he conveyed his views about the east to Gladstone, whose attacks on Disraeli's imperialist policy appealed to him. A result of the Liberal victory was Lord Lytton's return from India, and his encouragement led Blunt to publish *The Love Sonnets of Proteus*, with a dedication to Lytton. Some of the sonnets reprinted from the earlier volume *Sonnets and Songs* were strengthened, other new poems reflect the love affairs in which Blunt was, as usual, intensely involved. But a new interest occupied him. A conversation with the Persian Ambassador in London had suggest his studying Mohammedan doctrine; he disliked the Ottoman rule, and had tried to persuade Gladstone and Sir Charles Dilke, then under-secretary for Foreign Affairs, that the Caliphate was not necessarily part of Ottoman power; indeed, he thought that he might himself restore it to the Arabs.

Now forty, Blunt went to Egypt to study the Mohammedan religion. Sheik Mohammed Khalil was his first teacher; through him he met Sheik Mohammed Abdu, who wanted to create new intellectual approaches to social and political reform for Islam. The Blunts then travelled to Jeddah and there experienced the strength of feeling which was developing among the reformists; after that came a trip to the Sinai peninsula, and visits to Jerusalem and Damascus to try to effect the release of some Bedouin Sheiks who had been imprisoned by the Ottoman government. It seemed that a pan-Islamic feeling was developing, and when the Blunts returned to England after visiting Aleppo the summer of 1881 was largely occupied in the writing of *The Future of Islam*, in which Blunt tried to make clear to English readers the nature of the new liberal spirit in Moslem thought, the movement to bring to Islam a religious revival, a regeneration of spiritual forces which would in turn generate political freedom, and ultimately establish the Caliphate in Mecca.

When Blunt had been there on earlier visits he had tended to accept some of the official attitudes to Egypt; now, in 1881, when he found that Sir Edward Malet, whom he had known earlier in the Foreign Service, was Consul-General, he also developed friendships with various Egyptian Nationalists and was able to act as an intermediary between them and Malet. He wanted Gladstone to support the new movement in Egypt which seemed, after Ahmed Bey Arabi's peaceful revolution, to be embarked upon a series of useful reforms. He met and was impressed by Arabi, drew up a manifesto of the views of the Nationalist party, and sent it to Gladstone and the *Times*. Blunt persuaded the Nationalists to act moderately over a budgetary matter concerning the army but Malet did not give credit for this in his dispatch, and though it seemed that the Nationalists' policies could be accepted, in January 1882 the English and French assured the Khedive rather than the Nationalists of their support. Blunt found it impossible to justify this policy to Arabi; he had himself come to distrust both Malet and Sir Auckland Colvin, the English controller of Egyptian finance. He decided to return to England to put forward the Nationalists' views. Before he left he bought Sheykh Obeyd, a house and forty acre garden on the edge of the desert about ten miles from Cairo. He was to live there through many winters and with reason, for it was a beautiful place.

On his return to England Blunt found the Foreign Office firmly opposed to the Nationalists, and turned his attention to influencing

Gladstone, finding him, at first, impressive. He spoke at public meetings, wrote and talked to individuals; he persuaded Egyptian leaders to send suitable telegrams; but in the end he became completely disillusioned with Gladstone, regarding him as a 'mere parliamentarian' after his House of Commons speech on Egypt. In May the British and French fleets arrived at Alexandria, but Blunt continued to influence the Nationalist leaders; in a letter to the *Times*, he attacked the British officials for not knowing the reality of the Egyptian situation and misrepresenting it. Matters, however, came to head when Admiral Seymour demanded that the forts at Alexandria should be handed over by the Nationalists, – something to which Blunt thought they could not possibly agree; in July Alexandria was bombarded; and in September the Nationalists were decisively defeated at Tel-el-Kebir. Once war between his country and the Nationalists had begun Blunt withdrew from action, but after Arabi's surrender he was active in aiding his defence – it took an open letter to the *Times* to get Gladstone and the Foreign Office to agree to allow the counsel Blunt had arranged to send to Egypt access to Arabi. Blunt's efforts on behalf of Egypt and Arabi were regarded by many as the acts of a renegade. However, Blunt spent freely – over £5,000 on fees for one of the lawyers alone – in the hopes of an acquittal, but, faced with the prospect of a long trial with a double outcome, he agreed that Arabi and the other leaders would plead guilty of rebellion and accept exile, and financial compensation, while an amnesty would be granted to most of the nationalists. He had saved the lives of Arabi and his friends – and the place of exile agreed was Ceylon.

Blunt had first met Lady Gregory on 2 December 1881 in Egypt[3]; he had enlisted her support for the Egyptian nationalist cause, and she helped him greatly during 1882-3. Both she and her husband, Sir William Gregory, who had been a most successful governor of Ceylon, agreed with Blunt's views. They remained friendly with him when he was estranged from most of the English people in Egypt in 1882. Sir William later took a different view of Egyptian affairs but praised Blunt for the 'bold and indefatigable manner' in which he fought on Arabi's behalf in 1882. Lady Gregory's letter to *The Times* of 23 October 1882 (later published as a booklet) entitled 'Arabi and his Household' did much to enlist sympathy for Arabi, as it combatted the scurrilous rumours as to his lavish way of life, when in reality it was a very simple one. It may have saved his life.

Her letter followed the 'tragic climax' of Wolseley's attack on Tel-el-Kebir, about which Blunt wrote in his *Secret Diaries*. While Sir William carefully drew back from supporting the Egyptian cause his wife continued to serve its interests. She and Blunt were drawn more closely together and 'at the climax of the tragedy by a spontaneous impulse we found comfort in one another's arms'. Blunt called it a new experience in her quiet life and recorded how the passionate element in their intercourse was a source of inspiration and strength. The affair ended in the summer of 1883, to be replaced by 'a saner and less passionate kind' of friendship. She wrote 'A Woman's Sonnets', a sonnet sequence he included with her consent but, obviously not under her name, in his *Proteus* ten years later; she gave it to him the morning after their last night together. The secret of their love affair was well kept. Lady Longford thinks that only two contemporaries may have suspected that Blunt and Augusta Gregory were lovers, 'the husband of one and wife of the other'.[4] From the experience, the light once dimmed, the dream past, Lady Gregory learnt to be charitable to others who had practised similar deceit; she had experienced a 'moment's glimpse of Paradise' and had 'made some happiness' for Blunt.

The terms of the amnesty in Egypt were not defined, and Blunt, with the effective aid of Lord Randolph Churchill, had continued to fight against the imprisonments and hanging of Nationalists there until in the summer of 1883 these political punishments were halted. His activities, told in *The Secret History of the English Occupation of Egypt being a Personal Narrative of Events*, published by Fisher Unwin in 1907, show how he had come to develop a hatred of imperialism, a distrust in the English government. It was a peculiarly personal attitude. He saw issues in idealistic, even simplistic terms, and he attacked with savagery those who opposed him politically. He wanted his countrymen to see through hypocrisy. He had hoped England would support the Nationalists because they were the government the Egyptians wanted. This was what he himself wanted, that people should be governed by those whom they accepted as rulers. 'All nations' he said in India in 1883, were 'fit for self government'.

On his way to visit the Nationalist leaders in Ceylon he visited Egypt and was instrumental in persuading the new British resident, Major Evelyn Baring (later the 1st Earl of Cromer) to empty the gaols of Nationalist prisoners. He had, however, gone to the Zaptich gaol without permission, and Baring excluded him from Egypt for three years. He was ill on the voyage to Ceylon, where he admired the relationship between the Governor and the Singalese – in part a result of Sir William Gregory's earlier rule – then visited India for four months, being warmly received, particularly by the Mohammedan community, and helping to draw up plans – which didn't eventuate – for the founding of a Mohammedan university at Hyderabad. When he got back to England he wrote four articles in the *Fortnightly Review* which led to his *Ideas About India* (1885) – not for any separation of India from England, or rather from 'an Imperial Government' – which were based upon his liberal attitudes, not always upon accurate material, although he did not scruple to use information from private conversations. The second part of his *Secret History of the English Occupation of Egypt*, privately printed in London in 1907, often malicious, indicates some of his superficiality. He had, ultimately, a dilettante's privilege of recommending reform without any responsibility for realising the remedies and redressing the wrongs.

His instincts, however, were right. When he heard of General Gordon's mission to Khartoum he wrote him a letter prophesying what would happen – the powers of the Mahdi were not, Blunt felt, fully understood. He thought that Gordon should make peace between the Mahdi and the British troops in Egypt, evacuate Khartoum and acknowledge the Mahdi's sovereignty in the Soudan. Gordon's death could only lead to a war of conquest. He offered himself as a mediator, brought Sheykh Mohammed Abu to London, went to Constantinople to try, vainly, to see the Sultan, in an attempt to persuade him to appoint another Khedive in Egypt who could reach agreement with the Mahdi. But General Wolseley's army marched on towards Khartoum and General Steward's towards Metemneh, and negotiation seemed out of the question. Then news of the fall of Khartoum and of Gordon's death suddenly altered attitudes and it was decided to move the British army out of the Soudan.

After Gladstone's government fell in June 1884 Blunt began to think of entering political life. He lacked a solid base in any party, and his often immoderate language, his espousal of causes that were unpopular, and often lost, meant that he was not taken as seriously as he wished to be. Even the failure of his Arab horses to win the Newmarket race seemed a political loss of face. After much heart searching he decided to join Lord Randolph Churchill as a Tory Democrat, and stood unsuccessfully for Camberwell. He wanted Home Rule for Ireland, and when Gladstone included this in his policy, he decided to become a Liberal. He stood for West Birmingham against Joseph Chamberlain in the June election in 1885, losing by 288 votes, but feeling quite pleased to have lost by such a narrow margin. Afterwards, disillusioned about politics, he visited Rome, then was allowed to visit Egypt again in 1887. Egypt refreshed him, he began to set Sheykh Obeyd to rights, and when he returned to England decided to stand for parliament for a third and, as it turned out, final time, being candidate for Deptford.

His interest in Ireland was strong; he was elected a member of the Irish National League. His anti-Imperial views, his catholicism, his being an English rather than an Irish landowner made him welcome; he went to Roscommon and realised that land tenure was a basic problem, that the Land Laws administered by English legal ideas were foreign to the traditions and morality of the Irish peasantry. Evictions were in full swing – George Moore captures the uneasy spirit of the countryside at this time very effectively in his novel *Drama in Muslin* (1886) – and Blunt was sickened by witnessing an eviction on Lord Kingstone's estate at Arigna (as Maud Gonne was to be at Falcarragh in Donegal in 1888). He wrote fierce letters to the *Pall Mall Gazette* – and on his return to England reduced the rents on his own farms in Sussex. His Irish visit led him to the belief that the laws about land lacked justice. He made several more visits to Ireland, he made speeches, he supported the Land League, and then he met Arthur Balfour, Chief Secretary for Ireland.

They discussed Ireland on two occasions, Balfour regarding the Home Rule movement as the work of half a dozen leaders, who, he thought, could be dealt with through the Crimes Act. Blunt, aware of the feelings and characters of the Irish leaders – John Dillon, William Smith O'Brien and Michael Davitt – told him that they would go to prison rather than leave the country. Balfour replied that the severe imprisonment with hard labour they would get would probably kill those of them – particularly Dillon – who had not very strong health. No doubt this conversation added to Blunt's desire to aid William Smith O'Brien who had been sentenced to three months' imprisonment, and whom he persuaded to appeal, and further, to involve Blunt himself when there was any large demonstration. This occurred quickly, the venue being Woodford in Co.Galway on Lord Clanricarde's estate. There was a secret meeting which Blunt attended, then a public one was announced, to show that under the Crimes Act Blunt as an Englishman could not do in Ireland what would be his normal right as a citizen in England. He held the meeting in defiance of the Act, was arrested and charged with resisting the police. Sentenced to two months' imprisonment at Loughrea, he obtained bail, and had a popular reception in England, as having advanced the cause of the Liberal party and of Irish Home Rule.

After five days of his appeal trial Blunt was convicted for the full term and sent to Galway gaol. There he was not allowed writing materials, and then the prison governor was admonished for allowing him to retain his own overcoat and a travelling rug. His coat was taken by force; he appealed to the Visiting Judges, clad only in his blanket, and in the course of his deposition repeated his conversation with Balfour to them, since he thought the literal meaning of Balfour's words would indeed be applied to prisoners held under the Crimes Act in Ireland as part of the policy of coercion. He was allowed a coat made of prison material after this meeting with the Judges, to whom Lady Gregory had appealed on his behalf. She wrote him four prison sonnets in 1888. The tone of these was less passionate than those that had marked the end of their affair, though there was a clear residue of her love informing her declaration that

> My heart is in a prison cell
> My own true love beside
> Where more I worth and beauty dwell
> Than in the whole worldwide.

Blunt was transferred from Galway to Kilmainham gaol in Dublin, and lost his action for assault against Byrne, the magistrate in charge of the police who had arrested him at Woodford. This trial was by jury who had to return a unanimous vote; eleven were for his acquittal, but one against. He also lost the election at Deptford, and found his last weeks of imprisonment depressing in the extreme. On his release he found many of his friends disapproved of his use of Balfour's private conversation, and he decided not to stand for an English constituency; he refused the offers of Irish ones made to him because he felt an Englishman should not offer for election in Ireland. The record of his experiences in Ireland is recorded in *The Land War in Ireland, Being a Personal Narrative of Events in continuation of A Secret History of the English Occupation of Egypt* (1912), a more detached volume than his two earlier *Secret Histories*, perhaps because it was written some years after the events told in it had occurred.

After his return to England in 1888 he recuperated, at Crabbet, by busying himself with his Arab stud, then by travelling to Egypt to get Sheykh Obeyd in order; and after returning to England again by writing poetry. The pattern of his life was established for a time, with winters spent in Egypt and summers in Sussex and with visits to Scotland, France, Poland, the Ukraine, Tunis, and other places. He gradually re-established many of his friendships and even met Balfour again. He suffered a severe loss in the deaths of his close friends Francis Currie and Robert Lytton. Various love affairs occupied him, and he found William Morris a stimulating new friend. He took to driving a brake with a four-in-hand of his Arab horses; he had moved to Newbuildings place from Crabbet in 1895, and added to it, using a local bricklayer to make the additions to his own plans.

His Irish poems appeared in 1889, mainly sonnets composed on the fly leaf of his Bible. Lady Gregory, who had written him amused letters about his articles on India in 1884, had also liked his poem 'The Canon of Augrim' in 1886, but she found his Irish activities unpalatable the same year. She had not yet come round to the idea of Home Rule and he accused her of suffering from 'property-owning blindness'. This was the only break in a friendship which lasted forty years. She praised his Galway prison sonnets, *In Vinculis*, and she read the proofs of this book as well as many of his others for him.

Despite the fact that his relationship with Lady Anne and his daughter Judith became difficult about 1896, Blunt enjoyed life in the 'nineties enormously. The Crabbet Club of which he was president – an offshoot of another club, the Wilton or Wagger Club – visited him in Sussex every year: it was a convivial association, with intellectual interests, discouraging any over-serious views of life – anyone becoming a Cabinet Minister, an archbishop, an ambassador or Viceroy of India had to submit to re-election, anyone marrying had to be suspended for a year. It was a small privileged, carefree circle which stimulated conversation and had a literary turn.

A particularly valued member of the Crabbet Club was George Wyndham, Blunt's cousin and a close friend[5], who stimulated his writing of poetry. *Esther, Love Lyrics and Natalia's Resurrection* (1892) contained the sonnet sequence which retells his love of Skittles. It did not at first receive the reception for which he had hoped. However, Meredith, whose own love poetry has also been underrated, praised it warmly. And, also in 1892, William Morris showed his liking for Blunt's poetry by publishing a Kelmscott press edition of *Love Lyrics and Songs of Proteus with the Love Sonnets of Proteus* (this is the volume which contains Lady Gregory's 'A Woman's Sonnets'); and a selection of *The Poetry of Wilfrid Blunt*, made by W R Henley, was published in 1893. Blunt wrote prolifically during the 'nineties, even trying his hand at drama with *The Bride of the Nile* in 1903 (it was privately printed in 1907), which suggested a parallel between Roman-Egyptian relations in the period of the Roman Empire and those of the British with Egypt.

Blunt's relations with Baring had been good since his visit to Egypt in 1889, and he hoped that Baring, who became Baron Cromer in 1892, the year Tewfik died, might be able to improve affairs in Egypt with Tewfik's son Abbas II as the new Khedive. Blunt himself got on well with Abbas and began to play a part in Egyptian politics again, visiting Constantinople in 1893 – with as little result as in 1884. But the following summer he decided not to intervene in Egyptian affairs.

The Blunts' last joint desert adventure took place in 1896, a twenty day journey through the eastern desert, making a map which Blunt himself completed in 1898 on a fast six day excursion. In 1897 he had made a tough trip to the oasis of Siwah in the deserts of Tripoli among the Senussi. Here he was attacked in the last days of Ramadan and released when it was discovered that he was an Englishman; he thought he owed his life to his passive behaviour when he camp was stormed. He became convinced after this that the less religion in the world the better; but the trip had left him in very bad health, in great pain, and he was finally cured, he believed, after a pilgrimage to St Winifred's Well at Holywell near Chester. In his recovery from the breaking of a blood vessel he became friendly with Sidney Cockerell, newly appointed as his secretary.

His literary work included *Satan Absolved* (1899), in part prompted by his feelings about the Omdurman battle, his general dislike of the whole Soudan campaign, and the preliminary troubles in the Transvaal which were leading to the Boer War, in part by Herbert Spencer's suggestion that he should write a dialogue set in Heaven, where Satan complains that mankind has outdone him in wickedness. Blunt was attacking what he saw at the hypocrisy and greed of contemporary England, as well as what he regarded as the perversion of Christian teaching.

In 1900 he decided to make a pilgrimage to Mount Sinai and embarked at Suez on the *Chibine*; this was a ship carrying pilgrims on their way to Mecca and Medina; through bad seamanship it struck a reef and the passengers were eventually rescued after four nights. It was his last experience of travel in the East, bar a brief visit to Damascus in 1904. His involvement was kept up, however, for in 1901 when a party of English officers with foxhounds broke into Sheykh Obeyd and hunted the half-tame foxes there, they were attacked by the servants and assaulted them in return. The struggle became a political affair and the servants were imprisoned and beaten, while the officers could not be prosecuted, nor tried by courtmartial; indeed it seemed to the Egyptians an incident typical of the way military occupation interfered with administration of the law. Blunt did his best, writing letters to the papers, promoting questions in the House of Commons, and drawing unfavourable attention to aspects of Cromer's policy. An opportunity to play a positive part in political action came when he was able to help George Wyndham, now Chief Secretary for Ireland, with his enlightened Irish Land Act, which, undoubtedly had a large effect in the creation of modern Ireland. Blunt acted as go-between and finally brought Wyndham and John Redmond together for a private meeting in his house in London, where they reached agreement, the bill becoming law in 1903.

Lady Gregory and Yeats interested Blunt in the Irish literary revival; he supported the idea of a patent for the Abbey Theatre with George Wyndham; and in 1904 he wrote *Fand of the Fair Cheek*, a dramatised episode from the Cuchulain saga. Yeats and Lady Gregory told him they would put it on in the Abbey. As the years went by he assumed that this wouldn't happen, but then, without his prior knowledge, it was produced successfully in 1907.

In 1904 he settled Crabbet Park on his daughter Judith, who had married Neville Lytton in 1899 and had a son in 1904. In December he was badly afflicted by fever at Sheykh Obeyd, but by mid-April 1905, when he got back to England, Malta fever had laid him very low indeed. After his recovery from the danger of death he had to spend three months on his back and by the end of the year he wrote in his journal that he would not travel any more and had ceased to worry himself about public affairs.

Lady Anne had had much to put up with over the years; they quarrelled in London in 1905 when she came back from Egypt at the news of his illness. She had naturally resented his statement that his nurse, Miss Lawrence, was more important to him than she was; and, though she had written a moving appeal to him in June 1905 recalling their days together in desert places and hoping they could make the best of what might be left to them of life, she finally left him in 1906. That year Dorothy Carleton, his adopted niece, became his mistress and remained so until his death.

His old enemy tuberculosis struck him again in 1908; he refused to have an operation on his throat, and the crisis passed, leaving him weak, and restricted in his activities, though he could still ride his Arab horses upon occasion and drive them too, though he could still shoot, but from a wheel chair. He read voraciously and visited the theatre; he even continued to keep in touch with politics and spent much time on his memoirs – those dealing with

Egyptian, Indian and Irish experiences had been privately printed in 1906, and when the Egyptian volume was published by Fisher Unwin in 1907, it received a mixed reception. His *India under Ripon* was published in 1909, a sensible article on prison reform in the *English Review* the next year, followed two years later by *Gordon at Khartoum* and *The Land War in Ireland*. The flow of polemic continued. There had been attacks on Cromer's policy over Akabah in 1906, and then the Denshawi affair that year stimulated his pamphlet *Atrocities of Justice under British Rule in Egypt*, published by Fisher Unwin. In 1907 he heard with great joy the news of Cromer's resignation, and felt that the future looked brighter for Egypt. He wrote articles on the new situation there and in 1911 financed a monthly paper called *Egypt* which lasted until its editor, Frederick Ryan, died in 1913.

Despite these activities Blunt found the period before the Great War disturbing: he felt from 1911 on that war was near. He thought Sir Edward Grey a bad Foreign Secretary, insular and ill-informed; his hopes for Islam's reform and revival now seemed vain; and he decided to leave London. He had often looked forward to withdrawing from the world, and in 1912 he resigned from his London clubs, left London for ever, and withdrew to Newbuildings. He experienced frustration, he thought he had failed in all his enterprises, and then, with George Wyndham's death, he felt finished, unimportant, lonely.

He found consolation in poetry. Lady Gregory had urged him – after Wyndham's death – to arrange to have such poetry as he wished to give the public published in a collected edition. And he was encouraged by several younger poets who had asked him to attend a dinner to honour him as a poet, an idea suggested by Lady Gregory to Yeats. As he did not visit London, Richard Aldington, F S Flint, T Sturge Moore, Victor Plarr, Ezra Pound and W B Yeats came to the famous lunch – the 'Poets' Party' – in January 1914 at Newbuildings where peacock was served, and Pound read him a tribute, in which Blunt's support of Arabi got mixed up with Mazzini, to Blunt's bafflement. (On another occasion when Aldington and Pound visited him he put on his Arab robes for dinner, complete with pistols in his belt, and proposed a toast of 'Damnation to the British Government'.) Though he disliked the way art and literature were going, he was pleased by the poets' visit (though he wrote to Lady Gregory that it 'lacked reality' without her being there), and by Macmillan publishing his *Poetical Works* in two volumes later in the same year. Many of these poems convey his exuberant zest for life, his capacity, also, for conveying sorrow at its losses. His message to the younger poets was that the more unconventional their subjects the more elaborately careful should be their style. And yet his own best contribution to litera- ture is the easy, racy, vigorous, apparently spontaneous prose of his *Diaries*, their contents as unconventional as the man himself.

The last two volumes of his 'Secret Histories' published as *My Diaries*, in 1919 and 1920 respectively, eventuated through Blunt's attitude to the political and historical events which led up to the first world war. He kept to the position he had adopted during the Egyptian war of 1882; he stayed quiet, for he knew his views were idiosyncratic. For instance, he thought the war's origins were to be found in the Anglo-French *entente* of 1904, and he wanted to see an allied victory over Germany which would not leave Germany at the mercy of the allies. He had really wanted England to stay neu- tral – he disliked the Belgian treatment of the Congo, the Italian conquest of Tripoli, the French theirs of Morocco, and the English annexation of Egypt and Cyprus – and he knew his private views would carry no weight in a public situation where patriotism was uncritical. Yet he wanted people to see beyond the official views, behind the propaganda, to understand what he thought were the causes of the conflagration. And so Part One of *My Diaries*, 'The Scramble for Africa', covers the period from 1888 to 1900 and Part Two, 'The Coalition against Germany', from 1900 to 1914. With his views on political events he blended a good deal of gossip, exceed- ingly lively social comment and illuminating anecdotage. He sensed the losses that the destruction of war would bring to the England he loved; he had no sympathy with the levelling democ- ratic world which he realised was being created. And these *Diaries* convey very well indeed the feeling he held that his own world was vanishing.

During the war it seemed that he and Lady Anne had reached agreement over their joint ownership of the Arabian stud. They met for the first time for eight years in 1915, and wrote to each other after that till her death in Egypt in 1917. One of his letters to her dealt with their daughter's plans about Crabbet, and also com- plained of her influencing her children against him., He had delighted in their visits to Newbuildings, and the Earl of Lytton's *Memoir* (1961) shows us how the grandchildren viewed 'the bril- liance of their most attractive grandfather'.[6] Lady Anne's will sur- prised him, for it seemed completely different from what he thought she had intended, although it was made six months before her death, and left the stud to her granddaughters. Her diaries eventually made clear to him the extent to which she had resented his behaviour before their apparent reconciliation. His attitude to her was never the same after her conversion to Catholicism in 1880; nobody, he wrote to her sister after her death, ever was as entirely and naturally good as she was. He thought that after her joining the Roman Catholic church she became 'necessarily less single hearted (for no one can serve two masters) and to my loss'. In fact, he expected complete devotion; God was not supposed to diminish this!

Blunt's years in Sussex, watched over by his devoted entourage, were enlivened by visits from many friends – among them Skittles – who brought him news of the outside world, the literary and political gossip of London. At times he had the air of an Old Testament prophet, so many of his gloomier predictions had come true, but he could still exercise great charm and he evinced a philosophical wisdom. This he needed, not only to control his increasing and irritating infirmity and pain, but to weather the lawsuit brought by his daughter and the public trustee on behalf of his granddaughters to gain control of the Arab stud. It seems fairly certain that both Blunt and Lady Anne had wanted to keep it as a unity, out of Judith's hands, and safe for their grandchildren; and this might have been clearer had Lady Anne survived to return to England. The story of the case makes sad reading, though Blunt, then seventy-nine, at times gave as good as he got during the cross examination which took place in his bedroom at Newbuildings. Finally Blunt lost the case and retained only six mares.

He was tired; he did not believe in a future life. Lady Gregory, whom he regarded as intellectually superior to every other woman he had known, was one of his last visitors. He trusted her literary judgment; he thought she had aided Yeats and Douglas Hyde by focusing on Ireland; and she was to write a new preface for his *My Diaries* (1921) as well as advising Dorothy Carleton, his executor, later about publishing Blunt's work in America. Dorothy Carleton, who knew of Lady Gregory's earlier affair with him, regarded her as 'a wonderful woman' in so many ways. Lady Gregory did not share Blunt's views about an after-life. She believed that they would meet again after death and said that she would say to him 'I told you so', but if they didn't meet he would have the worst of it, for he 'couldn't say anything to her'. He did, however, receive the last rites of the Catholic Church before he died on 12 September, 1922. A few weeks before his death he gave directions for his burial to take place without any religious ceremony in Newbuildings wood. His body was thus returned to Sussex, where he was born, to the countryside which he had so deeply loved.

GEORGE MOORE: PORTRAIT FOR RADIO

1 NARRATOR: In George Moore's *Confessions* he tells us that he came into the world

GEO. MOORE: apparently with a nature like a smooth sheet of wax, bearing no impress, but capable of receiving any; of being moulded into all shapes. Nor am I exaggerating when I say I think that I might equally have been a Pharoah, an ostler, a pimp, an archbishop, and that in the fulfilment of the duties of each a certain measure of success would have been mine.

1 NARRATOR: A certain measure of success? Well, he certainly achieved that – indeed far more than that in his career as novelist, essayist and conversationalist. When he was eighty – in February 1932 – the *Times* published a memorial signed by leading writers and by the British Prime Minister, Ramsay MacDonald, celebrating not only Moore's birthday but his success, his great achievement as a writer, his perfecting of his craft. It was an unusual and an eloquent tribute. The uses of the English language had been changed by Moore's influence, the signatories declared,

2 NARRATOR: As though in an ancient music you had discovered new melodies and rhythms that shall be in the air when young men in future time have stories to tell. You have taught narrative to flow again and anecdote to illumine it as the sun a stream. You have persuaded words and inventions to sing new songs together that would have been heard, as those of an equal, by the masters upon whom the tradition of our literature relies, and on your eightieth birthday your pen is still unfailing in your hand.

1 NARRATOR: Earlier in the memorial they addressed him as an artist who had not ceased to labour with a single mind in the perfecting of his craft.

2 NARRATOR: And Moore demonstrated this by foregoing the pleasure of spending three or four weeks in writing to those who had honoured him – because his pen was 'still unfailing' and busy on a story. He replied to them collectively instead, in a letter to the *Times:*

GEO. MOORE: The thread of a story is easily broken and characters grow dim if they are allowed to lie dormant in the imagination

... I am sure my friends and the signatories to the memorial would forego the pleasure of receiving letters of thanks if, by so doing, they would help me to write my book, which I trust they will like.

1 NARRATOR: Moore had decided to become a novelist over fifty years before. When he was approaching his thirtieth year he settled himself in London, in cheap lodgings off the Strand, and there he began to write. This was his final attempt to find a career for himself.

2 NARRATOR: As a boy he had grown up in County Mayo in the west of Ireland at Moore Hall, a tall Georgian house overlooking Lough Carra. His great-grandfather, another George Moore, had built the house after making a fortune in Spain. The family, originally protestant, traced itself back to Sir Thomas More but Moore's great grandfather was a Catholic. The family were good landlords. Moore's father behaved very well in the terrible mid-nineteenth century Irish famine, selling off his racing stable and foregoing his rents to help his starving tenantry. He became an MP but resigned in 1859 to take up his interest in racing again, winning large sums of money, some of which he spent on educating his sons – George was the eldest of four boys and a girl – at Oscott, the Catholic College in England where he himself had been educated. George enjoyed living at Moore Hall as a boy, and descriptions of the house and its surroundings can be found in many of his novels. He liked fishing in the lake, he enjoyed shooting, and he was fascinated by the life of his father's stables – indeed at one time he thought he'd become a jockey:

GEO. MOORE: I was given a hunter, I rode to hounds every week, I rode gallops every morning, I read the racing calendar, stud-book, latest betting, and looked forward with enthusiasm to the day when I should be known as a successful steeplechase rider. To ride the winner of the Liverpool seemed to me a final achievement and glory; and had not accident intervened, it is very possible that I might have succeeded in carrying it off, if not the meditated honour, something scarcely inferior, such as – alas, I cannot now recall the name of a race of the necessary value and importance.

1 NARRATOR: The 'accident' that intervened was Moore's father's decision to abandon racing a second time. He was re-elected to the House of Commons in 1869 and settled the family in a house in Kensington.

2 NARRATOR: George, who had left Oscott at sixteen, was sent to a crammer's by his father who thought the army was the place for

him. Soon, however, he gave up any pretence of studying for the army examinations. He had made the acquaintance of a painter who talked incessantly about beautiful women and painted them sometimes larger than life in somnolent attitudes and luxurious tints. 'How jolly it would be to be a painter' said George, and gradually began to form the idea of becoming one. Then his father was suddenly called to Ireland and fell ill there. George and his mother were summoned to his bedside.

GEO. MOORE: We journeyed over land and sea; and on a bleak country road, one winter's evening, a man approached us, and I heard him say that all was over, that my father was dead. I loved my father; and yet my soul said 'I am glad'. The thought came unhidden, undesired, and I turned aside, shocked at the sight it afforded of my soul.

2 NARRATOR: He felt freed by his father's death, which gave him the power to create himself – that is to say, to create

GEO. MOORE: a complete and absolute self out of the partial self which was all that the restraint of him had permitted.

2 NARRATOR: He was, after all, now the master of Moore Hall:

GEO. MOORE: Before me the crystal lake, the distant mountains, the swaying woods, said but one word and that word was – self; not the self that was then mine, but the self on whose creation I was enthusiastically determined. But I felt like a murderer when I turned to leave the place which I had so suddenly, and I could not but think unjustly, become possessed of. As I probe this poignant psychological moment, I find that, although I perfectly well realized that all pleasures were then in my reach – women, elegant dress, theatres, and supper-rooms – I hardly thought at all of them, but much more of certain drawings from the plaster cast. I would be an artist. More than ever I was determined to be an artist, and my brain was made of this desire as I journeyed as fast as railway and steamboat could take me to London. No further trammels, no further need of being a soldier, of being anything but eighteen with life and France before me.

1 NARRATOR: He would become a great artist, he decided, but though he was a landlord he was not yet of age, not yet master of his destiny. He had to obey his guardians and study art in London until he was twenty-one. Then as soon as possible after his birthday he was off to Paris.

Despite having led a decidedly lively life in London Moore was a very young twenty-one. He was full of self-doubt, and, for all his posturing, slightly naive:

GEO. MOORE: I was a childish boy of one-and-twenty who knew nothing, and to whom the world was astonishingly new.

1 NARRATOR: He tried working at the Beaux Arts but found the hours too exhausting, sought private tuition, then enrolled in Julien's Salon. He shared an apartment with a friend in an old house in Rue de la Tour des Dames where

GEO. MOORE: the windows there overlooked a bit of tangled garden with a dilapidated statue ... our salon was a pretty resort – English cretonne of a very happy design – vine leaves, dark green and golden, broken up by many fluttering jays. The walls were stretched with this colourful cloth, and the armchairs and the couches were to match. The drawing-room was in cardinal red, hung from the middle of the ceiling and looped up to give the appearance of a tent; a faun, in terra-cotta, laughed in the red gloom, and there were Turkish couches and lamps. In another room you faced an altar, a Buddhist temple, a statue of Apollo, and a bust of Shelley. The bedrooms were made unconventional with cushioned seats and rich canopies; and in picturesque corners there were censers, great church candlesticks, and palms; then think of the smell of burning incense and wax and you will have imagined the sentiment of our apartment in Rue de la Tour des Dames. I bought a Persian cat, and a python that made a monthly meal off guinea-pigs; Marshall, who did not care for pets, filled his rooms with flowers – he used to sleep beneath a tree of gardenias in full bloom.

2 NARRATOR: Moore went to Paris in 1873. There was a brief period in 1874 when he rented a studio in London. But by 1875 he realised he was not intended for a painter and turned to the idea of becoming a writer. He had began to move in French society, attending balls and dinner parties, and to frequent the cafés of Montmartre. At the Nouvelles Athènes he got to know Manet who invited him to his studio. Degas was another painter to exert a powerful influence on him, and he also met Daudet, Monet, Pissarro, Renoir, and Sisley. He was particularly interested in Edmond Goncourt, Turgenev and Zola, in the last because he wrote on painting, a thing Moore began to think he might do himself.

1 NARRATOR: This was the period of Moore's cafe education. Yeats described him in his later Paris days as 'sitting among art students, young writers about to become famous, in some cafés; a man carved out of a turnip, looking out of astonished eyes'. His appearance was certainly unusual: pale yellow hair above prominent grey-green eyes; a delicate pink complexion; a long

neck rising from sloping shoulders. His whole body, in Yeats's words, was 'insinuating, upflowing, circulative, curvicular, popeyed'; he had a receding chin, beneath a full but straggling moustache.

Moore tried his hand at poetry – *Flowers of Passion*, a slim volume in the manner of Baudelaire – at comedy – a three act comedy called *Worldliness* of which no copies can be found – and at tragedy – *Martin Luther*, a play never produced – and then at poetry again with *Pagan Poems*, a volume which gave him some instant notoriety in London. His move from Paris in 1881 was caused by the Land War in Ireland. His tenants weren't paying their rents, agricultural prices were down, and his uncle was an inefficient agent. He crossed to Ireland, appointed a new land agent, sold timber, raised money by a mortgage and then, no longer carefree about money, settled in London to eke out a frugal existence while he tried to make a living by his pen. He got some journalistic work. He wrote some short stories, reviews and articles, and then his first novel, *A Modern Lover*, was published in 1883.

2 NARRATOR: The modern lover of the title is an artist, Lewis Seymour – Moore rewrote the novel in 1917 as *Lewis Seymour and Some Women* – who is helped by women throughout his life. In part, no doubt, the story has autobiographical elements. George Bernard Shaw remembered Moore at this time, and described him as

GBS: *[slight Dublin accent]* Always telling stories about himself and women. In every story there was a room full of mirrors and chandeliers and the story usually ended with some woman throwing a lamp at George and driving him out of the house. Everybody used to laugh at George and no-one believed him, but he had an imperturbable good humour and if you said: 'But George, don't talk such nonsense, you are making it all up', he was not in the least put out or angry but just said: 'Don't interrupt me', and went on as before.

1 NARRATOR: The caddish behaviour of Seymour in *A Modern Lover* has been described as having its counterpart in Moore's fantasies, but what the novel does achieve is a sense of the excitement of Paris and the allure of the artist as a hero. Moore captured a carnival atmosphere: tourists and idlers enjoy the evening air, saunter into the brilliantly lit cafes, sit

GEO, MOORE: drinking, talking or watching the crowd as it surged past. Women, too, were not lacking, and a gleam of a white petticoat or the elegancy of a lace stocking relieved the monotonous regularity of trousers and men's boots. Out of this seething mass of life the tall houses, built in huge stocks of grey stone, arose and faded into darkness, whilst the boulevard with its immense *trottoirs*, and its two interminable lines of gas lamps running out and into a host of other lights, extended until lost in what appeared to be a piece of starry sky.

2 NARRATOR: Paris was a city of pleasure; the artist moved in an element of hedonistic delight. Moore created his Paris in the style of the Impressionists but his characters were described in detail and the story runs on with an over-obvious reliance on chronology. It was the story which attracted Moore; he had still to learn how to write English prose.

1 NARRATOR: Moore had begun: that was what mattered. In his next novel he followed Zola's example. He called himself 'Zola's ricochet' and he portrayed most realistically in *The Mummer's Wife* the tragedy of a woman who tries to escape a loveless marriage to an invalid by running off with Dick Lennox, an actor. She cannot come to terms with her conscience, takes to drink, loses her baby by neglect, alienates her lover and dies sordidly. Flaubert's *Madame Bovary* comes to mind, but Moore was involved in detail and the drama of the conflict between Kate and her lover. She attacks Dick, seizing the poker:

2 NARRATOR: With one sweep of the arm she cleared the mantelboard, and the mirror came in for a tremendous blow as she advanced round the table brandishing her weapon; but, heedless of the shattered glass, she followed in pursuit of Dick, who continued to defend himself dextrously with a chair. And it is difficult to say how long this combat might have lasted if Dick's attention had not been interrupted by the view of the landlady's face at the door; and so touched was he by the woman's dismay when she looked upon her broken furniture, that he forgot to guard himself from the poker. Kate took advantage of the occasion and whirled the weapon round her head. He saw it descending in time, and half warded off the blow; but it came down with awful force on the forearm, and glancing off, inflicted a severe scalp wound. The landlady screamed 'Murder' and Dick seeing that matters had come to a crisis, closed in upon his wife, and undeterred by yells and struggles, pinioned her and forced her into a chair.

'Oh dear! Oh, dear! You're all bleeding, sir,' cried the landlady: 'she has nearly killed you.'

'Never mind me. But what are we to do? I think she has gone mad this time.'

'That's what I think,' said the landlady, trying to make herself
heard above Kate's shrieks.
'Well, then, go and fetch a doctor, and let's hear what he has to
say.' ...
'Yes, yes, I'll run at once.'
'You'd better,' yelled the mad woman after her. 'I'll give it to
you! Let me go! Let me go, will you?'
But Dick never ceased his hold of her, and the blood, dripping
upon her, trickled in large drops into her ears, and down into
her neck and bosom.
'You're spitting on me, you beast! You filthy beast! I'll pay you
out for this.' Then, she perceived that it was blood; the intona-
tion of her voice changed, and in terror she screamed, 'Murder'
murder! He's murdering me! Is there no one here to save me?'

1 NARRATOR: Moore had portrayed how real people could behave,
not how most Victorian novelists' characters behaved.

Then came *A Drama in Muslin*. Moore had returned to Ireland to
observe the social scene there in the eighteen-eighties. How were
young girls educated? How did they achieve marriage? As one
of the characters, Mrs Barton, advises her daughter:

MRS BARTON: *[well bred woman's voice]* A woman can do nothing
until she is married. A husband is better than talent, better even
than fortune – without a husband, a woman is nothing; and
with a husband she may rise to any height. Marriage gives a girl
liberty, gives her admiration, gives her success, a woman's
whole position depends upon it.

1 NARRATOR: Moore was sorry for the girls who were unsuccessful
in the marriage market. He showed one girl, Alice Barton,
(unlike the others) achieving her independence and maturity of
judgement. And he drew another contrast, too, the different
between rich and poor. The rich travel in their carriages to
Dublin Castle, the centre of establishment life in Ireland.

2 NARRATOR: In the broad glare of the carriage lights the shape of
every feature, even the colour of the eyes, every glance, every
detail of dress, every stain of misery were revealed to the silken
exquisites who, a little frightened, strove to hide themselves
within the scented shadows of their broughams: and in like
manner the bloom on every aristocratic cheek, the glitter of
every diamond, the richness of every plume were visible to the
avid eyes of those who stood without in the wet and the cold.
'I wish they would not stare so,' said Mrs Barton; 'one would
think they were a lot of hungry children looking into a sweet-
meat shop. The police ought really to prevent it.'

1 NARRATOR: Moore viewed the country people as dispassionately as he did the landlords:

2 NARRATOR: The peasantry filled the body of the church. They prayed coarsely, ignorantly, with the same brutality as they lived. Just behind Alice a man groaned. He cleared his throat with loud guffaws: she listened to hear the saliva fall: it splashed on the earthen floor.... One man bent double, beat a ragged shirt with a clenched fist; the women of forty, with cloaks drawn over their foreheads and trailing on the ground in long black folds, crouched until only the lean hard-worked hands that held the rosary were seen over the bench-rail. The young men stared arrogantly, wearied by the length of the service.

2 NARRATOR: This novel is often unsatisfactory in technique but it remains most interesting to read. It carries the sinister undertones of the Land War, it shows the restrictive life lived by his heroines, and conveys a sense of impending change. Moore, of course, realised that notoriety helped to get his name before the public. He had sought from Colonel Dease an *entrée* to the entertainments of Dublin Castle.

GEO. MOORE: I am actively engaged on a book, in the interests of which I came to Dublin last year to attend the Levée, the Drawing Rooms and the Castle balls. I was not fortunate enough to receive an invitation for a State dinner party. Now, as my book deals with the social and political power of the Castle in Modern Ireland, I should be glad to attend the Levée in February, if I could make sure of being asked to one of the big dinner parties. My books, as you are probably aware, are extensively read; this particular one will attract a good deal of attention. It would therefore be well to render my picture as complete, as true, as vivid as possible.

1 NARRATOR: Finally he was told the guest lists were 'at present closed' and he enjoyed himself enormously, publishing the correspondence:

GEO. MOORE: The 'at present' is amiable. Who are the people entitled to share in the entertainments given in Dublin Castle? Every year large sums are voted in Parliament for the maintenance of this court. Surely this is not done solely for the purpose of feasting and feting – and – I am of course unable as I am unwilling to argue that my social position entitles me to be asked to the Castle, but I cannot refrain from saying that Lord Fingall and Col. Dease would find it difficult to show I was not. Be that as it may, it was as a man of letters, it was for the purpose of studying, not of amusing myself, that I applied for an invitation. Was that the reason I was refused? One would feel almost inclined to think so.... It would be presumptuous on my part to hope to unearth any fresh crime, the lists of shame are already filled.... The opinions I hold on the subject [of the Castle] will be found in my next novel, my writing table is covered with human documents – fragments of conversations overheard, notes on character, anecdotes of all kinds. I came to the Castle, not as a patriot nor as a place hunter, but as the passionless observer, who, unbiassed by political creed, comments impartially on the matter submitted to him for analysis. I confess I would have liked to have seen one of the State dinner parties, but we cannot have all things, and I am not sure that Lord Fingall was not right to refuse my application. Fame comes to us in unexpected ways, and I believe that when this somnolent earl is overtaken by that sleep which overtakes us all, and for which, it appears, he is qualifying himself daily as well as nightly, his claim to be remembered will be that he refused to invite me to dinner at the Castle.

1 NARRATOR: There are moments of tension; and there are, too, Moore's memorably rhapsodic accounts of the dresses of the girls. Here is his famous description of the dressmaker's shop:

2 NARRATOR OR 3 NARRATOR [*woman*]: Lengths of white silk clear as the notes of violins playing in a minor key; white poplin falling into folds statuesque as the bass of a fugue by Bach; yards of ruby velvet, rich as an air from Verdi played on the piano; tender green velvet, pastoral as hautboys heard beneath trees in a fair Arcadian vale; blue turquoise *faille Française* fanciful as the twinkling or of a guitar twanged by a Watteau shepherd; gold brocade, sumptuous as organ tones swelling through the jewelled twilight of a nave; scarves and trains of midnight blue profound as the harmonic snoring of a bassoon.

The Misses Robinson, whom he he used to visit, read him out a passage which they had added in the margin of their copy: 'Everything was represented there, from the light clarinette of the embroidered lace handkerchief to the profound trombone of the red flannel pantaloons.' How could he write such a thing, they asked, and he fell into their trap and defended the phrase he had never used.

1 NARRATOR: Moore next launched himself into society's treatment of an unmarried mother and her moral restoration. *Esther Waters* was his first financial success and of his novels it is probably one the students of English literature are most likely to read. In

it he presents his heroine Esther Waters in various dramatic situations

GEO. MOORE: .... it is all about servants – servants devoured by betting. It begins in a house in the country where there are race
horses. Towards the end of the book – past the middle – the servants set up a public house. They cannot get custom unless they
have betting. Then come the various tragedies of the bar – the
hairdresser who cuts his throat – the servant who loses thirty
years' character for six shillings – the woman who pledges the
plate to give her lover money to bet with. The human drama is
the story of the servant girl with an illegitimate child, how she
saves the child from the baby farmers, her endless temptations
to get rid of it and to steal for it. She succeeds in bringing up her
boy, and in the last scene is living with her first mistress in the
old place, ruined and deserted. The race horses have ruined
masters as well as the servants.

2 NARRATOR: He disliked the treatment meted out to the poor. His
heroine Esther Waters gets a position as a servant:

1 NARRATOR: And it was into this house that Esther entered as general servant, with wages fixed at sixteen pounds a year; and for
seventeen long hours every day, for two hundred and thirty
hours every fortnight, she washed, she scrubbed, she cooked,
she ran errands, with never a moment that she might call her
own. She was allowed every second Sunday out of four, perhaps
for four and a half hours.

2 NARRATOR: The story's main background is the world of horse
racing, which Moore knew well. There are great descriptions of
Derby day, the boom of the great mob, the cockney crowd:

1 NARRATOR: The Cockney pilgrimage passed into a pleasant lane
overhung with chestnut- and laburnum-trees. The spring had
been late and the white blossoms stood up like candles – the yellow dropped like tassels, and the streaming sunlight filled the
leaves with tints of pale gold, and their light shadows patterned
the red earth of the pathway. But very soon this pleasant pathway debouched on a thirsting roadway where tired horses har-
nessed to heavy vehicles toiled up a long hill leading to the
downs. The trees intercepted the view, and the blown dust
whitened the foliage and the wayside grass, now in possession
of hawker and vagrant. The crowd made way for the vehicles;
and the young men in blue and grey trousers, and their girls in
white dresses, turned and watched the four horses bringing
along the tall drag crowned with London fashion, and the
unwieldy omnibus, and the brake filled with fat girls in pink

dresses and yellow hats, and the spring cart drawn up under a
hedge. The cottage gates were crowded with folk come to see
London going to the Derby. Outhouses had been converted into
refreshment bars, and from these came a smell of beer and
oranges; farther on there was a lamentable harmonium – a blind
man singing hymns to its accompaniment, and a one-legged
man holding his hat for alms; and not far away there stood an
earnest-eyed woman offering tracts, warning folk of their danger, beseeching them to retrace their steps.

What had attracted Sarah's attention was a boy walking
through the crowd on a pair of stilts fully eight feet high. He
uttered short warning cries from time to time, held out his wide
trousers and caught pennies in his conical cap. Drags and carriages continued to arrive. The sweating horses were unyoked,
and grooms and helpers rolled the vehicle into position along
the rails. Lackeys drew forth cases of wine and provisions, and
the flutter of table-cloths had begun to attract vagrants, itinerant
musicians, fortune-tellers, begging children. All these plied their
trades round the fashion of grey frock-coats, and silk sunshades.
All along the rails rough fellows lay asleep with their hats over
their faces, clay pipes sticking from under the brims, their
brown-red hands upon the grey grass.

The sun had risen high, and what clouds remained floated
away like filaments of white cotton. The Grand Stand, dotted
like a ceiling with flies, stood out distinct and harsh upon a
burning plain of blue. The light beat fiercely upon the booths,
the carriages, the vehicles, the rings, the various stands. The
country around was in the haze and dazzle of the sunlight; but
a square mile of downland fluttered with flags and canvas, and
the great mob swelled, and smoked, and drank, shied sticks at
Aunt Sally, and rode wooden horses. And through this crash of
perspiring, shrieking humanity Journeyman, Esther, and Sarah
sought vainly for William.

2 NARRATOR: The events in the story are treated with detachment.
Moore did not sentimentalize nor did he patronise the poor.
Esther is heroic in her battle to bring up her child; she has a stoic
capacity for endurance.

Moore went on conducting his education in public. *Evelyn Innes*,
his next novel, published in 1898, showed his interest in aes-
theticism, in furniture, in an Aubusson carpet – he was furnishing his own home in London – and in his new discovery,
Wagner. Then he wrote a sequel, *Sister Teresa*, exploring life in a
convent. Yeats said of the novel 'everything is there of the con-

vent except the religious life'. Indeed Moore may have begun the story through his interest in his friend Mrs Craigie, a rich American authoress converting to Roman Catholicism. He collaborated with her in several plays and seems to have fallen in love with her, though she dismissed him – probably hoping to marry Lord Curzon. She and Moore agreed in 1904 to collaborate in writing another play together, but they had a final quarrel. Moore told his friend Dujardin what had happened:

GEO. MOORE: I was walking in the Green Park and I saw her in front of me. I was blind with rage and I ran up behind her and kicked her.

1 NARRATOR: At first he related this story with some embarrassment, but when he grew accustomed to his invention, with relish. The scene in the Green Park was afterwards used in the sketch 'Lui et Elles' where a heartless woman on whose face he detected a mocking smile, receives the assault

GEO. MOORE: nearly in the centre of the backside, a little to the right.

1 NARRATOR: She seems highly gratified to find that she has aroused such a display of feeling.

GEO. MOORE: It was inevitable, I said, part of the world's history, and I lost sight of all things but the track of my boot on the black crêpe de Chine.

2 NARRATOR: By the time *Sister Teresa* was published Moore had left London for Dublin. He was deeply opposed to the Boer War and disliked jingoistic Imperialism. And Dublin offered him new material. He was excited by the Irish literary revival which Yeats had brought into being and by the Gaelic League, formed by Douglas Hyde. Edward Martyn, a Galway landlord, who was involved in the plans Yeats and Lady Gregory had for creating an Irish Theatre, was Moore's cousin and a very close friend. They were, said Yeats 'bound one to the other by mutual contempt.' He told Martyn Moore had good points, but Martyn replied that he knew Moore a good deal longer than Yeats did, and he had no good points. Moore thought Martyn the most selfish man alive because he thought Moore was damned and didn't care. Yeats later put the two of them and their friendship into his play *The Cat and the Moon* using the name of Laban, a townland where Edward Martyn – a most devout Catholic – went to chapel, to make the point clear. A blind beggar is talking

1 NARRATOR OR *BLIND BEGGAR* : Did you ever know a holy man but had a wicked man for his comrade and his heart's darling?

There is not a more holy man in the barony than the man who
has the big house at Laban, and he goes knocking about the
roads day and night with that old lecher from the country of
Mayo, and he a woman-hater from the day of his birth. And
well you know and all the neighbours know what they talk of
by daylight and candlelight. The old lecher does be telling over
all the sins he committed, or maybe never committed at all, and
the man of Laban does be trying to head him off and quiet him
down that he may quit telling them.

2 NARRATOR: Yeats, of course, had many scores to pay back. Moore
had compared him to a cunning rook enticing Martyn, a profound owl, from his belfry. Again he envisaged Yeats

GEO. MOORE: standing lost in meditation before a white congregation of swans assembled on [Coole] lake, looking himself in his
old cloak like a huge umbrella left behind by some picnic-party.

2 NARRATOR: Lady Gregory did not escape his satire. He described
her out walking with Yeats

GEO. MOORE: Seeking living speech from cottage to cottage, Yeats
remaining seated under the stunted hawthorn usually found
growing at the corner of the field, Lady Gregory braving the suf-
focating interior for the sacred cause of Idiom.

2 NARRATOR: Yeats – and Lady Gregory – were to find Moore's
jibing irritating to say the least. Here is Moore's evocation of his
meeting Yeats in St Stephen's Green in Dublin; it shows his
mocking attitude to his friend Martyn as well.

GEO. MOORE: I wandered on, now enchanted by the going and coming of the sun, one moment implanting a delicious warmth
between my shoulder-blades, and at the next leaving me cold,
forgetful of Yeats until I saw him in his black cloak striding in a
green alley, his gait more than ever like a rook's. But the smile
that had once amused me began to weary me from repetition,
and resolving to banish it from my mind for evermore, I listened
to him telling that he had been to the Kildare Street Club without finding Edward. Mr Martyn had gone out earlier than usual
that morning, the hall-porter had said, and I growled out to
Yeats: Why couldn't he come to see the tulips in the Green
instead of bustling off in search of a theologian... listening to
nonsense in some frowsy presbytery? The sparrows, Yeats! How
full of quarrel they are! And now they have all gone away into
that thorn-bush.

By the water's edge we met a willing duck pursued by two
drakes – a lover and a moralist. In my good nature I intervened,
for the lover was being hustled off again and again, but mistak-

ing the moralist for the lover, I drove the lover away, and left the moralist, who feeling that he could not give the duck the explanation expected from him, looked extremely vexed and embarrassed. And this little incident seemed to me full of human nature, but Yeats's thoughts were far above nature that morning, and he refused to listen, even when a boy pinched a nursemaid and she answered his rude question very prettily with – she would be badly off without one.

The spring-time! The spring-time! Wake up and see it, Yeats, I cried, poking him up with this objection – that before he met the Indian who had taught him metaphysics his wont was to take pleasure in the otter in the stream, the magpie in the hawthorn and the heron in the marsh, the brown mice in and out of the corn-bin, and the ousel that had her nest in the willow under the bank. Your best poems came to you through your eyes. You were never olfactory. I don't remember any poems about flowers or flowering trees. But is there anything, Yeats, in the world more beautiful than a pink hawthorn in flower? For all the world like one of those purpled waistcoats that men wore in the sixteenth century. And then, changing the conversation, I told him about an article which I should write, entitled, The Soul of Edward Martyn ...

2 NARRATOR: Moore, of course, could see the absurd in himself; indeed he could play the clown quite happily.

GEO. MOORE: The slight success that has attended my writings did not surprise my relatives as much as it has surprised me, and what seems curious is that, if the success had been twice what it was, it would not have restored the confidence in myself that I lost in childhood. I am always a novice, publishing his first book wondering if it is the worst thing ever written and I am as timid in life as in literature

2 NARRATOR: He was ready to seek advice and take it. Grammar, for instance, baffled him; but the mysteries of 'should' and 'would' intrigued him; and he decided he would use the subjunctive from the moment he was told about it by his friend Richard Best:

1 NARRATOR OR R. BEST: I said to him at one time 'Oh Moore, what you want there is the subjunctive; the subjunctive of that will get you out of the sentence' 'But what is the subjunctive?' he said. 'Oh well,' I said, 'the subjunctive mood is if you say 'If it rains we shall not go. Qu'il soit in French, you know.' Moore was delighted with the subjunctive, so I told him or there were various subjunctives, for instance there was the jussive subjunc-

tive; well, I don't think I gave him an instance but one might well have said, 'Jussive subjunctive is like the Ten Commandments – 'Thou shalt not commit adultery would be a jussive subjunctive.' I could imagine Moore saying 'Oh, but why not? I've been doing it all my life.'

2 NARRATOR: Moore had been able to help Yeats and Lady Gregory in the early stages of the Irish dramatic movement because he knew something of the actualities of the theatre. But his lasting contributions to the literary revival were in his writings. *The Untilled Field*, his famous collection of short stories, was about life in the west of Ireland, which he wanted to reveal in the way Tugenev had shown the realities of life in Russia. Moore was excited by the setting up of a Gaelic League; he was too old to learn Irish himself – after all he was 49 when he came to live in Dublin in 1901 – but he would encourage others to learn and use the Irish language, which he thought fresh, vivid, and concrete in its lack of abstraction. He even went so far as to threaten to disinherit his nephews if they were not brought up to know and use Irish. In this spirit, in this desire to make Ireland bilingual, he had the stories of *The Untilled Field* translated into Irish. They deal with the power of rural priests over the peasants.

1 NARRATOR: They convey Moore's love for the country people and despair at their weakness. He had, however, little in common with them. Those who avoid the constraints of orthodoxy in his stories are not necessarily happier; most of them seek escape in exile. But basically Moore was a landlord and regarded the peasants from a distance. His enthusiasm for the language was like his attitude to country people; it contained a certain repulsion – a point made clear in his account of a famous dinner given by *The Daily Express* to celebrate the Irish Literary Theatre when he heard the language used:

GEO. MOORE: It seems to be a language suitable for the celebration of an antique Celtic rite, but too remote for modern use. It had never been spoken by ladies in silken gown with fans in their hands or by gentlemen going out to kill each other with engraved rapiers or pistols. Men had merely cudgelled each other, yelling strange oaths the while in Irish, and I remembered it in the mouths of old fellows dressed in breeches and worsted stockings, swallowtail coats and tall hats full of dirty bank-notes, which they used to give my father. Since those days I had not heard Irish, and when [Douglas] Hyde began to speak it an instinctive repulsion rose up in me, quelled with difficulty, for I was already a Gaelic Leaguer.

2 NARRATOR: Moore was disappointed that no writers in Irish were emerging – they were to come later in the persons of Pearse, Liam O'Flaherty and many others – but his idea about translating English and continental classics into Irish eventuated in 1926. By the time of his next achievement, *The Lake*, Moore had lost much of the enthusiasm with which he had returned to Ireland. If the realistic stories of *The Untilled Field* were like Joyce's subsequent stories in *Dubliners*, 'scrupulously mean' in their treatment of the poverty-stricken paralysis of the west of Ireland, *The Lake* was like Joyce's subsequent *A Portrait of the Artist as a Young Man* in its development of individual style. *The Lake*, published in 1906, has a fairly simple plot: Joyce may have found sanction in it for *A Portrait of the Artist as a Young Man*.

1 NARRATOR: Father Gogarty, a priest in charge of a parish on the shores of Lough Cara, ejects Nora Glynn, a young schoolmistress who has become pregnant, by speaking against her from the altar. Gradually through a correspondence with a priest who looked after Nora when she came to London, and with Nora herself, Gogarty comes to realise that he has loved her, and attacked her out of sexual jealousy. Finally he came to think his own life empty; he leaves his clothes by the lake shore so that he will seem to have drowned and swims across the lake, intending to go to America.

The Lake, as the title suggests, dominates the story. It opens with a passage that shows Moore creating association between scene and mood. He was, of course, writing about the place in which he had himself grown up, and he writes with deep feeling:

GEO. MOORE: It was one of those enticing days at the beginning of May when white clouds are drawn about the earth like curtains. The lake lay like a mirror that someone had breathed upon, the brown islands showing through the mist faintly, with gray shadows falling into the water, blurred at the edges. The ducks were talking softly in the reeds, the reeds themselves were talking; and the water lapped softly about the smooth limestone shores. But there was an impulse in the gentle day, and, turning from the sandy spit, Father Oliver walked to and fro along the disused court-track about the edge of the wood, asking himself if he were going home, knowing quite well that he could not bring himself to interview his parishioners that morning. On a sudden resolve to escape from anyone that might be seeking him, he went into the wood and lay down on the warm grass, and admired the thickly-tasselled branches of the tall arches swinging above him.

1 NARRATOR: Moore talked of the difficulties he had to overcome:

GEO. MOORE: The one vital event in the priest's life befell him before the story opens, and to keep the story in the key in which it was conceived, it was necessary to recount the priest's life during the course of his walk by the shores of the lake, weaving his memories continually, without losing sight, however, of the long, winding, mere-like lake, wooded to its shores, with hills appearing and disappearing into mist and distance. The difficulty overcome is a joy to the artist, for in his conquest over the material he draws nigh to his idea, and in this book mine was the essential rather than the daily life of the priest, and as I read for this edition, I seemed to hear it. The drama passes within the priest's soul; it is tied and untied by the flux and reflux of sentiments, inherent in and proper to his nature, and the weaving of a story out of the soul substance without ever seeking the aid of external circumstance seems to me a little triumph. It may be that all ears are not tuned, or are too indifferent or indolent to listen; it is easier to hear 'Esther Waters' and to watch her struggle for her child's life than to hear the mysterious warble, soft as lake water, that abides in the heart.

2 NARRATOR: Moore was creating his famous melodic line, apparently simple but superb in its impressionistic effects. 'Every man has a lake in his heart', says the priest, having reached his decision to leave his parish:

1 NARRATOR OR GEO. MOORE: He walked along the shore feeling like an instrument that had been tuned. His perception seemed to have been indefinitely increased, so that it seemed to him as if he were in communion with the stones in the earth and the clouds in heaven; it seemed to him as if the past and the future had become one.

The moment was one of extraordinary sweetness, never might such a moment happen in his life again. The earth and sky were enfolding in one tender harmony of rose and blue, the blue shading down to grey, and the lake floated amid vague shores, vaguely as a dream floats through sleep. The swallows were flying high, quivering overhead in the blue air. There was a sense of security and persuasion and loveliness in the evening.

2 NARRATOR: This is a symbolist novel, a picture of skillfully presented daily life in an Irish backwater which nonetheless relates to all men in its humanism. Moore was pleased with it:

GEO. MOORE: The weaving of the soul substance without ever seeking the aid of external circumstances seems to me a little triumph.

1 NARRATOR: And in a letter to Lady Cunard he mentioned its 'Siegfried music', a reference, no doubt, to the repeated motifs echoing Wagner's style – which Moore's friend Dujardin saw as the parent of the interior monologue.

2 NARRATOR: Moore's stay in Dublin gave rise to many legends. There was the simple story, retailed by many, of how he had asked someone a vital question:

GEO. MOORE: How do you manage to keep up your under-drawers? Mine are always slipping down as I walk along the street.

VOICE OR 1 NARRATOR: Don't you know there are little loops on the drawers or – you put your suspenders [your braces] under them

GEO. MOORE: Here have I been for years suffering tortures in this way, and I never knew what these things were for.

1 NARRATOR: He was delighted with his house in Ely Place but he had his doorway painted green – a demonstration of his nationalistic views – and this enraged his neighbours, particularly the Misses Deam, maiden ladies who lived next door to him. All the tenants had an agreement with the landlord that all doors in Ely Place should be painted white. A lively correspondence ensued between the landlord and Moore, who maintained that, as a art critic, he had the right to match his door to his total scheme of decoration. The maiden ladies then bought a copy of Moore's *Esther Waters*, tore it into fragments and put these in a large envelope labelled 'Too filthy to keep in the house' and dropped it through the letterbox in his green door. At night Moore used to retaliate by going out at eleven, twelve and one to rattle his stick on the railings to make the ladies' dog bark. They hired organ grinders to play under his windows when he was writing; he prosecuted the organ-grinders. Another story has it that they encouraged their cat's amorous catterwauling outside his windows, that he then hired a pipe band to play outside their house in the small hours. And so on.

2 NARRATOR: Moore appreciated the singing of a blackbird in his garden, and told his friends at one of the Saturday evenings when he was at home

GEO. MOORE: I enjoy its song. If I were the bad man people say I am, could I enjoy its song?

2 NARRATOR: But when he was writing one morning he saw the maiden ladies' cat crossing the street and thought:

GEO. MOORE: That cat will get my bird.

2 NARRATOR: He filled the pocket of his dressing gown with stones but heard that cats are nocturnal and throwing stones in the

dark was ineffective. His cook suggested a trap and he told
Yeats who was passing through Dublin to stay with Lady
Gregory at Coole Park in Galway:

GEO. MOORE: I remembered how early that cat got up. I thought it
might get the blackbird if I was not there to protect it, so I set a
trap. The Miss Beams wrote to the Society for the Prevention of
Cruelty to Animals and I am carrying on a correspondence with
its secretary, cat versus birds.

2 NARRATOR: Yeats was again in Dublin on his return from Coole
Park and Moore came to see him, seemingly greatly depressed:

GEO. MOORE: Remember that trap?

2 NARRATOR: Yes.

GEO. MOORE: Remember that bird?

1 NARRATOR: Yes.

GEO. MOORE: I have caught the bird.

2 NARRATOR: Moore needed quiet. He worked exceedingly hard.
His secretary said there was nothing else in life he liked better
than to write and write and write. He dictated, corrected and
recorrected.

3 NARRATOR OR WOMAN SEC: He'd spend half a day on one paragraph, and after lunch we'd tackle that paragraph again, and
maybe the next morning when I'd come in we had to face the
whole thing again. The table was crowded with bits of paper, all
scribbled on, diagonally and everything. He was the despair of
editors and printers. If your final page proofs have more than a
certain number of corrections, there's a publishers' agreement
that you have to pay more – they must have cost him hundreds
of pounds ... I had to be there all the time – to type, and retype
and retype.

1 NARRATOR: He wrote something every day and advised other
writers to do the same. At first he sat quietly when dictating but
after a few sentences:

3 NARRATOR: the rhythm would unfold and they'd begin to move,
waving to and fro, keeping time to the rhythm. He had a wonderful sense of words. They just came in a regular flowing
stream – not a turbulent stream but a very gentle stream ... I
think somebody called it the melodic line.

2 NARRATOR: What Moore was writing so industriously after *The
Lake* was the story of his Dublin life, *Hail and Farewell*. He
worked till about four or five o'clock in the afternoon when he
could be seen emerging from Ely Place.

GEO. MOORE: The strain of composition has left my countenance, so
I'm going out.

2 NARRATOR: He would take his short walk, watched anxiously by many a citizen of Dublin for rumour had it that Moore was going to put half Dublin into it as a set of characters. Brinsely MacNamara the novelist commented:

1 NARRATOR OR B. MACN: Nobody knew which half. The anxiety of those who felt they were going to be in it for certain was only equalled by the rising jealousy of those who felt he mightn't be going to put them in it at all. Mr Moore walked, therefore, with a slight air of suspense surrounding him as he went. People would see him smiling to himself, and wonder who he might be turning over in his mind for a character just at that moment.

2 NARRATOR: *Hail and Farewell* was preceded by a lively rehearsal, the *Memoirs of My dead Life*, published in 1906, memories of various love affairs ... After various adventures, after various attempts to marry – an Irish heiress in Paris, an Irish cousin, the authoress Ada Leverson, the critic and translator Lena Mildman, the authoress Pearl Craigie – there came Moore's meeting in 1893 with Maud Alice Burke, a wealthy American heiress. He wrote to his brother Maurice Moore about her:

GEO. MOORE: I nearly died of seasickness coming over from France. I had a most delicious love adventure there. Generally my loves are mature but this one is a young girl of 18 – I think the most beautiful girl I ever saw in my life. Beauty generally doesn't fetch me but this one did. What she could see in me to rave about I cannot think. I have been wondering ever since, a blasé roué like me, rotten with literature and art to which Wagnerism has lately been added ... My golden-haired siren is an heiress; she wanted me to marry her but I said that that would be dishonourable, that I never went after a girl for her money. Only five days but when the lady is amorous and the aunt is complacent or witless a good deal can be done. 'J'ai rêvé dans la grotte ou nage la sirène'. That women may lose their virtue certainly makes life worth living.

2 NARRATOR: Maud Burke, however, married Sir Bache Cunard, the shipping magnate, in New York. The marriage has been described as 'loveless but not childless' And there are strong suggestions in Moore's letters to his brother Maurice and his friends the Edens to suggest that he was the father of Nancy Cunard who was born in 1896. Certainly he seems to have fallen deeply in love with Nancy's mother who kept over a thousand of his letters to her. Most of these have vanished, probably locked away in some safe-deposit box in America, but Moore told his official biographer, Charles Morgan, that, apart

from his memory and autobiographical writings, these letters were 'the most valuable source' of information existing about his life. In various editions of *Memoirs of my Dead Life* Moore altered the emotive account of their relationship, sometimes adding, sometimes removing sections of the story. His affection for Nancy Cunard is shown delightfully in her book *Memories of George Moore*; this chimes with a persistent theory that he was her father. She described him well:

3 NARRATOR OR WOMAN: I think I must have watched him a lot. No one spoke at all like him, no one else's mind worked like his in all its paradoxical, individual Irish brilliance. That long-drawn 'Oh' of stupor, suggesting that something portentous had just occurred, was merely surprise, but it sounded like awe. His sudden bouts of mimicry, the way he had of taking the words out of someone's mouth.... That person was heading one way, but G.M. would deliberately go and finish the thought himself in an entirely different direction, discomfiting or delighting his interlocutor. This generally led to that great and joyful laugh of his, ending with the characteristic chuckle, 'Khk, Khk, Khk' – long, rotund and juicy.

Never again in life have I heard such a rich voice, nor anything like its peculiar emphasis, a bubbling hot dish of a voice. Some words were pronounced much articulated, the word 'Well', constantly used at the beginning of a remark, often achieving two syllables. An example (how it returns to my ear) can be got out of a wasp:

'Wel'le if you will leave him a-lone, hee will go a-way.'

1 NARRATOR: She also captures his desire to shock. He had been asked to comment on young American widows – he said he supposed 'fast' women means what he would call 'dashing' women, and then he broke off with

GEO. MOORE: a beautiful story going round now about Oh, what is that woman's name?'

1 NARRATOR OR 3 NARRATOR [WOMAN]: He was notorious for forgetting people's names

GEO. MOORE: 'She was losing her husband's affections, you see. So she went to Paris and took lessons from some of the ladies in the Chabanel. A French cocotte has a good deal to teach, you may be sure. When she returned she began to·put these lessons into practice in bed with her husband. Oh, it must have been a dreadful moment when she heard him say: 'Dora, ladies never move.' Khk, Khk, Khk.'

1 NARRATOR: The frankness characterising Moore's account of this

scandal developed further in the trilogy of *Hail and Farewell* (1911-14). Moore called this three volume work, *Salve, Ave* and *Vale*, fiction, but what is it really? Probably a blend of fact and fiction, like the *Confessions of a Young Man* and *Memoirs of My Dead Life*. Even outrageous anecdotes or episodes have a kind of factual basis, and Moore treated chronology – *and* facts – to suit his artistic purpose – he was to go on doing so throughout his life, for *Avowals* (1919), *Conversations in Ebury Street* (1924) and *A Communication to My Friends* (1933) continue this kind of writing.

2 NARRATOR: It maddened many people. When *Hail and Farewell* appeared it was time for Moore to leave Dublin, many of whose streets and parks he had portrayed so lovingly and many of whose citizens he had treated with less than respect, with an awareness of their potential as actors in his great comedy. He returned to London, to Ebury Street, where he lived the rest of his life. What he left behind was a brilliant portrait of the Dublin of the literary Renaissance: utterly outspoken, utterly malicious. Yeats looking like an umbrella, AE the benign but efficient mystic, Martyn with his passion for Palestrina, John O'Leary, T.W. Rolleston, known for a single lyric, Douglas Hyde, Standish O'Grady the adaptor and translator of Gaelic, T.P. Gill, the newspaper editor, Horace Plunkett who dreaded laughter as a cat dreads cold water, all the characters made into a great panoramic pantomime – though despite laughing at his friends – or, as some of them rapidly became, his enemies – he conveyed his deep interest in them as subjects for his art, his appreciation of them and their individuality. Moore had a great capacity for wonder. He had, as Geraint Goodwin remarked, the purity of a child's thought and the vision of a child's eye. He came freshly to everything and could recapture – even seventy years later – freshness, that sense that life is wonderful:

GEO. MOORE: I can see the great hay-ricks over against the stables and the old pine in which the goldfinches built their nests, and brighter than day now is the day when the old servant took me out one morning and showed me the nest up on the high bough.... By my fireside in Ebury Street I can relive the delightful life of the 'sixties again, seeing everyone in his or her occupation, and every room unchanged, unaltered; my nursery with a print between window and door showing three wild riders leaping a wooden fence in a forest. The schoolroom overlooking the yard is before my eyes – the yard is in ruins but its homely life lives on – the mule, toiling always, bringing up water from the lake .... through the long bog to the next bridge, to discover a crayfish in the brook – it is a wonderful thing to see a crayfish and not to know it is a crayfish – and to remember Primrose and Ivory, two ponies dead fifty years or more, and the day my mother drove me to Ballyglass to see the mail coach swing round the hillside.

1 NARRATOR: He was to convey this wonder magnificently in *The Brook Kerith* of 1916. In this he envisaged Christ 'as an epitome of human goodness', and he thought – with considerable   justification – that *The Brook Kerith* was his finest literary achievement. First, as often in Moore's life, came a rehearsal, a play called *The Apostle* (1911) about Paul finding Jesus still alive. Then Moore spent fourteen months writing *The Brook Kerith*. In this Christ survives the crucifixion and lives a contemplative life among the Essenes. The attention is now focussed not on Paul but on Jesus Christ. Moore wanted to demystify Christ, yet to portray him without contradicting or unduly departing from the synoptic gospels. He visited the Holy Land in 1914, steeping himself in the biblical past:

1 NARRATOR: He gave an interview before he left:

GEO. MOORE: I feel I cannot describe a country I have never seen, if I don't know whether this place is on a hill or that in a plain, whether there is a river in sight or not. The smallest doubt of this kind stops the pen; it bothers you. You can't idealise when you don't know how far it is from the monastery to the Jordan. The monastery is in the wilderness. Is there a river there? If there is, I should like to see the river and spend a morning by its banks. There is sure to be a spring or well; if so, what sort of a spring? Can you see the Dead Sea or can't you? These are the questions I must get answered before I begin writing, and so I am going to the Holy Land.

What I should like to describe is the contrast between the two characters: between an ironical mystic that is Jesus – and Paul, the man in the full tide of belief. This is what I am going to try to write – mind you, I don't say that I shall succeed and I think I shall write it first as a story. That will enable me to become familiar with the subject, to get into it. The play will follow later.

2 NARRATOR: He had indeed a clear idea of what he wanted to create:

GEO. MOORE: Jesus is a legendary figure, illusive and illusory, and not an historical figure, incoherent and contradictory: a completion from various sources like all legendary characters. Out of this chaos I have tried to create a human being and the question at issue is: have I succeeded in creating a human being out of this chaos?

2 NARRATOR: Moore kept the stream of his ideas flowing along with his narrative. *The Brook Kerith* is a kind of epic in prose; its conversational style is fresh, spontaneous, warm. At first when Paul discovers Jesus living as a shepherd in the wilderness among the Essenes he thinks him a madman, then fears that he may return to Jerusalem to destroy his own work, his organisation of the church. Jesus, however, tells Paul that we must learn to live for ourselves and to suffer our fellows to do likewise. Learning he says, comes out of ourselves. No one can communicate his thought, for that thought is his alone. Moore has a masterly capacity for conveying profound ideas in a way that is dignified, in way where the high seriousness of the author's artistic purpose is underpinned by the inconsequential trivia, the concrete detail which make the story convincing, just as it is enlivened by subtle humour. Speech blends with thought, action with description; it is easy to read and it is worth reading aloud, for the style is simple yet flexible, the narrative backed by the Biblical echoes, the imagery and rhythms. Here is a passage which conveys its nature:

1 NARRATOR: Hast slept well, Paul, and hath sleep refreshed thee and given thee strength to pursue thy journey? Paul answered that he was very weary, but however weary must struggle on to Caesarea. Thy strength will not suffer thee to get farther than Bethennabrio, and thy sandals will need mending even to reach the village. And seating himself on a smooth stone Paul watched Jesus's hand tying new thongs, wondering if the madman's mind was still set on Jerusalem and if he would go thither as soon as he (Paul) was safely out of the ways of the Jews. Each shut himself within the circle of his own mind, and the silence was not broken till Paul began to fear that Jesus was plotting against him; and to distract Jesus's mind from his plots, if he were weaving any, he began to compare the country they were passing through with Galilee, and forthright Jesus began to talk to Paul of Peter and John and James, sons of Zebedee, mentioning their appearances, voices, manner of speech, telling of their boats, their fishing tackle, the fish-salting factory of Magdala, Dan, and Joseph his son. He spoke a winning story of the fishing life round the lake, without mention of miracles, for it was not to his purpose to convince Paul of any spiritual power he might have enjoyed, but rather of his own simple humanity. And Paul listened, still believing his guide to be a madman. If

thou hadst not run away crying: 'He is mad, he is mad, thou
wouldst have heard how my crucifixion was brought about;
how my eyes opened in the tomb and interrupting Jesus, Paul
hastened to assure him that if he cried out: 'He is mad, he is
mad' he had spoken unwittingly, the words being put into his
mouth by the sickness in which Jesus had discovered him. And
the sickness, he admitted, might have been brought about by the
shock of hearing thee speak of thyself as the Messiah. But, Paul
I did not speak of myself as the Messiah, but as an Essene who
during some frenzied months believed himself to be the
Messiah. But shepherd, Paul answered, the Messiah promised to
the Jews was Jesus of Nazareth, who was raised by his Father
from the dead, and thou sayest that thou art the same. If thou
didst once believe thyself to be the Messiah thou hast repented
thy blasphemy. In the desert these twenty years, Jesus answered.
But not till now did I know my folly had borne fruit, and that
Joseph knew a story had been set going; or it may be that the
story was not set going till after his death. Now it seems too late
to go into the field thou hast sown with tares instead of corn. To
which Paul answered: It is my knowledge of thy life among
rocks that prompts me to listen to thee. The field I have sown
like every other field has some tares in it, but it is full of corn
ripening fast which will be ready for the reaping when it shall
please the Lord to descend with his own son, Jesus of Nazareth,
from the skies. As soon as the words: Jesus of Nazareth, had left
his lips Paul regretted them, and upon a sudden resolve not to
utter another word that might offend the madman's beliefs, he
began to tell that he had brought hope to the beggar, to the outcast, to the slave; though this world was but a den of misery to
them, another world was coming to which they might look forward in full surety. And many, he said, that led vile lives are
now God-fearing men and women who, when the daily work is
done, go forth in the evening to beseech the multitude to give
some time to God. In every field there are tares, but there are
fewer in my field than in any other, and that I hold to be the
truth; and seeing that Jesus was listening to his story he began
to relate his theology, perplexing Jesus with his doctrines, but
interesting him with the glad tidings that the burden of the law
had been lifted from all. If he had stopped there all would have
been well, so it seemed to Jesus, whose mind was not able to
grasp why a miracle should be necessary to prove to men that
the love of God was in the heart rather than in observances, and
the miracle that Paul continued to relate with much unction

seemed to him crude; yet he once believed that God was pleased to send his only begotten son to redeem the world by his death on a cross. A strange conception truly. And while he was thinking these things Paul fell to telling his dogma concerning predestination, and he was anxious that Jesus should digest his reply to Mathias, who had said that predestination conflicted with the doctrine of salvation for all. But Jesus, who was of Mathias's opinion, refrained from expressing himself definitely on the point, preferring to forget Paul, so that he might better consider if he would be able to make plain to Paul that miracles bring no real knowledge of God to man, and that our conscience is the source of our knowledge of God and that perhaps a providence flourishes beyond the world.

2 NARRATOR: Moore defended *The Brook Kerith* characteristically in the *Pall Mall Gazette* after the novel was published in 1916:

GEO. MOORE: You write: 'Following a fairly common practice, the author discredits the Resurrection and endows Jesus with a further term of moral life, during which Jesus renounces all pretentions of divinity and embraces a sort of lachrymose pantheism.'

But Jesus does not lay claim to divinity in *The Brook Kerith*. He merely tries to convince Himself that He is the Messiah promised to the Jews, and I thought I had made this very important point quite clear, and that everybody would see that I was following certain well-known texts in Matthew and Mark, texts in which Jesus repudiates any comparison between Him and the Father. The prelates have tried to explain away these texts, but they have not succeeded in doing so to the satisfaction of many people. The Arians, who pointed to the text 'Why do you call me good, none is good but God', which they said was enforced by texts from St Paul's Epistles, were persecuted by the so-called Orthodox Church about the year 385, and the so-called Arian heresy has lasted into the present day under the name of Unitarianism. Many very intelligent and respectable people have belonged to this sect and have looked upon themselves as Christians, John Milton, among others of less poetical celebrity, but not less religious fervour.

It has always seemed to a great number of people that the claim to the divinity of Jesus did not begin to emerge until the Gospel of John was published about the middle of the second century, nearly a hundred years after the death of Jesus. This Gospel is looked upon by all critics, Agnostic, Protestant, and Roman Catholic, as an ecclesiastical work of no historical value. It contains scenes at which the author was not present and could not have had any knowledge of, notably the scene in which Pilate calls Jesus into the Praetorium and talks with Him alone. The Evangelist supplies Pilate and Jesus with some admirable dialogue, plausible enough, but which must have come out of the Evangelist's imagination in the same way as many scenes in *The Brook of Kerith* came out of mine. In writing *The Brook Kerith* I have followed the example of the Evangelist by including scenes at which I was certainly not present, and if I have done this on a larger scale than John I may still plead that it was he who set the example.

2 NARRATOR: After *The Brook Kerith* came a philosophical romance. He spent three years on this, travelling in France to absorb atmosphere, dictating about 1500 or 2000 words a day and later revising the whole book. The result was a blend of thought and tragedy, description and story, the moving story of Canon Fulbert's niece Heloise and her lover, the brilliant academic Abélard. Tension begins in the Canon's house overlooking the Seine. The fated lovers travel through the forests to Britanny, the background of their journey spring sights and sounds. This background is unobtrusive but atmospheric:

1 NARRATOR: But to reach Chécy before nightfall they would have to hasten, and the innkeeper told them that the road through the forest looped so that the village of Lorris might be taken into the circuit; but there was no need for him to follow this winding, he would find a by-path across certain low hills which he could not miss. Abélard did not feel sure that the by-path might not be missed, but to hear the road explained out again would be merely a waste of time, and so they hastened towards the forest in a sort of half- knowledge of the way, allowing the horses to trot a little, thinking that they might draw rein when they passed through the fringe of birch-trees that encircled with their pallor the great district of pines that showed in black masses over against Etampes. Now we are well within the forest, Abélard said, as much in the forest as if we were in the middle of it; and he asked Héloise to peep over the undergrowth that lined the rutted path down which they were riding, so that she might see the pines rising up naked and bare some fifty or sixty feet, some straight, some leaning, in endless aisles. Like the spears, Héloise said, of Crusaders going into battle; and how penetrating is the smell of the resin. But the pines were in patches only, and the forest passed quickly into rocky hillsides overgrown with oak and beech; and so faint was the path they followed that Abélard

often asked Héloise and Madelon to draw rein while he went forward in search of the path. For if we all went forward together, he said, we should not be able to go back to where the path ends: a tree is not a sure landmark; one forgets which tree, and wanders in a circle. I've got it, he cried to them, and they came forward, the forest getting lonelier as they proceeded into it. All bird cries have ceased, and we hear only the sighing of the boughs, Héloise said, and the smell of the forest is different from all other smells; a more mysterious smell is about, a smell of earth and moss. There is also a warm smell, said Madelon, that reminds me of our Brittany forests, the great forest about Clisson, where we shall be – Héloise, myself and my boy – before the month's end, should we catch a fast-sailing barge from Orléans. Did he not say that a little over three leagues from Etampes we should find the by-path that would save us several leagues' journey? Abélard asked, and some hundreds of feet after he told them to rein in while he went on ahead in search of the path. Here it is he cried, from a clearing; we have but to follow the path that leads through the hollows yonder up to the rising ground that the innkeeper spoke of. He spoke to me of oak-trees, and here they are. And they rode beneath the boughs not yet in full leaf, following the path as it wound through hollows, losing it and finding it amid rocks, pushing their way through thickets that seemed impenetrable at a distance but did not prove so hard to force through as they had appeared. There is a rutted way under the brambles, Abélard said; cattle and horses had been through here; and stooping low in their saddles, they broke through somehow, losing bits of clothing in the passage. Soon after the path led them up hills, through thorn and hazel mingled with inter-spaces, till it brought them to a heath, and Abélard said: those pines standing so solitary at the end of the lake embedded in rocks are the trees the inn-keeper told me I was to look out for. We have not missed the way, he continued; look back and see the forest that we have come through. And he pointed to a dark ragged line of pines flowing down the northern sky. But is our way to the right or to the left? Madelon asked. To the left, he answered; we have to ride southward, keeping the setting sun on our right.

2 NARRATOR: Moore balances the intellectualism of the lovers – the arrogance of the ambitious Abélard and the agonising of the amorous Héloise – against the earthiness of Madelon, the Canon's serving woman, and the peasant driving his cart. Here is the teeming bustle of eleventh century life: cities, convents,

classical culture, even the contentions between nominalists and realists. Moore blended the pulls of spiritual and erotic love, he sympathised with individuals – notably women – he was careful to reflect the ceaseless searching of human minds, to convey the human will to believe in heaven and immortal happiness.

1 NARRATOR: He went on writing, developing his interest in the medieval with an exploration of the thirteenth century in *Ulick and Soracha* in 1926, and then writing a play, *The Passing of the Essenes*, to treat the theme of *The Brook Kerith* dramatically as he had promised he would. He wrote more essays, but finally he didn't seem able to finish *A Communication to My Friends* which told

GEO. MOORE: how writing was forced on me, and the persecution I have undergone for forty years and which is just ended, leaving me a wreck.

2 NARRATOR: He searched endlessly for material. Here is how Harold Sharp, son of the Steward of Neville Holt, the Cunard estate near Market Harboro, remembered Moore:

VOICE: We all loved him, simply loved him. My father was fascinated by his talk; my mother thought he had a wonderful mind and a charmingly courteous manner. To me, as a boy, it was a delight to hear him speak. He put you at your ease at once. You know how he was always raking about, talking to everyone and asking questions, because this or that might go into a book. One often saw him walking alone around the place, and not only near the house. I was about twelve at the time I am thinking of and I had just bought a penny whistle. You remember how many grass-snakes there were round Holt Spa, where one would see them sunning themselves? It occurred to me I might try and charm these snakes with my tin whistle, so I went and sat down and played it by the Spa. Suddenly there was a loud chuckle in the bushes and G.M. appeared. He was alone, but you had surely taken him there, certainly no one else would have done that. He must have liked the place and gone back to see if it would give him something for his writing. My snake-charming amused him a lot and he stayed there talking to me for a long time.

1 NARRATOR: He had devoted himself to his art. He had a cousin who was a Carmelite nun who begged him to burn his books and make his peace with the Church he had left. He replied

GEO. MOORE: We are the two dreamers of a family little given to dreams; the two who have known how to make sacrifices – you for God, I for art. You tell me that you are perfectly happy, and that there is no greater happiness than to live with God and His Sacraments. I also can say that I am perfectly happy with my art; it fills my life from one end to the other.

1 NARRATOR: He was always aware of the shortness, the terrifying mystery and the speed of life. Though he could be naive, he could also be very shrewd; his mischeviousness allowed him to see his own limitations in comic terms. He became sharply apprehensive of beauty and ecstasy. He outgrew his youthful exhibitionism.

2 NARRATOR: A possible reason for it was that he was insecure and wanted to be interesting, to entertain. Many Irish authors have made butts of themselves to amuse others – Goldsmith is the supreme example. He hated a conversational vacuum. Moore, too, tried to fill the gaps:

GEO MOORE: I am never quite sure that I am not a bore – an unpleasant belief, no doubt, but a beneficial one for it saves me from blunders, and I owe to it many pleasant surprises: that day at Steer's when Tonks interrupted me in one of my usual disquisitions on art with Isn't it nice to have him among us criticizing our paintings? I had come back from Ireland after an absence of two years, and I shall never forget the delicious emotion that his words caused me. I never suspected my friends would miss me, or that it would mean much to them to have me back again. I was overwhelmed and were I Rousseau my pages would be filled with instances of my inherent modesty of character, but my way is not Rousseau's.

2 NARRATOR: No, indeed. But Moore saw that Rousseau realised in middle age what a shy silly lad he had been, always blundering and never with the right word on his lips, with no indication of the genius that awaited him in middle age. No, Moore may have been like Rousseau in his own *Confessions of a Young Man* but in middle age he also had the energy to be eccentric. His friend Oliver St John Gogarty tells how they were dining at Moore's one night and Moore said:

GEO. MOORE: We'll know exactly what's happening to us when the omelette comes up.

2 NARRATOR: So the omelette arrived on the table, Moore took up the cover and then went out into the hall and blew a police whistle. Presently a policeman came in and Moore said

GEO. MOORE: Go down and arrest that cook.

POLICEMAN: But on what charge Mr Moore?

GEO. MOORE: Well, look at that omelette, she calls that an omelette.

POLICEMAN: Well, what should it be?

GEO. MOORE: It should be food but it isn't. She's obtaining money...
   POLICEMAN: Oh, yes, on false pretences. That'll be all right, Mr
   Moore.
1 NARRATOR: As well as a capacity to create his own legend, for he
   knew well the value of publicity – indeed in modern terms he
   knew how to market himself – he retained a capacity to absorb
   the ideas and facts he got from others and their work, to reflect
   them and to adapt them in his own writings.
GEO. MOORE: Taking something from one man and making it worse
   is plagiarism. But taking something from one man and making
   it better – what is that? Certainly not plagiarism.
2 NARRATOR: We should let him have the last word.
GEO. MOORE: Should I ever have a tombstone, I should like this
   written on it – let us phrase it correctly

[.....pause.....]

Here lies George Moore, who looked Upon Corrections as the one
morality.

SOMERVILLE AND ROSS: AN INTRODUCTION

IRATE VOICE: The first time I read it, I read it at top speed. And the second time I read it very slowly chewing every word. And then I read it a third time, going over the bits I liked best. And then – and I thank God not till then – I heard it was written by two women.

NARRATOR: And what was it?

IRATE VOICE: Why sir, what could it be but *Some Experiences of an Irish R.M.?* What else would I read about but the pleasures and perils of fox-hunting, eh? Besides, I've hunted that Carbery country myself. Could believe anything of those people in that part of Cork. Amazin' place. Amazin' women, those two. Amazin' book, come to that. Lots of good laughs in it heh, heh.

NARRATOR: Yes, indeed. I've read it myself. And most of their other books too. They were clever women, those two, who created Flurry Knox and Major Yeates, the Englishman become Resident Magistrate in a remote part of Ireland, whose absurd adventures brought fame to his creators. They were for a time a mystery. Nobody knew who Somerville and Martin Ross were. There was a lot of speculation. Some said both writers were men, one of them an old man, the other young; others suggested a very old lady and her young nephew, a soldier. But then it became known that they were Edith Oenone Somerville and Violet Florence Martin. They met in 1886 in Castle Townshend in County Cork, and almost immediately began their career of literary collaboration which lasted until Violet Martin's death in 1915. Indeed the collaboration, in a sense, lasted on after her death, for Edith Somerville continued to issue her books under the joint signature. What they had in common was their upbringing. Both were children of Irish country houses, both grew up in that halcyon time at the end of the nineteenth century, when days were spacious and time went slowly. Time for boating excursions, picnics, shooting, fishing and hunting. Oh yes, certainly hunting. Here's how Major Yeates was introduced to hunting in Ireland, mounted on a horse called Quaker which Flurry Knox had sold to him.

READER: The next step in the day's enjoyment consisted in trotting in cavalcade through the streets of Drumcurran, with another

northerly shower descending on us, the mud splashing on my
face, and my feet coming torturingly to life. Every man and boy
in the town ran with us; the harriers were somewhere in the
tumult ahead and the Quaker began to pull and hump his back
ominously. I arrived at the meet considerably heated, and found
myself one of some thirty or forty riders, who, with traps and
bicycles and foot-people, were jammed in a narrow muddy
road. We were late, and a move was immediately made across a
series of grass fields, all considerably furnished with gates.
There was a glacial gleam of sunshine, and people began to turn
down the collars of their coats....It was at about this moment
that the hounds began to run, fast and silently, and everyone
began to canter. 'This is nothing at all' said Dr Hickey, thundering alongside of me on a huge young chestnut; 'there might
have been a hare here last week, or a red herring this morning.
I wouldn't care if we only got what'd warm us. For the matter
of that, I'd as soon hunt a cat as a hare.'
I was already getting quite enough to warm me. The Quaker's
respectable grey head had twice disappeared between his
forelegs in a brace of most unsettling bucks, and all my experiences at the riding school at Sandhurst did not prepare me for
the sensation of jumping a briary wall with a heavy drop into a
lane so narrow that each horse had to turn at right angles as he
landed. I did not so turn, but saved myself from entire disgrace
by a timely clutch at the mane. We scrambled out of the lane
over a pile of stones and furze bushes, and at the end of the next
field were confronted by a tall, stone-faced bank.
Every one, always excepting myself, was riding with that furious valour which is so conspicuous when neighbouring hunts
meet, and the leading half dozen charged the obstacle at steeplechase speed. I followed in their wake, with a blind confidence in
the Quaker and none at all in myself. He refused it. I suppose it
was in token of affection and gratitude that I fell upon his neck;
at all events, I had reason to respect his judgment, as before I
had recovered myself, the hounds were straggling back into the
field by a gap lower down.
....After the first five minutes I had discovered several facts
about the Quaker. If the bank was above a certain height he
refused it irrevocably, if it accorded with his ideas he got his
forelegs over and ploughed through the rest of it on his stifle
joints, or, if a gripe made that inexpedient, he remained poised
on top till the fabric crumbled under his weight. In the case of
walls he butted them down with his knees, or squandered them

with his hind legs. These operations took time, and the leaders of the hunt streamed farther and farther away over the crest of a hill, while the Quaker pursued at the equable gallop of a horse in the Bayeux Tapestry.

NARRATOR: Yes, that's the authentic note. They could write simply and effectively. And Flurry Knox is the horse coper incarnate, but a likeable character. He operates on heights where Major Yeates can never follow. There's a passage somewhere in one of the stories where Major Yeates has been asked by a friend in England to get him a horse. He finds Flurry Knox and asks him if he could find a good four year old, adding that he'd rather be stuck by a friend than a dealer....

READER: Flurry poured himself out another cup of tea, and dropped three lumps of sugar into it in silence.

Finally he said, 'There isn't a four year old in this country that I'd be seen dead with at a pig fair.'

This was discouraging, from the premier authority on horse flesh in the district. 'But it isn't six weeks since you told me you had the finest filly in your stables that was ever foaled in the County Cork', I protested; 'what's wrong with her?'

'Oh, is it that filly?' said Mr Knox with a lenient smile; 'she's gone these three weeks from me. I swapped her and six pounds for a three year old Ironmonger colt, and after that I swapped the colt and nineteen pounds for that Bandon horse I rode last week at your place, and after that I sold the Bandon horse for seventy-five pounds to old Welply, and I had to give him back a couple of sovereigns luck-money.

You see I did pretty well with the filly after all.'

'Yes, yes, – oh, rather,' I assented, as one dizzily accepts the propositions of a bimetellist; 'and you don't know of anything else – ?'

NARRATOR: But of course Flurry did. He remembered his grandmother had promised him a colt for his twenty-first birthday which he'd never got. He could sell that to Major Yeates's friend. So they both go and dine at old Mrs Knox's house. And on the way home Flurry collected the colt from a shed. It had not been discussed at dinner. Eventually Mrs Knox sends policemen to Flurry's to see if they can discover it. How she and Major Yeates do find it provides the startling dénouement of this tale. But old Mrs Knox is one of their great creations, and her house the key to the Irish Big House, of the last days of English and Anglo-Irish rule in Ireland.

READER: Old Mrs Knox received us in the library where she was seated by a roaring turf fire which lit the room more effectively than the pair of candles that stood beside her in tall silver candlesticks. Ceaseless and implacable growls from under her chair indicated the presence of the woolly dog. She talked with confounding culture of the books that rose all round her to the ceiling; her evening dress was accomplished by means of an additional white shawl, rather dirtier than its congeners; as I took her into dinner she quoted Virgil to me, and in the same breath screeched an objurgation at a being whose matted head rose suddenly into view from behind an ancient Chinese screen, as I have seen the head of a Zulu woman peer over a bush. Dinner was as incongruous as everything else. Detestable soup in a splendid silver tureen that was nearly as dark in hue as the Robinson Crusoe-like coachman's thumb, a perfect salmon, perfectly cooked on a chipped kitchen dish; such cut glass as is not easy to find nowadays, sherry that as Flurry subsequently remarked, would burn the skin off an egg; and a bottle of port, draped in immemorial cobwebs, wan with age and probably priceless.

NARRATOR: That is a good vignette of one of those old grey stone houses sitting in their demesnes, surrounded with grey stone walls built in the time of the famine of 1845. Houses with good libraries and all kinds of curios which were brought from service overseas, for the Anglo-Irish were great travellers and administrators and soldiers and sailors. They had their portraits painted and hung them in the dark halls and galleries to become blackened by turf smoke and age. They were an active aristocracy, fond of outdoor life. They liked practical joking, they had become infected with the liveliness of the native Irish with whom they had intermarried in the past. Indeed, on one occasion Flurry Knox hears that an enemy of his, one Tomsy Flood, is plotting to feed his hounds before a meet; and he ends up his evening's dancing and drinking by putting his hounds in Tomsy Flood's bedroom and waiting upstairs with his friends to see the result when Tomsy arrives home the worse for wear. The poet WB Yeats tells of an occasion when one of Lady Gregory's brothers turned a hose on the crowd of guests at a family wedding. It was a boisterous, high spirited gaiety which we find in the stories of Flurry Knox and the Irish R.M.

And Somerville and Ross also captured the liveliness of the speech of the peasants, their graphic imaginative twists of English. Here's an example of how they recreate the turns of English as it was then spoken in Ireland:

READER: At the top of the pass we stood and looked out over half a mile to the pale peaks of Killarney.

'There's Fahoura now, gentlemen,' said the carman, pointing downwards with his whip to a group of whitewashed farm buildings, that had gathered themselves incongruously about a square grey tower. 'I'm told old Mr O'Reilly's sick this good while'.

'What ails him?' said Flurry.

'You wouldn't know,' said the carman; 'sure he's very old, and that 'fluenzy has the country destroyed; there's people dying now that never died before.'

'That's bad,' said Flurry sympathetically; 'I had a letter from him a week ago, and he said he was parting the hounds because he couldn't run with them anymore.'

'Ah, don't mind him!', said the carman, 'it's what it is he'd sooner sell them now, than to give the nephew the satisfaction of them, after himself'd be dead.'

'Is that the chap that's been hunting for him?' said Flurry, while I, for the hundredth time, longed for Flurry's incommunicable gift of being talked to.

'It is, sir; Lukey O'Reilly' – the carman gave a short laugh. 'That's the lad! They say he often thried to go to America, but he never got south of Mallow; he gets that drunk saying good-bye to his friends!'

'Maybe the old fellow will live a while yet, just to spite him.' suggested Flurry.

'Well maybe he would, faith!' agreed the carman, 'didn't the dochter say to meself that maybe it's walking the road I'd be, and I to fall down dead!' he continued complacently; 'but sure them dochters, when they wouldn't know what was in it, they should be saying something!'

NARRATOR: Many Irish critics have written off Somerville and Ross because of similar lively passages. They maintain that the view of Ireland given in the Irish R.M. short stories is a superficial one, that there is no real understanding of the native mind. This is probably due to the fact that nationalism doesn't usually take kindly to humour. Somerville and Ross loved their country; but they were not nationalists. They loved their country with an affectionate ability to laugh at it; they could also, in the best traditions of the Anglo-Irish, laugh at themselves. The funniest of all their stories is probably 'The House of Fahy', begun in typically low key manner by Major Yeates: 'Nothing could shake the conviction of Maria that she was by nature and by practice a house dog.' And Maria has, in every sense, the last word.

VOICE: But aren't you forgetting the serious novels?

NARRATOR: No, I was going on to say that critics who dismiss the Irish R.M. stories as lightweight should remember that *The Real Charlotte*, though not nearly as popular when it was first published in 1894 as the later Irish R.M. stories became, was a profoundly tragic novel. It is Balzacian in its detail and scope, and as writers they should be judged by it.

VOICE: Yes, I agree, And anyone who says they didn't know their Ireland is very mistaken indeed. *The Real Charlotte* is a subtle analysis of differing nuances in the social life of Victorian Ireland.

NARRATOR: It's more than that, though. It's Tolstoyan in its sweep and vigour. A story of jealousy and revenge, really. Charlotte Mullen makes her plans, and makes her money. She plans that her cousin Francie will marry Christopher Dysart, the son who will inherit the Big House. But Francie refuses him, flirts with an English officer, and then marries Roddie Lambert, Christopher Dysart's agent. Charlotte's weakness has been her fondness and doting upon him.

VOICE: Do you remember the scene where she brings about the death of Roddie Lambert's first wife?

NARRATOR: Yes, indeed. It is what we might expect after the earlier indications of her ruthless pursuit of money and land. She has forced Lambert's wife to open his despatch box by telling her that he is involved with Francie:

READER: 'Mrs Lambert made no further demur. She took out the bundle that Charlotte pointed to, and drew the top one from its retaining india-rubber strap. Even in affairs of the heart Mr Lambert was a tidy man....'

'Get out, ye damned cur!' she exclaimed, the coarse, superstitious side of her nature coming uppermost now that the absorbing stress of those acts of self-preservation was over. Her big foot lifted the dog and sent him flying across the room, and she dropped on her knees beside the motionless, tumbled figure on the floor. 'She's dead! She's dead!' she cried out, and as if in protest against her own words she flung water upon the unresisting face, and tried to force the drops between her closed teeth. But the face never altered; it only acquired momentarily the immovable placidity of death, that asserted itself in silence, and gave the feeble features a supreme dignity, in spite of the thin dabbled fringe and the gold ear-rings and brooch, that were instinct with the vulgarities of life.

NARRATOR: Yes, it's also a study of vulgarity. Charlotte's crudity and coarseness of mind is measured by the refinement of Christopher Dysart. But poor silly Francie is also vulgar. Hers is the vulgarity of the city, and in the long run she is no match for Charlotte. Nor, of course, is Lambert, whose flashiness and vanity drive him deeper into Charlotte's debt. Charlotte is a powerful, terrifying figure, massive, and irresistible.

VOICE: Greed and thwarted passion are a nasty mixture. Especially when they are set in a novel which is convincingly realistic in all its details.

NARRATOR: The details which make it most moving for me are those which establish its realism most securely, and which many realistic novelists leave out in their seriousness.

VOICE: What details do you mean?

NARRATOR: The touches of humour and pathos that abound throughout the novel. They are like a three dimensional background. This element sets the major characters into an almost Chechovian atmosphere, but does not detract from the massive march of tragedy through the steady progress of the story. You'll remember the vignette of the bored English girl and her host. She is viewed by Lady Dysart as a possible wife for her son, but he is not interested in her, nor she in him:

READER: 'Miss Evelyn Hope-Drummond stood at the bow-window of the Bruff drawing-room and looked out over the gravelled terrace, across the flower-garden and the sunk fence, to the clump of horse chestnuts by the lake-side. Beyond these the cattle were standing knee-deep in the water, and on the flat margin a pair of legs in white flannel trousers was all that the guest, whom his mother delighted to honour, could see of Christopher Dysart. The remainder of him wrestled beneath a black velvet pall with the helplessly wilful legs of his camera, and all his mind, as Miss Hope-Drummond well knew, was concentrated upon cows. Her first visit to Ireland was proving less amusing than she had expected, she thought, and as she watched Christopher she wished fervently she had not to carry any of his horrid things across the park for him. In the flower-garden below she could see Lady Dysart and Pamela in deep consultation over an infirm rose-tree; a wheelbarrow full of pans of seedlings sufficiently indicated what their occupation would be for the rest of the morning, and she felt it was a piece with the absurdities of Irish life that the ladies of the house would enjoy doing the gardener's work for him. The strong scent of heated Gloire de Dijon roses came through the window, and suggested

to her how well one of them would suit with her fawn-coloured
Redfern gown, and she leaned out to pick a beautiful bud that
was swaying in the sun just within reach.

'Ha – a – ah! I see ye, missy! Stop picking my flowers! Push,
James Canavan, you devil, you! Push!'

A bath-chair, occupied by an old man in a tall hat, and pushed
also by a man in a tall hat, had suddenly turned the corner of
the house, and Miss Hope-Drummond drew back precipitately
to avoid the uplifted walking-stick of Sir Benjamin Dysart.

'Oh, fie, for shame, Sir Benjamin!' exclaimed the man who had
been addressed as James Canavan. 'Pray cull the rose, miss', he
continued, with a flourish of his hands; 'Sweets to the sweet!'

Sir Benjamin aimed a backward stroke with his oak stick at his
attendant, a stroke in which long practice had failed to make
him perfect, and in the exchange of further amenities the party
passed out of sight. This was not Miss Hope-Drummond's first
meeting with her host. His bath-chair had daily, as it seemed to
her, lain in wait in the shrubberies, to cause terror to the solitary,
and discomfiture to tête-à-têtes; and on one morning he had
stealthily protruded the crook of his stick from the door of his
room as she went by, and had all but hooked her round the
ankle with it.

'Really it is disgraceful that he is not locked up,' she said to herself crossly, as she gathered the contested bud, and sat down to
write letters; 'but in Ireland no one seems to think anything of
anything!'

NARRATOR: That is the Ireland they created for their larger reading
public, a country not unlike the parishes drawn with equally
light touch by George A. Birmingham. But the sombre side of
the peasant mind obviously interested them. Later, in 1925,
Edith Somerville wrote *The Big House of Inver*. This grew out of
a letter from Martin Ross, written to her in 1912.

READER: Yesterday I drove to see X House. A great cut stone house
of three stories.... Perfectly empty... it is on a long promontory
by the sea and there rioted three or four generations of X—s,
living with country women, occasionally marrying them, all illegitimate four times over.... About one hundred and fifty years
ago a very grand Lady – married the head of the family and
lived there, and was so corroded with pride that she would not
allow her two daughters to associate with the neighbours of
their own class. She lived to see them marry two of the men in
the yard.... Yesterday as we left, an old Miss X, daughter of the
last owner, was at the door in a little donkey-trap. She lives near

in an old castle, and since her people died she will not go into X House, or the beautiful old garden. She was a strange mixture of distinction and commonness, like her breeding, and it was very sad to see her at the door of that great house. If we dared to write up that subject – ! Yours ever, Martin.

NARRATOR: Well, though one partner died before they could, the partnership continued on, and *The Big House of Inver* explores the possibilities of such a situation. Not, I think, as well as both writers had explored the character of the real Charlotte. This story of the evil household and its tragedy does not hang together so well as the earlier, less stark, more tragic story.

VOICE: Ultimately I suppose their inspiration drew upon the clash – and the fusion – of cultures in their Ireland, the aristocratic and the peasant?

NARRATOR: That is the framework. But their real merit comes out not so much in investigating the differences of outlook between county and country people, as in their sensitive portraits of those who are betwixt and between. They show the pathos of a Francie as well as her vulgarity, they understand the grasping and increasingly greedy clutching at power which marks Charlotte Mullen's progress.

IRATE VOICE: Never could understand why they didn't stick to the good old Irish RM stories all the time. Jolly good fun, and they knew that hardgoing country all right. Took their jumps cleanly, too. But I never could have believed they were written by two women. Amazin'.

NARRATOR: That used to be the verdict on them. Now we realise that *The Real Charlotte* is a classic, that *The Big House of Inver* has more to it than many of the realistic novels about Ireland written by younger novelists in the 'twenties and 'thirties. And if we want to know more about these two original and intelligent women writers we can read their other books, *Irish Memories* (1917) and *Notions in Garrison* (1942). These books, along with Lady Gregory's *Journals*, are a fine expression of the lively, outgoing and courageous spirit which inhabited the Big Houses of Ireland before Land Acts and Death Duties and Political Differences emptied them of their hunting, shooting, fishing – and writing – aristocracy.

YEATS'S GREAT BLACK RAGGED BIRD

I

W B Yeats's poem 'The Pilgrim'[1] was first published in *A Broadside*, No 10 (NS) in October 1937. It is a ballad put in the mouth of a pilgrim to Lough Derg, 'a return', suggests T R Henn,[2] 'to the thought that the holy places of Ireland might effect a union of the two religions. It is a ballad that recalls, intensely, the world of some of Jack Yeats's paintings, and the ritual of pilgrimage; the very sight and smell of the peasantry'. The pilgrim tells us in the first stanza that he has fasted for some forty days on bread and buttermilk:

> For passing round the bottle with girls in rags or silk,
> In country shawl or Paris cloak, had put my wits astray,
> And what's the good of women, for all that they can say
> Is fol de rol de rolly O.

He describes his experiences at Lough Derg in the next three stanzas:

> Round Lough Derg's holy island I went upon the stones,
> I prayed at all the Stations upon my marrow-bones,
> And there I found an old man, and though I prayed all day
> And that old man beside me, nothing would he say
> But fol de rol de rolly O.

> All know that all the dead in the world about that place are stuck,
> And that should mother seek her son she'd have but little luck
> Because the fires of Purgatory have ate their shapes away;
> I swear to God I questioned them,. and all they had to say
> Was fol de rol de rolly O.

> A great black ragged bird appeared when I was in the boat;
> Some twenty feet from tip to tip had it stretched rightly out,
> With flopping and with flapping it made a great display,
> But I never stopped to question, what could the boatmen say
> But fol de rol de rolly O.

The last stanza places him in the public-house, for he

> ...can put the whole lot down, and all I have to say
> Is fol de rol de rolly O.[3]

Yeats had written about Lough Derg earlier in 'If I were Four and Twenty,' an essay dated 1919, and first published in the *Irish Statesman* on 23 and 30 August, 1919:

I think I would go – though certainly I am no Catholic and never shall be one – upon both of our great pilgrimages, to Croagh Patrick and to Lough Derg. Our churches have been unroofed or stripped; the stained glass of Saint Canice, once famous throughout Europe, was destroyed three centuries ago, and Christ Church looks as clean and unhistorical as a Methodist chapel, its sculptured tombs and tablets broken up or heaped one on t'other in the crypt; no congregation has climbed to the Rock of Cashel since the stout Church of Ireland bishop took the lead roof from the Gothic church to save his legs: but Europe has nothing older than our pilgrimages. In many little lyrics I would claim that stony mountain for all Christian and pagan faith in Ireland, believing, in the exultation of my youth, that in three generations I should have made it as vivid in the memory of all imaginative men among us as the sacred mountain of Japan is in that of the collectors of prints: and I would, being but four-and-twenty and a lover of lost causes, memorialise bishops to open once again that Lough Derg cave of vision once beset by an evil spirit in the form of a long-legged bird with no feathers on its wings.[4]

II

Where did Yeats get his knowledge of the Lough Derg pilgrimage, and particularly of 'the evil spirit in the form of a long-legged bird with no feathers on its wings'? Mrs Yeats suggested[5] that the evil spirit came from Lady Wilde's *Ancient Legends of Ireland*: 'In another lake there is a huge-winged creature, it is said, which escaped the power of St Patrick, and when he gambols in the water such storms arise that no boat can withstand the strength of the waves.' This does not cover the 'cave of vision', and Yeats's reference to the closure of 'that Lough Derg cave of vision' which the evil spirit beset suggests that he knew more of the traditions of the place than Lady Wilde provided.

III

He had read William Carleton's account of the pilgrimage; as a young man in the middle of his nineteenth year Carleton had made the journey in 1813, and his first published work was 'A

Pilgrimage to Patrick's Purgatory', published by Caesar Otway in
the *Christian Examiner* and *Church of Ireland Magazine* (1826, pp.268-
86, 343-62).[6] Yeats edited *Stories from Carleton* (1889) and in his
essay on Carleton suggests that the pilgrimage (about which
Carleton's father had told him, describing St Patrick's Purgatory on
an island in Lough Derg) set Carleton thinking. He pays tribute to
the account, and to the revised version:

> As we have it now the tale is a most wonderful piece of work. The dim
> chapel at night, the praying peasants, the fear of a supernatural madness if
> they sleep, the fall of the young man from the gallery – no one who has
> read it forgets these things.[7]

In each of his comments on Carleton, the second one a headnote
in *Representative Irish Tales* (1891), Yeats mentions the Spanish
author Calderón de la Barca (1600-81). In the first he alludes to 'the
grey island consecrated by the verse of Calderón', for which 'the
lean controversial Caesar Otway' had felt no veneration. Here he is
referring indirectly to Caesar Otway, *Sketches in Ireland: Descriptive
of Interesting, and hitherto unnoticed Districts, in the North and South*
(1827), pp.150-54. Otway was an aggressively polemical protestant
clergyman who found the place 'filthy, dreary and utterly
detestible', and associated Lough Derg and its island with 'the
monstrous birth of a degraded superstition, the enemy of mental
cultivation', and saw it as 'destined to keep the human understanding in the dark unproductive state as the moorland waste that
lay outstretched around' (Otway also wrote *A Tour in Connaught*
(1839). In his second comment on Carleton Yeats refers to the
Purgatory as 'celebrated by Calderón'.

Yeats had, then, obviously met the legend in Calderón's play *The
Purgatory of St Patrick*, as a young man, and, presumably, he
renewed his acquaintance with it when a production of it was considered for the Abbey Theatre in 1910. He probably read it in the
metrical translation by Dennis Florence Mac-Carthy, included in
his *Calderón's Dramas* (1887) which was based upon the text in
Calderón's Comedies, (ed.Hartzenbusch, Madrid, 1856). Some of the
material in this play by Calderón goes back to a Spanish source,
Juan Perez de Montalvan's *Vida y Purgatorio de San Patricio* (1627),
a very popular work of which the fifth impression 'improved and
enlarged by the author', appeared in 1628. It was translated into
various languages, into French (1637 and 1642), Dutch (1668) and
Portuguese (1738) as well as into Italian and German. Montalvan's
book was compiled from Thomas Messingham's *Florilegium Insulae
Sanctorum, Seu vitae et actae sanctorum Hiberniae*, published in Paris

in 1624. Messingham was Superior of the Irish Seminary in Paris.

In his play Calderón took over various parts of Montalvan's material (though, surprisingly, he invented Egerius as King of Ireland, ignoring Montalvan's attribution of the kingship to Leogaire), probably the story of Luis Ennius on whom the dramatic interest of the play centres. Ennius, who resembles the Owen of Henry Saltrey's earlier account (described below) decided, in Act II, scene V, to go to the Purgatory to offer public penance for his sins. (He has had a disturbing encounter with a cloaked figure which turns out to be his own skeleton); these sins include the killing of Polonia, the King's daughter who is restored to life by St Patrick. The Saint has been told by an angel about the 'vast and darksome cave' where a truly contrite person can see where the soul is purged of sin, see Hell itself and the places where the happy spirits dwell. (The King has challenged Patrick to show Purgatory for a proof of his religious affirmations). The cave is consequently described in Act II, scenes XVI, XVIII and XVX, and Polonia, who has nobly forgiven Luis Ennius for murdering her, gives him directions for finding it:

> This darksome lake doth all surround
> The lofty mountain's rugged base
> And so to reach the awful place
> An easy passage may be found:
> A sacred convent in the island stands,
> Midway between the mountains and the sands.

He finds the place pleasant in contrast to the dismal mountain with its mournful birds of prey which 'Hoarsely croak, presaging woe'. In the play he emerges, repentant and purged of his sins, to tell the story of his adventures to the Canons who have admitted him to the cave; he has met Saint Patrick there, and he finally begs to be allowed to stay at the monastery there for the rest of his life.

In the notes to his translation of Calderón's *The Purgatory of St Patrick* Dennis Florence Mac-Carthy cites not only the Latin text of Messingham but extracts from it, printed in English in Paris in 1718 under the title *A Brief History of Saint Patrick's Purgatory. Collected by the Reverend Mr Thomas Messingham, formerly Superior of the Irish Seminary in Paris. And now made English in favour of those who are curious to know the Particulars of that Famous Place and Pilgrimage so much celebrated by Antiquity*. The extract given is based on the MS of Henry of Saltrey, a Benedictine monk of the Abbey of Saltrey in Huntingdonshire. It tells the story of the soldier (or knight) Owen (whose native country is Northern Ireland), who makes known to a Bishop his resolve to do penance for his sins by going into St Patrick's Purgatory. This account tells how the Bishop introduced Owen to the Prior at the Purgatory, who prescribes fifteen days' fasting and prayer, after which he conducts Owen to the door of the cave, sprinkles him with holy water and tells him to walk through the cave to a field containing an artificially wrought Hell where he will meet messengers sent by God to tell him what he is to do and suffer, adding that, once God's messengers had gone, he would be tempted by evil spirits. Owen goes through the door, which the Prior prudently locks on the outside. In the Hell he is met by fifteen men in white garments who warn him that he will be destroyed body and soul if he gives way to the unclean spirits, but, if he is strong in faith, he will not only be purged of his sins but see the torments sinners endure and the place of Rest and Bliss which the just enjoy. A multitude of Devils appears and they attempt to terrify or flatter Owen into returning to the door. After he tries to resist them, Owen is cast into a fire from which he escapes by calling upon the name of his Redeemer. The devils then drag him to a field where an infinite number of men and women lying flat on their bellies are being cruelly tortured; again he invokes Jesus and is now brought to another field where people lay only on their buttocks, bitten by dragons, stung by serpents or gnawed by vultures. The third penal field contains people of both sexes fastened to the ground and pierced throughout their bodies by iron spikes which are on fire; the fourth field has several forms of fire torture, including frying, roasting, and dipping in boiling sulphur. All of these victims in the fields are constantly scourged by the devils, who show the soldier an iron wheel on which men are bound with flaming crooks; the devils spin this round at high speed, but Owen again escapes, as he does from a house full of cauldrons of boiling liquors into which the devils plunge their victims.

A high mountain is the next place of torture from which a whirlwind hurls naked men and women into an intolerably cold and stinking river. There follows what the devils call the Entrance to Hell, a sulphurous pit erupting men 'like sparks of fire' who fall back into the pit: into this the devils cast themselves headlong, bringing Owen with them. He is just able to utter God's name and is then shot up on to the brink of the pit. His next torment is to be told by another lot of devils that the previous ones had lied to him and that he must now go over a bridge, so slippery, straight and narrow and high up that no one could cross it. He crosses safely, to the rage of the devils, and sees a new world through which he is conducted by two Archbishops: all was 'peaceable, quiet, still, agreeable': he is shown the gate of Paradise and tastes Heavenly food. He is, however, told, to his great distress, that he must return to the world. He eventually returns, having met the fifteen who had given him his first instruction and now tell him to hasten to the cave door in case the Prior comes to the door, and, not finding Owen there, despairs of his salvation and locks it again.

This vision has been thought to have influenced Dante. Owen himself eventually becomes a monk, having helped Gilbert of Louth (from whom Henry of Saltrey said he had heard Owen's story) – who has been appointed by the King of Ulster to erect a monastery – as an interpreter, since Gilbert knows no Irish. He becomes responsible for the external relationships of the Monastery (built in two and a half years), the internal regime of which was presided over by Gilbert.

IV

Yeats's interest in the Lough Derg pilgrimage, evinced in his essay of 1919, was probably rekindled by a book on St Patrick's Purgatory written by Archdeacon St John Seymour upon whose other works he drew. (Mrs Yeats told me he had read all the Archdeacon's works.) Seymour's *Irish Witchcraft and Demonology*, for instance, provided the poet with information on the love-lorn Dame Alice Kyteler and the insolent fiend Robert Artisson for 'Nineteen hundred and nineteen', vi,[9] and his *Anglo-Irish Literature* contained a version of 'The Irish Dancer' used by Yeats for 'I am of Ireland'.[10]

Archdeacon Seymour's book, *St Patrick's Purgatory. A Medieval Pilgrimage in Ireland*, was published in May 1919, some months before Yeats's essay appeared. In it the Archdeacon gives an account of the early legendary history of Lough Derg. The lake, about thirteen miles in circumference, and 2,200 acres in area, lies in the extreme south of Co.Donegal, close to Co.Tyrone, four miles north of Lough Erne. It is surrounded by mountains and contains 'forty or more' islands. The reason for the arrival of pilgrims at this lough for over seven centuries was that it was believed that by a pilgrim's entering St Patrick's Purgatory and spending twenty-four hours there, in the midst of unspeakable horrors, he could purge himself of his sins in this world and avoid the pains of purgatory, entering heaven immediately after his death.

Archdeacon Seymour traced the Celtic legends about the place. The name Lough Derg, meaning the Red Lake, probably came from the reddish colour of its water, fed from bogs and moorland and by chalybeate springs. Legend, however, provided a different reason. The Lough was originally Lough Finn, the Fair Lake. Finn MacCumhaill hunted a venomous witch, and shot her with a silver arrow as her son, a giant, ran away with her on his back. Such was his haste that he ran to Donegal without noticing she was dead, but when he arrived there he was carrying little more than her bones, the rest of her body having been worn away by hitting trees, bushes and stones in his headlong flight. The giant threw down her bones. A hunting party of the Fianna found them, but were warned by a dwarf not to touch the thigh bone for it contained a venomous worm which would destroy the world if it could get out and find water to drink. Conan Maol, a notoriously bad-tempered hero, broke the bone, and threw the hairy worm which appeared from it into the Lough, remarking 'there is water enough for you'. A terrible beast thereupon rushed out of the lake and devastated the country, devouring people wholesale until Finn MacCumhaill himself attacked it, plunging his sword into its one vulnerable area, a mole on its left side. It lay writhing by the lough shore and its blood stained the water red. Finally St Patrick came by and compelled it to go to the bottom of the lake.

Archdeacon Seymour records variants of the legend, in one of which Conan allowed the beast to swallow him, then cut his way out through its belly, being balded by the heat of its entrails in the process (hence his nickname Maol, or bald). He decapitated it and the lough was reddened with its blood for forty-eight hours. Another version tells how St Patrick came to Lough Finn and found the monster on an island. He threw his crozier at it, piercing its heart. When its blood stained the lough he said that the lough would be called Lough Derg till the Day of Judgment. The combination of Pagan and Christian legend is reminiscent of Yeats's *The Wanderings of Oisin* where Oisin, the son of Finn MacCumhaill, tells St Patrick of his three hundred years in the otherworld with Niamh, and is urged by the Saint not to boast, but to pray for his soul, lost

> Through the demon love of its youth and its godless and passionate age.[11]

There was, however, another view of the lough's name, given by O'Donovan, that the name should not be Lough Derg but Lough Dearc, the lough of the cave. What is apparently the earliest account of the foundation of the purgatory, given by Henry of Saltrey, describes a round pit shown by Our Lord to Patrick who was in despair at the impossibility of converting the Irish to Christianity unless their demand that one of them should see the torments of the damned and the bliss of the sacred was met. The Lord said that any man entering the pit and staying there a day and a night would, provided his faith was strong, be purged of his sins and see the torments of hell, the joys of heaven. There are other accounts of the creation of the purgatory. In one Patrick was ordered to trace a circle on the ground which became the deep pit; in another he struck the ground with his staff. Later a cave into which St Patrick had retired to pray became the site. In yet another version this cave was tenanted by all the evil spirits banished by the saint from other parts of Ireland. Not unreasonably no one dared approach it, but the Saint rowed out in a little boat to the island where the cave was and prayed and fasted there for forty days. While there he expelled Satan from his last stronghold in Ireland 'but also obtained from God the privilege of seeing the pains by which the temporal punishment due to sin is expiated in purgatory'.

A celtic monastery did flourish at Lough Derg (Henry of Saltrey anachronistically described Patrick as placing canons regular of St Augustine to guard the church and the purgatory), probably comprising both Saints' Island and Station Island. The remains of an oratory and cemetery, and of a circular earthen enclosure are on Saints' island, and on Station Island are the so-called 'penal beds', possibly remains of bee-hive oratories, of the ninth century. The Four Masters record the death of Cillene of Lough Derg in 721: but the history of the monastery is vague. Archdeacon Seymour suggests it may have been sacked in the Danish invasions. But between 1130 and 1134 the canons regular of St Augustine established a priory there. Archdeacon Seymour examined the statements of four twelfth century writers, David of Wurzburg, Joscelin, a monk from the Cistercian Community of Furness, Giraldus Cambrensis and Henry of Saltrey. David of Wurzburg testified to the existence of a purgatory he believed St Patrick to have founded. Joscelin connected the purgatory with Croagh-Patrick in Co.Mayo where he described St Patrick as fasting and praying for the forty days of Lent, beset by devils in the shape of hideous black birds; his comments were made in about 1185. Two years later, Giraldus Cambrensis placed the purgatory at an Ulster lake in his *Topographica Hibernica* and gave virtually the same details as Henry of Saltrey whose account of the pilgrimage of the Knight Owen was probably written by 1190. This account may have helped to make the purgatory well known.

Archdeacon Seymour adds to his second chapter a list of the pilgrims, many of them from overseas, known to have visited the purgatory between the end of the twelfth century and 1497, when the Pope ordered the cave to be demolished. These pilgrims included George Crissaphan, a Hungarian knight who was there in 1353 (he was stripped naked after he left the cave, his clothes having an 'ineffable odour of Paradise'), Guillebert de Lannoy, a French diplomat, who was there in 1430 and Cardinal Merenio Chievati, Papal legate to the Court of Henry VIII who was there in 1515.

V

Of the accounts of the pilgrims the most interesting is that of a Florentine merchant, Antonio Mannini, who visited the purgatory in 1411. He sent this in letter form to a friend in London, Corso di Giovanni Rustichi, who sent it to Florence. There Antonio's brother Salvestro Mannini copied it, and added material to it from his brother's verbal account given when he returned to Florence. Antonio's account – which includes a quotation from Dante's *Paradiso* in its opening – tells the story plainly:

Many times I made ready to start, sometimes there was no ship, sometimes the wind was contrary, and sometimes I was without money. I had but two horses with which I desired to come, and I knew myself well-nigh forsaken by all men, and with no counsel or comfort, or hope of anything save the grace and mercy of God in whom I have hoped. And being in this state of mind it pleased God that there should come hither a noble gentleman of Hungary, named M Lorenzo Rattoldi, on his way to the purgatory of St Patrick. I visited the gentleman, and held long converse with him; and seeing his holy intention and devotion, for he had come from the head of all Christianity in the world to the end of the earth for the good of his soul, and that I was here close to the said Purgatory, and in such pain and trouble, considering what my life had been hitherto, sinful, and thinking but of worldly things, comforted by good hope I turned to God, and inspired by His mercy I resolved and determined for the good of my soul to go to the said Purgatory, hoping and believing in the divine mercy that perhaps in the future I might have better grace and fortune and an end to my long tribulations; and though I had long wished to go to that Purgatory, especially since I came to Ireland, I was dissuaded there from until then by a Roman gentleman, a priest called Master Antonio da Focha, by whom I sent you a letter long since. He went to the said Purgatory, and upon his return he persuaded me I should not go thither, saying that I was of a delicate constitution for so much hardship, with many other reasons which there is no need to give you here. Nevertheless, as I have already told you, fortified by the will of God, I resolved to make the said journey and pilgrimage with the said gentleman, and we set out from Dublin in the name of God on Friday the 25th of September, 1411. I thought indeed to go and return in three weeks at the longest, but through the perilous roads and other occasions we have spent three months and half in going and returning.

The Purgatory lies in a lake among high mountains, and is like a well, ten miles in circumference, in which there are thirty-four islands, great and small. We reached the island in that lake on which the priory stands in safety on Thursday the 4th of November [1411], which island is a mile measured by water from the island of the Purgatory; and the said island of the Purgatory is 129 paces long and 30 paces wide, and is in the very centre of the said lake. That day, as soon as I arrived, I confessed myself to the prior of the said priory and began the usual fast on bread and water as observed by others, according to their desire to do so and the constitution of the pilgrimage. I wished to fast for more days, but the prior, urging that it was winter and very cold, would not allow me to fast for more than three days one after the other.

On Saturday the 7th of November, 1411, preparing to enter the Purgatory that day, though the prior was very unwilling, I rose before dawn, and when he had confessed me he said the Mass of our Lord Jesus Christ for me, and then gave me Communion; and after that I heard another Mass of the Annunciation of Our Lady, and then I urged the prior that he should send me to the Purgatory. When he at last consented with great trouble and difficulty, the canon who said the Mass of Our Lady for me, whose name is brother John, and who is one of the canons of the said priory, was commanded to take me to the island of the Purgatory and put me into it. The said canon put me in a little boat, which was like a piece of roughly-hewn hollow tree-trunk, and four persons could hardly find room in it. The prior accompanied me as far as the water, and put me into the boat himself, first kissing me and giving me his blessing; you must note that I was barefoot and bareheaded, and was wearing a riding tunic and a doublet over my shirt. Then, the canon, who sat facing me with his back to the island, began to row with two small oars, and I sat facing him, with my face to the island of the Purgatory.

The weather was still and fine, and it was calm. When we were within half a bowshot of the said island of the Purgatory I saw a bird blacker than coal take flight; it had not a single plume or feather on its back, save only four or five on each wing, and it was shaped like a heron, but rather larger. And when I saw and noticed it I thought it a great marvel, and I began to tremble, and my heart beat fast with fear, and my hair stood straight upon end so that I could scarcely smooth it down with my hands and make it lie flat. The canon knew quite well what it was, for he began to make the sign of the cross, and he signed himself four or five times. I asked him what it meant, and what this bird might be and the reason of the great fear which had come upon me.

But he answered, trying to put me off, as if he did not wish to tell me, saying [in Latin] *Nothing! it's nothing! don't ask questions! don't ask questions!* and bidding me be of good cheer, and hope in God, and commend myself to Him. This made me the more suspicious, and I instantly and piteously besought him in God's name to tell me fully what this might be. Thereupon he replied that since I asked him in the Lord's name and in such a manner, he could not refuse, and he began as follows:

'At the time when our Lord shewed St Patrick this Purgatory, after him, and one of his disciples called St Nicholas, many went in, and most of them perished and came forth no more and were never heard of again. St Patrick marvelled greatly at this, and devoutly prayed to God with constant prayer and discipline, until he saw by the Holy Spirit that the reason of it was a wicked demon called Corna, who by his many and various temptations caused all the people to perish. Then St Patrick made special prayer to God, beseeching Him to destroy the power of this demon: and God heard his prayer, and appeared to him in visible form in this place on the island, and said:- 'Patrick, I have heard thy prayer,' and shewed him the wicked bird, saying: 'I have bound him in this shape, and he shall never again have power to harm any man, and he shall retain this shape until the Day of Judgment, and he shall not have power to abide anywhere but on a stone or a withered tree. And when any Christian comes to this island, he shall go forth there from and abide in some other island, but he shall not be able to leave the lake.'

Then the canon added that

when the accursed bird Corna blows the horn with his beak, like a man, it is a sign of perdition for him who is about to enter the Purgatory; but, God be praised he did not blow the horn for me, and I heard nothing. If I marvelled do you likewise now marvel, when you hear these words, for to this hour my heart beats when I think of it.[12]

When the boat was within twelve feet of the island the Florentine merchant was flung out into three fathoms of water, but rose to the surface, to the obvious relief of the canon 'who cried aloud *good! good!*' He described the chapel and his experiences there:

And as I was praying thus I fell asleep and whether my soul was rapt in ecstasy out of my body, and in what way I cannot tell you. What I saw, and what was shown to me, and what I did, I may not write in a letter, nor can I utter it save in confession, but if it ever pleases God that we should meet again I will tell you all things in due order.[13]

The canon returned at night, found him colder than ice, 'so that he doubted of his life', but woke him up and brought him back to the island of the priory:

In my judgment I was five hours in the Purgatory. It is usual to remain there for an ordinary day – that is, twenty-four hours, but in such cold weather the prior would not suffer me to remain longer. I think that place – that is, the whole of the lake, is the coldest country in which I have ever been; the mountains of Brigha are not cold in winter compared to that place. I wonder now how I endured it so long almost naked. Be certain, Corso, it would have been impossible, save by the grace and mercy of God.[14]

The account of Laurence Rathold de Pasztho, who went to Lough Derg with Antonio Mannini, is more elaborate. When the knight returned to Dublin and was waiting a ship, he told his friends of his adventures and they asked for a written account. So James Yonge, who acted as his secretary and scribe in Dublin, wrote down a Latin description of the pilgrimage. He had several conversations with the Hungarian knight but the account was not dictated. When Laurence arrived at Lough Derg he was warned of the dangers by the prior, who told him some pilgrims had died, some gone mad as a result of the attacks of evil spirits and others had simply disappeared and never been heard of again. He was allowed a five day fast instead of the usual fifteen days before being rowed to the island of the purgatory. It is at this point in the narrative that Yonge interpolated a description of the island, including Satan and his satellites who have lived there from time immemorial. Among these is a demon

called in the Irish language 'Cornu' in appearance resembling a heron without feathers, who when he utters a cry like the blare of a trumpet, foretells the death of the pilgrim who is about to enter the Purgatory.[15]

Yonge tells us that the knight was attacked by the evil spirits in the second cave, but he made the sign of the cross and uttered a prayer which drove them off. Then another devil disguised as an old pilgrim tried unsuccessfully to persuade him Jesus was a deceiver of the people. The third trial was the appearance of a seductive woman. There followed a visit from Michael the Archangel, who showed him, at Laurence's request, his family in purgatory. He was not allowed to see Heaven or Hell being judged unwilling to relinquish the world. He was given messages and revelations, but was not judged worthy to kiss the feet of the archangel, who brought him back to the cave by a shorter way. When he left Lough Derg the prior gave him a cautiously worded certificate in Latin translated by Seymour as follows:

> To all the faithful in Christ who shall see or hear these letters brother Matthew, Prior of St Patrick's Purgatory in the diocese of Clogher, sends continual greeting in the Lord. Know ye that the Magnifico, Laurence Rathold de Pasztho, visited our place, and exhibited letter of recommendation from the Archbishop of Armagh; and after he had done penance in fasting and prayer he entered the Purgatory. When he had heard the Mass of the Holy Cross, and had observed all the other attendant solemnities of the pilgrimage, with procession and litany he entered St Patrick's cave fasting and naked, except for *rosetis* and a *femoral*, and abiding there suffered the attacks of unclean spirits, as we are given to understand, and also saw and heard divine revelations in that cave wherein holy Nicholas and George Crissaphan, and Eugene O'Brien of England (formerly) bore the attacks of evil spirits. In testimony of which premises we have affixed our seal to these presents. Given in the island of saints on the fifth day after St Martin's day [Nov. 15] in the year 1411.[16]

VI

Some pilgrims, however, experienced nothing in the cave and a spirit of scepticism began to arise. About 1394 Froissart recorded discussing the experiences of Sir William de Lisle at Lough Derg with him, and Sir William with a touch of *phlegm anglais* told how he had been oppressed with strange fancies and wonderful dreams: ...and in the morning when they went out they had clean forgotten their dreams and visions; whereupon he concluded that the whole matter was fancy.[17]

Caxton's *Mirror of the World* (1481) recorded a high Canon of Waterford reporting that though he had been there eight or nine times he neither saw nor suffered any such strange things. The cave became part of some romance writers' material. But its mysteries were debunked by a monk of Enystadt who had had difficulty in getting permission to enter it. He could not afford the sums at first demanded by the local bishop, by the chieftain of the district, and by the prior, but eventually he persuaded all three to allow him to enter the cave. After spending a night in the pit into which he was lowered by a sacristan, he decided the whole affair was a deception, went to Rome, and told the Penitentiary, who informed the Pope. The Pope sent the monk back to Ireland with letters to the bishop, the chieftain and the prior ordering them to destroy the place, which they did in 1497. The reasons given were that the place had become one of shameful avarice, that it was not the purgatory which Patrick had obtained from God. Seymour comments that the monk's description differs from those of other pilgrims who described the cave as a kind of vault which could be entered unaided, not at all like the pit into which the monk was lowered. But some pilgrims had said that there was a stone at the extreme end of the cave which covered the true purgatory.

The Archbishop of Armagh petitioned the Pope in 1521 for a re-opening of the cave, the monastic community having continued to exist at Lough Derg. At the time of dissolution the prior was seized of a very ruinous old church and recently levelled walls. By 1603 it seems to have been derelict for some time. The pilgrimage, however, continued to be popular, some pilgrims having to leave without even reaching the island, so many were the visitors. In 1632 the pilgrimage was suspended and the buildings demolished by order of the Priory.[18] This work was carried out by the Bishop of Clogher, James Spottiswood, after Sir William Stuart had visited the island and caused four hundred people and seventy one people 'to be put safe to shore', an act accomplished without violence. But some buildings must have been rebuilt, for there is a record of their being demolished again in 1680. An act of 1764 forbade pilgrimages, and especially those to Lough Derg. But from then on this pilgrimage flourished.

VII

It is likely that Yeats's image of the great black ragged bird comes from Mannini's bird 'blacker than coal' which had not a single plume or feather on its back, 'save only four or five on each wing, and it was shaped like a heron, but rather larger'.

The 'stones' of the holy island may derive from contemporary accounts of the pilgrimage, though Archdeacon Seymour quotes a passage from Bishop David Rothe incorporated in Messingham's *Florilegium* which describes the ceremonies the pilgrim had to observe before entering the purgatorial cave:

The austerities lasted for nine days, during which the pilgrims only received one meal of dry bread and lake-water in twenty-four hours. Each day the stations had to be gone around three times, at morning, mid-day, and evening, and during the night they lay on hay or straw without any bed-clothes. 'The stations themselves are gone around in this order. Being admitted by the spiritual father, who is over the Purgatory, to make the peregrination, the devotees take off their shoes and stockings, and barefoot enter the church which is dedicated to St Patrick. Having prayed there, they go around the sacred enclosures seven times within the church itself, and as many times without in the cemetery. When this is finished they go to the penal houses, or penitential cells of the saints, which are [in the shape of] a circle. They go around the outside of these seven times barefoot, and around the inside on bended knees. In a similar manner they approach the cross in the cemetery, and then to another which is fixed to a heap of stones. So many rounds having being completed on rough and stony paths they come to the lake and place their feet, which are sometimes lacerated and always tired, on a stone under the water; and [being there] for at least a quarter of an hour they feel themselves so refreshed by the stone under their feet (on which St Patrick is said to have prayed, and to have left his footprints) that they are ready to commence a second round, which is not permitted unless a certain space of time intervenes.'[19]

Why Yeats should have thought of the Lough Derg pilgrimage in 1937 is difficult to say. The idea of pilgrimage attracted him and the poem also echoes his own interest in purgation.[20] In his general comment on the poems of *The King of the Great Clock Tower* (1934) he wrote of how:

An Irish poet during a country walk talked of the Church of Ireland, he had preferences for this or that preacher, Archbishop Gregg had pleased him by accepting certain recent Lambeth decrees; one could be a devout communicant and accept all counsels before the Great Schism that separated Western from Eastern Christianity in the ninth century. In course of time the Church of Ireland would feel itself more in sympathy with early Christian Ireland than could a Church that admitted later developments of doctrine. I said that for the moment I associated early Christian Ireland with India: Shri Purohit Swami, protected during his pilgrimage to a remote Himalayan shrine by a strange great dog that disappeared when danger was past, might have been that blessed Cellach who sang upon his deathbed of bird and beast; Bagwas Shri Hamsa's pilgrimage to Mount Kailas, the legendary Meru, and to lake Manas Sarowa, suggested pilgrimages to Croagh Patrick and to Lough Derg. A famous philosopher believed that every civilisation began, no matter what its geographical origin, with Asia, certain men of science that all of us when still in the nursery were, if not African, exceedingly Asiatic. Saint Patrick must have found in Ireland, for he was not its first missionary, men whose Christianity had come from Egypt, and retained characteristics of those older faiths that have become so important to our invention.[21]

In 'Meru'[22] he wrote (probably between August 1933 and June 1934) of Mount Meru, then in his mind because he was about to write an Introduction to Shri Purohit Swami's book *The Holy Mountain* (1934). The Swami had not accompanied a friend to Mount Kailas, 'the legendary Meru'. Holy places in general were in Yeats's thought at this time and especially the two Irish pilgrimages to Croagh Patrick and Lough Derg. And the publication in 1932 of an elegant book, *Saint Patrick's Purgatory. A Record from History and Literature* compiled by Shane Leslie, may also have rekindled his interest in Lough Derg and its legends a little earlier,[23] for Leslie's book includes Antonio Mannini's and Laurence Rathold's accounts of their pilgrimages with the great black bird flapping above the island in the lake. A final comment on the demon in heron form, the 'Cornu' or 'Corna' can be given from Seymour's study:

Richardson records in his *Folly of Pilgrimages* that towards the close of the seventeenth century a Frenchman, named Ludovicus Pyrrhus, came to Lough Derg for the purpose of discovering the purgatorial cave. In this respect his efforts were not crowned with success, but in the course of his excavations he happened upon an image 'which is said to be the image of Caoranach, and is kept on the lesser island [Station I.] for the satisfaction of the pilgrims.' According to the same authority the monster which came out of the lake, and was slain by Conan Maol, its bones being subsequently metamorphosed into great stones, was named Caoranach. He also states that the figure of this monster was cut on a flat stone at the angle of the little chapel, and denotes its position on his map by the letter (*a*). Skelton adds the interesting genealogical fact that this was the Devil's mother. In appearance this figure was said to represent a wolf with a serpent's tail between its legs and thrown over its back; in other words it was one of these pieces of grotesque medieval stone-cutting which are found so frequently in connection with ecclesiastical structures all over Ireland and Europe. Whether such are emblematic of the vices, or whether they are merely sprung from the sculptor's impish fancy, is just the question. At all events it would seem that the image cut on the chapel was shewn to the pilgrims as the representation of the terrible monster slain by the patron saint, the abundant streams of blood from which gave the lake its name and colour. Thus, as no doubt happened elsewhere, an incidental piece of Christian carved work and a centuries-old pagan legend were brought into connection. That Corna and Caoranach are one and the same is beyond question, the words being radically identical. We have little doubt that what Mannini saw was a heron, or a bird of kindred species; possibly it was remarkable for its longevity, and chose the lonely isle

as being a place where it would not be disturbed, and for this reason was regarded by the community with superstitious awe, local
legend furnishing the explanation given by the canon of Mannini.
Apparently when the heron died the legend was transferred to the
image.[24]

MEMORIES OF MAUD GONNE

In my teens I used to talk to Maud Gonne. She lived about a quarter of a mile away in Roebuck House and occasionally took a walk along our road, dressed in black from head to foot of her tall, bent but graceful body, her eyes large and luminous with a hint of mesmeric qualities, her voice elegantly modulated. She admired our cats, she liked flowers, she seemed to drift along, just a little tired, just a little detached from the life around her, yet recording what she saw with clarity, apprehending its details effortlessly.

I went to call on her when I was writing a Ph.D. on the sources and symbolism of Yeats's middle and later poetry. Roebuck House had a faintly mysterious air to me: doors swung on double hinges: there were large dogs about. I wondered how Madame MacBride – then seventy-seven – would react to someone obviously curious about her relationship to Yeats but brought up in Dublin where in those days privacy was still to be respected, decorum still to be preserved.

Maud, for so I always thought of her, was sitting by the fire. She was very frail now, more bent, her face criss-crossed with lines. The setting – with harp and spinning-wheel – was superb. Moving stiffly, she took down from a shelf a volume of Yeats's poems and read me 'When You are Old'. She read it in that most evocative voice of hers, clearly, unaffectedly, and murmured 'I think Willie would have liked me to read you that poem'. We discussed other poems she particularly liked; 'Red Hanrahan's Song about Ireland' was her favourite, she said, quoting it. And she told me of the day they spent on Howth after he had first proposed to her in 1891. It was a place that meant a great deal to them both, for both had spent part of their youth there and loved the then somewhat isolated peninsula. They were resting in the heather by the cliff path, when two seagulls flew overhead and out to sea, and she had said that if she were to have the choice of being any bird she would above all prefer to be a seagull 'and in three days he sent me the poem with its gentle theme "I would that we were, my beloved, white birds on the foam of the sea".' (The second stanza of that poem, 'The White Birds', alters it, to chime with her wish, to 'For I would we were changed to white birds on the wandering foam: I and you!'). She went on to tell me how she had replied to him whenever he proposed to her: 'No, Willie, the world will thank me for not marrying you. Let us go on being such good friends. And go on writing me these lovely poems.'

To a certain extent the impression she gave me in this first conversation about Yeats was that she had a prepared script. She had, after all, a great ability as an actress, and had first attempted to create a life of her own on the stage -she had the makings, too, of a secret agent (commenting to me that Willie could never keep anything secret) with that disregard for danger, for death itself, that her father had inculcated in her. My sense of her having a well-rehearsed script predominated when she discussed politics. It was obviously easier for her to enact a political monologue, as if she were switched to an automatic pilot.[1] But this was not inevitable, however much in old age she had manufactured and depended upon her own mythology, for she responded to suggestions about poems and people which arose from questions that, to my delight, drifted into discussion. She was touched by Yeats's remembering their plans of forty years before – for a Castle of Heroes upon that island in Lough Key – when they last met in old age at Riversdale in 1938. I thought that symbolised the gulfs between them: perhaps she had never realised how much she meant to him, how obsessed with her he was – and remained. He had not kindled in her any kindred yearnings; he had helped her, he was a friend, perhaps the brother she never had and may have needed; she accepted his help, indeed she expected it.

One way of discovering her views on particular poems was, I found, to tell her some of the sources I had been discovering for them, by following up references to authors in Yeats's prose, by reading his diaries, letters and manuscripts, and by working on books in his library (which Mrs Yeats had preserved). Out of such conversations came her most interesting reactions to my queries – and there were many of them – about specific poems. For instance, 'The Cold Heaven' seemed to me then to relate to Yeats's belief, expressed in 'The Trembling of the Veil' (*Autobiographies*, p.378) that men live their lives backwards after death. This remark of mine elicited her comment that when she had asked Willie the meaning of the poem, which first appears in *The Green Helmet and other Poems* (1912), he had told her it was an attempt to describe the feelings aroused in him by the cold detached sky in winter. It was a mood of loneliness when he felt responsible for mistakes made in the past which were now disturbing his peace of mind.

It has been a strange experience after so many years – Maud died in April 1953, at the age of eighty-six – to read her letters to

Yeats. Those he had kept Mrs Yeats returned to Maud after his death. His own letters to her were mainly destroyed when Irish Free State soldiers raided her house in St Stephen's Green during the Irish Civil War, though some few have survived and will be included in the volume of her letters to him, which her granddaughter Anna White has preserved and which I am editing with her.[2] They range from 1893 to 1938 and give an idea of the friendship between two remarkable people: the great poet of the twentieth century, playwright, essayist, editor, and occultist, the creator of the Abbey Theatre with Lady Gregory, the Senator of the Irish Free State and Nobel Prize Winner for Literature; and the independent woman who did so much to help other women to play their independent parts in Irish political life, the supporter of evicted tenants, of treason-felony prisoners, the mother of two children by her French lover Lucien Millevoye, of Sean, her son by her husband John MacBride, a son she loved deeply who became IRA commandant, then Irish government minister, then United Nations Commissioner in S.W. Africa.

Maud Gonne, a women who learnt to draw and paint skilfully, was a powerful public speaker in her youth and middle age; she had endured imprisonment and hunger-striking. She campaigned ceaselessly for prisoners, beginning with those in Portland Gaol and later for those in Irish gaols. She made her house in Dublin a refuge for many in want. There were often refugees of one kind and other there, for Maud not only sympathised with the oppressed and those in need but took practical steps to help them. Her kindness extended to children. An educational programme of free classes for children in Irish, history, music, dance and drama was set up by Inghinidhe na hEireann, the organisation of which she was president. In 1910 she worked with the flood relief committee in Paris set up to deal with the victims of the devastating floods. This experience may have turned her attention to the effects of poverty on the health of children in Dublin. She was mainly responsible for creating a canteen for children in St Audeon's parish in 1910, and for another in Ringsend in 1911.

Seen by many as a Woman of the Sidhe in her early days in Donegal, aiding the evicted tenants in the second phase of the Land War, her public image was enhanced by the presence of Dagda, her Great Dane, whose potential menace she did not scruple to exploit upon occasion. A dog of Dagda's impressive size was a suitable companion to accompany a heroic figure. While Yeats in writing his first play for her thought of her as the Countess Cathleen who sold her goods and finally her soul to save her people, and later saw her enact, indeed embody, the symbolic Cathleen ni Houlihan in the famous first production of *Cathleen ni Houlihan* in Dublin in 1902, he generally thought of her as being like a goddess – a view shared by H W Nevinson, among others. Yeats described her as resembling Pallas Athene, though Diana with her passion for dogs might in some ways have been suitable. Dagda was the first of a long line of large dogs. There was a very large Great Dane – rather like a Dalmatian, a spotty dog as we used to call them, in its markings – at Roebuck House when I first visited it and there was one Alsatian – or perhaps more – padding around too. Maud gave me a large photograph of herself with the Great Dane taken with the red brick wall of the garden as background.

Her early habit of travelling with cages of singing birds was described briefly by Yeats in his *Autobiographies*, while Sarah Purser (who painted her portrait with her pet marmoset 'Chaperone') recorded the din of the canaries in Maud's apartment in Paris with some irritation. Several people commented on the menagerie-like menage in France at Colleville, where there was a troop of black dogs, cats, bantams and parrots and, as ever, the singing birds. (Maud managed to have one with her later when she was in Holloway Gaol in 1918 and she sometimes released them at public meetings.) Ella Young, for instance, remarked on the number of dogs 'large and small: Great Danes, Toy Pomeranians, haughty court-bred Pekinese, and one Persian cat' and on the parrot that cursed in Spanish and its comrade that yelled in a language of its own. (*Flowering Dusk* (1945), pp.101-2). Yeats however, had become philosophical about it, wryly describing Maud's house to Lady Gregory in a letter of 15 August 1917 (*The Letters of W.B. Yeats*, ed.Allan Wade (1954) pp.629-30) as having the usual number of cage birds, a parrot, a monkey, a goat, two dogs, a cat and seven rabbits.

The parrot has one accomplishment, a scream of laughter, and if anyone laughs in its hearing the scream comes at once. As I write the monkey is on the window outside scratching to draw my attention. Two days ago a neighbour called, a young widow, and she and the parrot became hysterical with laughter – each setting the other off. I have just driven the monkey off the window sill.

On 17 August he recorded how the monkey had tried to pluck the parrot.

The letters written by Maud to Yeats which survive – there are approximately three hundred and fifty of them (some are fragments of letters) – show some of the high and low points in their

friendship. They throw much light on details of their long relationship, from 1889 to 1939, and they demonstrate their early shared
and later conflicting interests in Irish politics, their interest in and
knowledge of Celtic mythology – Maud sometimes saw herself as
Maeve; it was the name she used among her friends in Inghinidhe
na hEireann; and Yeats's poem of 1903, 'The Old Age of Queen
Maeve', moves from the Gaelic queen to Maud with poignant
effect:

> Friend of these many years, you too had stood
> With equal courage in that whirling rout;
> For you, although you've not her wandering heart,
> Have all that greatness, and not hers alone,
> For there is no high story about queens
> In any ancient book, but tells of you;
> And when I've heard how they grew old and died,
> Or fell into unhappiness, I've said,
> 'She will grow old and die, and she has wept!'
> And when I'd write it out anew, the words,
> Half crazy with the thought, She too has wept!
> Outrun the measure.

The letters also reveal how much both friends travelled – something easier for Maud, whose finances were ample until the first
world war, but often a problem for Yeats in his youth and early
middle age. They show the extent of their capacity to experience
visions (some in the 'nineties induced by hashish and others by
mescalin supplied by Havelock Ellis – though the latter did not
seem very effective) and to convey them and their dreams in some
detail. They demonstrate their involvement in the lives of other
people who impinged on their own intense and immensely complex lives. Reading them has brought back to me with great vivid-
ness the drive and energy Maud still had in late years; though but
a very diminished force compared to that which she had put into
what she called her work in her more politically active days, this
vitality was the more remarkable because of her frequent lapses
into illness. Her writing conveys this dominating desire of hers to
get things done. Yeats, too, was remarkable for his capacity to cope
with breakdowns and various illnesses, as well as reading on such
a large scale with very defective vision. His letters to her we can
but guess at; those few preserved among her correspondence certainly convey his concern for her as well as his later awareness of
the gulf between their political beliefs. Their lives were indeed
lived on an Olympian scale.

THE FORTUNES OF RICHARD MAHONY:
AN ANGLO-IRISHMAN RECONSIDERED

When I went to Australia in 1951 it seemed a long way off from Edinburgh, where I had been a university lecturer for nearly three years. Academics didn't fly in those days, and the romantic prospect of a month's voyage emphasised the fact that I was taking my family to the other side of the world. My sister wrote to me to say she didn't advise my reading Henry Handel Richardson's *The Fortunes of Richard Mahony*, because, if it didn't completely put me off going to Australia, it would depress me about the nature of life there. However, in the course of what turned out to be a delightful stay of nearly seven years in Adelaide, South Australia, I did read the novel, and I realised what she had meant. For this novel can indeed seem forbidding – its description of a land frighteningly unlike the British Isles in size and climate, in flora and fauna, an environment both tough and demanding, peopled by a pioneering colonial society.

Not for nothing did Henry Handel Richardson use *qui trans mare currunt* as the heading to the proem of the second book of *The Fortunes of Richard Mahony*, for the trilogy is about emigration, which can often and easily become another word for exile. Richard Mahony recalls the full quotation toward the end of the first book; like a half-remembered tune the words float into his mind: 'Horace, he thought, but whatever their source words that fitted case to a nicety. *Coelum, non animum, mutant, qui trans mare currunt.* 'Non animum?' Ah! Could we have but foreseen this – foreknown it.' The quotation (from Virgil's *Aeneid*) suggests the epic scale of the whole novel, and its somewhat sardonic comment -'Those who cross the seas change their climate not their character'- applies to the novel's main figure. The story is about Richard Mahony's life and death.[1] He is an Anglo-Irishman, a graduate in medicine of the University of Edinburgh, who emigrates to work in the Australian goldfields as the keeper of a shanty store in the hope of rebuilding his family's fortunes. He seeks material success but that success, once gained (when he becomes a doctor in Ballarat), hinders his desire for intellectual independence. He is torn between these material and spiritual aims; his life falls into recurring patterns of success and failure. He escapes from a society in which he feels trapped, but two attempts to settle in practices in England fail and he returns to Australia. He gains money and position, and then loses both; his decaying body overcomes his restless mind, and the land to which he exiled himself, from which he sought escape, finally takes him to itself in death.

The opening quotation of the book, from Sir Thomas Browne's *Religio Medici*, reminds us that 'Everyman is not only himself;- Men are lived over again; the word is now as it was in ages past; there was none then, but there hath been some one since, that parallels him, and is, as it were, his revived self.' As we sailed back in 1955 (on study leave for me to work in libraries in Dublin, London, and Oxford), leaving the fierce sunshine of South Australia to enjoy the fainter wintry sunshine of the Mediterranean before eventually corkscrewing out of the Bay of Biscay into the thick grey fog of the English Channel, insistent images came to mind of Roman officers cursing their luck at leaving the Mediterranean for the damp and fogs of England. But these images were soon replaced by my recollections of a more modern 'living it over again' in *The Fortunes of Richard Mahony*. When Mahony made enough money from his practice in Ballarat, he brought his Australian wife to England; and as they neared the English coast there was a cold iron-grey sky above them, a 'cold and stony aspect of things.' Mahony, however, was elated by the sight of the freshness that the rain brought to the landscape. It was lovely as a garden but with a garden's limitations: suddenly Mahony was conscious of 'England's littleness, her tiny, tight compactness, the narrow compass that allowed of so intense a cultivation.' But soon 'the whole dirty, cold, cheerless reality of arrival' in London chilled them. There followed the depressing experience of Leicester's red-brick streets, its 'stickiest provinciality,' and after this the enclosed petty snobberies of Buddlecomb in Devonshire where, realising that his wife's warm-hearted hospitality and generosity were not appreciated, Mahony suddenly faced the fact that he himself felt no more at home in England than she. He was an outcast and a wanderer, he told himself; but his feelings about Australia were mixed. In one mood it seemed humiliating to return to the land that had eaten up his prime; in another he looked forward to the sunshine, the uplifting effect of Australia's vast space. The return – landfall after eighty-four days out from Liverpool – emphasises the differences, with a gaudy brilliancy of light and colouring, no frail tints or misty trimmings: 'everything stood out hard, clear, emphatic.'

There followed a second period of prosperity: his shares rose and he bought a large house, *Ultima Thule*, by the sea near Melbourne. A magnificent description of Melbourne's social and intellectual life follows. Then Mahony tired of Melbourne and decided on a tour in Europe with his family. This tour was broken off at the news that all his money had been lost. For the third time he tried again in Australia:

> Twice in the past he had plucked up his roots from this soil, to which neither gratitude nor affection bound him. Now fresh from foreign travel, from a wider knowledge of the beauties of the old world, he felt doubly alien; and with his eyes still full of greenery and lushness, he could see less beauty than ever in its dun and arid landscape. It was left to a later generation to discover this: to those who, with their mother's milk, drank in a love of sunlight and space; of inimitable blue distances and gentian-blue skies... [There follows a lyric description of Australian scenery.] He returned to the colony at heart the stranger he had always been.

Mahony however had also discovered, on his first return to Europe, that he was a stranger both in Dublin and in Edinburgh. The feelings of depression and guilt aroused by his visits to his mother in Dublin and his awareness of his own age in Edinburgh are economically portrayed. He had the exile's point of view. When he had done with a place he had done with it: he had no desire to return anywhere. Mahony's temperament was forever driving him on; settled in Hawthorn, a Melbourne suburb, he next moved north, to a country town where he realised the nature of his illness. There is a firm account of his decline while he works as a health officer boarding ships at Shortlands. (It was typical of him to have bought *Ultima Thule* near the sea, and now to choose to work beside the sea. It was his means of discovery and escape, and his delight in the ships that carried him across the seas is symptomatic of his love of changing surroundings.) Then comes his incarceration in a madhouse, for he was by now suffering from cerebral arteriosclerosis and inexorably moving to the state of general paralysis of the insane.[2] His wife became postmistress in Gymgurra, a small town two hundred miles from Melbourne. She realised Mahony's sufferings in the asylum and successfully sought to get him out of it, bringing him to Gymgurra, where he achieved some peace, his brain becoming feebler, his paralysed body weakening into death.

The symbolic contrasts between European and Australian life and the complex repetitions of pattern in Mahony's own life are given an inevitability, an inexorable movement. His wife's failure to understand his sensibility emphasises his sense of isolation; yet despite their differences in temperament – for she is practical and pragmatic – they love each other, and her gradual movement into a more active role as he weakens is convincing. Yet her lack of imagination has been stressed throughout the novel, and though she displays heroic qualities in his decline, no matter-of-fact energetic efficiency can cope with his restlessness.

Rereading the novel recently with students at Aarhus University in Denmark made me realise the reasons for Mahony's waywardness, his vagrancy of spirit. Like many earlier novelists writing of Australia, Richardson is very conscious that Australia's beginnings as a convict settlement cannot be ignored. The continent itself seemed a vast prison – and material success for Mahony, as for other fictional characters, could mean escape. The land imprisoned those who came to plunder it. Thus in the opening chapter a man is buried alive in a mining shaft; the novel begins and ends with burial. And Mahony's 'success' had, ironically, seemed to imprison him in an inadequate suburbia. What he sought was an ideal state, evoked in nostalgia for a world that never was, imagined as a return to a state before his family experienced genteel poverty (such as that which enveloped the families of many Anglo-Irish writers – those, say of the Goldsmiths, or the Yeatses, or the Shaws). Mahony's interest for the reader lies not in the account of his vicissitudes, nor in the sometimes overlong conversations and dialogue, but in the narration of his thoughts, his attempts to understand his lonely situation, his alienation. The running commentary on his variability of mood, his tension, is well done. He sees himself like a Jew weeping by the rivers of Babylon: his movements enact the over-optimism of dreams and ambition; his careering across the seas does not change his capacity for destructive self-analysis, for the logic which destroys his ability to believe, yet drives him to speculate and experiment.

* * *

Henry Handel Richardson, who was born Ethel Florence Lindesay Richardson in 1870, was well equipped to write the novel. It concerns her father, whose life was its basis. He had graduated in medicine in 1849, emigrated to Victoria, and been a prospector and storekeeper before setting up his successful practice. In Europe he heard that his investments had failed, and the story follows his subsequent return to Australia, his practice at Queenscliff, his incarceration in an asylum, and his wife's becoming postmistress at Koroit in southwest Victoria, where he died in 1878.

Not only did she have her father's life to explore,[3] but she her-

self knew the meaning of exile. After her education at the
Presbyterian Ladies' College in Melbourne, brilliantly described in
Myself When Young (1948), she went to Leipzig in 1887 with the aim
of becoming a concert pianist. She faced the fact that she wasn't
gifted enough to have a successful career in music, so decided to
write. She began by translating *Niels Lyhne*, a novel by the Danish
novelist J P Jacobsen, then in 1895 married J G Robertson and lived
with him in Strasbourg and later in London, where he became professor of German at London University. She returned once to
Australia for a brief trip of a few weeks in 1912.

   Maurice Guest (1908), her first novel, which took her eleven
years to write, portrays a world of artists and traces the effect of
passion upon Maurice Guest, who is a weak character, unable to
measure up to the demands of his musical milieu. This novel, however, is not merely what Henry Handel Richardson wanted to say
'about love and lovers,' as she wrote in 'Some Notes on My Books';
nor is it a record of Leipzig life (though the city is observed precisely and at times evocatively): it is primarily preoccupied with
exile and failure. As she herself admitted, she had a youthful desire
to leave nothing unsaid, and the novel exhibited longueurs. But it
is an early-twentieth-century urban novel about temporary exile,
for the students are birds of passage in Leipzig; they have chosen
this exile to get their training, to discover themselves, to experience
sexual selection and some of the moral problems sex creates.

   Maurice Guest fails to become an artist: he fails to shape his life
to his dreams. In the novel a powerful irony is at work, verging
upon the comic at times in part one, whereas in part three the story
is tragic in the outcome of its sentimental education. Maurice cannot fathom himself, let alone Shilsky the Polish genius. And
Shilsky, not Maurice, is loved by Louise Dufrayer. Maurice cannot
dominate her; unlike Shilsky, he chooses her rather than his work
and pays for this romantic mistake. This story has an intensity that
is reminiscent of Dostoevsky, though Flaubert and Stendhal influenced the presentation. It is difficult to realise how 'advanced' the
novel seemed to many British readers in 1908: the use of dreams, of
psychology, of symbolism, of Nietzschean characters such as Kraft,
and of Nietzschean themes such as the contrast between 'free' and
'servile' spirits. (A.D. Hope has an essay on this subject.) Its presentation of homosexuality and of Maurice's sexual relations with
Louise (whose sensual side probably derived from Fennimae, an
outspokenly passionate woman in Jacobsen's *Niels Lyhne*) seemed
to some – to list the adjectives Henry Handel Richardson remembered – 'morbid, depressing, dull, verbose, degraded, coarse,

erotic and neurotic.' She was, she realised later, writing a European novel and invading England with it. Despite its obvious flaws – of length, of a crude technique which isn't always flexible enough for its task (how interior monologue would have helped the characters' self-analysis!) – the novel is worth reading. (She achieved a better technique for dealing with revelation of thought and reverie in *The Fortunes of Richard Mahony*, particularly in the second volume.) The narrative in *Maurice Guest* is skilful, and analysis and explanations follow descriptions effectively. And the novel exhibits surprising moments of realism – the drunken students' party, for instance – while its continuous contrast of dream and reality, its ironic picture of the romantic fatal woman's effect upon a passionate prig, convinces us that the action is not only possible but inevitable.

Henry Handel Richardson had originally intended to carry the story of the Mahonys to a second and even third generation, and she wrote some chapters on Richard Mahony's son, Cuffy; they remained a fragment. But the impetus to put more of the family on paper was spent. In 1931 she had formed the idea of writing on Cosima Wagner's life. She thought that 'the tangle of her intimate relations with Bülow and Wagner had never been fairly or honestly treated.' Her husband helped to assemble the books she needed to track down the motives and circumstances which led to Cosima's adherence to one man, her deception and desertion of the other; but the complexity was staggering. It is probable that her husband's death in 1933 had an adverse effect on this further study of the nature of genius. *The Young Cosima* (1939) is not a book that I would reread, for it is merely the product of research which lacks the conviction, the sheer scope of her other work in which creative imagination was firmly built upon personal and family experience and was slowly shaped out of a delight in what she called playing with words and pondering phrases.

There is however a timeless lasting quality about *The Getting of Wisdom* which shows us the development of not a genius but an intelligent sensitive child. Henry Handel Richardson understood the problem of pride, the theological sin that can also be seen as self-respect. When her characters break down, as Maurice Guest does, as Richard Mahony does, we realise the extent of their failure. The massing of detail, the passing of time, and scope of space are so managed in *The Fortunes of Richard Mahony* that coursing from continent to continent cannot, of itself, bring content to characters. These people are caught in those quotations from Virgil and Sir Thomas Browne, caught, as Yeats said of himself, in the cold snows of a dream. She created, this withdrawn woman 'with a Dantesque profile and heavy-lidded eyes,' the solitary in the crowd, the dreamer among the active, the lonely alienated man among the alien everymen. Although Mahony was an early Victorian with all the prejudices and limitations of his time, she saw him as 'a seeker' who was crushed physically, dissipated mentally, both dazed and confused by the ultimate demands of life. 'He was never once equal to it.'

JOYCE'S PRECURSORS

In Joyce's end is my beginning. You will remember that *Finnegans Wake* ends thus:

On shandymount Finn's body lies.

Shandymound? Echo of Sandymount? Tristram Shandymount? On *Tristram Shandy* Joyce mounted his style.

A keyword is to be found in a bracket in *Finnegans Wake:* '(that his pumps may ship awhoyle shandymound of the dussard)'. The dussard or desert follows naturally on the Shand or sand in Shandymound and suggests to anyone knowing their Joyce, or merely the geography of Dublin, Sandymount, on the south side of Dublin facing Howth across the waters of the Bay. In an early draft of *Finnegans Wake* Finn's body is buried under Dublin, stretching from the Phoenix Park to Howth and Joyce ended one version with 'On Shandymound Finn's body lies' but is this Shandymound with its suggestion of Dublin Bay as Finn's burial place all that flows through Joyce's stream of consciousness? No, for Shandy also suggests the Tristram Shandymound on which Joyce mounted his style. 'I am trying', said he, 'to build many places of narrative with a single aesthetic purpose. Did you ever read Laurence Sterne?'

Joyce's question is the right kind of question to be asked in the dark. You get into the train of education and no sooner are you off than you are plunged into the dark tunnel of specialisation. But when you do emerge into the light how much there is to see. Did you ever read Laurence Sterne? If you reply by asking 'Was he on the syllabus?' you should get a firm answer. That is no way to consider Joyce, the builder of many places of narrative. As our train races past, we can see some of them in the broad sweep of country into which we have burst from the narrow confines of the tunnel.

An old and complex landscape we see, long-settled, but repaired, expanded, contracted; the styles of literary building alter over the years. We race through this landscape heading for the future when we may leave the train and build a place for ourselves, our own words ordered in the pattern of our own style.

Where did Joyce begin? 'Begin at the beginning', was the terse advice of the King in *Alice in Wonderland,* one of Lewis Carroll's memorable characters – and Carroll was one of Joyce's beginnings,

Carroll equipped for the journey, Victorian style, with his portmanteau full of his portmanteau-words. But Joyce escaping from
an Aquininian tunnel saw Homer's building first of all: the epic:
the beginning of his beginning. Shall we discuss the *Odyssey* then?
Ah, you say, you can see Mr Bloom as the wandering, eventually
homecoming Ulysses; Gerty as lovely Nausicaa on the strand, sea
shells sherry and sand-shoes alive o so alive-oh; and Molly bloom-
ing not fading, no pensive prohibiting prohibitive Penelope she.
What did Joyce really get from Homer? Take a prospect of
Odysseyland, bring out your Claude glass before we leave it
behind in our mad rush to modernism, post-modernism, struc-
turalism, poststructuralism, deconstruction, post-deconstruction,
post-post-post, the mileage posts pass by, you crane your neck to
look back but it's difficult, we are moving so fast, so fast, so fast.

Isn't the structure what Joyce needed? All God's artists need a
structure, but Joyce needed one more than most. Because he overflowed, because without a structure he would have run into the
sands, built on them a Hindu temple ambling, seemingly out of
any architectural control? No, but because he had a need to marry
his imagination and his intellect, a greater need than that of most
artists. And because he naturally turned to Homer, because like
Homer he came from an oral tradition, because he was a story-
teller, he needed form, he needed a skeleton beneath the surface
skin of style. By modelling the skeleton of *Ulysses* upon that of the
Odyssey he gained freedom – for what? He needed to hold himself
to his purpose, to his grand overall design, to keep the natural
exuberance of his creativity under control. Why? Ah, there's the
nub of it.

Joyce was concerned with the stuff of life, the experience of it.
He sought in part by wit and humour (those vital elements in him
so often unduly neglected by the prolific professors) to illuminate
the way our minds work, consciously *and* subconsciously.

This is not – as the literary histories or the critical textbooks at
which we have peered in the artificial light of the carriage as we
moved through the restrictive tunnel of prescribed reading may
have told us – a twentieth century phenomenon, this exploration of
the way the mind works at several levels. Jung Joyce was not early
Freudened into self-examinification; he did it, to be sure, all on his
oney-oh in Dublin's 'fair city'. But others built their places of narrative before Joyce and some of their building anticipated his way
of doing it. And he knew that. It is my theme.

Very well, we will begin at the beginning, the epic, the long narrative poem in elevated style about superhuman heroes. From our

train speeding through time we see that virtually no sooner was *Gilgamesh* recited in Sumeria (say about 2700 BC) than Homer was composing his primary epics, the *Iliad* and the *Odyssey* (about the eighth century BC) and *Beowulf* was beaten out with mugs of mead in some eighth-century AD alehouse, followed by the *Chanson de Roland* fabricated about 169 years before the French language and Anglo-Norman armour invaded Ireland.

The secondary, literary epic got going with Virgil's *Aeneid* (say, 30-20 BC), the process accelerating in the Renaissance with Dante's *Divine Comedy* (1307-21), Camoens's *The Lusiads* (1572), Tasso's *Jerusalem Liberata* (1575) and Milton's *Paradise Lost* (1667 – revised in 1674).

Then came tertiary epic: the translations by Dryden of the *Aeneid*, by Pope of the *Iliad* and the *Odyssey*. Perhaps we should have another label, that of Quaternary epic (sometimes to be thought of even as Quartan epic for it sometimes gives you the shivers) for the kind of poem known as mock-epic – Pope's *Rape of the Lock*, for example, and *The Dunciad*.

The novel, too, has learned from primary, secondary, tertiary and quaternary epic. Here the genre had barely begun when it began to mock itself. Fielding's *Shamela* parodies Richardson's *Pamela;* he refined his attack in his second attempt, the novel that is a novel as well as a parody, *Joseph Andrews*. In that novel he showed he had begun to learn from Homer the usefulness of a journey, as a structure to hold the action together. But only begun, for Joseph is a young simple soul, no Ulysses of the many middle-aged wiles, nor yet the tolerant decent Everyman Fielding wanted to create.

Fielding realised the novel needed status: he provided it in *Tom Jones* with its very conscious linkage to the epic; indeed it is the mock-epic at its best. He took Homer's voyage and modified it, moving it from the sea to the roads, giving it three parts: the country; the journey on the roads; the city. The tale is told with a fine enjoyment of the parallels between the actions of its nonheroic characters and the heroes of Homer. Though here a digression is demanded, for Homer was not above a bit of irreverence. When the goddesses have a row one calls another a bitchface; and what of the nightclub song that is prescribed by that paragon of hosts King Alcinous of Phaeacia when he sees Odysseus is sad, thinking of home with an exile's intense loneliness? The King tells the blind harpist to get cracking with something cheerful, and Demodocus tells the story – a ballad or short narrative – of Ares, god of war, having an affair with Aphrodite, goddess of love and beauty, the wife of Hephaestus, the lame blacksmith god. Hephaestus suspects them, and constructs a device, a metal net which closes on the adulterous lovers and traps them when they are in bed together. Once he is sure they are immobilised Hephaestus summons the other gods and goddesses to see the trapped couple, and they all stand round and have their sweet fill of laughter. After this Ares is released upon payment of recompense – a hefty fine – no doubt for 'alienation of affections'. The Victorians were perhaps right to translate this flippant, cynical, Tom Lehrer-ish song as 'The Lay of Ares and Aphrodite.'

But back to the mainline out of the siding, and we see that Fielding used the epic structure because it gave him a model for the novel, a structure, a mould, a form into which he could pour his ideas. It suited written as opposed to oral composition, and yet, paradoxically, the form came from an oral tradition; for the *Iliad* and the *Odyssey* were recited, passed on through memory; they have all the devices of such work: repetitions, stock descriptions, stock similes that gave the reciter a kind of mental breather (for reciting at length is no easy task) and must have allowed his audience, too, a moment to relax, munch an olive and snatch a gulp from a goatskin before the narrative got going again. You can almost hear them say to themselves 'Oh, it's the old eagle descending-on-a-lamb simile again – did you get those olives in Hymettus? Very good. Have a swig of this, it's last year's Chian red'.

Fielding knew the value of the oral tradition. He tries to talk to his reader when he gives his literary views. He needed humour: it had its place in what he was creating: a story of a man growing up, having adventures, developing in character and winning his girl; all of this happening within a stylised framework, character neatly balanced by character, and the action moving fast all the time.

Like all great writers Fielding developed. His sexy girls were called Molly – a name, the *OED* remarks, occasionally applied to a prostitute. Molly Straddle, for instance, in Fielding's *Jonathan Wild* is certainly one. Here she is, complete with Irish connections. The situation is that Heartfree has been robbed of his money. When an apprentice comes in with a £500 note which a gentlewoman, who is looking at jewels in the shop, wishes to change, Heartfree recognises the number as being that of one of those stolen from him and tells Wild this.

Wild . . . with the notable presence of mind, and unchanged complexion, so essential to a great character, advised him to proceed cautiously; and offered (as Mr Heartfree himself was, he said, too much flustered to examine the woman with sufficient art) to take her into a room in his house alone. He would, he said, personate the master of the shop, would pretend to show her some jewels, and would undertake to get sufficient information out of her to secure the rogues, and most probably all their booty. This proposal was readily and thankfully accepted by Heartfree. Wild went immediately upstairs into the room appointed, whither the apprentice, according to appointment, conducted the lady.

The apprentice was ordered downstairs the moment the lady entered the room; and Wild, having shut the door, approached her with great feroc-ity in his looks, and began to expatiate on the complicated baseness of the crime she had been guilty of; but though he uttered many good lessons of morality, as we doubt whether from a particular reason they may work any very good effect on our reader, we shall omit his speech, and only mention his conclusion, which was by asking her what mercy she could not expect from him? Miss Straddle, for that was the young lady, who had had a good education, and had been more than once present at the Old Bailey, very confidently denied the whole charge, and said she had received the note from a friend. Wild then, raising his voice, told her she should be immedi-ately committed, and she might depend on being convicted: 'but', added he, changing his tone, 'as I have a violent affection for thee, my dear Straddle, if you will follow my advice, I promise you on my honour to for-give you, nor shall you be ever called in question on this account'. – 'Why, what would you have me to do, Mr Wild?' replied the young lady, with a pleasanter aspect. 'You must know then', said Wild, 'the money you picked out of my pocket (nay, by G-d you did, and if you offer to flinch, you shall be convicted of it) I won at play of a fellow who it seems robbed my friend of it; you must, therefore, give an information on oath against one Thomas Fierce, and say that you received the note from him, and leave the rest to me. I am certain, Molly, you must be sensible of your obligations to me, who return good for evil to you in this manner'. The lady readily consent-ed, and advanced to embrace Mr Wild who stepped a little back and cried, 'Hold, Molly; there are two other notes of £200 each to be accounted for – where are they?' The lady protested with the most solemn asseverations that she knew of no more; with which when Wild was not satisfied, she cried, 'I will stand search'. 'That you shall', answered Wild, 'and stand strip too'. He then proceeded to tumble and search her, but to no purpose, till at last she burst into tears, and declared she would tell the truth (as indeed she did); she then confessed that she had disposed of the one to Jack Swagger, a great favourite of the ladies, being an Irish gentleman, who had been clerk to an attorney, afterwards whipped out of a regiment of dragoons, and was then a Newgate solicitor, and bawdyhouse bully; and as for the other, she had laid it out that very morning in brocaded silks and Flanders lace.[1]

Wild's Molly Straddle was not so much a Molly as a gangster's

Moll. Molly Seagrim is rather different. She is a forward piece of sixteen when she begins to impress the nearly-nineteen year-old Tom Jones. He casts 'eyes of affection' on her:

And this affection he had fixed on the girl long before he could bring himself to attempt the possession of her person: for though his constitution urged him greatly to this, his principles no less forcibly restrained him. To debauch a young woman, however low her condition was, appeared to him a very heinous crime; and the good-will he bore the father, with the compassion he had for his family, very strongly corroborated all such sober reflections; so that he once resolved to get the better of his inclinations, and he actually abstained three whole months without ever going to Seagrim's house, or seeing his daughter.

Now though Molly was, as we have said, generally thought a very fine girl, and in reality she was so, yet her beauty was not of the most amiable kind. It had indeed very little of feminine in it, and would at least have become a man as well as a woman; for, to say the truth, youth and florid health had a very considerable share in the composition.

Nor was her mind more effeminate than her person. As this was tall and robust, so was that bold and forward. So little had she of modesty, that Jones had more regard for her virtue than she herself. And as most probably she liked Tom as well as he liked her, so when she perceived his backwardness, she herself grew proportionately forward; and when she saw he had entirely deserted the house, she found means of throwing herself in his way, and behaved in such a manner, that the youth must have had very much, or very little of the hero, if her endeavours had proved unsuccessful. In a word, she soon triumphed over all the virtuous resolutions of Jones: for though she behaved at last with all decent reluctance, yet I rather choose to attribute the triumph to her, since, in fact, it was her design which succeeded.

In the conduct of this matter, Molly so well played her part, that Jones attributed the conquest entirely to himself, and considered the young woman as one who had yielded to the violent attacks of his passion. He likewise imputed her yielding, to the ungovernable force of her love towards him; and this the reader will allow to have been a very natural and probable supposition, as we have more than once mentioned the uncommon comelinesss of his person: and indeed he was one of the handsomest young fellows in the world.[2]

Perhaps in an age of female chauvinism we should ask why the term 'Yes-Man' is frequently in use. The Mollies of Fielding are, Yes-women, and the supreme Yes-woman of literature will be Molly Bloom. 'And yes, I said, yes I will, Yes'. Fielding changed. His last work of fiction, *Amelia*, moves from models of primary

epic to those of secondary. Virgil's story of Dido and Aeneas is paralleled by the amour of Booth and Miss Matthews in prison. It has,
as Claude Rawson remarked,[3] 'a wry Joycean quality' about it.
Booth is an older Tom Jones, and like Tom, his sexual sins reflect a
generosity of spirit – matched by his wife Amelia who has all the
tolerance of a Penelope.

Here we stop at the wayside halt called Ithaca. It's not Homer's
Ithaca but one invented by a French author in which Odysseus has
settled back into the routine of pre-Troy days, to the annoyance of
his son Telemachus who wants to change the way they run the
farm. Odysseus, in fact, has become just a bit of a bore and psychologically they are all ready for him to take off again. One morning he rhapsodises about the weather to his now less patient
Penelope. 'Ah, dear', he says, 'do you remember on mornings like
this we used to crush the grapes against the infant lips of
Telemachus?' 'No, Odysseus', she replies with an edge in her voice,
'We have never had grapes on Ithaca. Some other island, some
other woman, some other child . . .'

Back on our way again, we realise that in *Amelia* there is a deepening of feeling, of sensibility. Fielding no longer needs to under-
cut the portrayal of emotions with irony or mock-heroic mockery.
The story becomes more serious, more complex. Booth's inner feelings are bursting to be fully explored, but somehow Fielding can
only describe them from outside. As yet the mechanism for portraying inner ideas is not there. But cheer up, look out of the train
window. The landscape is changing from Fielding's rustic England.
There is Dr Smelfungus in view, the egregious Tobias Smollett who
discovered and began the popularisation of the curative climate of
the French Riviera. His *Travels* are full of reflections; they blend the
rationalism of the eighteenth century with sharp Scottish intelligence. Here is Smollett recording his first glimpses of the Pont du
Gard:

I would not willingly pass for a false enthusiast in taste; but I cannot
help observing, that from the first distant view of this noble monument, till
we came near enough to see it perfectly, I felt the strongest emotions of
impatience that I had ever known; and obliged our driver to put his mules
to the full gallop, in the apprehension that it would be dark before we
reached the place. I expected to find the building, in some measure,
ruinous; but was agreeably disappointed to see it look as fresh as the
bridge at Westminster. The climate is either so pure and dry, or the free-
stone, with which it is built, so hard, that the very angles of them remain
as acute as if they had been cut last year. Indeed, some large stones have
dropped out of the arches; but the whole is admirably preserved, and pre-

sents the eye with a piece of architecture so unaffectedly elegant, so simple, and majestic, that I will defy the most phlegmatic and stupid spectator
to behold it without admiration. It was raised in the Augustan age, by the
Roman colony of Nîmes, to convey a stream of water between two mountains, for the use of that city. It stands over the river Gardon, which is a
beautiful pastoral stream, brawling among rocks, which form a number of
pretty natural cascades, and overshadowed on each side with trees and
shrubs, which greatly add to the rural beauties of the scene . . . If I lived at
Nismes, or Avignon (which last city is within four short leagues of it), I
should take pleasure in forming parties to come hither, in summer, to dine
under one of the arches of the Pont du Garde, on a cold collation.[4]

There is practicality for you! Being a well-educated eighteenth
century Scot, Smollett tended to reflect rather than to indulge in
reverie. And he did reflect the stream of consciousness in his last
novel *The Expedition of Humphry Clinker*. Here is Jenkins writing to
Mary – not Molly, please note – Jones. But, by an interesting and
revealing kink, the letter ends up by addressing Mary Jones as
Molly. What would the Freudian critics make of that? After it I
should not allude to the spelling, which is part of the pleasure of
the letter, but draw your attention to its orthography:

Dear Mary,
     The squire has been so kind as to rap my bit of nonsense under the
kiver of his own sheet – O Mary Jones! Mary Jones! I have had trials and
trembulation. God help me! I have been a vixen and a griffin these many
days – sattin has had the power to temp me in the shape of van Ditton, the
young squire's wally de shamble; but by God's grease he did not purvail –
I thoft as how there was no harm in going to a play in Newcastle, with my
hair dressed in the Parish fashion; and as for the trifle of paint, he said as
how my complexion wanted rouch, and so I let him put it on with a little
Spanish owl; but a mischievous mob of colliers, and such promiscuous rib-
ble rabble, that could bare no smut but their own, attacked us in the street,
and called me *hoar* and *painted Issabel*, and splashed my ciofe, and spoiled
me a complete set of blond lace triple ruffles, not a pin the worse for the
ware. – They cost me seven good sillings to Lady Griskin's woman at
London.
     When I axed Mr Clinker what they meant by calling me Issabel, he put
the byebill into my hand, and I read of van Issabel, a painted harlot, that
was thrown out of a vindore, and the dogs came and licked her blood – But
I am no harlot; and, with God's blessing, no dog shall have my poor blood
to lick; Marry, Heaven forbid, amen! As for Ditton, after all his courting
and his compliment, he stole away an Irishman's bride, and took a French
leave of me and his master; but I vally not his going a farting; but I have

had hanger on his account – Mistress scoulded like mad; thos I have the comfit that all the family took my part, and even Mr Clinker pleaded for me on his bended knee; thos, God he knows, he had raisins enuff to complain; but he's a good sole, abounding with Christian meekness, and one day will meet with his reward.

And now, dear Mary, we have got to Haddingborough, among the Scots, who are civil enuff for our money, thos I don't speak their lingo – But they should not go for to impose upon foreigners; for the bills on their houses say, they have different *easements* to let; and behold there is nurra geaks in the whole kingdom, nor anything for pore servants, but a barrel with a pair of tongs thrown across; and all the chairs in the family are emptied into this here barrel once a day; and at ten o'clock at night the whole cargo is flung out of a back window that looks into some street or lane, and the maid calls *Gardy loo* to the passengers, which signifies, *Lord have mercy upon you!* and this is done every night in every house in Haddingborough; so you may guess, Mary Jones, what a sweet savour comes from such a number of profuming pans: But they say it is wholesome, and truly I believe it is; for being in the vapours, and thinking of Issabel and Mr Clinker, I was going into a fit of astericks, when this siss, saving your presence, took me by the nose so powerfully, that I sneezed three times, and found myself wonderfully refreshed; and this to be sure is the raisin why there are no fits in Haddingborough.

I was likewise made believe, that there was nothing to be had but *oatmeal* and *seeps-heads;* but if I hadn't been a fool, I mought have known there could be no *heads* without carcasses – This very blessed day I dined upon a delicate leg of Velsh mutton and cully-flower; and as for oat-meal, I leave that to the servants of the country, which are pore drudges, many of them without shoes or stockings – Mr Clinker tells me here is a great call of the gospel; but I wish, I wish some of our family be not fallen off from the rite way – O, if I was given to tail-baring, I have my own secrets to discover – There has been a deal of huggling and flurtation betwixt Mrs and an ould Scots officer called Kismycago. He looks for all the world like the scarecrow that our gardener set up to frite away the sparrows; and what will come of it the Lord nows; but come what will, it shall never be said that I mentioned a syllabub of the matter – Remember me kindly to Saul and the kitten I hope they got the horn-buck, and will put it to a good use, which is the constant prayer of,
   Dear Molly
      Your living friend,
         WIN. JENKINS.[5]

We are coming near the very stream of consciousness and as we peer ahead we can see it dividing off Sterne from his contemporaries. His work seemed for a time a kind of genetic sport in the novel, because what Sterne was creating wasn't fully understood. Said Dr Johnson in 1776, 'Nothing odd will do long. *Tristram Shandy* did not last'.[6] An odd comment, that seems to us, and *it* hasn't lasted, for he was wrong, the old Cham; Sterne *has* lasted. He challenged the assumption that straight chronological order is the only structure for narrative fiction. His own structure was very carefully constructed, none the less.[7] What William James said in a *locus classicus* on consciousness[8] in his *Principles of Psychology* applies well to Sterne:

Every definite image in the mind is steeped and dyed in the free water that flows around it. The significance, the value of the image is all in this halo or penumbra that surrounds and escorts it . . . .

Consciousness does not appear to itself chopped up in bits. It is nothing jointed; it flows . . . let us call it the stream of thought, of consciousness, or of subjective life.

Consciousness, then, is not chopped up into divisions of time. How well Auden put it in *New Year Letter* when he said that all our intentions 'Mock the formal logic of the clock'. Sterne revolts against that formal logic in *Tristram Shandy*. At the moment of Tristram's conception Mr Shandy is interrupted by the clock striking. This may be what motivated Mr Shandy's intellectual interest in time. He is predetermined in his mind to give Uncle Toby a clear account of the matter by a 'metaphysical dissertation upon the subject of duration'. Here we meet another philosopher, for Mr Shandy, describing duration more fully and considering the succession of ideas, draws upon John Locke:

In our computations of time, we are so used to minutes, hours, weeks and months – and of clocks (I wish there was not a clock in the Kingdom) to measure out their several portions to us . . . Now whether we observe it or not, continued my father, in every sound man's head there is a regular succession of ideas, of one sort or another, which follow each other in train.

In train? Imprisoned in space in our train we can the more easily, perhaps, understand imprisonment in time. It can be the routine of realists. Sir Roger Stevens, formerly an Ambassador in Sweden and Persia, when asked the difference between being a diplomat and the University Vice-Chancellor he subsequently became, said he felt imprisoned by his University diary, the routine of meetings of Council, of Senate, of Senate Business Committee, Honorary Degrees Committee, and endless appointment committees, meetings of the Vice-Chancellors' and Principals' Committee. As an Ambassador he rarely had engagements more than two or three weeks ahead in his diary. There was something inexorable, he thought, in the conventions of the University Calendar, in the way the time of the university's world had, realistically, to be arranged in the fixed routine of the terms that make up the academic year.

What Sterne was doing was reacting against realism and the realists; in his case against the rationale, the conventions of the world of the novel. He reacted by creating his own world, one of ideas and memories, of sensitivity, of mood. The Shandean world is not for the solemn. Dr Leavis, for instance, called it 'irresponsible and nasty trifling'. But it is an attempt, a brave one involving turning the novel inside out, to show that human life, a living, moving, changing thing, the mystery that it is, is *fixed* in a novel, an orthodox novel. Sterne had absorbed that classical sentence *Fixum restat in orbe nihil*. Writing when properly managed, he said, is but a different name for conversation. Here we realise he was born in Ireland, a land of oral culture. Dr Leavis was a product of a print-orientated culture. Ireland is a land of talkers. Wilde said of the Irish, 'We are the greatest talkers since the Greeks, too poetical to be poets, a nation of brilliant failures'. Here our diesel-electric locomotive blows a fanfare on its airhorn.

Sterne knew what good conversation was. One thing leads to another. There may be no logical connection between them; there may be no *apparent* connection. But there is the stream of individual consciousness that carries on the flow of ideas and images. Sterne exploits it, for comic purposes, to shock the reader with surprises. (Joyce does the same). He seems to say to his readers, 'Your Worships, look, you appear to think logically, as if your mind is a machine; *but it is not*'. Locke had the idea of discrete elements capable of being arranged beside each other in space. But Sterne overflows, like Joyce. This may be the Irish mind at work, full of imaginative, oral exuberance. Why should this be so? Because conversation has to hold interest. It is the poor man's entertainment; it flourishes best when there are no other distractions. But why pick out the Irish? For the perennial contrast with the English, obviously. The late Professor Stanford maintained the difference between the English and the Irish was a matter of truth. The English tell you less than the truth, the Irish tell you more. Both are liars in their different ways. If you think of the decoration of the Book of Kells, the sheer exuberance of it, you will probably be reminded of the best kind of Irish talk, the kind of thing that Synge well understood when he puts 'a fine bit of talk' in the mouth of the tramp in *The Shadow of the Glen*. But after the verbal exuberance of the Renaissance, perhaps under the influence of the Puritans, the

English tradition became instead one of restrained speech, reaching its crescendo of constraint in the clipped chat of the public school boys who ran the Empire with stiff upper lips closed tight in understatement. In the recent words of a Cabinet secretary, this is being economical with the truth. We Irish – as Berkeley might have said – are generous with it: it doesn't cost much. But the English are now catching up under the cultural pressure of working class attitudes of letting emotion rip at least once a week – in the pub, of course, on pay day – and under the subtler pressure of a not fully understood movement into an oral culture, of persons passive in the face of squarefaced screens, active in using the telephone rather than the letter, the luncheon rather than the memoir. Perhaps this oral culture will condone the seriousness of intellectual clowning; it is, after all, a form of exploration.

What Sterne does is to take Locke's ideas (as Joyce did Vico's) and clown with them. Here, in the fourth book of *Tristram Shandy*, he is playing with Locke's view that the association of ideas in the mind is a highly irrational process:

I am this month one whole year older than I was this time twelvemonth: and having got, as you may perceive, almost into the middle of my fourth volume – and no further than to my first day's life – 'tis demonstrative that I have 364 days' more life to write just now than when I set out; so that instead of advancing, as a common writer, in my work with what I have been doing at it – on the contrary, I am just thrown so many volumes back – was every day of my life to be as busy a day as this? – And why not? – and the transactions and opinions of it to take up as much description – And for what reason should they be cut short? As at this rate I should just live 364 times faster than I should write – It must follow, an' please your Worships, that the more I write, the more I shall have to write – and consequently, the more your Worships read, the more your Worships will have to read.

Will this be good for your Worships' eyes? It will do well for mine; and, was it not that my opinions will be the death of me, I perceive I shall lead a fine life of it out of this selfsame life of mine; or, in other words, I shall lead a couple of fine lives together.

What Sterne does is to control the flowing of ideas; he comments freely on them. He *selects* the comic, the pathetic, the sentimental. His characters are eccentrics. Uncle Toby, a retired soldier, plays soldiers. Mr Shandy is full of theories. All this exuberance of creation comes from the countryside of Rabelais, of Burton; it reemerges into view again in Thackeray and Thurber. Remember the latter's cartoon in which a man, accompanied by two women, comments to one, obviously a visitor, about a third woman crouching on a glass case, 'That's my first wife up there and this is the *present* Mrs Harris'. This has a logic of its own; it is zany; the mixture makes it supremely memorable. Mrs Shandy, however, could never remember:

It was a consuming vexation to my father that my mother never asked the meaning of a thing she did not understand. That she is not a woman of science, my father would say, is her misfortune; but she might ask a question. My mother never did. In short, she went out of the world at last without knowing whether it turned round or stood still; my father had officiously told her above a thousand times which way it was, but she always forgot.

There is a different stream of consciousness to be observed: the linguistic one. Smollett, for instance, again ponders an example of it in the speech of Mrs Jones; it is full of meanings at different levels:

Providinch hath bin pleased to make great halteration in the pasture of our affairs. We were yesterday three kiple chined, by the grease of God, in the holy bonds of matter-money, and I now subscrive myself at your service . . . Present my compliments to Mrs Gwyllim and I hope she and I may live on dissent terms of civility.[9]

Here are ambiguities, fusions, telescoping of words and ideas, incongruities and congeries, double meanings. This leads to the telegram-style and the portmanteau word so beloved of Lewis Carroll. Sometimes this flow is based on visual detail, as in the opening chapter of *Great Expectations* Pip tells how he got his ideas of his dead parents from seeing their tombstones:

The shape of the letters on my father's, gave me an odd idea that he was a square, stout, dark man, with curly black hair. From the character and turn of the inscription, 'ALSO GEORGIANA, WIFE OF THE ABOVE', I drew a childish conclusion that my mother was freckled and sickly. To five little stone lozenges, each about a foot and a half long, which were arranged in a neat row beside their grave, and were sacred to the memory of five little brothers of mine . . . I am indebted for a belief I religiously entertained that they had all been born on their backs with their hands in their trouser pockets, and had never taken them out in this state of existence.

Thus runs the sharp insight of Dickens into a child's way of thinking, into the flow of consciousness. He could recreate adults' ways of remembering things too. Here is Jack Hopkins at Bob Sawyer's party telling the story of the child that swallowed his sister's necklace:

'Next day, child swallowed two beads; the day after that, he treated himself to three, and so on, till in a week's time he had got through the necklace – five-and-twenty beads in all. The sister, who was an industrious girl and seldom treated herself to a bit of finery, cried her eyes out at the loss of the necklace; looked high and low for it; but I needn't say, didn't find it. A few days afterwards, the family were at dinner – baked shoulder of mutton and potatoes under it – the child, who wasn't hungry, was playing about the room, when suddenly there was heard the devil of a noise, like a small hailstorm. 'Don't do that, my boy', says the father. 'I ain't a-doin nothing', said the child. 'Well, don't do it again', said the father. There was a short silence, and then the noise began again, worse than ever. 'If you don't mind what I say, my boy', said the father, 'you'll find yourself in bed, in something less than a pig's whisper'. He gave the child a shake to make him obedient, and such a rattling ensued as nobody ever heard before. 'Why, dam'me, it's in the child', said the father, 'he's got the croup in the wrong place!' 'No, I haven't, father', said the child, beginning to cry, 'it's the necklace; I swallowed it, father'. The father caught the child up, and ran with him to the hospital, the beads in the boy's stomach rattling all the way with the jolting; and the people looking up in the air, and down in the cellars, to see where the unusual sound came from. 'He's in the hospital now', said Jack Hopkins, 'and he makes such a devil of a noise when he walks about, that they're obliged to muffle him in a watchman's coat, for fear he should wake the patients.'

George Orwell has pointed out[10] the detail that he says only Dickens would have noticed, such things as 'baked shoulder of mutton and potatoes under it'. We may be travelling fast but time is relative, so is speed; to Alfred Jingle in *Pickwick Papers* the stage coach seemed every bit as fast as our diesel electric, as he travelled past local landmarks:

'Terrible place – dangerous work – other day – five children – mother – tall lady, eating sandwiches – forgot the arch – crash – knock – children look around – mother's head off – sandwich in her hand – no mouth to put it in – head of a family off – shocking, shocking! Looking at Whitehall, sir? – fine place – little window – somebody else's head off there, eh, sir? – he didn't keep a sharp lookout enough either – eh, sir, eh?'[11]

You can find this kind of thing in Fenimore Cooper's *The Spy* (in the speech of Caesar the slave) and Melville's *Moby Dick* (where Ahab scans the sea 'What I've dared I've willed, and what I've willed I'll do . . . I now prophesy, I will dismember my dismemberer'). It is reminiscent of the selfcommunion in Stephen Dedalus' soliloquy on the sea shore, in some ways; but it goes back further, to Shakespeare's Llewellen or, if we want an Irish example, to Maria Edgeworth's *The Absentee*. Reflection; reverie; soliloquy: here, then, is Maria Edgeworth:

'It will do very well, never mind', repeated Petito, muttering to herself as she looked after the ladies whilst they ran downstairs 'I can't abide to dress any young lady who says never mind and it will do very well. That and her never talking to one confidentially or trusting one with the least bit of her secrets, is the thing I can't put up with from Miss Nugent; and Miss Broadhurst holding the pins to me, as much to say, do your business, Petito, and don't talk. Now that's so impertinent, as if one wasn't the same flesh and blood, and had not as good a right to talk of everything, and hear of everything, as themselves. And Mrs Broadhurst, too, cabinet counselling with my lady, and pursing up her city mouth, when I come in, and turning off the discourse to snuff, forsooth, as if I was an ignoramus, to think they closetted themselves to talk of snuff. Now, I think a lady of quality's woman has as good a right to be trusted with her lady's secrets as with her jewels: and if my Lady Clonbrony was a real lady of quality, she'd know that, and consider the one as much my paraphanalia as the other. So I shall tell my lady tonight as I always do when she vexes me, that I never lived in an Irish family before, and don't know the ways of it. Then she'll tell me she was born in Hoxfordshire; then I shall say with my saucy look 'Oh was you my lady? I always forget that you was an Englishwoman'. Then maybe she'll say, 'Forget! You forget yourself strangely, Petito'. Then I shall say with a great deal of dignity 'If your Ladyship thinks so, my Lady, I'd better go'. And I'd desire no better than that she should take me at my word, for my Lady Dashfort's is a much better place, I'm told, and she's dying to have me I know.

Soliloquy, by Reflection out of *Reverie*. This horse is cantering beside our train, drawing attention to *Ironical Comedy*, a fast runner out of *Restoration Situation* by *Witty Dramatist*. And in the blood line there runs *Irish Talk*. Remember Yeats, who hated Locke, deliberately acting out his poems in imitation of Irving's Hamlet, of Irving and his plume of pride. 'Oh, well', said the policeman in Harold's Cross, disturbed by seeing the young man walking equally unconcerned over clean footpaths and muddy puddles, 'If it's only the poetry working in his head'. Here is the inner soliloquy becoming the outer, as drama demands.

There is a midway point – the diary. Fanny Burney soliloquises in hers. Who would have thought *her* a maidenly Molly Bloom? And a hundred years before Molly, too!

Well, I am going to bed – Sweet dreams attend me – and may you sympa-

thize with me. Heigh ho! I wonder when I shall return to London! – Not
that we are very dull here no, really – tolerably happy – I wish Kitty Cooke
would write to me – I long to hear how my dear, dear, beloved Mr Crisp
does. My papa always mentions him by the name of my Flame. Indeed he
is not mistaken – himself is the only man on earth I prefer to him. Well – I
must write a word more – only to end my paper – so! – that's done and
now good night to you.[12]

And what of Miss Bates? In *Emma* her stream of consciousness
flows meanderingly round oxbow bends in mesmeric murmurings,
in what Jane Austen permitted herself to call her 'incessant flow':

'So very obliging of you! – No rain at all. Nothing to signify. I do not care
for myself. Quite thick shoes. And Jane declares – Well!' (as soon as she
was within the door), 'Well! This is brilliant indeed! This is admirable!
Excellently contrived, upon my word. Nothing wanting. Could not have
imagined it. So well lighted up! Jane, Jane, look! did you ever see anything
-? Oh! Mr Weston, you must really have had Aladdin's lamp. Good Mrs
Stokes would not know her own room again. I saw her as I came in; she
was standing in the entrance. 'Oh! Mrs Stokes', said I – but I had not time
for more'. She was now met by Mrs Weston. 'Very well, I thank you,
ma'am. I hope you are quite well. Very happy to hear it. So afraid you
might have a headache! seeing you pass by so often, and knowing how
much trouble you must have. Delighted to hear it indeed! Ah! dear Mrs
Elton, so obliged to you for the carriage; excellent time; Jane and I quite
ready. Did not keep the horses a moment. Most comfortable carriage. Oh!
and I am sure our thanks are due to you, Mrs Weston, on that score. Mrs
Elton had most kindly sent Jane a note, or we should have been. But two
such offers in one day! Never were such neighbours. I said to my mother,
'Upon my word, ma'am – 'Thank you, my mother is remarkably well.
Gone to Mr Woodhouse's. I made her take her shawl – for the evenings are
not warm – her large new shawl, Mrs Dixon's wedding present. So kind of
her to think of my mother! Bought at Weymouth, you know; Mr Dixon's
choice. There were three others, Jane says, which they hesitated about
some time. Colonel Campbell rather preferred an olive. My dear Jane, are
you sure you did not wet your feet? It was but a drop or two, but I am so
afraid; but Mr Frank Churchill was so extremely – and there was a mat to
step upon. I shall never forget his extreme politeness. Oh! Mr Frank
Churchill, I must tell you my mother's spectacles have never been in fault
since; the rivet never came out again. My mother often talks of your good-
nature; does not she, Jane? Do not we often talk of Mr Frank Churchill? Ah!
here's Miss Woodhouse. Dear Miss Woodhouse, how do you do? Very well,
I thank you, quite well. This is meeting quite in fairyland. Such a transformation! Must not compliment, I know' (eyeing Emma most complacently)

– 'that would be rude; but upon my word, Miss Woodhouse, you do look
– how do you like Jane's hair? You are a judge. She did it all herself. Quite
wonderful how she does her hair! No hairdresser from London, I think,
could – Ah! Dr Hughes, I declare – and Mrs Hughes. Must go and speak to
Dr and Mrs Hughes for a moment. How do you do? How do you do? Very
well I thank you. This is delightful, is not it? Where's dear Mr Richard? Oh!
there he is. Don't disturb him. Much better employed talking to the young
ladies. How do you do, Mr Richard? I saw you the other day as you rode
through the town. Mrs Otway, I protest, and good Mr Otway, and Miss
Otway, and Miss Caroline. Such a host of friends! and Mr George and Mr
Arthur! How do you do? How do you all do? Quite well, I am much obliged to you. Never better. Don't I hear another carriage? Who can this be? –
very likely the worthy Coles. Upon my word, this is charming, to be standing about among such friends! And such a noble fire! I am quite roasted.
No coffee, I thank you, for me; never take coffee. A little tea, if you please,
sir, by-and-by; no hurry. Oh! here it comes. Everything is so good![13]

The question of the relationship of soliloquy and reverie is
raised in any contemplation of George Moore's now unduly
neglected writing. His development is in some ways akin to that of
Joyce.[14] After his career as Zola's richochet with *Esther Waters* and
A Mummer's Wife came his career as an Irish writer. His short stories in *The Untilled Field* explore the sordid, the dreary, the static in
the countryside of the west of Ireland, whereas Joyce drew upon
what seemed to him the paralysis, the decay of Dublin in the east.

Moore next created the melodic line, wanting to avoid transi-
tions, interpolated retrospects, struggling movements from one
consciousness to another. And an audience is much less conscious
of these when listening to a story told orally. 'I often', he remarked,
'tell my stories better than I write them'. The presence of the story-
teller carries the story along; he skips obstacles without the listener
perceiving the skips and bounds. The equivalent in Moore's career
to Joyce's *A Portrait of the Artist as a Young Man* is *The Lake*, where
Moore's capacity to blend imaginative reverie with thought is magnificently achieved. Father Gogarty is affected by his beautiful surroundings. Here is the first version of 1905:

The earth and sky were enfolding in one tender harmony of rose and blue,
the blue shading down to gray, and the lake floated amid vague shores,
vaguely as a dream floats through sleep. The swallows were flying high,
quivering overhead in the blue air. There was a sense of security and persuasion and loveliness in the evening.

And here is the rewritten version of 1921:

And he watched the earth and sky enfolded in one tender harmony of rose and blue – blue fading to grey, and the lake afloat amid vague shores, receding like a dream through sleep.

After his superb evocations, the more effective as he worked on them, cutting them to simpler patterns, came his parallel to *Ulysses*, a *Portrait of Himself as Impotent Sigfried*, or to give it its proper title, *Hail and Farewell*. Like Joyce after him, Moore needed a model; but he chose Wagner rather than Homer. He was writing out of established success; though a landlord, he was hardly of the establishment, as his portraits in A *Drama in Muslin* and his vain efforts to be invited to Dublin Castle – in his preparation for writing that devastating exposé of the marriage market – clearly, and most amusingly, demonstrate. *Enfant terrible* he remained. But his Dublin is very different from Joyce's; *Hail and Farewell* moves among the figures of the literary movement whom Joyce affected to despise. Moore had, by landlord's standards, to live on very little money indeed when beginning his writing career; shortage of money has been the spur that urged on many Irish writers – the list is long. Farquhar, Goldsmith, Sheridan, Wilde, Shaw and Yeats, for example, had to make their way in the world by writing. And so indeed had Joyce, more than any of them. None of the other families had to burn the wood of staircases in the fireplaces of rented houses. But Moore's Dublin in *Hail and Farewell* is decidedly not short of funds; though Moore mocks and satirises, he does this at a social level different from Joyce's, and from a position of success.

After finishing *Hail and Farewell* Moore had, in every sense, exhausted Dublin. There followed his *Finnegans Wake* in *The Brook Kerith*, his movement into historical phantasy matched by the contemplation of *Heloise and Abelard*, all conveying the flow of thought easily, convincingly, in their stylised narrative.

But *The Lake* is *the* novel of Moore to leave with you – here is narrative, reflection, speech; the flow of inner and outer consciousness. This is not only the stream of consciousness but the fountain of human creativity:

His thoughts melted into nothingness, and when he awoke from his reverie he was thinking that Norah Glynn had come into his life like a fountain, shedding living water upon it, awakening it. And taking pleasure in the simile, he said, 'A fountain better than anything else expresses this natural woman', controlled, no doubt, by a law, but one hidden from him. 'A fountain springs out of earth into air; it sings a tune that cannot be caught and written down in notes; the rising and falling water is full of iridescent colour, and to the wilting roses the fountain must seem not a natural thing, but a spirit, and I, too, think of her as a spirit'. And his thoughts falling away again he became vaguely but intensely conscious of all the beauty and grace and the enchantment of the senses that appeared to him in the name of Nora Glynn.

The stream of consciousness uses the imperfect rather than the past tense: the author aims often at the continuous present; it is a tense, incidentally, peculiar to Irish, whose writers 'do be' using it continuously, and it is one of which Irish writers in English are well aware. It becomes a matter of montage, then. Moore achieved flow by adding 'and', Joyce by removing it. Why? Because he strives to represent a piece of objectivity through what can be called montage, because his art is to create reality through artifice, through trying to unite art and life. He was well aware of Bergson's views – Bergson is Bitchson in *Finnegans Wake* and so each moment in *Ulysses* necessarily is unique. Always passing the stream of life, says Bloom; and to repeat that previously cited *locus classicus* of William James: 'every definite image in the mind is steeped and dyed in the free water that flows around it'. Perhaps Joyce remembered James's *Principles of Psychology?*) 'How can you own water really? It's always flowing in a stream, never the same, which is the stream of life we trace?'

The idea was taken over into literary criticism by a reviewer, May Sinclair, who was reviewing Dorothy Richardson's novels in 1918. *Pointed Roofs* (1915) has in the accepted sense, no plot, no tragedy, no comedy, no love interest, no catastrophe – only Miriam Henderson who lives, experiences, reacts to the stimuli of others and the world of things – life to her is 'an incessant shower of innumerable atoms'. What does it all add up to? A governess in a school in Germany returns to England, is disappointed in love. Dorothy Richardson creates in her an over-sensible woman to whom the world exists as material for her sensibility to assimilate. How does one select? This is something that Virginia Woolf's characters search for: the paring down of experience. She puts it thus in *Orlando:*

But Time, unfortunately, though it makes animals and vegetables bloom and fade with amazing punctuality, has no such simple effect on the mind of man. The mind of man, moreover, works with equal strangeness upon the body of time. An hour, once it lodges in the queer element of the human spirit, may be stretched to fifty or a hundred times its clock length; on the other hand, an hour may be accurately represented on the timepiece of the mind by one second. This extraordinary discrepancy between time on the clock and time in the mind is less known than it should be and deserves fuller investigation.

Time is the crux as well as the multiplicity:

And indeed it cannot be decried that the most successful practitioners of
the art of life – somehow continue to synchronise the 60 or 70 different
times which beat simultaneously in every normal human system so that
when 11 strikes all the rest chime in unison. Now as she stood with her
hand on the door of her motor car – the present again struck her on the
head 11 times she was violently assaulted. 'Confound it all' she cried, for it
is a great shock to the nervous system hearing a clock strike.

And talking of hearing the clock about to strike, I should leave
you with two points to consider about Joyce, and, especially, about
his predecessors. He and Édouard Dujardin did not invent the
stream of consciousness, nor the monology of the interiors – the
interior monologue. Joyce paid tribute to Dujardin's *Les Lauriers
sont Coupés* (a short novel published in 1887 in which a young man
rambles on in the present tense) and Dujardin's own rambling
shambling definition is worth considering:

The internal monologue, in its nature on the order of poetry, is that
unheard and unspoken speech by which a character expresses his inmost
thoughts (those lying nearest the unconscious) without regard to logical
organisations that is, in their original state – by means of direct sentences
reduced to the syntactic minimum, and in such a way as to give the
impression of reproducing the thoughts just as they come into the mind.

This is worth considering because the interior monologue is
unheard, unspoken. And the artist reduces it to the syntactic minimum. Joyce cut out 'and'. And the telegram-style, the portmanteau
words of Lewis Carroll and earlier writers achieved this out of a
Victorian attitude, not a modernist one. Art is not a matter of time.

The second point is that the poets knew about it too. Once the
inhibitions of the eighteenth century were shed (perhaps more
through Coleridge's ideas than is often thought) Browning's dramatic monologues are 'heard' by convention. They too demand
elliptic syntax. And Coleridge paved the way in 'Frost at Midnight'
which shows the range of the romantic mind:

> The Frost performs its secret ministry,
> Unhelped by any wind. The owlets's cry
> Came loud – and hark, again! loud as before.
> The inmates of my cottage, all at rest,
> Have left me to that solitude, which suits
> Abstruser musings: save that at my side

My cradled infant slumbers peacefully.
'Tis calm indeed! so calm, that it disturbs
And vexes meditation with its strange
And extreme silentness. Sea, hill, and wood,
This populous village! Sea, and hill, and wood,
With all the numberless goings-on of life,
Inaudible as dreams! the thin blue flame
Lies on my low-burnt fire, and quivers not;
Only that film, which fluttered on the grate,
Still flutters there, the sole unquiet thing.
Methinks, its motion in this hush of Nature
Gives it dim sympathies with me who live.
Making it a companionable form,
Whose puny flaps and freaks the idling spirit
By its own moods interprets, everywhere
Echo or mirror seeking of itself,
And makes a toy of Thought.

The theme, like our train, has reached its terminus. Now I offer you a return ticket, to return you to thoughts of that great writer washed by the lapping waters, to the Shandymount of Joyce, to Laurence Sterne, the greatest of Joyce's precursors.

JOYCE'S 'DONE HALF BY DESIGN'

'Done half by design'; was Joyce's allusion to the *Faugh-a-Ballagh* anachronistic?

Coincidence, you could call it. When re-reading *Ulysses* in the course of selecting passages for *Joycechoyce* I was prompted – as so often happens in reading Joyce – to memories of my own. Mr Bloom is regarding Dublin Bay:

Howth. Bailey Light. Two, four, six, eight, nine. See.

I remembered swimming when I was a schoolboy late at night in a coastal pool below Howth Head and seeing the beam of light from the Bailey, its regularity offsetting the unpredictability of the waves that occasionally lapped over the concrete wall between the rocks that held in enough water for diving and a dozen strokes or so. I read on, remembering a fire on the headland:

Howth a while ago amethyst. Glass flashing. That's how that wise man what's his name with the burning glass. Then the heather goes on fire. It can't be tourists' matches. What? Perhaps the sticks rub together in the wind and light. Or broken bottles in the breeze act as a burning glass in the sun. Archimedes. I have it! My memory's not so bad.

Neither is mine, particularly as Mr Bloom continues his ruminations, moving from bees to birds, praising the latter for their bravery and thinking of perils at sea:

Nerve? they have to fly over the ocean and back. Lot must be killed in storms, telegraph wires. Dreadful life sailors have too. Big brutes of ocean-going steamers floundering along in the dark, lowing out like seacows. *Faugh-a-ballagh*. Out of that, bloody curse to you.

What is the allusion to *Faugh-a-ballagh*? Suddenly I remember the drab grey paint of a purposeful vessel moored in the Liffey at Sir John Rogerson's Quay, a long pipe its main feature. 'A Sandsucker', said my father who had brought me on a walk down from Butt Bridge, under which there chuffed a Guinness barge, steam enveloping both bridge and barge until the crew pulled the funnel vertical again once they had emerged from the low clearance of the bridge. Drays laden with Guinness barrels and drawn by vast horses clattered over the cobbles. Cranes rattled, steam enshrouded, as they hoisted barrels into Guinness vessels. At the stern of the silent sandsucker ran the name: *Faugh-a-Ballagh*. 'It means clear the way there,' said my father, 'it's the motto of the Inniskilling Dragoons.' He walked on. 'Irish' he added.

An epiphany? Hardly. But a clear memory of seeing something unusual amid the normality of Dublin's flow of Guinness. My father went on to talk of the need for dredgers to keep the Liffey deep enough for ships to use it, spoke of sand bars, and how a sandsucker could shift them. Later I was to hear the clatter of the endless chain of buckets from another grey painted vessel in the Liffey. As Maurice James Craig has reminded me, this was the aptly named *Sisyphus*, which he too remembers from his schooldays. That dredger, he has told me, was purchased in 1904. He got this information from the annual reports of the Board of Works for 1904 and 1905 (which contained nothing about the *Faugh-a-Ballagh*) in answer to a query of mine, wondering if the *Faugh-a-Ballagh* existed in 1904. Was Joyce, too, remembering that sandsucker when he put the Inniskilling Dragoons' apt battle cry in the mouth of some member of the crew of one vessel bearing down upon another?

I began my enquiry into this possible link with the Liffey away from likely sources, for I live at Fife Ness, the nose of Fife that sticks out into the North Sea between the Firth of Forth and the Firth of Tay. Turning the idea over in my head I thought I must try to discover if the *Faugh-a-Ballagh* existed on Bloomsday, 16 June 1904. If so, it was likely Joyce had it in his mind when he was writing of Dublin Bay. I thought of our coastguard David Whitehead, a former ship's officer, and asked his advice. Would Lloyds know of it? Not, he thought, if it were merely a local, coastal vessel, but worth trying. He provided me with the phone number of Lloyds in Colchester; there I made contact with Conor McFadden, who knew the passage in *Ulysses*. He suggested that I should try the Guildhall Library in London and ask for the aid of Declan Barriskill there.

Mr Barriskill, too, knew his *Ulysses*! He very kindly consulted the Mercantile Navy List 1904-1907 and the *Lloyds Register of Shipping* 1904-5. The Mercantile Navy List had an entry for *Faugh-a-Ballagh* and he gave me the details. It was built of iron in Belfast in 1878, of 372 gross tons, 150 feet 6 inches in length, 25 feet 6 inches in breadth and it drew 12 feet 2 inches. It had a 53 h.p. engine driving a single screw propeller, was registered in Londonderry under the British flag and was owned by John Best, 21st Duke of Edinburgh. A negative result. There was another *Faugh-a-Ballagh*. This was listed in the *Mercantile Navy List*, 1935-1939. It was a motor vessel, built in 1912 by Tarbert of Loch Fyne, and owned by the Royal Technical College, Glasgow. Another negative result. And yet another, for from 1900 to 1930 *Lloyd's Register* of Shipowners did not record that the Dublin Port and Docks Board owned a vessel called *Faugh-a-Ballagh*. Mr Barriskill, however, did point out that Lloyds were not interested in vessels under 300 to 400 tons, and so he was unable to research into the smaller types of craft. This information, though it was negative, was none the less very helpful.

I had decided to go to the Dublin Port and Docks Board as well as Lloyds, and Gerry Daly, yet another close reader of Joyce, told me that there was a dredger called *Faugh-a-Ballagh* in existence in the early part of the century – I had wondered if the name had been in existence on an earlier sandsucker. Mr Daly has a photograph of it dated 1912. He told me that the dredger did not belong to the Dublin Port and Docks Board but to the Board of Works, now the Office of Public Works. The dredging operations of the Office of Public Works were taken over by the Department of the Marine. Mr Daly contacted them, but found that most of their old records had been destroyed. They did, however, confirm that there was a vessel called the *Faugh-a-Ballagh*, and gave the date of purchase as 1905. So near to 16 June 1904! I wonder did Joyce see the sandsucker on one of the occasions when he returned to Ireland (in 1909, 1910 and 1912) or did he, when writing *Ulysses* (he began it in 1914; the complete book was published in 1922), see some mention of it in an Irish paper? He might have forgotten it was purchased in Dublin (?new) in 1905, or never known whether or not it was working in 1904, or – dare one suggest it – never cared to find out?

He did have an interest in dredgers. Mr Daly has pointed out to me that there is reference to a bucket dredger, the *Eblana*, in *Ulysses* (see the Bodley Head edn, 3rd impression (1963) p. 712). Mr Daly has never been able to find any such craft in the Dublin Port and Docks Board records (the name *Eblana* is an old name of Dublin); he did, however, find that the Dublin corporation owned a barge called *Eblana* in 1904. He thinks no bucket dredger carried a name before 1920, when the *Deepworker* was purchased. The Dublin Port and Docks Board did, however, have a suction dredger in 1904, the recently purchased *Sandpiper* which survived to the early 1960s. (Was this so useful that the *Faugh-a-Ballagh* was added to other vessels, dredgers, sandsuckers and hoppers, that kept the port of Dublin viable?)

Mr Daly very kindly wrote to me a second time, and I quote from this letter, referring to the passage in *Ulysses*:

It does seem that it might refer to a vessel called the 'Faugh a ballagh' and, of course, the words mean 'clear the way', (or 'leave the way' literally) which fits in with the 'lowing out' of the steamers in that passage. Dredgers have right or way by the law of the sea and every other vessel must get out of their way, hence the appropriate name chosen for the B.of W. dredger. There may have been a previous dredger of the same name, but my contact, formerly of the Board of Works did not know of it.

I seem to remember that 'Faugh a ballagh' was also the motto of one of the Irish regiments in the British Army. These troops were known as the 'Faugh a ballaghs', but I do not think this has any connection with the passage in Joyce.

He ends this letter with the comment 'To the making of discoveries in Joyce there is no end.' In the absence of further evidence a reader must decide if this ambulatory speculation leads to a negative result or is a discovery of an anachronism in *Ulysses*. Mr Bloom should have the last word, as Howth settled for slumber, 'And far on Kish bank the anchored lightship twinkled, winked at Mr Bloom.' He effaces what he has written on the sand:

Hopeless thing sand. Nothing grows in it. All fades. No fear of big vessels coming up here. Except Guinness's barges. Round the Kish in eighty days. Done half by design.

THE REALIST NOVEL IN IRELAND: 1900-1945

When I was asked to comment on *The Irish Realist Novel before the Second World War* my first reaction was to think of George Moore's brilliant picture of Dublin in *Hail and Farewell* (1911, 1912, 1914), that exciting, evocative, entertaining blend of realistic fact and imaginative fiction, and then to think of James Joyce's *Dubliners* (1914), *A Portrait of the Artist as a Young Man* (1916), *Ulysses* (1922) and *Finnegans Wake* (1939) which capture very different aspects of Dublin. But there was a difference in the attitude of these two writers to the countryside, I thought, to the other Ireland. Joyce avoided it, city dweller that he was, but Moore had shown his realistic view of the countryside in the stories of *The Untilled Field* (1903). Then the word 'realist' began to strike home to me, for others were to treat of Moore and Joyce and my brief was to discuss other realistic writers. My mind turned to a wet night in 1915 when Sean O'Faolain saw Lennox Robinson's play *Patriots* on the stage of the Cork Opera House and realised with a shock of recognition that the Ireland he knew could be put on the stage. One of the Cork realists, those early dramatists of the Abbey Theatre, had brought him strange and wonderful news, he thought; that the streets of his native Cork might also be 'full of unsuspected drama'.[1] He was ready, he said, to explore, to respond to, for the first time to see the actuality of life in Ireland. So literature need not be idealistic nor romantic, but could reflect upon and interpret the realities of life.

My mind began to range over the map of Ireland, away from Cork city, away from Frank O'Connor and Sean O'Faolain and the man who influenced them both, Daniel Corkery, and away from Edith Somerville, County Cork's partner in that great literary combination of Somerville and Ross, away up to thoughts of Liam O'Flaherty and the storm-tossed western Aran Islands, further up to Donegal and Peadar O'Donnell's realistic and moving novel *Islanders* (1928) and across to Dromore and Omagh, Benedict Kiely country, then to the Erne countryside of Shan Bullock's *The Squireen* (1903), *Dan the Dollar* (1906), and *The Loughsiders* (1924). And after that away from Forrest Reid's *Peter Waring* (1937), his well-known rewritten portrayal of adolescence, to his less well-known realistic fiction, *The Kingdom of Twilight* (1904) and *At the*

Door of the Gate (1915) with its harsh portrayal of working class Belfast. Michael McLaverty's *Call My Brother Back* (1939) has pictured the rural area of the north-east with its grinding poverty as the industrial city of Belfast grew, and the depopulated land seemed blighted. And realism informs that undervalued comic novelist – and supporter of the Gaelic League – George A. Birmingham, whose serious political novels include *The Seething Pot* (1905) and *The Red Hand of Ulster* (1912). Red, I thought. The stop sign. Is there an amber left? The whimsy of James Stephens's *The Crock of Gold* (1912) at once glowed warmly, an image of bright sunlight on the golden flowers and the green gorse bushes of the Dublin mountains. But how very different Stephens's bleaker picture of Dublin in *The Charwoman's Daughter* (1912) where the charwoman had to send her daughter out to work. And she saw the failure which this work meant, the expanding of ther daughter's life-ripples to a bleak and miserable horizon where the clouds were soap-suds and floor-cloths, and beyond a blank resignation only made energetic by hunger. Mrs Makebelieve, rightly named, wants to keep her daughter Mary out of the world. Unrealistically. But Mrs Cafferty, mother of six, the Makebelieves' neighbour, a comic figure, reminds us of the realities of life: 'An infant and a fireplace act upon each other like magnets; a small boy is always trying to eat a kettle or a piece of coal or the backbone of a herring; a little girl and a slop-bucket are in immediate contact; the baby has a knife in its mouth; the twin is on the point of swallowing a marble, or is trying to wash itself in the butter, or the cat is about to take a nap on its face,'[2]. Despite the irony – and, at times, the romance – in this novel, what remains in the reader's mind is Stephens's realistic attack on what he thought the only 'grave and debasing vice in the world – poverty'. But there are other vices that the realistic novelists have portrayed. Do you remember the dark black qualities of Brinsley MacNamara's notorious novel, *The Valley of The Squinting Windows* (1918)? Its bitter portrayal of provincial narrowness had the terrifying quality I found in some of Carleton's stories when I was a child.

But to the present; even leaving out Moore and Joyce, I had been given a shuffled pack of cards, only there were far more than fifty-two novels in the pack, even more than 52 novelists, come to that. And more to it than recognising the aces, kings, queen, jacks and jackeens. How was one to arrange them patiently, in a game of patience where black clubs become green shamrocks, black spades bog-stained loys? But realism called, and I reached for the reference books for precise dates, to see if there was a pattern of

decades, of rosaries and anti-rosaries, of pre-war and post-war repetitions, and perhaps the three-card-trick of class: big house, cottage and semi, or a trumping the ace of Westminster rule by Dublin
or Belfast rule, or a shift from land hunger to sexual hunger, or a
move from milk-and-white maidens to archetypally menacing
Maeves and demanding Deirdres.

Enough, enough. Apart from Moore and Joyce should any other
realist novelist besides Gerald O'Donovan be considered to exist
before the nineteen-twenties? Gradually the subject seemed to be
the realist novel *between* the wars. O'Donovan, however, came of a
pre-war liberal generation that had hoped for improvement in the
second decade of our century. Born Jeremiah O'Donovan, he
became a priest and was an enlightened administrator in
Loughrea, gaining for a new cathedral there the work of Irish
artists – Sarah Purser and Jack Yeats – bringing John MacCormack
to sing there, and the Irish National Theatre also to act before a
large audience. O'Donovan was in favour of modernism, and
refused to submit to the Papal encyclical against it of 1909, which
he condemned with a cool analytic anger in his first novel *Father
Ralph*, published in 1913. The world O'Donovan creates is that of
small-town Ireland, that of the bourgeoisie, fast developing, and
expanding in influence. And his second realistic novel, *Waiting* of
1914, tackled the problems raised for mixed marriages in Ireland
by the *Ne Temere* Papal decree of 1904. He tried his hand at the
political situation in *Conquest*, published in 1920, but in this novel,
which ends with the British suppression of the Dáil in 1919, the
conversations too often turn into debates, and the flow of the narrative suffers as a result.

If O'Donovan's novels capture superbly the atmosphere of the
Irish small town in the period before 1914, then Daniel Corkery's *A
Munster Twilight* (1916) and *The Threshold of Quiet* (1917) reflect
something rather different. Theirs is the world of what has been
called 'puritanism and local self-satisfaction', for the urban
Corkery remained a puritanical provincial. There are limits in *The
Hounds of Banba* (1920) that reveal his moving away from creative
literature into the literary criticism, politically – indeed almost
racially – slanted, for which he is now best known. But at its best
his fiction could be atmospheric, evocative and melancholic.

Corkery, however, is a pre-revolutionary figure, one of those
who kept revolutionary traditions going, who helped to set the fire
of 1916. What of the crucial shifts in Irish life which created the
subject matter of the realist novel after 1916, between the two
world wars? Joyce had left Dublin for a life of exile in 1904, and

O'Donovan left Loughrea and the priesthood for his exile that same year. In doing so he provided George Moore, himself to leave Dublin six years later, with some of the subject matter for that carefully observed and psychologically persuasive experimental novel, *The Lake*.

When Moore wrote the realistic stories of *The Untilled Field* of 1903 he was portraying the after-effects of the appalling mid-nineteenth century famine, when emigration was a more effective answer to rural poverty than, for instance, the no doubt well-meant but often ill-directed efforts of the Congested Districts Board in the west of Ireland. And emigration was also an answer to the power of the priests, which Moore attacked. Influenced by Zola, parallel to Turgenev, he set down the markers for some subsequent fiction in stories such as 'Julia Cahill's Curse', and 'The Exile', which reflect the Jansenist puritanism which shaped much rural life after the famine. More striking than the negative effects of the famine, however, were those of the Wyndham Land Act of 1903 which effectively turned Ireland into a land of small farmers. Its results were that the large estate was replaced by the small farm, the big house by the small town or the streets of the expanding city.

Realistic fiction mirrored this crucial change. Maria Edgeworth's *Castle Rackrent* (1800), scrupulously realistic in its speech and its facts, a story of disintegration, tells of the decay and collapse of the big house and the landlords who inhabited it in the 1780s. But the big house has continued to decay and collapse ever since, with wonderful results in realistic fiction: novels with a vertical stretch of society from gentry to peasantry, peasantry to gentry. Generated out of these tensions came the under-rated, indeed largely un-read, novels of Charles Lever, the later ones in which he depicted so realistically the decline of the landlords in the nineteenth century, their failure of nerve, their inability to recognise political realities. George Moore then pursued the theme further with equally savage satire of the administration in Dublin Castle in *A Drama in Muslin* (1887). The impermanence of the big house, the great estate, and the landlords as a cohesive class, a political force, is there also in that great achievement of Somerville and Ross, *The Real Charlotte* (1894). This novel, however, showed the way society was going, for it was no longer just the story of landlord and tenants, but of a snobbish, stratified society. Somerville and Ross carried Maria Edgeworth's observation and realism into twentieth-century fiction. They observed the countryside closely, drew it lovingly in the magnificently atmospheric descriptions of *The Real Charlotte* and their other novels. They also recorded tellingly the nuances of speech; their differing kinds – and classes – of people speak and behave convincingly, and this realistic technique was at Edith Somerville's disposal when she wrote *The Big House at Inver* in 1925. This is a powerful, sombre attempt to capture a theme suggested much earlier to Martin Ross by a visit to Tyrone House, where, in her words, there had rioted three or four generations, 'living with the countrywomen, occasionally marrying them, all illegitimate four times over.'[3] This novel was published in 1925, thirty-one years after *The Real Charlotte*, a century and a quarter after *Castle Rackrent* – which itself had been followed by the other realistic Irish novels of Maria Edgeworth – *Ennui, The Absentee* and *Ormond*. And the theme continued to occupy Irish writers. Seumas O'Kelly in *The Lady of Deerpark* (1917) for instance, created a novel in which realism portrays such events as the suicide of the owner so succinctly and effectively in its opening pages as to set the tone of the rest of the story with a precise particularity, marred only by an unconvincing ending. Pádraig Colum's *Castle Conquer* took up the theme of the big house in 1923; but the theme alters as time moves on. Elizabeth Bowen's *The Last September* of 1929, for instance, evokes the somewhat sinister atmosphere of a big house, its inhabitants surrounded by a countryside alive with people, still mysterious after centuries of propinquity. Here is a vignette from it of the undertones of the impending troubles. Lois, the young girl in the house, walks towards the woods where, the rumour is, someone has been seen burying guns. She is alone. Nobody wants to be involved; indeed nobody really wants to know.

'First, she did not hear footsteps coming, and as she began to notice the displaced darkness thought what she dreaded was coming, was there within her – she was indeed clairvoyant, exposed to horror and going to see a ghost. Then steps, hard on the smooth earth; branches slipped against a trench-coat. The trench-coat rustled across the path ahead, to the swing of a steady walker. She stood by the holly immovable, blotted out in her black, and there passed within reach of her hand, with the rise and fall of the strike, a resolute profile, powerful as a thought.'[4]

The impermanence of the settler in the landscape is there, as it was in Maria Edgeworth, and in the later Charles Lever, and in Somerville and Ross and in George Moore. Lois thinks:

'It must be because of Ireland he was in a hurry; down from the mountains, making a short cut through their demesne. Here was something else she could not share. She could not conceive of her country emotionally: it was a way of living, an abstract of several landscapes, or an oblique frayed island, moored at the north but with an air of being detached and washed out west from the British coast.'[5]

What had happened? Elizabeth Bowen's answer is succinct: 'A Man in a trench-coat passed without seeing her: that was what it had amounted to.' Less full of foreboding was Joyce Cary in *Castle Corner* (1938) but he, like Elizabeth Bowen, tempered his realism with romance, or rather was pulled each way by the two impulses. His *A House of Children* (1941) is a better, more realistic picture of ideal, timeless childhood days spent in Donegal. And the decay of the big house continues in our own time with Aidan Higgins's powerful novel *Langrishe Go Down* (1962) and Jennifer Johnston's masterly, very realistic evocations of the melancholia of disintegration and decay in *The Captains and the Kings* (1972) and *The Gates* (1973).

These novels, however, are themselves survivals of the theme of the survivors in the big house. What happened to the realistic novel between the wars was a reflection of the new, changed Ireland. The vertical range of society gives way to the horizontal – parallels with the drama are there, for Yeats's imaginative heroic plays gave way to realistic cottage comedies, with Synge's great art mediating between tragedy and comedy, between imagination and reality. Realistic novelists turned to the individual character as Ireland moved into a middle society. After the acquisition of the land what could follow? Acquisition of wealth, of social standing, made marriages, enforced respectability. Individuals could serve the despotism of an ambitious father while waiting to inherit, could conform to a society moulded by an often repressive clergy. The choice could lie between conformity or emigration to individualistic freedom. This is how Moore had seen it and how many later realistic novelists were also to interpret it after the establishment of the Irish Free State.

The way that the state came into being was, however, not convincingly treated at first. Writers were too close to it. Eimar O'Duffy in *The Wasted Island* of 1919 was over-ambitious in his picture, and, as in Gerald O'Donovan's *Conquest* of 1920, there is too much debating. Darrell Figgis in *The House of Success* (1922) was perhaps too satirical, while Liam O'Flaherty's *Insurrection* of 1950 is too fragmentary, and succumbs too much to over-melodramatic handling to be fully realistic. Iris Murdoch has recently tried her hand at it in *The Red and the Green* in 1965 but this centres too much on the characters involved. Michael Farrell's *Thy Tears May Cease* (1963), however, is a deeply personal and moving blend of realism and romance which probably captures the essence of the period better than any other novel.

After the civil war came a virtually inevitable disillusionment. To some realistic writers the fight for a republic had ended in total defeat; defeat by a combination of 'an acquisitive middle class and a vigorous and uncultivated church'.[6] These are the words of John Whelan, a pupil of Daniel Corkery; another pupil, Michael O'Donovan, and he were, as the writers we know as Sean O'Faolain and Frank O'Connor, to present Ireland with a forceful picture of itself. Idealism was indeed over. The mythology of the heroic past called into fresh life in the period of the Revival, however much it had inspired the leaders of 1916, was no longer adequate for an age where there was a steady shift from country to city. This was an age when rebellion – many of the authors of the 1920s and 1930s had taken part in the actual fighting – rebellion on behalf of nationalism and its ideals turned to rebellion against the state which that nationalism had brought into being. This new state, this new Irish society seemed to the writers, particularly the realistic novelists, to threaten the restriction of the individual's development. It was certainly one which showed its dislike of those who had fought to bring it into being by banning their writing.

O'Faolain's *Bird Alone* (1936) conveys this post-independence struggle, this querying of assumptions of the realistic novelists. In it Corney Crone asserts his personal independence, but the society that surrounds him and Elsie Sherlock is unsympathetic, and sectarian conformity proves destructive in the end. Similar destructive forces are at work in O'Faolain's realistic stories. Restrictions upon individuals imposed by social and religious attitudes continue to occupy his later work – in those superb series of short stories, more tolerant now but still sharp in their reality, their radicalism and their ability to reveal the interior ideas of individuals.

Sean O'Faolain was upset when his *Midsummer Night Madness and Other Stories* was banned in Ireland in 1932. And Frank O'Connor was too, when his *The Saint and Mary Kate*, published the same year, was also banned. This is another study of obsessive religion. Like O'Faolain, O'Connor put the material of the troubles and the civil war into fiction, and his story of the shooting of hostages, 'Guests of the Nation', shows the inhuman madness, in human terms, that possessed so many. In part it may have been a purgation of experience. But in part O'Connor was getting at the ultimate loneliness of the individual, and his realism, like O'Faolain's, retained a certain undercurrent of idealistic romance. Asked in the civil war to shoot unarmed Free State soldiers courting in Cork he refused 'because this was a basic violation of the imaginative concept of life, whether of boy's weeklies or the Irish sagas'. He added to the realism of his other Chekovian stories by conveying the sound of real men and women speaking, and as a result his narrative convinces us, sweeps us along as the story unfolds.

Liam O'Flaherty is a different kind of writer. His dynamic novels centre upon the solitary, obsessed nature of central characters. He is factual in his treatment of them; Gypo Nolan of *The Informer* (1925), and the main characters of his other novels such as *The Black Soul* (1924) or *Mr Gilhooley* (1926) or *The Assassin* (1928) or *The Puritan* (1931) or *The Martyr* (1933) are all clearly in focus. Society is a backdrop in front of which they act out their rebellions. The exception is, of course, *Famine* (1937), more a picture of the whole community under stress. *Skerrett* of 1932 deals with a feud between a teacher and a priest in Inismore, and its tension is typical, as the emotional turmoil, pent up in this quarrel, spills onto O'Flaherty's pages, violently, convincingly, menacingly. It goes back to the Gothic strain in nineteenth-century Irish fiction, to the horror of Maturin's *Melmoth the Wanderer* (1820), to some of Carleton – *The Black Prophet* (1947), or *Wild Goose Lodge* in the *Traits and Stories of the Irish Peasantry* (1830; 1833) – to Sheridan Le Fanu's *The House by the Churchyard* (1863) and *Uncle Silas* (1864), even to Somerville and Ross's *An Irish Cousin* or to Bram Stoker's *Dracula*. This Gothic element, this murmuring of melodrama, lurks beneath the realism every bit as much as the romance of, say, Emily Lawless's nineteenth-century realistic novel *Hurrish* (1886), or Elizabeth Bowen's modern *The Last September* (1924). And the romantic element lurks there too, as idealism gone temporarily to ground, in the realistic novels of O'Connor and O'Faolain.

To return to O'Flaherty and to his early collection of short stories, such as *Spring Sowing* of 1924, is to realise how good he is at conveying the reality of the rural scenes he loved. A similar interest in the land dominated much of Patrick Kavanagh's writing about Monaghan. *Tarry Flynn* (1948) contains the essence of rural life on a small farm with all its restrictions: and yet the realism must include the dream. Tarry walks backwards up the daisied slope of Callan's Hill:

He gazed across the valley right across to the plains of Louth, and gazing he dreamed into the past. O the thrilling daisies in the sun-baked hoof-tracks. O the wonder of the dry clay. O the mystery of Eternity... the heavy slumbrous time and place made him forget the sting of the thorn of a dream in his heart. Why should a man want to climb out of this anonymous happiness in the conscious day.[7]

But his sister's cry of 'Tarry, Tarry, Tarry' recalls him to reality. "What?', he shouted down. 'Come down and give us a hand to teem the pot'.[8] Yes, the dream is there, however restrictive the milieu, the routine that hems it in. This contrast of dream and reality continues in the nineteen-twenties and thirties. Mary Lavin, for instance, has understood it well. She prefers the short story, she says, but one of her two novels, *The House in Clewe Street* (1945) is a masterly, faithful picture of small town life. She focuses upon apparently irrelevant details only to incorporate them tellingly in the pattern of her analyses of bereavement, of love.

She is probably right when she argues that the short story provides a necessary curb upon the oral exuberance that swirls below the surface of the prose of those Irish writers who seek, however realistically, to tell the story. Concentrated compression pays off. Compare Frank O'Connor's novel *Dutch Interior* (1940) with, say, his stories in *My Oedipus Complex and Other Stories* (1963), or compare Sean O'Faolain's novel *A Nest of Simple Folk* (1933) with, say, his *Foreign Affairs and Other Stories* (1976) and you will probably agree with me that, however good the novels, the stories have it every time.

In general the techniques used by the realistic novelists of the nineteen-twenties and thirties were not revolutionary – Moore and Joyce had done enough innovating for the time being, perhaps – but where did the thwarted idealism go, where the mythology? Perhaps one answer is to be found in the Chinese box-like satire, the realism of the word play, in Flann O'Brien's *At Swim-Two-Birds* (1939). Sometimes one is forced to the conclusion that T S Eliot was right when he said, 'Mankind cannot bear very much reality', for throughout the Irish novel and realistic short stories there seems to be a satirising of the present through the past (and not always the heroic past of Gaeldom either) – as in the work of Darrell Figgis, or of Eimar O'Duffy, and more recently in that of Benedict Kiely (notably in *A Journey to the Seven Streams*) or in the later novels of Mervyn Wall. But picking at the itching dry scabs of social change, or the after-effects of the violence that ushered in modern Ireland is not wholly natural to the Irish temperament. We cannot forget the everlasting foibles of human nature that George A. Birmingham presents so lightheartedly, or James Stephens so quizzically, or Seumas O'Kelly so drastically in the rural humour of *The Weaver's Grave*. The best ultimate human realism is surely to be found in the realistic comedy of the authors which I cannot begin to discuss within the confines of this essay, and they are Joyce, and Beckett, and Flann O'Brien.

NOTES

SWIFT AND THE IRELAND OF HIS DAY

1   Edmund Curtis, *A History of Ireland* (London 1936), p.267.
2   William Molyneux *The Case of Ireland's being bound by Acts of Parliament in England, Stated*, 1725 ed., p.36.
3   *Ibid.*, p.116.
4   *Ibid.*, p.100.
5   *Miscellanies* (2nd ed. London 1861), p.111.
6   State Papers Domestic (Public Records Office) 63/3,64 quoted by Oliver W. Ferguson, *Jonathan Swift and Ireland* (Urbana 1962), p.18.
7   See Charles H. McTwain, *The American Revolution* (New York 1923), pp.36-37.
8   See Constantine Fitzgibbon, *Out of the Lion's Paw* (1970), p.5: 'The English had not grasped the fact that... it was precisely these Protestant gentlemen, Grattan, Tone, Parnell and so on, who had led the Irish in their longing to be free of alien rule. Were they not traitors thus to align themselves with the 'mere Irish' who were, by legal and religious definition and economic subjugation, reduced to the status of second class citizens in their own country? At least Washington, Jefferson and Franklin had never sided with the Redskins against the Redcoats'.
9   See *The Correspondence of Jonathan Swift*, ed. F. Elrington Ball (1910-1914), Vol. VI, 127.
10 Letter to Ford, 12 Nov.1708. See *The Letters of Jonathan Swift to Charles Ford*, ed. D. Nichol Smith (Oxford 1935).
11 *The Correspondence of Jonathan Swift*, ed. F. Elrington Ball, IV, pp.76-7.
12 *Autobiography*, ff 7 v.8, quoted by Irvin Ehrenpreis, *Swift. The Man; His Works, and the Age* (1962), I, p.60.
13 *The Prose Works of Jonathan Swift*, ed. H. Davis (Oxford 1939-68), IV, p.282.
14 See I. Ehrenpreis, *Swift*, I, p.43.
15 *Autobiography* f.9, quoted Ehrenpreis, *op.cit.*, p.146.
16 See Evelyn Hardy, *The Conjured Spirit-Swift* (1949), pp.50-51.
17 *The Correspondence of Jonathan Swift*, ed. F. Elrington Ball, I, p.10.
18 See Ehrenpreis *op.cit.*, I, p.187.
19 *The Correspondence of Jonathan Swift*, ed. F. Elrington Ball, I, p.465.
20 *Swift, Journal to Stella*, ed. H. Williams (Oxford), I, 194.
21 *Ibid.*, I, 220.
22 *Ibid.*, II, 472.
23 *Ibid.*, II, 525.
24 *Ibid.*, II, 573.

25   See his *Journal to Stella*, II, 655-666: 'They say here 'tis much to my
     Reputation that I have a Bp in spight of all the wor[ld], to get the best
     Deanery in Ireld'.
26   See Swift *Prose Works*, ed. H. Davis, IX.
27   Swift, *Drapier's Letters*, ed. H. Davis (1935), pp.39-40.
28   *Prose Works*, XII, p.65.
29   For discussion of this apostrophe and the views of others upon it, see W.
     J. McCormack, 'Vision and Revision in the Study of Eighteenth-Century
     Irish Parliamentary Rhetoric', *Eighteenth Century Ireland. Iris an dá
     Chullúr, II*, 1987, p.7-13.

FARQUHAR'S FINAL COMEDIES

1   Quoted by James Sutherland, 'New Light on George Farquhar', *Times
     Literary Supplement*, 6 March 1937, p. 371.
2   See Sybil Rosenfeld, 'Notes on *The Recruiting Officer*', *Theatre Notebook*
     XVIII, Winter 1963-4, 47-48.
3   Quoted by Charles Stonehill (ed.) *The Complete Works of George Farquhar*
     (1930), p. xxvi.
4   See Connely, *Young George Farquhar* (1949), pp. 243-4.
5   See Robert L. Hough, 'An Error in "The Recruiting Officer",' *N & Q*,
     CXCVIII, August 1953, pp. 340-41, and 'Farquhar: "The Recruiting
     Officer"', *N & Q* New Series 1, Nov. 1954, p. 454.
6   See Eric Rothstein, *George Farquhar*. (New York, 1967), p. 130.
7   *Ibid.*, p. 129.
8   *Ibid.*, pp. 28-9.
9   See Thomas Harwood, *The History and Antiquities of the Church and City
     of Lichfield*, (Gloucester 1806) p. 501.
10   Vanbrugh, *The Provok'd Wife, III. III.*
11   Vanbrugh, *The Relapse*, II. I.
12   Milton, *Doctrine and Discipline of Divorce*, in *Prose Works*, ed. J. A. St. John,
     (1848-744) III, p. 249. See Martin A. Larson, 'The Influence of Milton's
     Divorce Tracts on Farquhar's *Beaux' Stratagem*,' in *P.M.L.A.*, XXXIX
     (1924), pp. 174-8.
13   Milton, *op. cit.*, III, p. 265.

GOOD-NATURED GOLDSMITH

1   In *Goldsmith: The Gentle Master*, ed.Seán Lucy (1984).

MATURIN THE INNOVATOR

1   His novels are: *Fatal Revenge; or, The Family of Montorio*, 1807; *The Wild
     Irish Boy*, 1808; *The Milesian Chief*, 1812; *Women; or, Pour et Contre*, 1818;

Melmoth the Wanderer, 1820; *The Albigenses*, 1824. His plays are: *Bertram*, 1816; *Manuel*, 1817; *Fredolfo*, 1817.

2 A Dublin edition of 1802 is supposed to have existed, but no copies survive. See Lionel Stevenson, *The Wild Irish Girl* (London, 1936), p. 317.

3 Maria Edgeworth regarded the peasants as dependents, her father's and later her own responsibility. Both she and her father wished that the English and the Anglo-Irish would not despise the Gaelic Irish peasantry as savages. They themselves proved that decent treatment would be reciprocated, for very few of Mr. Edgeworth's tenants had not remained loyal in the rebellion of 1798. Maria Edgeworth's views were akin to those of Sir Jonah Barrington, *Personal Sketches and Recollections* (1876), p. 341: 'No people under Heaven could be so easily tranquillised and governed as the Irish; but that desirable end is alone attainable by the personal endeavour of a liberal, humane and resident aristocracy.' The peasants, once educated, were to remain in a subordinate position in society.

4 A letter of Mr. Edgeworth's, dated Dec. 23, 1806, quoted by Mona Wilson, *These Were Muses* (London, 1924), pp. 70 ff., refers to the 'just character' given by Lady Morgan to the 'lower Irish'.

5 He, as well as Edward Lysaght, assisted Lady Morgan with information and encouragement.

6 Cf. Donal O'Sullivan, *Irish Folk Music and Song* (Dublin, 1952), p. 10.

7 See for general discussion and particular references Constantia Maxwell, *The Stranger in Ireland* (London, 1954), pp. 125-135, 209-221. See also her *Dublin under the Georges* (London and Dublin, 1946), pp. 247-277.

8 *A Tour in Ireland; With General Observations on the Present State of That Kingdom; Made in 1776, 1777 and 1778 and Brought Down to the End of 1779* (London, 1780).

9 *A Tour Through Ireland* (Dublin, 1791). For the depressed condition of the peasantry see p. 159, and for their native music, pp. 105, 165, 219. For discussion of conditions in the countryside see Maxwell, *Country and Town in Ireland under the Georges* (London, 1940), *passim*.

10 This enterprising line in hardware prompted the circulation of a motto attributed to Lady Clare, wife of the Lord Chancellor:
>Here you may behold a liar
>Well deserving of hell-fire:
>Every one who likes may p . . .
>Upon the learned Doctor T . . .

Cf. Maurice Craig, *Dublin 1660-1860* (Dublin and London, 1952), p. 210, and Maxwell, *Dublin under the Georges*, p. 276.

11 Cf. Niilo Idman, *Charles Robert Maturin, His Life and Works* (Helsingfors and London, 1923), p. 12.

12 *Fatal Revenge*, 4th ed. (London, 1840), p. 24.

13 *The Milesian Chief* (London, 1812), p. iv.

14 *The Wild Irish Boy*, 2nd ed. (London, 1814), p. 102.

15   The hero's death is perhaps a development of the noble savage's inevitable fate at the hands of civilization; cf. the end of Oroonoko in Mrs. Behn's novel.

16   *Sermons* (London, 1819), p. 364.

17   *The Milesian Chief*, p. v.

17a Idman, p. 70.

18   Cf. *Fatal Revenge* (1807), Ch. iv, p. 61: 'When the talents and taste of Cyprian failed, even the pensiveness of the little monitor would yield to the solicitude for his pupil; in the graceful petulance of airy command, he would wind his slender arms around Ippolito and with female blandishments declare he should not quit the palace, blandishments to which he bowed with the pouting smile of reluctance.'
Cf. also Ch. vii, p. 118: 'The obscurity of his introduction, the peculiarity of his manners, gave even a hovering shade of awe to impressions, of which the character had otherwise been faint and fugitive. Not of a sex to inspire love, and still too female for the solid feelings of manly friendship, Cyprian hovered around his master, like his guardian sylph, with the officiousness of unwearied zeal and the delight of communicated purity.'
In Ch. ix Cyprian is reading letters, asks Ippolito to kiss him, and then faints.

19   AIaric Watts called it a 'horrible anatomy of the moral frame,' *The New Monthly Magazine, and Universal Register,* XI (1819), 167.

20   Scott thought her to be originally derived from Madame de Stael's Corinne *(The Quarterly Review,* June 1818). *See* also Willem Scholten, *Charles Robert Maturin the Terror-Novelist* (Amsterdam, 1933), p. 64.

21   The storm scene possesses humour, as did the scene with Macowen in the Wentworth house. Maturin unfortunately reserved his wit and humour for his own conversations.

22   *Women* (Edinburgh and London, 1818), p, 38.

23   Hyacinth breath always seems to have been exuded by Maturin's heroes or heroines when they were in close physical contact with their lovers. There was an element of the commercial copywriter lost in him.

24   *Melmoth the Wanderer* (Edinburgh and London, 1820), I, pp. 51-52.

25   Cf. Stevenson, *The Wild Irish Girl,* p. 65: 'The praises of Provençal minstrelsy, and the elaborate account of how the language and culture of Provence survived in defiance of oppression, could be transferred to Ireland by any alert reader. The sufferings of the poor, under a system of absentee landlordism, were shown with similar insinuation. Even more prominent was the insistence on the evils of a religious antagonism which filled otherwise admirable people, Catholics and Protestants alike, with prejudice, hatred, and vengeance, leading to the horrors of civil war. The eloquent pleading for tolerance and cancellation of ancient feuds had as much relevauce to contemporary Ireland as to France of two centuries before.'

26   *Sermons* (1821), p. 81.

READING LEVER

1 Charles Lever, *The O'Donoghue; A Tale of Ireland Fifty Years Ago* (Dublin, 1845), p. 1.
2 The Right Honourable Benjamin Disraeli, *Alroy* ('New Edition', London, n.d.), chapter 3, p. 24.
3 'Yeats and the Wrong Lever', originally published in *Yeats, Sligo and Ireland*, (Gerrards Cross & New York, 1980), pp 98-111.
4 Roger McHugh, 'Charles Lever', *Studies* XXVII, 1939, pp.247-60.
5 Edmund Downey, *Charles Lever, His Life in His Letters*, 2 vols. (London, 1906), pp. 196-7.

YEATS AND THE WRONG LEVER

1 Reprinted in William Butler Yeats, *Letters to the New Ireland*. Edited Horace Reynolds (Oxford, 1970), pp.163-74.
2 Reprinted in William Butler Yeats, *Letters to the New Ireland*, pp.168.
3 *Ibid.*, p.168.
4 *Ibid.*, p.173.
5 Published in the *Leisure Hour*, November 1889, p.35; reprinted in *Uncollected Prose by W.B. Yeats*, ed. John P. Frayne, I, 1970, pp.146-162.
6 *Ibid.*, p.162.
7 *Ibid.*, p.161.
8 W.B. Yeats (ed.), *Representative Irish Tales* (New York, 1891), pp.5-6.
9 From reprinted version of *United Ireland* article, *Uncollected Prose*, I, p.207.
10 From reprinted version of *United Ireland* article, *Uncollected Prose*, I, p.208.
11 *The Letters of W. B. Yeats*, ed. Allan Wade, (1954), p.246.
12 *Ibid.*, p.248.
13 'First Principles' *Samhain*: 1908, included in W. B. Yeats, *Explorations* (1962), p.235.
14 W. B. Yeats, *Autobiographies* (1956), p.138.
15 *Ibid*, p.207.
16 W. J. Fitzpatrick, *The Life of Charles Lever*, (1884), p.11.
17 Charles Lever, Introduction to *Charles O'Malley*, 1897, I.
18 Edmund Downey, *Charles Lever, His Life in his Letters*, 2 vols (1906) I, 308.
19 *Ibid.*, p. 337.
20 Charles Lever, *Jack Hinton*, New Edition with Autobiographical Introduction, n.d., p.240.
21 *Ibid.*, p.257.
22 *Ibid.*, p.257.
23 *Ibid.*, p.2.
24 *Ibid.*, pp.190-191.
25 *Ibid.*, p.xv.
26 *Ibid.*, p.143.

27 *Ibid.*, pp.142-144.
28 *Ibid.*, p.344.
29 *Ibid.*, p.275. This was also developed in *Roland Cashel* (1848) I.38 and 209-210.
30 *The Martins of Cro' Martin*, 1854, I p.xx.
31 Preface to Charles Lever, *The Martins of Cro' Martin*, (2 vols, 1872), p.ix.
32 *Sir Brooke Fossbrooke*, p.277.
33 *Ibid.*, p.280.

TORRENS: AN IRISHMAN IN SOUTH AUSTRALIA

1 In *Plan of An Association in aid of the Irish Poor Law*, 1838, he attacked the use of workhouses as a solution to the problem of poverty. For his economic theories see Lionel C. Robbins, *Robert Torrens and the Evolution of Classical Economics*, (1958).
2 See his *Thoughts on the Catholic Question by a Protestant*, 1807 and his novel *The Victim of Intolerance, or the Hermit of Killarney – a Catholic Tale*, 1814.
3 A proposal was made to government in 1831 to found a colony on the southern coast of Australia and a company was formed to organise this. For details, see J. J. Eddy, *Britain and the Australian Colonies 1818-31. The Technique of Government*, 1975. See also Robert Torrens, *Colonisation of South Australia*, 1835.
4 Torrens to Lord Russell, 24 March 1841, in *Parliamentary Papers*, 1841, 394a p.271.
5 It is very hard to understand, in view of the facts, why Douglas Pike's comments on Torrens are sneering in tone. In *Paradise of Dissent, South Australia 1829-1857*, (1957), p.42, he remarked that 'the Anglo-Irishman Torrens was an insensitive schemer whose blarney won him authority more easily than it covered his blunders'. The remark seems to indicate a bias against Irishmen in general and Torrens in particular.
6 Stephens to Lord John Russell, 22 December 1839, *Colonial Office*, 13/15.
7 It met for the last time on 3 January 1840.
8 See his *Emigration from Ireland to South Australia*, 1839. See Geoffrey Blainey, *The Tyranny of Distance. How Distance Shaped Australia's History* (1968), pp.164-65 for the time taken on the voyage and its hardships.
9 *The Budget, a series of letters on financial, commercial and colonial matters by a member of the Political Economy Club*, 'Letter VIII addressed to the friends of extended colonialism' (1848), p.241.
10 See the South Australian *Mining Journal*, 25 April 1849 and 3 May 1850.
11 See *The Budget*, Letter VIII, p.191.
12 Parliamentary Debates, Series 3, vol.XVI, pp.492-95.
13 See Torrens, *Emigration from Ireland to South Australia* (1839), p.21.
14 See his *Colonisation particular in southern Australia with some remarks on small farms and over populations* (1835), p.6.
15 Gouger to Florance, 19 January 1835, *Colonial Office*, 286/11.

16 She was probably his second wife, as Robert Richard was born in 1814 and there is a record of a Robert Torrens marrying Arabella Harmon of St Peter's Parish, Dublin, in 1801. The *Dictionary of National Biography* gives the date of his marriage to Charity Herbert Chute as 1801, but see S. A. Meenai, 'Robert Torrens 1780-1864' *Economica*, XXIII, February 1956, p.89. The Torrens family was reputedly descended from a Swedish count, a cavalry captain who had fought in William's army and settled near Derry.

17 *South Australian Gazette and Register* 2 August 1845. The phrase about theory and practice echoes his father's frequent use of the words.

18 For restrictions on trade, see Geoffrey Blainey *op.cit.*

19 The letter was published in the *South Australian Register*, 27 March 1841.

20 See, for example, the *South Australian Register*, 3 May 1841, 16 and 19 October 1844 and 17 January and 2 August 1845. See also G. A. Jessup, *Torrens of the Torrens System*, unpublished manuscript in South Australian Archives.

21 See *South Australian Register*, 19 and 26 January 1848.

22 See *South Australian Register*, 17 April 1841 and 5 June 1841.

23 In the *Mining Journal*, of which he was editor at the time. See the later venomous attacks in the *Mining Journal* of 9 October 1847 and 28 January 1848.

24 *South Australian Register*, 10 March 1849.

25 The wits then said that Stevenson had collected £250 for damages under false pretences and should return the money to Torrens.

26 Douglas Pike, *Paradise of Dissent*, p.500.

27 Hindmarsh to Lord Glenely, 19 May 1837. *Colonial Office*, 13/16, cited by Pike, *op.cit.*, p.112.

28 See Pike, *op.cit.*, p.104.

29 Edwin Hodder, *The History of South Australia*, 1893.

30 *Proceedings of the Royal Colonial Institute*, XII. 1875-1876, p.203.

31 Cited in J.J. Eddy, *op,cit.*, p.307.

32 *South Australian System of conveyancing by Registration of Title etc.* (1839), p. v.

33 *Adelaide Observer*, 21 May 1859.

34 An Act similar to his was passed in New Zealand in 1870.

35 Queensland in 1861, New South Wales, Tasmania and Victoria in 1862 and Western Australia in 1874. For his reception in these other states, see his unpublished *Autobiographical and genealogical notes*, in the South Australian archives.

36 *A Handy Book on the Real Property Act of South Australia*, a paper read to the Society for the Amendment of the Law in 1862 and subsequently published in Adelaide.

37 He thought he had excluded himself 'from all favourable notice in Downing Street' because of the paper he had read to the British Association for the Advancement of Science at Newcastle on 29 August 1863, a forceful, closely reasoned and cogent attack on transportation and the sacred cow of a recent Royal Commission's report on it.

38   A letter to his agents, Wright Brothers, in the South Australian archives provides information on his attitudes.
39   Before his resignation from the Registrar-Generalship in 1865, his income had been about £2,700 per annum. This was made up of his salary as Registrar-General, £1,000; his income from an annuity, £500; and the rest came from land and property in North Adelaide and other parts of South Australia and his interest in the *Globe* newspaper. Mrs Torrens owned a farm on the Port Adelaide Road. To make up for the loss of his salary of £1,000, he had the proceeds of the sale of Torrens Park.
40   See *Hansard*, 199, 1670, p.1002 *seq.* and p.10098 *seq.*

BLUNT: ALMOST AN HONORARY IRISHMAN

1   *Wilfrid Scawen Blunt. A Memoir* by his Grandson The Earl of Lytton (London, 1961).
2   Elizabeth Longford (The Countess of Longford), *A Pilgrimage of Passion: The Life of Wilfrid Scawen Blunt* (1979).
3   First diary entry in which he appears.
4   Elizabeth Longford, 'Lady Gregory and Wilfrid Scawen Blunt' *Lady Gregory Fifty Years After*, ed.Ann Saddlemyer and Colin Smythe (1987), p.84.
5   Their friendship has been well described by Max Egremont in *The Cousins* (1977).
6   The Earl of Lytton, *Wilfrid Scawen Blunt, A Memoir by his Grandson* (1961), p.12.

YEATS'S GREAT BLACK RAGGED BIRD

1   *Yeats's Poems*, ed. A. Norman Jeffares (1989), p. 431.
2   T. R. Henn, *The Lonely Tower* (1950), p. 311.
3   *Yeats's Poems*, p. 432.
4   W. B. Yeats, *Explorations* (1962) pp. 266-27.
5   In conversation with me, and also with T. R. Henn (see *The Lonely Tower*, p. 146).
6   This was reprinted as 'Lough Dearg Pilgrim' in *Father Butler: The Lough Dearg Pilgrim, being Sketches of Irish Manners* (Dublin, 1829), pp. 201-302. Professor Barbara Hayley has commented on the revisions in her *Carleton's Traits and Stories and the 19th Century Anglo-Irish Tradition* (1983), p. 334 seq. See also her Foreword to *Traits and Stories of the Irish Peasantry* (2 vols. 1990).
7   W.B. Yeats, *Prefaces and Introductions,* Ed. William H. O'Donnell (1988), p. 27.
9   *Yeats's Poems*, p. 318.
10 *Ibid.*, p. 382.

11   *Yeats's Poems*, p. 34.
12   St. John D. Seymour, *St. Patrick's Purgatory* (1919), pp. 55-57.
13   *Ibid.*, p. 59.
14   *Ibid.*, p. 60.
15   *Ibid.*, p. 64.
16   *Ibid.*, pp. 68-69.
17   *Ibid.*, p. 75.
18   See William Pinkerton 'Saint Patrick's Purgatory', *Ulster Journal of Archaeology*, 5, 1857, p. 71. I owe this reference to a lively, well-informed article by J.E., 'St. Patrick's Purgatory', *Canadian Journal of Irish Studies*, June 1984, vol. X, No. 1. pp. 7-40.
19   St. John D. Seymour, *St. Patrick's Purgatory*, p. 86. He gives as his source Migne, *Patr. Lat.* CLXXX.
20   Cf. 'If I were Four and Twenty', *Explorations* (1862), p. 267: Then, too, I would associate that doctrine of purgatory which Christianity has shared with Neo-Platonism, with the countryman's belief in the nearness of his dead 'working out their penance in rath or at garden end...'
21   W. B. Yeats, Commentary on Supernatural Songs, *The King of the Great Clock Tower* (1934). The 'Irish poet' was F. R. Higgins.
22   *Yeats's Poems*, p. 407.
23   He wrote an Introduction to Shri Purohit Swami, *An Indian Monk: His Life and Adventures* (1932). In this Yeats traced parallels between Indian mysticism and Celtic Christianity. In this volume the Swami doctor described his austerity on a pilgrimage. The Mount Girnar pilgrimage may also have suggested Croagh Patrick. See W. B. Yeats, *Essays and Introductions* (1961) pp. 426-437.
24   St. John D. Seymour, *op. cit.* p. 71.

MEMORIES OF MAUD GONNE

1   For instance, she more or less repeated parts of the text of her autobiography verbatim to me. The autobiography is now once more in print: see Maud Gonne MacBride, *A Servant of the Queen. Reminiscences*, ed. A. Norman Jeffares and Anna MacBride White (Gerrards Cross, 1994).
2   They have now been published at *The Gonne-Yeats Letters 1893-1938. Always Your Friend*, ed. Anna MacBride White and A. Norman Jeffares (1992).

THE FORTUNES OF RICHARD MAHONY:
AN ANGLO-IRISHMAN RECONSIDERED

1   See my 'Richard Mahony, Exile', *Journal of Commonwealth Literature* 6 (January 1969): 106-119, for critical exegesis of the trilogy.

2   In 'Diagnosis of Mahony' (*Australian Quarterly*) C. H. Hadgraft argued against the novel's being a tragedy because of this inevitability; whereas V. Buckley, in *Henry Handel Richardson*, argued that the intention of the novel is to present a comprehensive case-history.

3   He died, she said, when she was too young to know much about him, but she used his diaries as well as such books as William Howitt's *Land, Labour and Gold: or Two Years in Victoria* (1855) and William Kelly's *Life in Victoria* (1858). Other sources are given in Leonie Kramer, *A Companion to Australia Felix* (1962).

JOYCE'S PRECURSORS

1   Henry Fielding, *Jonathan Wild*, II, v.

2   Henry Fielding, *Tom Jones*, IV, vi.

3   C. J. Rawson, *Henry Fielding* (1968), p.8.

4   Tobias Smollett, *Travels through France and Italy*, text from *The Miscellaneous Works* (1800) V, p.312.

5   Tobias Smollett, *The Expedition of Humphry Clinker*, text from *The Miscellaneous Works* (1800) VI, pp. 237-9.

6   See, in this connection, Peter Quennell, *Samuel Johnson his Friends and Enemies*, (1972) pp. 214-16.

7   In this he resembles David Hume, who in his *A Treatise of Human Nature: Being an Attempt to introduce the experimental Method of Reasoning into Moral Subjects* (1739) regarded human personality as a 'bundle of perceptions' and put his views elegantly in a carefully constructed style: elegance and neatness were to allow his writing to command 'the Attention of the World' with its ironic scepticism, its presentation of personal identity as a mere legend, perceptions 'in perpetual flux and movement'.

8   I first met this in Melvin Friedman, *Stream of Consciousness. A Study in Literary Method* (1955), a stimulating book which prompted me to reread several of the texts from which quotations are made subsequently. Two other useful studies of the stream of consciousness are *The Stream of Consciousness in the Modern Novel*, ed.Robert Humphrey (1958) and *The Stream of Consciousness: scientific investigations in the flow of human experience*, ed.Kenneth F. Pope (1975).

9   Tobias Smollett, *The Expedition of Humphry Clinker*, text from *The Miscellaneous Works* (1800) VI, pp.383-4.

10 See his *Critical Essays* (1946), p.46.

11 Jingle's telegram-style has to be translated by Job Trotter in 'the final suit' of the couple in Chapter LIII. Jingle, when Perker points out that Mr Pickwick by 'corresponding with Jingle's creditor, releasing his clothes from the pawnbrokers, relieving him in prison, and paying for his passage' has 'already lost upwards of fifty pounds'. Jingle hastily rebuffs this. 'Not lost. Pay it all – stick to business – cash up – every farthing. Yellow fever, perhaps can't help that – if –' Job translates: 'He means to

say that if he is not carried off by fever, he will pay the money back again. If he lives, he will, Mr Pickwick'.

12 When Fanny Burney was being courted by the chevalier Alexander-Jean-Baptiste Piochard d'Arblay in the first seven months of 1793 – they married on 28 July of that year – her accounts of their relationship convey her hesitant reactions with great charm. Here is her account of her feelings on 10 April 1793:

Tuesday [9 April] nothing passed whatsoever; but *Wednesday April* 10th., I received early a Note from Mrs Lock, to invite me to Dine, though mentioning an Engagement for the Evening, but preferring Dinner to nothing, & adding "And poor M.D'Arblay will be quite delighted". This amazed me – but was too open to alarm me, & I resolved to go. I expected M^c de Ronchrolle would be there, & mentioned that for my inducement here.

'And now comes an account of the sweetest Hour or two that ever – I fear – will fall to my lot. I dare hope no repetition, circumstanced as I am every way! – more than passed now would distress & disturb -less, perhaps, now, would be uninteresting & flat. – To this Morning, just as it passed, I look, back with unmixt pleasure.

'I had begged the Carriage to take me to Portland Place, & to bring me home early, as Mrs Lock was engaged for the Evening. My Father had consented; his indisposition still preventing his using the Horses for himself.

'About one o'clock, while I was with my Father in the study, Sarah came flying from the Parlour, exclaiming "Sister Fanny, here's M.D'Arblay!" –
I did not affect being much grieved! – but I fear I was less calm than my Father knew how to account for: however, I had no time for such investigation; & hurried to the Parlour with what speed I could –

'My mother had flown the premises, into the next Room; & Sarah did not re-appear: I found him therefore alone: & the moment he had enquired after my Health, he would have begun – without an instant's procrastination, upon a subject I had entreated him to leave out of our discourse.

'I made an immediate check – & most truly in earnest – as he could not but see – my firm wish & plan being to avoid all further engagement or tie or entanglement, till I had settled my own doubts for HIM, & seen more of probabilities for myself. He resisted me gently, but not importunately, &, though he looked disappointed, looked, also, too just to attribute my averseness to any thing that ought to offend him.'
Less than a week later she is considerably less hesitant in confiding her feelings to her sister Susanna Elizabeth Phillips in the blend of journal and letter that recorded, minuted down the tension and excitement created in Fanny by d'Arblay's courtship:

'My Father came in very gravely, & full of reserve & thought. M.d'A not aware how little this was his custom, used every effort to inspire the gaiety with which his own mind was teeming; & my dear Father, never

insensible to such exertions, was soon brought round to appear more like himself; &, in a short time, his amiable Nature took the reins from his fears & his prejudices, & they entered into literary discussions with all the animation & interest of old friends. My Father then produced sundry of his most choice literary curiosities, & particularly Italian, when he found that language familiar to his Guest. His fine Editions of Ariosto, Dante, Petrarch & Tasso, were appreciated with delight. Then came forth the select Prints, &c, & then the collection of French Classics, which gave birth to disquisitions, interrogatories, anecdotes, and literary contentions, of the gayest & most entertaining nature: – while, though not a word passed between us, I received, by every opportunity, des regards si touchans, si heureux! – Ah, my dearest Susanna! – with a Mind thus formed to meet mine – would my dearest Father listen ONLY TO HIMSELF, how blest would be my lot! –'
Extracts from Fanny Burney, *Journals and Letters* ed.Joyce Henslow, 2 vols (1972), pp.59 and 81.

13   Jane Austen, *Emma* (1876) Chapter XXXVIII.
14   Melvin Friedman, *op.cit.*, pp.37-41, points out various experiments in Moore's *Mildred Lawson* (in *Celibates*, 1895) and *Mike Fletcher* (1889), remarking that Moore said of *Ave Atque Vale* that 'my nonsense thoughts amuse me; I follow my thoughts as a child follows butterflies' (*Memoirs of my Dead Life* (1911) p.3). He regards Moore as an anticipator of the stream of consciousness, citing his appreciation of his friend Dujardin's *Les Lauriers Sont Coupés* (1887), where he thought Dujardin has 'discovered the form the archetypal form, the most original in our time; but the psychology is a little "naturalist"' *(see Letters from George Moore to Edward Dujardin, 1886-1922* (1929), p.40). Another letter to Dujardin, (of November 1930) is cited as a metaphorical definition of interior monologue, in terms of Moore's own procedures: 'When the novel stops going into the wings to ring down the curtain we begin to hear exquisite music. The cage is open and the birds (our thoughts) sing in free verse'. See Dujardin, *Le Monologue Interieur* (1931). p.79.

JOYCE'S 'DONE HALF BY DESIGN'

1   *Joycechoyce: The Poems in Verse and Prose of James Joyce*, ed. A. Norman Jeffares and Brendan Kennelly (London, 1992).

THE REALIST NOVEL IN IRELAND: 1900-1945

1   Sean O'Faolain, *Vive Moi* (Boston, 1964), p. 112.
2   James Stephens, The Charwoman's Daughter (London, 1912), pp. 115-16.
3   From a letter of Violet Martin to Edith Somerville, 8 March 1912.
4   Elizabeth Bowen, *The Last September* (London, 1929), p. 43.
5   *Ibid.*, p. 44.

6 Sean O'Faolain's remark about 'the alliance between the Church and new businessmen and politicians, all three nationalist, isolationist...? in 'Fifty Years of Irish Writing', *Studies*, Spring 1962, p. 97.

7 Patrick Kavanagh, *Tarry Flyn* (Dublin, 1948), p. 20.

8 *Ibid.*, p. 21.

INDEX

Page references in **bold** indicate complete chapters.

Abbas Hilmi Pasha (son of Tewfik Pasha), Khedive of Egypt 215
Abercorn, Marchioness of 123, 126–27, 128, 129
Abercorn, Marquis of 123, 126–27, 128
Abu, Sheik Mohammed 208, 211
Acheson, Lady 37, 38–39, 75
Acheson, Sir Arthur 37, 39
Addison, Joseph 22, 35, 59
Ahmed Arabi (Arabi Pasha) 208–09
Ainsworth, Harrison 153
Aldington, Richard 217
Allingham, William 90, 167
    Irish Songs and Poems 165–66
Anderson, Mrs 120
Anne, Queen of Great Britain and Ireland 24–27, 42, 49, 50, 51, 53–54, 56–58
Arabi Pasha *see* Ahmed Arabi
Arbuthnot, John 75
Ashe, St George 1, 11
Auden, W.H., *New Year Letter* 298
Austen, Jane 154, 160
    Emma 304–05
Austin, Dr 119
Austin, Mrs 119

Bagot, Captain 193, 194
Baker, Kate 171
Balfour, Arthur 212, 213, 214, 217
Balzac, Honoré de 181, 186, 256
Banim, John and Michael 167
Baring, Major Evelyn 210, 215, 216
Barrington, Sir Jonah, *Recollections of the Later Eighteenth Century* 155
Barriskill, Declan 311, 312
Baudelaire, Charles Pierre 224
Beauclerk, Topham 97
Beckett, Samuel 322
Bedford, 9th Duke of (Lord Lieutenant of Ireland) 121
Bee, The 95, 99
Bell, Sydney *see* MacOwen, Mrs Sydney
Benson, Captain White 123, 124
Beowulf 291
Bergson, Henri 307
Berkeley, Charles, 2nd Earl of 13, 20, 21, 48–49
Berkeley, George, Bishop of Cloyne 300
    The Querist 18
Berkeley, Lady Betty 20, 21
Best, Richard 233
Biddulph, Sir Michael 83
Billington, Mrs 119
Birmingham, George A. (pseud. of James Hannay) 258, 322
    The Red Hand of Ulster 315
    The Seething Pot 315
Black, W. 90
Blackwood's Magazine 179
Blakeway, E. 77
Blunt, Alice 202, 204
Blunt, Francis Scawen (brother of Wilfrid) 202, 204
Blunt, Francis Scawen (father of Wilfrid) 202
Blunt, Francis Scawen (son of Wilfrid) 204
Blunt, Judith 201, 205, 214, 216, 218, 219
Blunt, Lady Anne 201, 214, 216, 218–19
    Bedouin Tribes of the Euphrates 206
    A Pilgrimage to Nejd, The Cradle of the Arab Race 206
Blunt, Mary 202
Blunt, Samuel 202
Blunt, Wilfrid Scawen x, **201–19**

Atrocities of Justice under British Rule in Egypt 217
Bedouin Tribes of the Euphrates 206
The Bride of the Nile 214–15
'The Canon of Augrim' 214
Diaries 202
Esther, Love Lyrics and Natalia's Resurrection 204, 214
Fand of the Fair Cheek 216
The Future of Islam 208
Gordon at Khartoum 217
Ideas about India 211
In Vinculis 214
India under Ripon 217
The Land War in Ireland, Being a Personal Narrative of Events... 213, 217
Love Lyrics and Songs of Proteus (1892) 210, 214
The Love Sonnets of Proteus (1881) 204, 207, 214
A Pilgrimage to Nejd, The Cradle of the Arab Race 206
Poetical works 217–18
Satan Absolved 215
Secret Diaries 209
Secret Histories (*My Diaries*) 213, 218, 219
The Secret History of the English Occupation of Egypt being a Personal Narrative of Events 210, 211
Sonnets and Songs of Proteus (1875) 203–04, 205, 207
Blunt, William 202
Bolingbroke, Viscount *see* St John, Henry
Bolton, Theophilus 49
Bond, Thomas 83
Book of Kells 299
Bookman, The 158, 167
Boswell, James 90
Boucicault, Dion ix
Bowden, Charles Topham 134
Bowen, Elizabeth
The Last September 318–19, 321
Seven Winters x
Boyd, E.A. 158
Ireland's Literary Renaissance 180
Boyd, Reverend 119
Boyer, Abel 25
Broadside, A 260–61
Brooke, Charlotte, *Reliques of Irish*

Poetry 134
Browne, Peter 11
Browne, Sir Thomas 287
Religio Medici 283
Browning, Robert 308
Bryanton, Robert 98
Buckingham, John Sheffield, Duke of 52
Bullock, Shane
Dan the Dollar 314
The Loughsiders 314
The Squireen 314
Bülow, Hans Guido von 287
Bunting, Edward, *General Collection of the Ancient Irish Music* 134
Burke, Edmund 105, 159, 174
A Philosophical Enquiry into the Origin of our Ideas of the Sublime and Beautiful 97
Burke, Maude Alice 239
Burney, Fanny 303–04
Burton, Sir Richard Francis 204, 300
Bushe, Arthur 20
Byrne, Donn 164
Byron, George Gordon, Lord 203, 204
Byron, Lady 204

Cahir, Lady 129
Calderón de la Barca, Pedro
Calderón's Comedies 262
The Purgatory of St Patrick 262–63
Camoens, Luis de, *The Lusiads* 291
Carleton, Dorothy 216, 219
Carleton, William 158, 167, 179, 315
The Black Prophet 321
'A Pilgrimage to Patrick's Purgatory' 261–62
Traits and Stories of the Irish Peasantry 167, 321
Traits and Stories of the Peasantry 165
Valentine McClutchy 155
Wild Goose Lodge 321
Carlyle, Thomas 90
Carroll, Lewis (pseud. of Charles Dodgson) 153, 301, 308
Alice's Adventures in Wonderland 289–90
Carteret, John, 1st Earl Granville 35
Cary, Joyce
Castle Corner 319
A House of Children 319
Cassell, Mr 192–93

Castlereagh, Robert Stewart, Viscount 126
Catalini, Madame 136
Caxton, William, *Mirror of the World* 272
Cervantes Saavedra, Miguel de 170
    Don Quixote 83
Chamberlain, Joseph 211
Chandler, Mary 202
Chandler, Miss 168
Chanson de Roland 291
'Chaperone' (Maud Gonne's pet marmoset) 280
Charles I, King of Great Britain and Ireland 9
Charles II, King of Scotland and England 6
Chetwode, Knightley 69
Chievati, Cardinal Merenio 268
Christian Examiner and Church of Ireland Magazine 262
Churchill, Lord Randolph Henry Spencer 210, 211
Chute, Charity Herbert 190
Cibber, Colley 76
Clanricarde, Hubert George de Burgh-Canning, 4th Marquis and 15th Earl of 212
Clarendon, Edward Hyde, 1st Earl of 2
Clark, Sir Arthur 120
Clarke, Austin 171
    Twice Round the Black Church x
Coburn, Henry 123
Cockerell, Sidney 215
Colbourn, Henry 130
Coleridge, Samuel Taylor, 'Frost at Midnight' 308–09
Colum, Pádraig, *Castle Conquer* 318
Colvin, Sir Auckland 208
Congreve, William 10, 22, 35
    Love for Love 78, 81
Connely, Willard 78
Cooper, James Fenimore, *The Spy* 302
Corkery, Daniel 134, 158, 180, 314, 320
    The Hounds of Banba 316
    A Munster Twilight 316
    The Threshold of Quiet 316
Cowley, Abraham 19
Craig, Maurice James 44, 165, 311
Craigie, Pearl 231, 239
Crissaphan, George 268

Cristoph, Philipp, Count Konigsmark 25
Crofton, George 118
Crofton, Lady 117, 120
Crofton, Sir Malby 117, 118, 120
Croker, John Wilson, *Familiar Epistles on the Present State of the Irish Stage* 121
Croker, Thomas Crofton 166, 167
Cromwell, Oliver 1, 2, 9
Crossley, Francis 127
Cunard, Lady 237
Cunard, Nancy 239
    Memories of George Moore 240
Cunard, Sir Bache 239
Curll, Edmund 42
Curran, John Philpot 159, 174
Currie, Francis 214
Curtis, Professor Edmund 2
Curzon, George Nathaniel, Marquis Curzon of Kedleston 231
Cutts, John Cutts, Baron 22

Dagda (Maud Gonne's Great Dane) 279–80
Daily Express (Dublin) 158, 167, 234
Daly, Gerry 312
Daly, Richard 119
Dante Alighieri 265
    Divine Comedy 291
    Paradiso 268
Darwin, Charles, *Origin of Species* 203
Daudet, Alphonse 223
David of Wurzburg 267
Davis, Thomas 158, 167, 179
Davitt, Michael 212
de Lannoy, Guillebert *see* Lannoy, Guillebert de
de Lisle, Sir William 272
de Montalvan, Juan Perez *see* Montalvan, Juan Perez de
de Pasztho, Laurence Rathold *see* Rathold, Laurence
Dease, Colonel Sir Gerald Richard 227
Declaration Setting Forth How, and by What Means, the Laws and Statutes of England Came to be of Force in Ireland (Anon) 8
Degas, Edgar 223
Delaney, Reverend Patrick 34–36
Derby, Edward Geoffrey Smith

Stanley, 14th Earl 172, 189, 203
Dermody, Thomas 119, 124–25
di Giovanni Rustichi, Corso 268
Diaper, William, *Nereides: or Sea-Eclogues* 26
Dickens, Charles 153
  Barnaby Rudge 154
  Great Expectations 301
  Master Humphrey's Clock 154
  Nicholas Nickleby 154
  The Old Curiosity Shop 154
  Oliver Twist 154
  Pickwick Papers 154, 302
  Sketches by Boz 154
Dilke, Sir Charles Wentworth 207
Dillon, John 212
Dingley, Rebecca 21, 29–30, 32, 60, 64, 71
Disraeli, Benjamin 180, 207
  Alroy 153–54
  Coningsby 154
  Contarini Fleming 153
  Endymion 154
  Henrietta Temple 154
  Lothair 154
  Sybil 154
  Tancred 154
  The Young Duke 153
Donne, John 162
Dostoyevsky, Fyodor Mikhailovich 286
Doughty, Charles 206
Dowden, Professor Edward 167
Dryden, John 19, 23
  translation of the *Aeneid* 291
Dublin University Magazine 158, 161, 171, 172, 175, 187
Dujardin, Édouard 231, 237
  Les Lauriers sont Coupés 308

Earle, Captain 123, 124
Edgeworth, Maria 134, 158, 162, 167, 174, 180
  The Absentee 128–29, 155, 163, 177, 303, 318
  Belinda 141
  Castle Rackrent 117, 132–33, 154–55, 163, 185, 317, 318
  Ennui 117, 136, 155, 318
  Ormond 119, 155–56, 163, 318
  Patronage 181
Edgeworth, Richard Lovell 181

Egypt 217
Ehrenpreis, Professor Irwin 10, 11, 60
Eliot, George (Mary Ann Evans), *Middlemarch* 162
Eliot, T.S. 104, 322
Elliot, Frances 189
Elliot, Thomas Frederick 189
Ellis, Henry Havelock 281
Emmet, Robert 143
English Review 217
Estcourt, Richard 76
Everard, Ignatius 120, 121
Everard, Richard 121
Examiner, The 24, 51, 54, 56

Faris, Sheik of Shanmax tribe 206
Farquhar, George ix, **76–89**, 179, 306
  The Beaux Stratagem 76, 82–89, 152–53
  The Inconstant 81
  Love and a Bottle 81
  The Recruiting Officer 76–81, 83, 84, 152
  The Stage-Coach 77–78, 83
  The Twin Rivals 78, 83
Farrell, Michael, *Thy Tears May Cease* 319
Faugh-a-Ballagh (in *Ulysses*) 310–13
Ferguson, Sir Samuel 167
Ferrier, Susan 153
Fielding, Henry
  Amelia 294–95
  An Apology for the Life of Mrs Shamela Andrews 291
  Jonathan Wild 292–94
  Joseph Andrews 291
  Tom Jones 119, 291–92
Figgis, Darrell 322
  The House of Success 319
Finch, Edith, *Wilfred Scawen Blunt* 201
Fingall, Arthur James Plunkett, 11th Earl 227, 228
Finniss, B.T. 195
Fitzpatrick, W.J., *Life of Charles Lever* 169–70
Flanagan, Professor
  Irish Novel 159
  The Year of the French 159
Flaubert, Gustave 286
  Madame Bovary 225
Flint, F.S. 217
Flynn, Dr 118

Foley, John Henry 105
Fontaine (*maître de ballet*) 120
Ford, Charles 28, 32, 33, 36, 55, 71, 74
Forster, Anthony 196–97
Fortnightly Review 211
Freeman's Journal, The 121, 167
Froissart, Jean 272

Gale, Sarah 202
Galt, John 154
Garrick, David 118
Gaskill, William 82
Gawler, George 189, 190–91
Gay, John 35, 42
Geree, Reverend John 68
Germain, Lady Betty 75
Giffard, Lady 48, 60
Gifford, William 125
Gilgamesh 291
Gill, T.P. 241
Giordani, Tomaso 120
Giovanni Rustichi, Corso di *see* di
    Giovanni Rustichi, Corso
Giraldus Cambrensis, *Topographica
    Hibernica* 267
Gladstone, William Ewart 182, 187,
    199, 207, 208–09, 211
Globe and Traveller 192
Godolphin, Sidney, 1st Earl of 23–24,
    49, 50, 52
Godwin, William 133
Goethe, Johann Wolfgang von 133
    Werther 115, 125
Gogarty, Oliver St John 249
Golding, William, *Lord of the Flies* 106
Goldsmith, Charles (brother of
    Oliver) 98
Goldsmith, Contarine (uncle of
    Oliver) 96
Goldsmith, Henry (brother of Oliver)
    94, 97
Goldsmith, Mr (father of Oliver) 94
Goldsmith, Oliver ix, 19, **90–105**, 118,
    170, 249, 306
    'A Comparative view of Races and
    Nations' 101
    The Deserted Village 90, 101–05,
    106–07
    'Elegy on the Death of a Mad Dog'
    90
    *A Enquiry into the State of Polite
    Learning in Europe* 92–93, 94, 98–99

The Good Natur'd Man 90–91
*History of the Earth and Animated
    Nature* 91
The History of the Man in Black
    95–96
Letters from a Citizen of the World 91
'The March of Intellect' 95
'Retaliation' 90
She Stoops to conquer 90–91, 113, 152
'Stanzas on Woman' 90
The Traveller 90, 99–101
The Vicar of Wakefield 90, **106–14**
'When lovely Woman stoops to
    folly' 90
Goncourt, Edmond 223
Gonne, Maud x, 212, **277–81**
Goodwin, Geraint 241
Gordon, General Charles 211
Gouger, Robert 190
Grattan, Henry 18, 130, 159, 174
Grattan brothers 32, 36
Gray, Sir Edward 217
Gregory, Lady Augusta x, 132, 238,
    279
    'Arabi and his Household' 209
    attitude to Charles Lever 158, 168,
    178
    Blunt and the Irish literary revival
    216, 217, 219
    Journals 259
    Moore and the Irish theatre 231–32,
    234
    in Somerville and Ross *Some
    Experiences of an Irish R.M.* 254
    sonnets to Wilfred Blunt 213
    'A Woman's Sonnets' 210, 214
Gregory, Sir William 209, 210
Grey, Henry, 3rd Earl 189
Griffin, Gerald 167
Griffiths, Ralph 97
Guarini, Giovanni Battista 133
Guiscard, Marquis de 52–53
Gwynn, Stephen 180

Halifax, Charles Montagu, Earl of 59
Hamilton, Edward 207
Harley, Robert (1st Earl of Oxford) 24,
    26–28, 50–54, 57, 59–60, 68, 72
Harrison, John 83
Harvey, Beauchamp Bagenal 143
Henley, W.R., *The Poetry of Wilfrid
    Blunt* 214

Henn, T.R. 260
Henry II, King of England 4, 5
Henry III, King of England 4
Henry VIII, King of England 2, 268
Henry of Saltrey 263–65, 266–67
Higgins, Aidan, *Langrishe Go Down*
　319
Hill, Jane 118
Hindmarsh, Sir John 192, 195
Hobbes, Thomas 43
Holt, Neville 248
Homer 306
　Iliad 107, 291, 292
　Odyssey 107, 290–91, 292, 295
Hood, Thomas 172
Hope, A.D. 286
Horace 165
Howard, Mrs, Countess of Orkney 75
Hudson, Edward 134
Hughes, Mr 198
Hyde, Douglas x, 167, 219, 231, 234,
　241

Ibn Arûk, Mohammed 206
Ibn Meshid, Mashur 206
Ibn Rashid, Mohammed 206
Ibn Shaalan, Sheik 206
Idman, Niilo 144
Inismore, Princess of 121
Irish Statesman 261
Irving, Sir Henry 303
Ismail Pasha, Khedive of Egypt 205

Jackson, Reverend Daniel 36
Jacobsen, J.P., *Niels Lynne* 286
James II, King of England 2, 3, 5, 6, 10
James, William, *Principles of*
　Psychology 298, 307
Jedaan, Sheik 206
Jeffcot, Sir John 195
John (Lackland), King of England 4, 5
Johnson, Dr Samuel 90, 91, 298
Johnson, Hester/Esther *see* Stella
Johnson, Mrs 64
Johnston, Jennifer
　The Captains and the Kings 319
　The Gates 319
Johnston (London Publisher) 121
Jones (? Sergeant) 77
Jonson, Ben, *Volpone* 78
Joscelin (Cistercian monk) 267
Jowett, Benjamin, *Essays and Reviews*

203
Joyce, James x, 162, **289–309, 310–13,**
　315, 316, 322
　Dubliners 235, 314
　Finnegan's Wake 289, 306, 307, 314
　A Portrait of the Artist as a Young
　Man 235, 305, 314
　Ulysses 290, 306, 307, 310–13, 314
Joyce, P.W., 'Celtic Romances' 167

Kavanagh, Patrick, *Tarry Flynn*
　321–22
Kells, Book of 299
Khalil, Sheik Mohammed 208
Kiely, Benedict 180, 314
　A Journey to the Seven Streams 322
　Modern Irish Fiction 180
King, William (Archbishop of Dublin)
　1, 50–53, 55–56, 74–75
King-Noel, Lady Anne Isabella 204
Kingsbury, Miss Henrietta 136
Kingstone, Henry Ernest Newcomen
　King, 8th Earl of 212
Konigsmark, Madam 26

la Chapelle, Jean de, *Les Carosses*
　d'Orléans 77–78, 83
Lamb, Lady Caroline 154
Landa, Professor Louis 49
Langton, Bennet 90
Lannoy, Guillebert de 268
Lavin, Mary, *The House in Clewe Street*
　322
Law, Hugh 180
Lawless, Emily, *Hurrish* 321
Lawrence, Miss 216
Le Fanu, Mrs 126–27
Le Fanu, Sheridan
　The House by the Churchyard 321
　Uncle Silas 321
Le Sage, Alain René 170
Leavis, Dr F.R. 299
Lecky, William Hartpole 8
Lehrer, Tom 292
Leisure Hour, The 158
Leslie, Shane, *Saint Patrick's*
　Purgatory. A Record from History and
　Literature 275
Leutwein, Helen 203
Lever, Charles ix, 139, **150–63, 164–78,**
　317, 318
　Arthur O'Leary 170, 179

'Barney O'Reirdan' 167
Barrington 155, 158, 159, 177
Charles O'Malley 157, 158, 167, 168, 171–74, 172, 179
Con Cregan 170
The Confessions of Harry Lorrequer 153, 157, 165, 171–73, 175, 179
Davenport Dunn 165
The Dodd Family Abroad 176
'Father Tom and the Pope' 167
Jack Hinton 158–59, 172, 174–76
The Knight of Gwynne 176
Lord Kilgobbin 153, 157, 158, 159, 173, 178, **179–87**
Luttrell of Arran 159
The Martins of Cro Martin 159, 172, 176–77
Maurice Tierney 159
The O'Donoghue; A Tale of Ireland Fifty Years Ago 150–52, 153, 155–57, 159–62, 172, 175
Roland Cashel 159, 165
St Patrick's Eve 159, 175
Sir Brook Fossbrooke 158, 159, 177, 185
Sir Jasper Carew 159
Tom Burke of 'Ours' 157, 159, 161, 165, 172
Lever, James (father of Charles) 168, 171
Lever, John (brother of Charles) 168
Leverson, Ada 239
Lewis, Erasmus 57, 58–59, 60, 67–68, 131, 154
Lintot, Bernard 76
Lloyd's Register of Shipowners 312
Lloyd's Register of Shipping 311
Locke, John 298, 299, 300, 303
Long, Miss 67
Longford, Lady Elizabeth 202, 210
Lovelace, Augusta Ada, Countess of 204
Lovelace, Earl of 204
Lover, Samuel 139, 158, 160, 166
    Handy Andy 165
Lytton, Anthony, Earl of, *Wilfrid Scawen Blunt. A Memoir* 201–02, 218
Lytton, Edward Robert Bulwer 153, 204, 207, 214
Lytton, Neville 216

MacBride, John 279

MacBride, Sean 279
MacCarthy, Dennis Florence
    A Brief History of Saint Patrick's Purgatory. Collected by... 263
    Calderón's Dramas 262
MacCormack, John 316
MacDermott of Coolavin 118
MacDermotts of Moylurg 118
MacDonald, Ramsay 220
McDonnell, Dr James 134
MacDonnell, Sir Richard Graves 195–96, 197
McFadden, Conor 311
McGlashan, James 160, 162
McHugh, Professor Roger 159
    'Charles Lever' 180
McLaverty, Michael, *Call My Brother Back* 315
MacNamara, Brinsley 239
    The Valley of the Squinting Windows 315
MacOwen, Mrs Sydney (née Bell) 118, 119
MacOwen, Walter 118
Macpherson, James, *Ossian* 115, 125, 137
Mahaffy, Arthur 165
Mahaffy, Sir John Pentland 165
Mahdi (Mohammed Ahmed) 211
Malet, Sir Edward 208
Manet, Édouard 223
Mangan, James Clarence 149, 167
Manning, Henry 203
Mannini, Antonio 268, 270, 271, 273, 275–76
Mannini, Salvestro 268
Marlborough, John Churchill, Duke of 23, 24, 41
Marlborough, Sarah, Duchess of 25
Marsh, Narcissus 48, 49
Martin, Violet Florence *see* Somerville and Ross
Martyn, Edward 231–33, 241
Mary II, Queen of Great Britain and Ireland 2
Masham, Lady Abigail 25, 58
Masham, Samuel 25
Mashur Ibn Meshid *see* Ibn Meshid, Mashur
Maturin, Charles Robert ix, **131–49**, 154, 158
    The Albigenses 148–49

Bertram 136
'Bruno-Lin, the Irish Outlaw' 132
*Fatal Revenge, or, The Family of
Montorio* 131–32, 134–35, 137,
140–41, 144
Melmoth the Wanderer 131, 135,
147–48, 321
The Milesian Chief 135, 136, 141–45,
146, 148, 156–57
The Wild Irish Boy 135–41, 145–46,
156
Women 135, 136, 145–47
Maxwell, William Hamilton
Tales of the Peninsula War 171
Wild Sports of the West 162, 171
Mazzini, Guiseppe 217
Melville, Herman, *Moby Dick* 302
Ménière, Dr Émile Antoine 27
Mercantile Navy List 311
Mercier, Vivian, *The Irish Comic
Tradition* 180
Meredith, George, *Vittoria* 160
Messingham, Thomas, *Florilegium
Insulae Sanctorum, Seu vitae et actae
sanctorum Hiberniae* 262–63, 273
Meynell, Charles 203
Millevoye, Lucien 279
Milne, William 13, 48, 49
Milton, John 245
Doctrine and Discipline of Divorce
84–86
Paradise Lost 291
Mitchel, John 167
Mohammed Abu *see* Abu, Sheik
Mohammed
Mohammed Ahmed (the Mahdi) 211
Mohammed Ibn Arûk *see* Ibn Arûk,
Mohammed
Mohammed Ibn Rashid *see* Ibn
Rashid, Mohammed
Mohammed Khalil *see* Khalil, Sheik
Mohammed
Moira, Countess of 119
Molière (Jean Baptiste Poquelin) 170
Molyneux, Thomas 1
Molyneux, William 1–3, 8, 10, 16–17,
18, 178, 187
*The Case of Ireland's being bound by
Acts of Parliament in England, Stated
(1698)* 4–5, 7
Montague, John, 'Exile and Prophecy'
103

Montalvan, Juan Perez de 263
Vida y Purgatorio de San Patricio 262
Monthly Review 97
Moore, George 163, 164, 166, **220–50**,
315, 316, 318
The Apostle 242
Avowals 241
The Brook Kerith 242–46, 248, 306
A Communication to My Friends 241,
248
Confessions of a Young Man 220, 241,
249
Conversations in Ebury Street 241
A Drama in Muslin 212, 226, 306,
317
Esther Waters 228–30, 237, 305
Evelyn Innes 230
'The Exile' 317
Flowers of Passion 224
Hail and Farewell! x, 238–39, 241,
306, 314
Héloïse and Abelard 246–48, 306
'Julia Cahill's Curse' 317
The Lake 235–37, 238, 305–07, 317
'Lui et Elles' 231
Martin Luther 224
Memoirs of my Dead Life 239, 240,
241
*A Modern Lover (Lewis Seymour and
Some Women)* 224
A Mummer's Wife 225, 305
Pagan Poems 224
The Passing of the Essenes 248
*Portrait of Himself as Impotent
Siegfried* 306
Sister Teresa 230–31
Ulick and Soracha 248
The Untilled field 234–35, 305, 314,
317
Worldliness 224
Moore, George (great-grandfather of
George) 221
Moore, Maurice (brother of George)
239
Moore, Thomas 122, 158, 167, 168
Irish Melodies 116, 134
Moore, Thomas Sturge 217
More, Sir Thomas 221
Morgan, Lady Sydney ix, 115, 154,
158
The O'Briens and the O'Flahertys 146,
157

O'Donnel **123–30**
see also Owenson, Sydney
Morgan, Miss 65
Morgan, Sir Charles 115, 123, 127–28, 239–40
Morris, William 214
Motteaux, Peter 83
Murdoch, Iris, *The Red and the Green* 319

Napier, Colonel Sir Charles 190
Nash, Richard 91
Nation, The 158, 179
Nevinson, H.W. 280
Nietzsche, Friedrich Wilhelm 286
Northumberland, Earl of 25
Nottingham, Earl of 7, 23

O'Brien, Flann, *At Swim-Two-Birds* 322
O'Brien, William Smith 212
O'Connell, Daniel 158, 159, 168, 179, 190
O'Connor, Frank (pseud. of Michael O'Donovan) 314, 321
Dutch Interior 322
'Guests of the Nation' 320–21
My Oedipus Complex and Other Stories 322
The Saint and Mary Kate 320
O'Donnell, Peadar, *Islanders* 314
O'Donovan, Gerald (pseud. of Jeremiah O'Donovan) 266, 316, 317
Conquest 316, 319
Father Ralph 316
Waiting 316
O'Donovan, Jeremiah *see* O'Donovan, Gerald
O'Donovan, Michael *see* O'Connor, Frank
O'Duffy, Eimar 322
The Wasted Land 319
O'Faolain, Sean 314, 321
Bird Alone 320
Foreign Affairs and Other Stories 322
Midsummer Night Madness and Other Stories 320
A Nest of Simple Folk 322
O'Flaherty, Liam 235, 314
The Assassin 321
The Black Soul 321
Famine 321

The Informer 321
Insurrection 319
The Martyr 321
Mr Gilhooley 321
The Puritan 321
Skerrett 321
Spring Sowing 321
O'Grady, Standish 167, 241
O'Halloran, Count (invented character in *The Absentee*) 128
O'Halloran, Sylvester
General History of Ireland from the earliest accounts to the close of the twelfth century 134
Introduction to the Study of the History and Antiquities of Ireland 134
O'Kelly, Seumas
The Lady of Deerpark 318
The Weaver's Grave 322
Oldfield, Anne 76
Oldham, Charles x
O'Leary, John 241
Ormonde, Duke of 3, 7, 9, 11, 14, 25, 28, 51, 52–59, 76
Ormsby, Sir Charles 125, 126, 127
Orrery, Boyd, Charles, 4th Earl of 76
Orwell, George 302
Otway, Caesar
Sketches in Ireland: Descriptive of Interesting and hitherto unnoticed Districts, in the North and South 262
A Tour in Connaught 262
Ovid, *Metamorphoses* 22
Owenson, Olivia 119, 120, 123–24
Owenson, Robert 118–20, 124
Owenson, Sydney 127, 141
The First Attempt, or the whim of a Moment 120
Midas 120
The Missionary, an Indian Tale 126
The Novice of St Dominick 116, 123, 125, 148
Patriotic Sketches of Ireland, Written in Connaught 117
Poems 115
St Clair; or, The Heiress of Desmond 115, 123, 132–33, 156
Twelve Original Hibernian Melodies 116, 123, 134
The West Indian 120
The Wild Irish Girl **115–22**, 123, 126, 132–33, 136, 142, 144, 156

Woman, or Ida of Athens 125–26
see also Morgan, Lady Sydney
Oxford, Earl of *see* Harley, Robert

Pall Mall Gazette 212, 245
Park, Mungo 190
Parkhurst, Charles 127
Parnell, Margaret 84
Partridge, Eric 44
Paztho, Laurence Rathold de *see*
Rathold, Laurence
Patrick (Swift's servant) 59
Peacock, Thomas Love 153, 154
Pearse, Patrick 235
Pelligrini, Dr Alphonse 120
Pembroke, Thomas Herbert, 8th Earl
of 49, 50
Percy, Elizabeth 25
Percy, Thomas, Bishop of Dropmore
77
Peterborough, Lord 52
Petty, Sir William 1, 24
Phillips, Richard 116, 121
Phiz (pseud. of Hablot Knight
Browne) 160, 163, 165
Pike, Douglas 195
Pissarro, Camille 223
Plarr, Victor 217
Plautus, Titus Maccius 153
Plunkett, Horace 241
Pollinson, William 61
Pope, Alexander 27, 35, 38, 43, 75
The Dunciad 291
The Rape of the Lock 291
translations of the *Iliad* and the
Odyssey 291
Postboy, The 56
Poulett, John Poulett, 1st Earl 52
Pound, Ezra 162, 217
Preston (London publisher) 116
Prior, Matthew 52
Private Eye 192
Providence Sunday Journal 165
Purohit, Swami *see* Swami Purohit
Purser, Sarah 280, 316
Pynchon, Thomas 162
Pyrrhus, Ludovicus 275

Quarterly Review 125–26

Rabelais, François 300
Radcliffe, Mrs 131

Rathold, Laurence 271–72, 275
Redmond, John 216
Reid, Forrest
At the door of the Gate 314–15
The Kingdom of Twilight 314
Peter Waring 314
Renoir, Pierre Auguste 223
Reynolds, Sir Joshua 90
Rich, Christopher 76
Richard I, King of England 4, 5
Richardson, Dorothy, *Pointed Roofs*
307
Richardson, Ethel Florence *see*
Richardson, Henry Handel
Richardson, Henry Handel
The Getting of Wisdom 287
Maurice Guest 286–87
Myself When Young 286
'Some Notes on My Books' 286
The Fortunes of Richard Mahony
282–88
The Young Cosima 287
Richardson, Reverend John, Rector of
Annal, *Folly of Pilgrimages* 275
Richardson, Samuel 97
Pamela 291
Robbins, Lionel Charles, Baron
Robbins of Clare Market 188
Robertson, J.G. 286
Robinson, Lennox, *Patriots* 314
Rochfort brothers 36
Rolleston, T.W. 241
Romney, Sidney, Earl of 20, 48
Ross, Martin (pseud. of Violet
Florence Martin) *see* Somerville and
Ross
Rothe, David, Bishop of Ossory 273
Rothstein, Professor 81
Rousseau, Jean Jacques 133, 249
La Nouvelle Héloïse 115
Russell, George William (pseud. AE)
241
Russell, John, 1st Earl Russell 188, 189
Ryan, Frederick 217

St John, Henry (1st Viscount
Bolingbroke) 24, 26, 27–28, 42,
52–53, 57–61, 68, 74, 75
St John, Mrs 52, 53
Salinger, J.D., *The Catcher in the Rye*
106
Scawen, Winifred 202

Scott, Sir Walter 128, 131, 146, 150,
    152, 163, 181–82
    Ivanhoe 148
    Memoirs of Swift 67
    Waverley 153–54
Seele (Provost of Trinity College,
    Dublin) 2
Seymour, Admiral Frederick
    Beauchamp Paget, 1st Baron
    Alcester 209
Seymour, St John D. 272, 273–74
    Anglo-Irish Literature 265
    Irish Witchcraft and Demonology 265
    *St Patrick's Purgatory. A Medieval
    Pilgrimage in Ireland* 265–72, 275–76
Shakespeare, William ix, 152, 153,
    170, 303
Sharp, Harold 248
Sharpe, John, Archbishop of York 25,
    26
Shaw, George Bernard 173, 224, 306
    Immaturity 93–94
    Major Barbara 180
Shelley, Mary 154
Sheridan, Richard Brinsley 159, 170,
    174, 306
    The Rivals 152
Sheridan, Thomas 34–35, 36, 44,
    71–73, 75
    Life of the Reverend Dr Jonathan Swift
    67
Shrewsbury, Charles Talbot, Duke of
    52
Sinclair, May 307
Sisley, Alfred 223
Skelton, John 275
Skene, James Henry 206
Smith, David Nichol 74
Smollett, Tobias 301
    The Expedition of Humphry Clinker
    296–97
    Travels in France and Italy 295–96
Solomon, Mr Vaiben 194
Somers, John, 1st Baron 59
Somerset, Duchess of 24–25, 54
Somerville, Edith 314
    The Big House at Inver 258–59, 318
    see also Somerville and Ross
Somerville and Ross x, **251–59**, 314
    'The House of Fahy' 255–56
    An Irish Cousin 321
    Irish Memories 259

Notions in Garrison 259
The Real Charlotte 256–58, 259,
    317–18
Some Experiences of an Irish R.M.
    251–55, 259
South Australian Register 191–95, 197
Spencer, Alexander 162
Spencer, Herbert 216
Spottiswood, James 273
Stanford, Professor W.B. 299
Stanley, Edward Geoffrey Smith, 14th
    Earl Derby 172, 189, 203
Stearne, John 15, 50, 55–56, 57, 58
Steele, Sir Richard 22, 35, 75
Stella (Hester/Esther Johnson) ix,
    21–22, 41
    'Jealousy' 31
    in *Journal* 28
    'On his Birthday, November 30,
    1721' 31–32
    Swift's letters to and about 54–58,
    60–62, 64–67, 69, 71–74
    Swift's poems to 29–33, 36–38
Stendhal (pseud. of Henri Marie
    Beyle) 286
Stephens, James 188, 322
    The Charwoman's Daughter 315
    The Crock of Gold 315
Sterne, Laurence 170, 289, 297, 309
    Tristram Shandy 298–301
Stevens, Sir Roger 298–99
Stevens, Wallace 162
Stevenson, George 192–95
Stewart, General Sir Charles James
    211
Stockdale (London publisher) 126
Stoker, Bram, *Dracula* 321
Stopford, Reverend James 72
Stuart, Sir William 273
Studies 159, 180
Sunderland, Charles Spencer, 3rd
    Earl of 59
Surtees, Robert, *Jorrocks Jaunts and
    Jollities* 154
Sutherland, John Gordon, Earl of 48
Swami Purohit, *The Holy Mountain*
    275
Swift, Adam (uncle to Jonathan) 63
Swift, Jonathan ix, **1–18**, **19–45**, **46–75**,
    92, 170, 178, 187
    'Apollo Outwitted' 22
    'An Apology to Lady Carteret' 35

'Ardelia' 22
'The Author upon Himself' 26
Autobiographical Fragment 47
'A Ballad on the Game of Traffic' 21
'A Ballad to the Tune of the
Cutpurse' 21
'Baucis and Philemon' 22
'A Beautiful Young Nymph going
to Bed' 40
Bickerstaff Papers 22
'Cadenus and Vanessa' 28–29, 70
'Cassinus and Peter' 40
'A Character Panygeric and
Description of the Legion Club' 44
'The Character of Sir Robert
Walpole' 41
'A City Shower' 40
*The Conduct of the Allies and the
Late Ministry, in Beginning and
Carrying on the Present War* 24, 54,
56
'Daphne' 38
'The Dean's Reasons for not
building at Drapier's Hill' 37
'Death and Daphne' 38
'A Description of a City Shower' 23
'A Description of the Morning' 23,
40
'The Description of a Salamander'
22
'Dick, a Maggot' 44
*A Discourse of the Contests and
Dissentions between the Nobles and
Commons in Athens and Rome*... 22,
58–59
*A Discourse to prove the Antiquity of
the English Tongue* 45
'The Discovery' 20
'Drapier's Hill' 37
Drapier's Letters 17–18, 34, 72
*An Enquiry into the Behaviour of the
Queen's Last Ministry* 28
'An Epigram on Wood's Brass
Money' 34
'An Epistle upon an Epistle' 35
The Examiner 24
'An Excellent New Song being the
Intended Speech of a famous
Orator against Peace' 23
'An Excellent New Song on a
Seditious Pamphlet' 33–34
'The Faggot' 26

'George Nim-Dan-Dean Esq. to Mr
Sheridan' 36
'George Nim-Dan-Dean's
Invitation to Mr Sheridan' 36
'The Grand Question Debated' 39
Gulliver's Travels 11, 34, 46, 71,
73–74
*The History of the Four Last Years of
the Queen* 56, 72–73
'Holyhead. September 25, 1727' 37,
73–74
'Horace, Lib 2, Sat. 6' 27
'In Sickness' 26, 27
'Ireland' 41
'The Journal of a Modern Lady' 39
Journal to Stella 14–15, 28, 46–47, 51,
62, 66–67
'Lady Acheson weary of the Dean'
38
'The Lady's Dressing Room' 40
'The Legion Club' 43
*A Letter from a Member of the House
of Commons of Ireland to a Member of
the House of Commons in England* 17
Letter to the Archbishop of Dublin 18
The Letter to a Young Clergyman 45
Letters 46
'Letters to Elisa' 63
'A Libel on the Reverent Dr
Delaney and his Excellency John,
Lord Carteret' 35
'Mad Mullinix and Timothy' 44
'Mary the Cook-Maid's Letter to Dr
Sheridan' 35
A Modest Proposal 18
'Mrs Harris's Petition' 19, 35
'My Lady's Lamentation and
Complaint against the Dean' 38
'Ode to Dr William Sancroft' 19
'On Censure' 30
'On Cutting Down the Old Thorn
at Market Hill' 39
'On His own Deafness' 44
'On Poetry: a Rhapsody' 43
'On Wood the Ironmonger' 34
'A Panegyric on the Dean in the
person of a Lady in the North' 38
'The Part of a Summer at the
House of George Rochefort, Esq.'
36
'A Pastoral Dialogue' 39
'penny papers' 56

'The Place of the Damned' 41
Polite Conversation 44–45
'The Problem' 20
'Prometheus: on Wood the Patentee's Irish Halfpence' 34
Proposal for Correcting the English Tongue 45
A Proposal for the Universal Use of Irish Manufacture... 17, 33
The Public Spirit of the Whigs 26–27
'A Receipt to Restore Stella's Youth' 36–37
'The Revolution at Market Hill' 39
'A Satirical Elegy on the Death of a Late Famous General' 41
'A Serious Poem on William Wood' 34
Sid Hamet 52
'A Simile' 34
'Stella at Woodpark' 36, 71
The Story of the Injured Lady, in a Letter to her Friend, with her Answer 16
'Strephon and Chloe' 40
A Tale of a Tub 11, 13, 22, 25, 40, 54, 59
'To an agreeable young Lady, but extremely Lean' 38
'To Dean Swift' 37
'To Dr Delaney, on the Libels writ against him' 35
'To a Friend who had been much abused in many inveterate Libels' 35
'To Mr Delaney' 35–36
'To Mr Sheridan, upon his Verses Written in Circles' 36
'To Quilca' 34
'Tom Mullinex and Dick' 44
'A Town Eclogue' 23
'Twelve Articles' 38
'Verses on the Death of Dr Swift' 41–42
'Verses Made for the Women Who Cry Apples, etc.' 45
'Verses occasioned by the sudden Drying up of St Patrick's Well near Trinity College, Dublin' 41
'Verses said to be Written on the Union' 24
'Verses on the Upright Judge who condemned the Drapier's Printer' 34
'Verses Wrote in a Lady's Ivory Table-Book' 19
'The Virtues of Sid Hamet the Magician's Rod' 23–24, 52
'Whitshed's Motto on His Coach' 34
'The Windsor Prophecy' 24–25, 26, 54
'Wood, an Insect' 34
Swift, Thomas (cousin of Jonathan) 11, 19
Swift, Thomas (grandfather of Jonathan) 9, 24
Swiney, Owen 76
Synge, J.M. 132, 319
    The Shadow of the Glen 299

Taín Bó Cuailnge 107
Tasso, Torquato, *Jerusalem Liberata* 291
Tatler 45
Temple, John 59
Temple, Lady 25
Temple, Sir William 25, 58, 66
    'An Essay upon the Advancement of Trade in Ireland' 7
    Swift at Moor Park 12, 13, 21, 37, 47–48, 61–62
Terence, Publius Terentius Afer 153, 170
Terson, Madame 119, 120
Tewfik Pasha, Mohammed, Khedive of Egypt 215
Thackeray, William Makepeace 300
    The Professor 154
    The Yellowplush Papers 154
Thurber, James 300–301
Thynne, Thomas 25
Times, The 196, 208, 209, 220
Tisdall, Reverend William 64–65
Tolstoy, Count Leo Nikolayevich 256
Torrens, Sir Robert Richard ix, **188–200**, 190
Trollope, Frances 153
Turgenev, Ivan Sergeevich 223, 234, 317
Twiss, Richard 134
Tynan, Kenneth 82
Tyrconnel, Richard Talbot, 1st Earl of 2, 10

United Ireland 158, 167

Vanbrugh, Sir John 22
  The Provok'd Wife 83–84
  The Relapse 84
Vanessa (Esther Vanhomrigh) 28–32,
  38, 62, 67–70, 74
Vanhomrigh, Bartholomew 28
Vanhomrigh, Esther *see* Vanessa
Vanhomrigh, Mary (Moll) 29, 68
Vanhomrigh, Mrs 28, 29, 67
Varina (Jane Waring) 14, 62–64, 65
Vico, Giovanni Battista 300
Villiers, Ernest 189
Virgil 23, 165, 287
  Aeneid 282, 291
Voltaire, François Marie Arouet de 91
von Bülow, Hans Guido *see* Bülow,
  Hans Guido von

Wagner, Cosima 287
Wagner, Richard 287, 306
Wakefield, Edward Gibbon 188
Walker, Alice 106
Walker, Joseph Cooper
  Historical Memoirs of the Irish Bards
  134
  Memoirs of the Irish Bards 117
Walkington, Edward 48
Wall, Mervyn 322
Wallace, Thomas 127
Walpole, Sir Robert 41, 42
Walters, Catherine ('Skittles') 203–04,
  214, 219
Waring, Jane *see* Varina
Weichsel, Madame 118, 119
Wharton, Thomas, 1st Earl of 50
Whelan, John *see* O'Faolain, Sean
White, Anna (granddaughter of
  Maud Gonne) 279
Whitehead, David 311
Whitshed, William 34
Wilde, Lady Jane Francesca
  ('Speranza') 167, 168
  Ancient Legends of Ireland 261
Wilde, Oscar x, 168, 299, 306
Wilde, Sir William 158
Wilder, Theaker 92, 94
Wilks, Robert 76, 82–83
William III, King of Great Britain and
  Ireland 2, 5, 6
Williams, Sir Harold 66
Winchelsea, Anne, Countess of 22
Winder, Reverend John 63

Wolseley, Garnet Joseph, Viscount
  209, 211
Wood, William 34, 35, 41
Woolf, Virginia 162
  Orlando 307–08
Wordsworth, William 134, 137, 143,
  147, 149
  Lyrical Ballads 131, 132
Worgan, Dr 118
Worrall, Reverend John 71–72
Wyndham, George 202, 214, 216, 217
Wyndham, Mrs 203

Yeats, J.B. 260, 316
Yeats, Mrs George (née Georgie Hyde
  Lees) 261, 265, 278, 279
Yeats, W.B. x, 19, 151, 238, 241, **260–76**
  attitude to Lever 159, 162, **164–78**,
  180
  Autobiographies 158, 168, 280
  Blunt and the Irish literary revival
  216, 217, 219
  The Cat and the Moon 231–32
  Cathleen ni Houlihan 279–80
  'The Cold Heaven' 278
  editor of *Stories from Carleton* 262
  The Green Helmet and Other Poems
  278
  'If I were Four and Twenty' 261,
  265
  imaginative heroic plays 319
  and Joyce 303, 306
  The King of the Great Clock Tower 274
  letter to Lady Gregory 280
  'Meru' 274–75
  Moore and the Irish theatre 223–24,
  230–31, 233–34
  'The Old Age of Queen Maeve' 281
  'The Pilgrim' 260
  'The Poet of Ballyshannon' 165–66
  'Popular Ballad Poetry of Ireland'
  158, 166
  'Red Hanrahan's song about
  Ireland' 277
  Representative Irish Tales 166, 262
  and *Richard Mahoney* 287–88
  in Somerville and Ross *Some
  Experiences of an Irish R.M.* 254
  on Stella's poem to Swift 32
  'The Trembling of the Veil' 168, 278
  The Wanderings of Oisin 266
  'When You are Old' 277

'The White Birds' 277
'The Young Ireland League' 158, 167
Yonge, James 271
Young, Arthur 134

Young, Ella, *Flowering dusk* 280
Young, Sir Henry Fox 189–90

Zola, Émile 223, 225, 305, 317